Mar ry

A Life Through Poetry:
Marina Tsvetaeva's Lyric Diary

by

Jane A. Taubman

Slavica Publishers, Inc.

PG
3476
.T75
Z89
1989

Slavica publishes a wide variety of books and journals dealing with the peoples, languages, literatures, history, folklore, and culture of the peoples of Eastern Europe and the USSR. For a complete catalog with prices and ordering information, please write to:

Slavica Publishers, Inc.
P.O. Box 14388
Columbus, Ohio 43214
USA

ISBN: 0-89357-197-0

Text set by Randy Bowlus and Karen Robblee at the East European Composition Center, supported by the Department of Slavic Languages and Literatures and the Center for Russian and East European Studies at UCLA.

Printed in the United States of America.

TABLE OF CONTENTS

PREFACE

I am indebted to the following for their support of this project: the Amherst College faculty research fund, the American Council of Learned Societies, and the American Philosophical Society. I owe a great debt of gratitude to Viktoria Schweitzer for her generosity and friendship, and to my husband and children for their patience. Katerina Clark, Jane G. Harris, Dale Peterson, Stanley Rabinowitz, and Stephanie Sandler all read the manuscript at various stages; I thank them for their suggestions and criticisms. I also want to thank the reference and interlibrary loan staff of the Robert Frost library at Amherst College for their cooperation and interest, and Margaret Ferro for her peerless word-processing.

Between 1910 and 1913, the five greatest poets of Russia's post-symbolist generation made their debuts. For nearly twenty years, their voices would form a magnificent contrapuntal quartet (Akhmatova, Mandel'stam, Pasternak, and Tsvetaeva) with a booming bass soloist (Mayakovsky) off to the left of stage. Coincidentally, the five were born one after another in successive years, Akhmatova first in 1889 and Mayakovsky last in 1893. Fate and history dealt with them severely: Mayakovsky shot himself in 1930, Mandel'stam died in 1938, starving and deranged, in a Siberian transit camp, and Tsvetaeva hanged herself in 1941, during the evacuation, in the provincial town of Elabuga two months after Hitler attacked Russia. Pasternak and Akhmatova managed to survive into the sixties, but there were long silences during which they published only translations or nothing at all, while those close to them were imprisoned as hostages. Of the quartet, two were women and two men, but the more important kinship was between the Petersburg poets (Akhmatova and Mandel'stam) and the Muscovites (Pasternak and Tsvetaeva).

Tsvetaeva is least known in the West, though this is no longer true in her native country, where she exerts a stronger influence over young poets than any of her contemporaries. Her poetry, published rarely and in limited editions generally available only in foreign-currency stores, is avidly sought on the book black markets and in *samizdat*. According to a recent article in a Soviet mass-circulation magazine, thousands of admirers and school excursions annually make the pilgrimage to the house where her suicide occurred and the graveyard where she is buried.

Her biography alone accounts for the years of neglect, both in Russia and the emigration, which followed her death. She lived what the Soviets euphemistically call a "complex life." The only one of the five to experience foreign, rather than "internal" emigration, she lived for seventeen years in shabby suburbs of Prague and Paris, grudgingly published, misunderstood, and often attacked by the emigre press. Her husband, Sergei Efron, who had fought with the White Army from 1918 to 1920, became a Soviet sympathizer and even a collaborator of the secret police. In 1937 he was involved in the murder of an NKVD defector in Switzerland, and escaped through Spain to the USSR. Their daughter, who shared her father's political views, had already returned to the Soviet Union. Though Tsvetaeva and Efron had been living separate lives for years, she followed him back to Russia in 1939 "like a dog," she wrote,[1] just as she had followed him into emigration in 1922. Her emigration did not endear her to the Soviets, nor did her return endear her to the emigres.

Why has the west been slow to discover Tsvetaeva? She did not live to enjoy (or suffer) Pasternak's Nobel Prize fame, or Akhmatova's Oxford doctorate *honoris causa*. She did not leave an eloquent and indomitable widow like Nadezhda Mandel'stam. Tsvetaeva's husband, arrested only months after her return to Russia, was shot in August, 1941. Their son, drafted into the Red Army in 1944, perished in unknown circumstances at the front. And their daughter Ariadna, arrested even before her father, spent seventeen years in camps and exile before she was able to devote the last years of her life to the publication and preservation of her mother's works. Her memoir of her mother, written for Soviet publication,[2] revealed a literary talent of her own, but Ariadna, cautiously pro-Soviet until her death, was never willing to tell her story as Nadezhda Mandel'stam did, indicting, Cassandra-like, an entire generation for their moral cowardice.

Yet more than biography or whim of fate have, until now, deprived Tsvetaeva of her due recognition in the west. Her poetry, to be frank, could be extremely difficult; so, too, could her personality. In both, she embraced self-contradictory opposites. Tsvetaeva wrought innovations in Russian meter and rhyme as radical as anything attempted by the Futurists, yet she found her moral ideals in the eighteenth-century aristocracy, and her image of the poet came straight out of high Romanticism. Her imagery could be as dense as Mandel'stam's, her syntax sometimes as puzzling as Pasternak's—which is not to say that her voice could ever be mistaken for theirs, for in this, as in everything else, Tsvetaeva was *sui generis*. Needless to say, she is not kind to the translator. No great poet is, of course, but Tsvetaeva's particular achievement was the rediscovery of lost meanings, and the creation of new ones, within the building-blocks of Russian—its roots and even its grammatical forms. English (or French, or German) simply puts itself together in a very different way. The translations I offer here (and there are many, for I have tried to let Tsvetaeva's voice be heard as much as possible) make no attempt to retain the meter or rhyme, the often elaborate formal organization of Tsvetaeva's verse. My hope is that they will give English readers some sense of Tsvetaeva's voice, and that readers with some Russian will use them as stepping-stones to the (often fiendishly difficult) originals.

Tsvetaeva's life was as full of contradictions as her work. Married young, and the mother of three children (her second daughter died of starvation during the Civil War) she insisted throughout her writing on the ideals of duty and loyalty. It was these ideals which sent her into emigration to join her husband, and which, years later, sent her back to Russia for the sake of her family. Yet within three years of her marriage, she embarked on a series of affairs, infatuations, and chance encounters, both hetero- and homosexual, which belie those very ideals.

This book will study the most important aspect of Tsvetaeva's work, her lyric poems—there are more than 2,000 of them in all—and attempt to "read" them (in most of the contemporary senses of that verb) as a continuously unfolding, self-referential diary. Though it must inevitably sort out the internal and external events of Tsvetaeva's life as it studies their transformation into poetry, it is not a literary biography as is Viktoria Schweitzer's monumental *Byt i byt'ie Mariny Tsvetaevoi.*[4]

It does not intend to be a comprehensive overview of her entire *oeuvre*, which fills more than seven thick volumes in the Russica editions.[3] Simon Karlinsky has already given us this in his fundamental *Marina Cvetaeva: Her Life and Art*, and in *Marina Tsvetaeva: The Woman, her World, and her Poetry.*[5] I will treat other aspects of Tsvetaeva's work (her prose, long narrative poems, verse dramas, and letters) only as they serve to illuminate the lyric diary. We must not forget that we will be using biography , when necessary, to illuminate some very difficult and complex poetry, not the other way around, and that it is Tsvetaeva's transformation of her life into art which makes that life of interest. She herself provided a valuable caveat in her essay on Mandel'stam:

> I do not know whether in general we need line-for-line "true life" translations for poems: who—when—where—with whom—in what circumstances, etc. as in the familiar high-school game. The lines of verse have ground up "life" and thrown it out, and now, from the residue which remains, crawling after it as if on his knees, the biographer struggles to reconstruct the past. Why? To bring us closer to the living poet. But does he not know that the poet lives *in his poems*, and *in his essence* is far away? (IP1, p.365)

What *is* Tsvetaeva's "essence?" That is a question she asked herself throughout her life, throughout her work, whose essence, we might say, was the search for an answer. Her world-view has often been described as dualistic, more recently as "dichotomous." In the words of one Tsvetaeva scholar:

> Tsvetaeva's various antithetical notions do not belong to distinct realms, hermetically sealed and mutually exclusive, but, on the contrary, are related and represent opposite sides of one and the same phenomenon.[6]

Such dichotomous pairings abound in Tsvetaeva: *byt* (everyday reality) and *byt'ie* (pronounced "byt-yo", a transcendental reality); earth and "that other world," flesh and spirit, Christianity and paganism, chastity and promiscuity. Each of these dichotomies was an attempt to define herself and her work. Thus, according to Anya Kroth, the importance of androgyny, the combination of male and female characteristics, in some of her characters, such as the Tsar-Maiden and her docile lover, and, I would add, in Tsvetaeva's own poetic personae.

In Tsvetaeva's earlier lyrics, the search for self-definition took the form of an unusual concentration on her contemporaries. Mandel'stam, Akhmatova, and Blok (the only poet of the symbolist generation who influenced her) were the addressees and subjects of important cycles of poems. These poems to other poets were an attempt to set up antitheses in which Tsvetaeva would be the other element. In other words, she sought to define herself as "not-Mandel'stam," "not-Akhmatova," "not-Blok." In the 1930's, with most of her poetic career behind her, Tsvetaeva wrote two prose essays in which she set other poets in *both* elements of the pairings: "The Epic and Lyric of Contemporary Russia" (Mayakovsky vs. Pasternak) and "Poets with a History and Poets Without a History" (Pushkin/Goethe vs. Pasternak/Lermontov). The reader of these essays cannot resist the question, "But where does Tsvetaeva see herself in these dichotomies?" The answer, clear to one with a knowledge of Tsvetaeva's work, is: Tsvetaeva subsumes both at once, she is *both* epic and lyric, a poet both with and without a history.

Tsvetaeva's "Poets Without a History" are pure lyric poets, whose career she represents as a circle, whose poetry she sees symbolized by the ocean. Ever renewing and rediscovering themselves, they yet remain essentially the same from birth. Such, according to Tsvetaeva, were Pasternak and Lermontov, Heine, Byron, Shelley, Verlaine. The career of "Poets with a History," by contrast, is like an arrow, their work like a river (she quotes Heraclitus: we never step twice into the same river). They are poets of themes and move from one to another as the dynamic of their genius propels them. Tsvetaeva's "Poets Without a History" are all, undeniably, romantics, and the sway of the romantic world-view and image of the poet over her are equally undeniable. Yet, when we read the whole lyric diary, it becomes clear that, uniting both halves of her dichotomy, she is an essentially lyric poet (of personal, rather than social themes) *with* a history.

A centrally important dichotomy in Tsvetaeva's work is the opposition of "illusion," or rather "imagination," to "reality." Tsvetaeva distinctly preferred imagination. The epigraph to her final collection of poetry (taken from the eighteenth-century poet-pedant Trediakovsky) declared:

> From the fact that the poet is a creator it does not follow that he is a liar: a lie is a word contrary to reason and conscience, but a poetic invention relates to reason [by showing] how a thing *can* and *should* be. (III, p.9)[7]

Was she not characterizing her art when she wrote, in 1915:

И как могу	And how can I
Не лгать, — раз голос мой нежнее, —	Not lie,—for my voice is more gentle
Когда я лгу. . .	When I lie. . .
	(I, 189)

These programmatic statements explain the importance of mythmaking in Tsvetaeva's poetry and biography—the transformation of everyday reality by her poetic imagination. While this was essential for her poetry, it often had a disastrous effect on the human relationships which were its most frequent subject. Tsvetaeva acted as if *her* reality were the operative one, and few, even of her brother poets, understood what she was doing.

Throughout her life Tsvetaeva attempted to reject *byt*, everyday reality, and all that it involved, be it household chores or politics. The irony of her fate was that circumstances, as if in revenge, thrust her into the very midst of *byt*, in which she could not, or would not, operate.

Reading the lyric diary offers us the opportunity to study Tsvetaeva's mythmaking, for we can often compare a poem with the event or other poem which inspired it.[8] Her brilliant and voluminous letters, when they form a parallel chronicle to the lyric diary, are an invaluable source, yet they are, to some extent, works of art themselves. Tsvetaeva tried to write every day. She carefully dated her poems, and when she could, published them in chronological order. The lyric diary that resulted is essentially an autobiography, though of Tsvetaeva's *byt'ie* rather than her *byt*. It is a version of her life, in Trediakovsky's words, "as it *could* and *should* have been", which gains added resonance when read against the background of how (in some hypothetically "objective" sense) it *was*. This book, therefore, will proceed chronologically, because experience has taught me to take Tsvetaeva at her word:

> Chronology is the key to understanding. . . . He who has not read all of me, from *Evening Album* (childhood) to "The Ratcatcher" (the present day) does not have the right to judge. (IP1, 224)

Her poems, when read in sequence, do illuminate one another: earlier poems become sub-texts for the later ones. (Sub-texts are earlier texts which the poet answers, contradicts, reaffirms, quotes, paraphrases, or otherwise uses in building the new structure of his or her work.) In poets like Mandel'-stam or Brodsky, the sub-texts are drawn from the whole range of Classical and European literature. In Tsvetaeva, the sub-texts are usually from her own poetry, or that of her poetic friends and contemporaries. I have found in Tsvetaeva's work a marked pattern of lexical and thematic repetition similar to the pattern in Mandel'stam's poetry so tellingly described by Clarence Brown, who coined for it the term, "drift."[9] Repetition of uncommon words and images calls up earlier poems *en bloc*, making them elements with which the later poems work.

All poets write with an eye (or rather an ear) to tradition.[10] But at the beginning of the twentieth century in Russia a poet, to a unique degree, had this tradition developing around her as she wrote, so complete had been the death, or at least the suppression, of poetry during the dominance of the Russian novel, and so rapidly explosive was the rebirth of poetic tradition in Russia beginning in the 1890's. For this reason, I have paid considerable attention to the work of Tsvetaeva's major contemporaries, which provide the essential context in which hers must be read. *Sui generis* she may have been, but she was not isolated from the poetic matrix of her generation—a matrix unique in Russian, and perhaps world, literature, for the presence, at one time, of so many strong poets. In Tsvetaeva's case, Harold Bloom's theories of influence and intertextuality need to be applied synchronically (looking at the poetry of her generation as a structure of meaning) rather than diachronically (over time). Bloom's theory about the strong poet's oedipal relationship to his predecessors needs particular re-evaluation in the case of a poet, herself female, who had no "strong" female predecessors in the Russian tradition, and who was, to complicate matters still further, androgynous in her ideology and bisexual in her erotic orientation.[11]

In the late seventies and early eighties, while I was working on this book, a large and increasingly sophisticated feminist literary scholarship was developing, largely in the United States, but also on the continent. Needless to say, nothing of the sort was appearing in the Soviet Union or even in the emigre Russian press; feminist scholarship of Russian literature is in an embryonic state compared to Anglo-American, French, and even German criticism. That new feminist scholarship has enriched my reading of Tsvetaeva's lyric diary, and enabled me to ask, and sometimes to answer, some fascinating questions. What similarities may she have shared with other women writers never known to her? What might be called "feminine" about her creativity? How was she unique? Were there aspects of the Russian tradition which made women writing in it different, in any fundamental ways, from other women writers?

But does such an approach not do violence to Tsvetaeva herself? It would be absurd to apply the term "feminist" in the traditional sense to her. She was not the least interested in the organized political elements of feminism, and her few explicit mentions of womens' groups and "the woman question" are laced with irony.

> . . . There are criteria of classification more essential than one's membership in the male or female sex, and, from birth I have been squeamish about everything that bore any stamp of feminine (mass) separateness, such as: female courses, suffragism, the Salvation Army, the celebrated "female question," with the exception of its military solution: the legendary kingdoms of Penthesilea, Brunhilde, Maria Morevna, and the no less legendary Petrograd female battalion. . . . There is no female question in art—there are female answers to human questions, like Sappho, Joan of Arc, St. Theresa, Bettina Brentano.[12]

Political feminism in Russia has never enjoyed the wide support it has in England or the United States. One reason, perhaps, is its cooptation by the most radical wings of the revolutionary movement in the nineteenth century, where discussion of the "woman question" was *de rigeur*. Indeed, a disproportionate number of the radical terrorists in such organizations as Land and Freedom were well-educated young daughters of the aristocracy, like Sergei Efron's mother, Elizaveta Durnovo. These were women who saw no outlet for their talents and aspirations in Russian society of their time, and turned those talents to the revolutionary movement in the hope of bringing about a new society which would give those opportunities to all.[13] But by the turn of the century, discussion of "the woman question" only produced boredom among the intelligentsia: witness the condescending treatment of Uncle Vanya's bluestocking mother in Chekov's play. Tsvetaeva's brief childhood infatuation with revolution and revolutionaries undoubtedly acquainted her with the tradition of these revolutionary heroines, but it was the romanticism, rather than the politics of revolution which captured her imagination. The Soviet regime, by claiming to have solved the problem of womens' rights, continues to attempt to co-opt feminism, alienating from it most contemporary Russian woman, as it did the militantly apolitical Tsvetaeva.

Yet in her own life and career, in the name of freedom of the spirit, Tsvetaeva was always confronting limitations imposed on her as a woman, not by explicitly protesting traditional sex roles and gender limitations, but simply by ignoring them.[14] She had before her her mother's negative example—a brilliant pianist who sacrificed her own life for the sake of others, giving up her first, unacceptable love for her father's sake, then giving up a career for the sake of Tsvetaeva's father, his museum, and his children. On the one hand, Tsvetaeva admired such loyalty, yet she could never find satisfaction by living through others. She found none of the available models for a Russian woman's life appealing: one good reason for her reluctance to abandon childhood, the closest state to androgyny that humans ever know.

Sandra Gilbert and Susan Gubar, in the introduction to their collection of essays on women poets, point out that:

> While a number of fine feminist studies have recently explored the relationship between gender and creativity in the work of women novelists, the problems as well as the triumphs of women poets in England and America still remain inexplicably obscure. Yet the obstructions such literary women confronted were even more formidable than those faced by female novelists.[15]

The feminist scholar of Russian literature cannot even begin with a tradition of successful nineteenth-century women novelists. Russia had no Jane Austen, Charlotte Bronte, George Eliot or even Harriet Beecher Stowe. (Indeed, for some strange reason, Austen remains almost unknown to the Russian reader: *Pride and Prejudice* was first translated only in 1960.) Tsvetaeva, as a young woman with literary aspirations, faced the same void. She of course knew George Sand and, as an adolescent, devoured her novels. But Tsvetaeva was never drawn to write fiction, perhaps because the Russian novel was a novel of ideas rather than experience, and experience— *life*—was what interested Tsvetaeva the most.

It is not accidental that her poetry grew out of the only two literary genres ordinarily open to nineteenth-century Russian women of breeding:

the intimate diary and the personal letter. Her achievement, essentially, was to bring these two modes into the mainstream of poetry, to canonize them, as it were. Both the diary and the letter raise interesting questions of audience, readership, and "interlocutor"—questions of considerable interest in contemporary critical theory. Tsvetaeva's engagement with her "implied reader" is always intimate, sometimes uncomfortably so. Her persona does not simply hint, describe, or demonstrate—she is forever demanding, requesting, proclaiming, and even haranguing her reader. Her characteristic diction grows not from the syntax of the written language, but out of Russian oral utterance: one-to-one speech, with its often incomplete thoughts, its anaphoric (that is, beginning several lines with the same word) parallel phrases, enjambements and internal rhymes. This, I think, is the reason why a specific addressee was so essential to her creative process, why so many of her poems were originally addressed to a specific "other." This, too, is an adaptation of yet another "genre" open to women—the intimate conversation.

The diary, in contrast to the letter, is a very ambiguous genre in terms of addressee. Whom, exactly, does the diarist address? ("Dear Diary" . . .) Surely not simply herself? A chance intruder who may stumble accross her notes? Posterity? Tsvetaeva's achievement was to take the diary-like intimacy of voice which characterized her juvenilia and retain that intimate voice, matured, deepened, wiser, yet still unmistakably hers alone in its engagement with her reader/listener, as her poetry grew to treat wider and more universal themes.

The same questions can be asked about any poet's "implied reader." But questions of the poetic voice and its authority are even more complex for the female poet. Of course, the very fact of Tsvetaeva's self-definition as "poet" (she regarded the term "poetess" as an insult) was a profoundly feminist gesture. Gubar and Gilbert observed that:

> Before the nineteenth century the poet had a nearly priestly role, and "he" had a wholly priestly role after the Romantic thinkers had appropriated the vocabulary of theology for the realm of aesthetics. But if in Western culture women cannot be priests, then how—since poets are priests—can they be poets?[16]

Russian romanticism was rather short-lived, but the neo-romantic revival at the turn of the century (better known as symbolism) was the dominant force in Tsvetaeva's youth. Bal'mont, Briusov, Bely, and even her adored Blok appropriated to themselves the role of priests of a new theurgy, and women, with the exception of Gippius, had little place except as the objects of their eroticism or idealization. Tsvetaeva's answer to this predicament was her discovery of the female priesthood in witches and fortune-tellers, a discovery which animates so much of her work in the years from 1916-1920.

In the 1920's, she turned to the sorceresses of Greek and Biblical myth. Tsvetaeva's use of word-play in the effort to discover ancient, buried meanings of words and connections between them finds a curious echo in the writing style of the American feminist theorist Mary Daly, (author of *Gyn/Ecology*) who also looks to the ancient female wisdom of witches for an answer to the violence and repression of the male-dominated "Sado-society."[17]

Jeanne Kammer finds a common thread in the work of three great Anglo-American poets: Dickinson, Marianne Moore, and H.D.: "Each developed her poetry as an art of silence where it has historically been treated as an art of speech." Kammer points to "devices of linguistic compression" which are equally characteristic of Tsvetaeva's work: "ellipsis, inversion, syntactic substitution, the omission of connectives in favor of dramatic juxtapositions of word and image, and complicated processes of sentence embedding."[18] Yet it is difficult to characterize Tsvetaeva's art as "the art of silence" contrasted to the art of speech, for living female speech, as opposed to written language, was the basis for her poetry. It may be the case that these "devices of linguistic compression" are in fact characteristic not of silence but of female speech and art. Still, Kammer's suggestion that: "For the reclusive, emotionally vulnerable personality . . . the ambiguity of saying and not saying may be the only acceptable axis for communication"[19] puts into perspective Tsvetaeva's predilection for using her poetry as a means of communication.

In the same very suggestive article, Kammer borrows Philip Wheelwright's distinction between two kinds of metaphor, epiphor and diaphor. Epiphor, the more traditional, produces a "primarily linear process of concretion to abstraction," in a language which "still fulfills syntactic expectations." Diaphor, on the other hand, produces new meaning simply by juxtaposing two or more images, each in itself concrete: their joining is unexplained, the meaning of their conjunction "rooted in the associational properties of the subconscious mind."[20] Kammer offers as an illustration of diaphor H.D.'s "Oread":

> Whirl up, sea—
> whirl your pointed pines,
> splash your great pines
> on our rocks,
> hurl your green over us,
> cover us with your pools of fir.

The reader of such a poem, explains Kammer, is forced by the lack of syntactic connectives and the "conspicuous absence of a named feeling or quality or abstraction" to "search for other, less rational entries" to it. Diaphor, thus defined, was increasingly frequent in Tsvetaeva's poetry and prose, built on just such unexplained juxtapositions, and is particularly characteristic of her last collection, *After Russia*:

Ночные шепота: шелка	Nocturnal whispers: a hand
Разбрасывающая рука.	Scattering silks.
Ночные шепота: шелка	Nocturnal whispers: lips
Разглаживающие уста.	Smoothing silks.
Счета	Accounts
Всех ревностей дневных —	Of all daytime jealousies—
и вспых	and a flash
Всех древностей — и стиснув челюсти —	Of all antiquities—and, jaws clenched—
И стих	And a controversy
Спор —	Of verses—
В шелесте. . .	In rustling. . .
И лист	And a leaf
В стекло. . .	Against the glass. . .
И первой птицы свист.	And the whistle of the first bird.
— Сколь чист! — И вздох.	—How pure!—And a sigh.
Не тот. — Ушло.	Not the one.—It went away.
Ушла.	She went away..
И вздрог	And the shrug
Плеча.	Of a shoulder.
Ничто.	Nothing.
Тшета.	Vanity.
Конец.	The end.
Как нет.	As null.
И в эту суету сует	And into this vanity of vanities
Сей меч: рассвет.	This sword: dawn.
	June 17, 1922 (III, 13)

It was exactly these missing connections Tsvetaeva felt she had to point out for her Soviet reader (and censor) when, in preparing her (never published) 1940 collection, she gave separate titles to scores of untitled poems from that book. (This particular poem was put into a cycle titled: "Dawn.")

Kammer explains the advantage of diaphor for the female poet: in such poetry, the poetic voice is "not the universal 'we' of bard or orator" (both, she points out, traditionally imaged as masculine), but "an individual quality as distinctly *other* as the objects of experience it describes. The sex of the speaker is unimportant: male and female speech has equal validity."[21] This was of prime importance to Tsvetaeva, who wanted to be heard as a soul speaking to other souls, without attention paid to her gender. The diaphoric impulse, Kammer continues, is at the root of modern poetry in general, characteristic of Pound, Eliot, Williams, and Stevens, and has its parallels in modern painting, music, sculpture and architecture (Picasso, Calder, Frank Lloyd Wright). There is nothing exclusively female about it. Nevertheless, she continues, "the point at which diaphor takes hold in art is also the historical point at which female artists of major rank begin to emerge and to receive recognition." Kammer's hypothesis helps explain Tsvetaeva's paradox: how, while she herself despised modernity and its values, her art could be at the cutting edge of modernism.

*****

My title is an attempt to convey in English a key phrase from one of Tsvetaeva's letters: "Zhivia stikhami"—"Though I've *lived* [by means of] *poems* since—well, since I was born!—only this summer I learned from my publisher the difference between a trochee and a dactyl.[22] Tsvetaeva lived in, by, and for poetry. Her lyric diary is both the achievement and the testament of such a poetic.

CHAPTER ONE

Mama and Papa

Nineteenth-century professorial families gave the twentieth century a disproportionate share of its writers and poets. In Russia, Tsvetaeva, the daughter of a classicist and art historian, shared her professorial heritage with Blok (son of a law professor at Warsaw University, grandson of a biologist, son-in-law of the great chemist Mendeleev) and Bely (son of a Moscow mathematician). Even Pasternak's artist father was a professor at the Moscow School of Painting, Sculpture, and Architecture, giving the family an ambience far more academic than Bohemian. Was this simply coincidence, or did some common factors in those staid but close-knit professorial households propel their gifted children into symbolism and modernism?

The poets of Russia's first Golden Age, in the early nineteenth century, had all come from the gentry, then the only class with enough education to attempt the writing of sophisticated verse and enough resources to afford the leisure for what was then a seldom remunerative activity. The professorial families of the late nineteenth century provided their children—both sons and daughters—with a superior, thoroughly European education, and the expectation that they would use that education to follow an intellectual career, though poetry was not usually what they had in mind (Bely, like Akhmatova, had to adopt a pseudonym to save his family the embarrassment of having spawned a poet.) In their late-Victorian love for order, classification, and propriety, professorial fathers also provided the perfect foil for the modernist rejection of science and rationality.

The personal and psychological parallels are even more curious if we compare Tsvetaeva's life with those of her near-contemporaries Virginia Woolf and Hilda Doolittle, (H.D.), the greatest of the very few female talents produced by Anglo-American modernism. Granted that Woolf's father, the eminent Victorian Leslie Stephen, gave up "the quiet life of a don at Cambridge because of religious doubt"[1] before Virginia's birth in 1882, scholarship still dominated the household. His immense *Dictionary of National Biography*, begun that same year, was the functional equivalent of Ivan Tsvetaev's art museum. Hilda Doolittle was born in 1886 to Charles Doolittle, an astronomer "so intent on his work that he literally froze to his telescope."[2] Though it is highly unlikely that Woolf and H.D. knew anything of Tsvetaeva and her work, or she of theirs, the parallels in the lives of the three women are uncanny. Each was born, the product of a second marriage, into a large and complex Victorian household, where her mother tirelessly filled the traditional role of "angel in the house." Both Tsvetaeva and Woolf lost their mothers at the crucial stage of early adolescence; H.D., descended from Moravian sectarians, shared Tsvetaeva's Germanic maternal heritage. Each struggled for self-definition as a writer in an exclusive literary elite that was overwhelmingly male; each was briefly courted by a leading writer of that elite (Mandel'stam, Strachey, Pound). Though all three married, for each the love of another woman was a pivotal event in her emotional development; all three were shattered by the outbreak of World War II, the ultimate expression of all they saw as hostilely "masculine" in culture. For H.D., the war brought emotional breakdown, for Woolf and Tsvetaeva, suicide (within five months of each other in 1941).

Both Woolf and H.D. struggled with madness all their lives. Are madness, "oddness" and suicide the inevitable price of female genius, or, conversely, are they inflicted by society on the woman who dares to be different? These are loaded questions which I have no intention of answering here. I pose them, however, to raise the question of why, with all the other striking parallels in the lives of these three women, there is scarcely a hint of mental illness in the record of Tsvetaeva's life. One obvious answer, of course, is that there simply wasn't any problem of psychic stability, and I am not about to build a strong case that there was. But I would like to play with the possibility for just a moment, since it raises some broader issues.

If we look at Tsvetaeva's creative chronicle, we find some dry spells in the late 1920's, not all of them explainable by lost works. Her letters to Anna Teskova and Vera Bunina in the 1930's frequently complain of deep, long-lasting depression. Is it because the conditions of her life seemed to justify that depression, even (if that is possible) her suicide, that we find Tsvetaeva's depression more "rational" than Woolf's? Or can we hypothesize that modern Russian history, by forcing Tsvetaeva to cope with enough concrete disasters for several lifetimes, saved her from disintegration of personality?

The extant memoir literature on Tsvetaeva contains no hint of mental illness but that is not surprising. The fullest and most important memoirs are those of her sister and daughter who would be unlikely to raise the issue if it existed, particularly in the Soviet press where both memoirs were published. Such a possibility could concretize the emigre assumption that "She must have been crazy to go back." Further, Russians of all political stripes have always been less receptive to Freud and more reticent in writing about aberrations of the psyche than have those in the West. It is not simply the Soviet puritanical and ideological rejection of the Viennese doctor and his theories. Emigre culture (first, second, and third wave) has shown little interest in Freud or Jung, preferring, when necessary, a traditional "psychologizing" with its roots in the nineteenth-century realistic novel.

Tsvetaeva, in emigration, could never have afforded the luxury of psychoanalysis (H.D. was analyzed by Freud himself), nor is it even likely she would have sought it had she needed it. But Freud and Freudianism were definitely part of the European *Zeitgeist* by the twenties, and Tsvetaeva, though she never mentions Freud by name, must have known something of his work. Though I have no proof other than intuition, I see her "childhood prose" of the 1930's, her revived interest in family history and her own early childhood, as a kind of "do-it-yourself" psychoanalysis comparable to Bely's *Kotik Letaev* or Zoshchenko's *Before Sunrise*. The Soviet scholar Irma Kudrova hints at such an interpretation when she attributes Tsvetaeva's turn to autobiographical prose to her realization of "her failure in her relationships with the world; she was deeply troubled by the communication which had gone completely out of order."[3] Though a Soviet reader or editor could easily interpret this to mean "her communication with the emigre world that surrrounded her" Kudrova cannily leaves the question open.

Tsvetaeva, who always paid great heed to dreams, could not have been totally uninterested in the great dream interpreter. Some pages of her childhood memoirs, particularly her description of her love for the Devil, have a distinctly "Freudian" erotic element discreetly ignored by most Russian critics and commentators, who also tread delicately around the forthright eroticism which characterizes much of her poetry.[4]

* * *

Marina (born 1892) and Anastasia (Asya, born 1894) were the children of Ivan Vladimirovich Tsvetaev's second marriage. When they were born, Tsvetaev was already in his late forties, and preoccupied with his life's obsession: the founding of Russia's first museum of classical and Western sculpture. The girls called it "our colossal younger brother." The Alexander III Museum of Fine Arts finally opened in May 1912, with great fanfare and the Tsar in attendance. The name did not survive the Revolution—it is now Moscow's Pushkin Museum of Fine Arts—but on the fiftieth anniversary of the opening, a commemorative plaque with Tsvetaev's portrait was placed by the main entrance. He would doubtless have been distressed to learn that he is better known today as the father of one of Russia's greatest poets than as the founder of one of its major museums.

Ivan Tsvetaev (1847–1913) was a self-made man. One of four sons of a village priest in the province of Vladimir, he doggedly pursued an education and became a professor of classical languages and art at Moscow University and the director of the Rumiantsev Museum, Moscow's largest library (its collection became the basis for the Lenin Library). With the same determination Tsvetaev pursued the dream of his museum, coaxing donations from wealthy Moscow merchants and their widows. He personally oversaw the construction and even travelled to the Urals to choose the marble for the museum's facade.

Tsvetaev's first wife was Varvara Ilovayskaya, beautiful daughter of the reactionary and anti-Semitic historian whose history textbook was required reading in all Russian schools before the Revolution. They had a daughter Valeria (1883–1966) and a son Andrey (1890–1933), but Varvara died shortly after her second childbirth. A year later, the still grieving Tsvetaev married Maria Mein, who, at 22, was exactly half his age. Maria Mein was the only daughter of a Moscow journalist and businessman. Her own mother, a young Polish aristocrat, had died giving birth to her. Maria's doting father gave his orphaned daughter an education then unusual for a young woman. Like Pasternak's mother, Rosa Kaufmann, she was a talented pianist who, a generation later, might well have had a concert career, but her father would not allow her to perform publicly. Fluent in German, French, and Italian, she read widely, particularly in the German Romantics. Hers was, according to her daughter Marina, "a claustrophobic, fantastic, unhealthy, bookish life."[5]

After their mother's death at the age of 36, Marina and Asya discovered and devoured her diary, which revealed aspects of her life they had never suspected. They learned that, at the age of sixteen, she fell in love with a man several years her senior. "But he was married, and grandfather considered divorce a sin. . . . Mama loved grandfather too much to agree to a marriage under such conditions."[6] Their mother devoted a whole volume of the diary to the affair, but Marina and Asya knew only the name and initial of its hero, Seryozha E. Her mother, who in life provided Marina with a model in so many ways, thus, posthumously, provided her with two more important examples: of self-abnegation, denial of fulfillment for the sake of another, and of the use of the diary form as an outlet for emotions and creativity.

Against her father's advice, Maria Mein married the widowed Professor Tsvetaev, hoping, in Anastasia's words, "to overcome the tragedy of her first love in the task of raising another's children. . . ."[7] She did not find her new life easy. Valeria resented her stepmother, and Tsvetaev was still in love with the memory of his first wife, whose enormous portrait dominated their living room. Maria Alexandrovna threw herself determinedly into helping him with his museum project, managing his household, and raising his children. She and a series of governesses took charge of the girls' schooling; only when Marina was nine was she enrolled in a private girls' school.

The family spent long, happy summers in Tarusa, a small town on the river Oka frequented by artists and writers; the landscapes which Marina loved most in her later life always had in them something of Tarusa. But this happy protected childhood ended abruptly in 1902. Maria Alexan-drovna fell ill with tuberculosis, and, on doctors' orders, she went abroad, taking the girls. Marina and Anastasia, aged ten and eight, suddenly found themselves by the unknown, magical ocean, in the Italian town of Nervi, with a new and unaccustomed freedom, no teachers and little discipline. They clambered over seaside cliffs in the sunshine and learned street Italian. Russian radical exiles staying at their *pension* befriended them, admired Marina's precocious verse, and planted some new ideas in their heads— among them populism and atheism.

In the spring of 1903, Marina and Asya were sent off to a *pension* in French-speaking Lausanne, where they spent the spring, summer, and fol-lowing academic year. The first step in their mother's reacclimatization to life in a colder climate took place in 1904. The girls and both parents spent an enchanted summer high in the hills of the Black Forest; here lie the roots of Tsvetaeva's ambivalent love for Germany. In the fall, Marina and Anastasia entered a German-speaking *pension* in Freiburg, while their mother took a room nearby. But in midwinter she caught a cold, and her tuberculosis went into a regression from which she was never to recover. In the revolutionary summer of 1905, after almost three years abroad, mother and daughters returned to Russia—at least to Yalta. But Maria Tsvetaeva's health continued to deteriorate, and in June 1906, after almost four years of wandering, they all went home to Tarusa. Three weeks later, on July 5, she died. Marina was not quite fourteen, Anastasia was almost twelve.

Their mother's death thrust the girls into a life of premature independ-ence. The sisters were unpredictable and "difficult." "Perhaps that is why after Mama's death not one of Papa's female relatives took upon herself our upbringing."[8] Though a kindly, gentle man, Tsvetaev, preoccupied with his museum, was more a grandfather than a father to his younger daughters. He never understood their Bohemian lifestyle, and was horrified at their early marriages (solemnized in both cases well after the fact). Nor did the girls, very different from him in temperament and interests, have much sympathy for his values. They seemed not to care that they caused him a great deal of grief. Marina came to appreciate him only as he was dying:

> He loved us very much, considered us "talented, capable, mature," but he was horrified at our laziness, independence, boldness, and love for what he called "eccentricity."[9]

Tsvetaeva attributed her creativity, intelligence and rebelliousness exclu-sively to her maternal heritage:

> Her tormented soul lives in us—only we reveal what she concealed. Her rebel-lion, her madness, her thirst have developed in us to the point of screaming.[10]

Or, as she wrote in a very early poem:

Все бледней лазурный остров — детство,
Мы одни на палубе стоим.
Видно грусть оставила в наследство
Ты, о мама, девочкам своим!

The azure island—childhood—
    grows ever paler,
We stand alone on the deck.
Clearly, Mama, you gave us,
    your little girls
Melancholy as our inheritance.
(I, 21)

Was the "melancholy" (*grust'*) of which the young Marina wrote just another commonplace of *fin de siècle* decadence, or was the adolescent Tsvetaeva already aware of a more concrete psychological legacy? Many of those qualities which would make Marina always a misfit in the world of *byt* did seem to come from her mother. Was the "sadness" that was mama's leitmotif in all Tsvetaeva's early poems also a depressive personality she passed on as well?

Maria Mein-Tsvetaeva's illness and death deprived Marina of more than simply maternal care and nurturance. Marina was forced into a quasi-adulthood which she did not want and for which she was not ready. Her mother's death, moreover, cut off at a crucial stage—the rebellious years of early adolescence—a complex relationship of two creative women, leaving the daughter, for the rest of her life, to struggle with the questions of female identity and creativity which inform and inspire so much of her work. A more concrete legacy was the comfortable inheritance which—until it vanished in the Revolution—allowed Tsvetaeva a considerable amount of financial, and therefore creative, independence.[11] Until the Revolution and Civil War turned her world upside down, poetry was for Tsvetaeva always a calling, a self-identification, a profession in that sense, but never a source of livelihood. Ironically, her mother's death, by providing that inheritance, enabled an artistic freedom which probably would never have been possible had she lived.

Maria Mein, sensing her elder daughter's special gifts, naturally assumed they were her own musical ones. She started her on the piano at the age of four, hoping to make her (and Asya) into pianists in her own image, "so my daughters will be the 'free artists' I wanted so much to be."[12] The quotation is from Tsvetaeva's 1934 prose memoir, "Mother and Music." Whether Maria Mein really felt that way is less important than that Marina believed or wanted to believe she did. She went on to recall: "Mother deluged us with music . . . with all the bitterness of her own unrealized vocation, her own unrealized life. . . ."[13] But Marina's undeniable lyric talent was made for poetic, not musical, expression. No matter how great her gift, a pianist always interprets *someone else's* notes, and it was precisely the *notes* at which the young Marina balked. Marina wanted to create her *own* songs, with her *own* melodies and rhythms, not bring to life someone else's. In the very first paragraph of "Mother and Music," Tsvetaeva "overcomes" music by turning the notes—her mother's kingdom—into a kind of poetry. Her mother's patiently repeated "*Do, re*" turned in Marina's mind into a melding of the French artist Gustave Dore and the literal meaning of the word in French ("gilded"). All the other notes of the scale, following their lead, then acquired a metaphorical color derived from verbal associations:

> *Do* is clearly white, empty, *do vsego*, "before everything else," *re* is light blue, *mi* is yellow (maybe—*midi?*), *fa* is brown (maybe mother's faille street dress, and *re* is blue—*reka*—river?)—and so on, . . .[14]

Music would remain with Marina, finding its expression in the unique rhythms of her poetry. The piano of her childhood would frequently appear as an image, particularly in the poems addressed to Boris Pasternak, who also renounced a career in music for poetry.

After her mother's death, Marina abandoned the piano and spent more time writing poetry. Several of the poems in her first collection, *Evening Album* (1910), are dated 1908; some undated ones may have been written even earlier. Her mother's presence dominates the first section of the book and much of Marina's second collection, *Magic Lantern* (1912). These early poems are an attempt to recreate, and thus preserve, a childhood irrevocably lost along with her mother. The wander years in Europe, though they gave Tsvetaeva a mastery of French and German that would stand her in good stead during her emigration, play only a small part in her poetry and in her memoirs. The world she most often evokes and idealizes is that of early childhood, the house at Three Ponds, the dacha at Tarusa, music and books and above all Mama, playing the piano or reading to the girls. It is an idealized world, and an idealized mama who moves through it, wise and loving, though sad.

One of the best of these early poems, hovever, gives a more complex picture:

МАМА ЗА КНИГОЙ

...Сдавленный шепот. . . Сверканье
                книжала. . .
— «Мама, построй мне из кубиков домик!»
Мама взволнованно к сердцу прижала
Маленький томик.

...Гневом глаза загорелись у графа:
«Здесь я, княгиня, по благости рока!»
— «Мама, а в море не тонет жирафа?»
Мама душою — далеко!

MAMA OVER A BOOK

"A Muffled whisper. . .The flash of a
    dagger. . ."
—"Mama, build me a house out of blocks!"
Mama, agitated, clasps to her heart
The little volume.

—The count's eyes lit up with thunder:
"I am here, princess, by the favor of fate!"
—"Mama, do giraffes drown in the sea?"
Mama's soul is far away!

— «Мама, смотри: паутинка в котлете!»
В голосе детском упрек и угроза.
Мама очнулась от вымыслов: дети —
Горькая проза!

—"Mama, look: there's a cobweb in the
     cutlet!"
In the childish voice, reproach and threat.
Mama's returned from her fantasies: children
Are bitter prose!
                    1909 or 1910
                       (I, 67)

Mama's reading matter is a parody of romantic fiction, underlined by the exaggerated alliteration of the line which begins the second stanza: "*Gnevom glaza zagorelis' u grafa,*" while the child's interruptions have the freshness of reality—the ploys of a verbally precocious daughter toying for her mother's attention.

This is one of the few hints in the early poems of the complex mother-daughter relationship Tsvetaeva draws in her childhood prose of the 1930's. Then, having experienced the storms of her own daughter's adolescence, she drew a far franker picture of a stern, almost cold, and impossibly demanding mother who, Tsvetaeva was convinced, favored the baby Asya and never forgave her first-born for not being a son, nor for lacking her own musical gift. We have no way of knowing how accurate a picture it is, but in many details it fits with what we know of Tsvetaeva herself as a mother to Ariadna Efron. Mothering may not have come naturally to Maria Mein, motherless herself, and she passed the awkwardness on to her elder daughter.

Significantly, the early poems mention "Papa" hardly at all. Busy with his work, and largely absent during their years in Europe, Tsvetaev played only a small role in his younger daughters' lives. Only on the twentieth anniversary of his death did Tsvetaeva write about him, in a series of prose sketches collectively titled "Father and his Museum" which opened the series of childhood prose. Even there, Tsvetaev is seen entirely against the background of his single-minded concern for the museum: wheedling money out of a wealthy industrialist, slyly smuggling in, duty free, a German lawn-mower for the museum yard, expressing dismay at the cost of the elaborate court uniform required for him to accept the honor bestowed for his achievement ("It would be better spent on the museum!"). In these later sketches, Tsvetaeva's portrait of her father is wryly amused and proud, as she acknowledges at least two inheritances from him: her addictions to hard, daily work, and to long vigorous walks.

But, at least as Tsvetaeva saw it, the creativity was all on her mother's side. Tsvetaev's most original idea, his museum, was, after all, to be a collection of *copies*, copies of the great works of Western sculpture to be studied and admired by poor boys like himself not similarly blessed by the good fortune to travel to Italy on scholarship. The concept of the museum reflected the immense social changes that had taken place in Russia in the

latter half of the nineteenth century. Who, till then, had concerned themselves with the aesthetic education of the lower classes? The aristocracy,
who travelled freely to Europe, hardly needed copies of Western art in
Moscow. Several pages into the memoir about her father, Tsvetaeva
launches into a long paragraph in praise of her *mother*:

> My father's closest co-worker was my mother .... She carried on all his
> voluminous foreign correspondence and often, *by her particular epistolary
> eloquence* [emphasis mine—J.T.], by a certain special grace of wit or flattery
> (with a French correspondent) a line from a poet (with an English one), some
> question about the children, the garden (with a German)—by using that
> human touch in a business letter, a personal note in an official communica-
> tion, and sometimes simply by an apt turn of phrase, she would succeed in
> something that my father might achieve only with labor and quite differently.[15]

Such "particular epistolary eloquence" was of course one of the characteristics of her daughter's art.

* * *

> He doesn't yet know our words. His speech seems to come from a desert
> island, from childhood, from the Garden of Eden: it doesn't quite make sense,
> and it knocks you over. At the age of three, this is common, and is called "a
> child"; at twenty-three it is uncommon, and is called, "a poet." (Tsvetaeva,
> speaking of Pasternak)[16]

Tsvetaeva always valued the child's eye and ear; the artist, she was convinced, is one who manages to carry that freshness of vision into his adult
life. Childhood was the major theme of her first two books of poetry, published when she was hardly more than a child herself; her reexamination of
that childhood in the 1930's broke new ground in Russian prose. Childhood,
of course, is the only period in human life when we are allowed the willful
rejection of reality in favor of fantasy, imagination, and "play-acting," precisely those processes which are the essence of the poet's craft. After childhood, as Tsvetaeva says more eloquently above, the creation of willful fic-
tions is allowed only (leaving aside politicians) to the creative artist.

Tsvetaeva began to write very early, at the age of six, she claimed. During
most of her creative life, one or more of her own children was a constant
companion, as she divided her time between writing and mothering. Ariadna
(Alya), the eldest, appears often in her mother's poems. She was a precocious writer, like her mother, and Tsvetaeva thought enough of her poems
to include some of them (written when Alya was seven) in one of her own
collections. In fact, Tsvetaeva's first book of prose—sketches reworked from
her diaries of revolutionary Moscow—remained unpublished because Tsvetaeva insisted that Alya's diaries be included as well.

We have three literary versions of Tsvetaeva's childhood: her own early poems (she published well over two hundred of them before she was twenty), her prose memoirs of the 1930's, and the memoirs of her younger sister Anastasia.[17] Obviously, the biographer seeking hard facts should approach all these sources with extreme caution. Yet these three versions of a single childhood do allow us to make some observations about the way the child Marina and the woman Marina transformed her life into art.

Anastasia's memoirs, despite their greater distance in time from their subject, are far richer in detail. In fact, they are *too* rich, with loving descriptions of treasured toys and the shops they came from, the layout of the family house at Three Ponds Lane, of Italian, Swiss, and German landscapes as seen by the girls at the beginning of the century. Marina's memoirs, in contrast, are strikingly bereft of "realistic" detail. Yet how much more evocative, and ultimately more interesting they are! She is concerned not with the particular, but with the whole question of the child's perception of the world and the roots of her own artistic imagination. Marina's primary aim in writing these pieces was not "literal truth" in the narrowly biographical sense. Anastasia complains that "Mama in Marina's writing seems to me. . .simplified, schematic."[18] Yet this simplification and schematization is the essence of Tsvetaeva's transformation of reality into art, something Anastasia never attains.[19]

Tsvetaeva's early poems assert, albeit rather naively, her belief in children's "special knowledge," their special understanding of other worlds, and other *words* which adults have lost.

Мы старших за то презираем,
Что скучны и просты их дни. . .
Мы знаем, мы многое знаем
Того, что не знают они!

We disdain our elders
Because their days are dull and simple. . .
We know, we know a great deal
That they don't know!
(I, 5)

One of the things her children know is the emptiness and banality of *this* world, and the joy of other worlds, be they beyond the grave, or only the products of fantasy. They are willing to "seize the beautiful moment" while they are still young, even at the price of early death. On her seventeenth birthday, Marina prayed:

Ты дал мне детство — лучше сказки
И дай мне смерть — в семнадцать лет!

You gave me a childhood better than a fairytale
Now give me death—at seventeen!
Tarusa, Sept. 26, 1909
(I, 57)

Occasionally the wished-for early death is self-imposed. A poem titled "Suicide," recounts, from a small boy's point of view, how he watched his mother drown herself in the pond of their summerhouse. We must not and

cannot forget that these poems were written when their author was sixteen
or seventeen, under the influence of her first exposure to Russia's "decadent"
turn-of-the-century culture. But this adolescent idealization of suicide seems
eerily frightening when we remember that Tsvetaeva, more than thirty years
later, would choose to take her own life, leaving her sixteen-year-old son to
the care of strangers and the mercy of fate.

In Tsvetaeva's early poetry we hear, now and then, the fiercely independent and unmistakable poetic voice—with its child-like directness and immediacy of address—which was to be hers to the end. Most, if not all the
poems in *Evening Album* and *Magic Lantern* are juvenilia. Nevertheless, there
are themes here which reemerge in more sophisticated form in Tsvetaeva's
mature verse. Most important of these is Tsvetaeva's preference for "that
other world," the "*byt'ie*" of imagination and spirit. At this early stage,
before those terms had entered her poetic vocabulary, Tsvetaeva posed the
opposition in terms of childhood (*byt'ie*) and adulthood (*byt*). Marriage
and motherhood were frightening prospects; Maria Mein's life of self-
sacrifice was not an appealing model. In Paris in the summer of 1909, Marina watched the children playing in the Jardin de Luxembourg and attempted to write a paean to motherhood: "I want to cry out to each mother
fondling her child, 'You own the whole world!'" But despite her brave conclusion, the poet's ambivalence is evident:

Я женщин люблю, что в бою не робели,	I love those women who did not fear battle,
Умевших и шпагу держать, и копье, —	Who knew how to hold both sword and spear,
Но знаю, что только в плену колыбели	But I know that only in captivity to the cradle
Обычное — женское — счастье мое!	Lies my ordinary—female—happiness!
(I, 11)	

A somewhat later poem, probably written in the winter of 1910, presents an
ominous portrait of a young girl about to be married off against her will:

ОБРЕЧЕННАЯ	THE DOOMED GIRL
Бледные ручки коснулись рояля	Her pale little hands touched the piano
Медленно, словно без сил.	'Slowly, as if without strength.
Звуки запели, томленьем печаля.	The sounds sang out, sad and pining.
Кто твои думы смутил,	Who has troubled your thoughts,
Бледная девушка, там, у рояля?	Pale maiden there at the keyboard?
Тот, кто следит за тобой,	He who follows after you
— Словно акула за маленькой рыбкой —	Like a shark after a little fish—
Он твоей будет судьбой!	He will be your fate!
И не о добром он мыслит с улыбкой,	He's not thinking of good with that smile,
Тот, кто стоит за тобой.	He who stands behind you!
С радостным видом хлопочут родные:	With joyous faces the relatives bustle,
Дочка — невеста! Их дочь!	Their little girl's engaged! Their daughter!
Если и снились ей грезы иные, —	If she had any other dreams—
Грезы развеются в ночь!	Those dreams will disperse in one night!
С радостным видом хлопочут родные.	With joyous faces the relatives bustle!

Светлая церковь, кольцо,	A brightly-lit church, a wedding band,
Шум, поздравления, с образом мальчик. . .	Noise, congratulations, a boy with an icon . . .
Девушка скрыла лицо,	The girl has hidden her face,
Смотрит с тоскою на узенький пальчик,	She looks with anguish at the slender finger
Где загорится кольцо.	Where the wedding band will soon blaze!

(I, 60)

Motherhood at least promised the opportunity to remain, in many ways, in the world of the nursery; the mother-child bond seemed close to Tsvetaeva's androgynous ideal of love between souls rather than bodies. Marriage, on the other hand, seemed to offer no consolations at all.

CHAPTER TWO

After Mama

Life resumed in the house at Three Ponds after their mother's death, but it was very different from the girls' early childhood. Thrust into a premature independence, Marina tried to prolong her childhood in her poetry.

In the fall of 1906, at her own request, Tsvetaeva entered the Von Derviz *gymnasium*. Its strict regimen scarcely suited her nonconforming spirit and she was expelled before the year was out. It was the first of three schools she would attend in three years. Anastasia tries to convince her Soviet readers that Marina was expelled for "revolutionary tendencies," but her rebelliousness was more adolescent and intellectual than political. Tsvetaeva frequently played hooky; alone at home she devoured the German romantics of her mother's bookshelf.

As she neared sixteen, Marina's literary infatuations shifted to the French, particularly to Edmund Rostand and his play *L'Aiglon* (The Eaglet, 1900), about Napoleon's son, the Duke of Reichstadt. Rostand's hero is a beautiful, noble youth, mesmerized by the achievements of a father he scarcely knew. Half Bonaparte, half Hapsburg, he is a but a prisoner in the gilded cage of Schoenbrunn, his jailor the Austrian emperor who is at once his father's nemesis and his own grandfather. Tempted to return to France at the head of a Bonapartist plot, he fails in resolve at the crucial moment, and soon dies of consumption. During the winter of 1908–1909, Marina created a private cult of Napoleon and his son. She ordered all the books she could find on them from the French bookstore in Moscow, and set Napoleon's portrait in place of the Virgin on her icon-stand, much to her father's dismay. With the hundredth anniversary of Borodino fast approaching, it was a particularly unconventional adulation for a Russian schoolgirl. Had she never read *War and Peace*? There is no mention of the novel, and scarcely a mention of Tolstoy, anywhere in her work or her letters.

Marina's adolescent fanaticism might seem hardly worth a passing mention, but in fact this first well-documented "love affair" is in many ways characteristic. Tsvetaeva was more attracted to the doomed, gentle Duke than to his martial father. Even more important, the role of the Duke was created and immortalized by Sarah Bernhardt—the fascinatingly androgynous feat of an aging actress of genius playing a handsome young man. There are important androgynous elements in the play itself: the leader of the Bonapartist plot is the Duke's cousin, the Countess Camerata, a bold Amazon and accomplished swordswoman. The Eaglet's escape from

Schoenbrunn is to be effected by a ruse in which the countess, dressed as his double, will distract the guards. An added sexual *frisson*: on the night of his planned escape, Reichstadt has arranged a rendezvous with a young Frenchwoman, a romantic appointment that will be kept by his cousin. Marina, not yet seventeen, spent the summer of 1909 in Paris, ostensibly studying French, but largely for the purpose (vain, it turned out) of seeing Bernhardt in the role.

In the fall of 1908, Marina had begun translating the play, working diligently throughout the winter only to discover that another translation existed. According to Anastasia, Marina could see that her version was far superior, but "the thought of giving a second translation evidently never entered her head."[1] The translation has evidently been lost, but the experience probably taught Tsvetaeva the poet a good deal more than she might have learned from the schoolwork she shirked while completing a verse translation of the 200-page work. Her abandonment of the project is also characteristic: Marina could not stand to share her loves; she always needed to be different, to love the underdog, the rejected of this world.

The orphaned Tsvetaeva sisters found a mother-substitute in a family friend, Lidia Alexandrovna Tamburer, whom the girls nicknamed "the Dragon Lady." Half-Italian and half-Ukrainian, a strong-minded middle-aged woman with a career (she was a dentist), Tamburer took the girls' intellectual life under her wing. She introduced Marina to her first live poet: Lev L'vovich Kobylinsky (1874–1947), who wrote under the pen name Ellis. Ellis, now relegated to a footnote in histories of Russian literature, was then a well-known poet, critic, and theoretician of Symbolism. After a youthful flirtation with Marxism, Ellis transferred his allegiance to Baudelaire, whom he translated.[2] It was Ellis who first turned Marina's attention to contemporary Russian poetry, then dominated by the Symbolist "B's:" Briusov, Bal'mont, Blok, and Bely, and began her introduction to the Moscow literary world. Though eighteen years her senior, the mercurial Ellis was a far from ideal mentor. He appears in Bely's memoirs (colored, undoubtedly, by their subsequent rift) as a scandalist and parodist extraordinaire, with a murderous gift for satiric imitations. These were qualities Tsvetaeva herself would soon demonstrate when she locked horns with the influential Valery Briusov. Ellis' ultimate influence on Tsvetaeva's development as a poet was minimal. But one of his traits, as depicted by Bely, is eerily similar to Tsvetaeva's predilection for "personal mythifications:"

> He would create for himself a pearl of creation, and immediately begin to commit acts of violence. . .out of love. "You are a pearl, don't dare grow dull; shine, shine, shine no matter what." If you want to eat, a scandal: diamonds don't defile themselves with food; you want to marry—don't dare; "diamonds" don't marry, they carry in their hearts the cult of the rose . . .[3]

Did Tsvetaeva learn her passion for mythification from Ellis or, more likely, was it this mutual tendency which brought them together?

Illegitimate son of the well-known educator Lev Polivanov, Ellis lacked regular employment, lived in modest furnished lodgings, and cultivated dinner invitations. In the spring of 1909, when Prof. Tsvetaev travelled to Cairo for a conference of archaeologists, the girls were left totally unsupervised. Ellis came almost every evening and stayed late into the night. Five years later, when he was living in Switzerland (Rudolf Steiner had succeeded Baudelaire, and was in turn succeeded by Catholicism), and their friendship was but a memory, Tsvetaeva paid tribute to Ellis in a long poem (*poema*) titled, "The Wizard" (the sisters' nickname for him). Marina recalled those endless evenings, undoubtedly exaggerating, as was her habit, the girls' adolescent exuberance:

Два скакуна в огне и мыле —	Two race horses in fire and lather
Вот мы! — Лови, когда не лень!	That's what we are! Catch us, if you're not lazy!
Мы говорим о том, как жили	We talk about how we spent
Вчерашний день.	Yesterday,
О том, как бегали по зале	How tonight, in the moonlight,
Сегодня ночью при луне	We raced about in the parlor,
И что и как ему сказали	And how and what we then said to him
Потом во сне.	In our dreams.
И как — и мы уже в экстазе! —	And how—and we're already in ecstasy!—
За наш непокоримый дух	The administration of our two schools
Начальство наших двух гимназий	Is persecuting us both
Нас гонит двух.	For our unruly spirit.
Как никогда не выйдем замуж,	And how we'll never marry
— Так и останемся втроем! —	—That way, we'll stay a threesome!
О, никогда не выйдем замуж,	Oh, we'll never marry
Скорей умрем!	We'd rather die!

                                            (I, 157)

In the fall of 1909, Ellis introduced the sisters to his friend Vladimir Ottonovich Nilender, a twenty-six-year-old student of their father who was translating Heraclitus. Behind him was a stint in the naval academy and a wife named Sophia, who was "no longer with him." Nilender became Tsvetaeva's first serious romantic involvement, but the exact nature of the affair is cloaked in mist and mythification. From Tsvetaeva herself, we have only a group of poems in her first collection, *Evening Album*, and two cryptic, seemingly offhand references in prose memoirs written decades later. Anastasia's account of the affair, which Karlinsky wisely judges "most likely laundered,"[4] is suspiciously rich in irrelevant detail and coyly silent about central issues.

The gist of her account is that Ellis made Marina a proposal of marriage in a letter sent via his friend. Shocked and embarrassed, she saw the proposal as a betrayal. Ellis was their first "adult" friend, her literary mentor, and knew of their intentions never to marry. Evidently, he saw her, after all, not as a "brother poet," but simply as an eligible young lady of good family and substantial dowry. Marina answered him in verse with a poem titled, "The Mistake."

Оставь полет снежникам с мотыльками
И не губи медузу на песках!
Нельзя мечту свою хватать руками,
Нельзя мечту свою держать в руках!

Don't disturb the flight of snowflakes and
  moths,
Don't crush the jellyfish in the sand!
You can't grasp your dream with your hands,
You can't hold your dream in your hands!

Нельзя тому, что было грустью зыбкой,
Сказать: «Будь страсть! Горя безумствуй,
                                         рдей!»
Твоя любовь была такой ошибкой, —
Но без любви мы гибнем, Чародей!

You can't say to that which has been unsteady
  melancholy
"Be a passion! Burn madly, glow!"
Your love was such a mistake,—
But without love we perish, Wizard!

(I, 34)

Why did Ellis chose such a roundabout route to propose? Anastasia doesn't even raise the question, though it soon became obvious that the messenger was himself attracted to Marina. The second section of *Evening Album*, titled "Love," is the lyric diary's version of these events. "Into the Other Camp," addresses both Nilender and Ellis with a maidenly rejection of male passion:

Ах, вы не братья, нет, не братья!
Пришли из тьмы, ушли в туман. . .
Для нас безумные объятья
Еще неведомый дурман.

Oh, you're not brothers, no, not brothers!
You came from shadows, you've vanished in
  mist. . .
For us your mad embraces
Are an as yet unknown intoxicant.

Пока вы рядом — смех и шутки,
Но чуть умолкнули шаги,
Уж ваши речи странно-жутки,
И чует сердце: вы враги.

While you're beside us—laughter and jokes,
But as soon as your steps have faded
Your speech is strange and terrifying
And the heart senses you are enemies.

(I, 29)

Tsvetaeva was barely seventeen, and though precocious as a poet, she was still naive, even immature for her years, in the art of human relationships. She had no mother to advise her; her closest confidante was a giddy fifteen-year-old sister. She had sought in Ellis and Nilender elder brothers, mentors, and colleagues; they answered with professions of a kind of love with which she was unprepared to cope, not only personally, but even artistically. The "grown up" sensuality they offered (and must have expected in exchange) directly challenged the ideal of an androgynous a-sexual childhood she had been creating in the poems of "Childhood," the first section of *Evening Album*. Moreover, Nilender was a classical philologist like her father, indeed, her father's *protege*. A future as his wife could only promise a recapitulation of her mother's fate.

It was not that she found Nilender unattractive. In fact, if we are to take the poems at their word, (and at this early stage of the lyric diary, we have no reason not to) *both* sisters were girlishly infatuated with him: the four-way friendship, it appears, contained *two* triangles. But the girls' shared infatuation, like the very existence of Nilender's estranged wife, seemed to assure Tsvetaeva that their friendship would remain in the idealized world of *byt'ie* where she could deal with it in her art. When his avowal threatened to push the relationship into the concrete world of *byt*, Tsvetaeva retreated, frightened. Years later, Tsvetaeva would claim that she published her first collection "for reasons alien to literature but akin to poetry—in place of a letter to a man with whom I was deprived of the possibility of communicating in any other way."[5] Because to do so would encourage Nilender's "unacceptable" passion? Because he was legally married? This version makes the book the first of Tsvetaeva's characteristic epistolary-poetic friendships with "impossible" correspondents.

In the midst of the Nilender poems, there is a bit of seeming nonsense—a poem addressed "To the Next (Man)." In it, the two sisters await an "enchanted prince" who is "blue-eyed," "tender as a maiden," "quiet as a child," an Eaglet-like prince who shares their childish delights and interests. Tsvetaeva had at least the self-knowledge to provide the poem with the epigraph "Quasi una fantasia." But that fantasy hero—delicate, gentle, childlike—would recur again and again in her lyric diary as the ideal "other" in a love relationship. His most vivid portrait is the androgynous tsarevich in her long narrative poem *The Tsar-Maiden*. It was the ideal which she sought in the men in her life, and came closest to finding in the man she married. Nearly all the other men who would play major roles in Tsvetaeva's lyric diary (Mandel'stam, Pasternak, Bakhrakh, to name a few) possessed some traits of that fantasy hero—childlike and non-threatening—and in her poems, Tsvetaeva transformed them further in that direction. The ideal had clearly been there from the beginning, but the glimpse Ellis and Nilender provided into the "enemy camp" must have colored her subsequent relationships with men. Seldom again would she let herself be involved in a relationship in which she did not feel herself in some way stronger and dominant.

In the abortive romance with Nilender, as in nearly all the love affairs that found their way into the lyric diary, separation proved to be a far more productive ground for art than union. It provided the situation which motivates so many of Tsvetaeva's greatest poems—intimate address to an "other," most often another poet, across some impenetrable boundary, a formula guaranteed to keep relationships in the world of *byt'ie*. Though the earlier poems in that central section of *Evening Album* deal with the Nilender-related drama of declarations and parting, the more numerous, and usually more interesting, later poems of the section are retrospective, exploring Tsvetaeva's memories and emotions in the months which followed. Most of them are directly addressed to Nilender; such direct address to a specific addressee became characteristic of Tsvetaeva's lyrics. Direct address gave her the opportunity to play with the rhythms of Russian conversational speech, a traditional female "genre." She never seemed as comfortable with the poetic equivalent of the omniscient third-person narrator, that authoritative voice beloved in the male tradition. That was the voice she had used, with less success, in the first section of *Evening Album*. The Nilender poems set still another pattern: though most of the poems in Tsvetaeva's first two books are undated, the cluster of poems dealing with the events of December 20, 1909 through January 17, 1910, pointedly bear dates, either beneath the poems themselves, or attached to a letter or diary excerpt that serves as an epigraph. Here, in fact, are the real beginnings of Tsvetaeva's lyric diary.

As those events slipped further into the past, Tsvetaeva began to regard them with increasing regret and greater poetic sophistication. It is less their theme than their form which makes these poems worthy of some attention. The thirty-five poems of "Love" are a workshop and showcase for Tsvetaeva's developing verse technique. Most of the poems in "Childhood" were written in conventional quatrains of straightforward binary or sing-song ternary meters. By contrast, nearly every poem in the second section of the book uses a different combination of meter, rhyme scheme, and stanza. Tsvetaeva began to experiment with very long lines (four-and five-foot ternary meters, with as many as sixteen syllables to the line), and there is even, at this early date, a debut of her trademark, the *logaed*, which mixes binary and ternary feet in a regular pattern within a single line.[6] She builds five-and six-line stanzas with more complicated rhyme schemes, and we more often encounter the characteristic shortened line at the end of the stanza (for breathless exclamations or a witty *pointe*). "The Nursery," addressed to Nilender, illustrates many of these innovations:

Наша встреча была — в полумраке беседа	Our meeting was a conversation in half-darkness
Полувзрослого с полудетьми.	Of a half-adult with half-children.
Хлопья снега за окнами, песни метели. . .	Flakes of snow outside the windows, songs of the snowstorm.
Мы из детской уйти не хотели,	We didn't want to leave the nursery—
Вместо сказки не жаждали бреда. . .	We didn't want delerium in place of fairy-tale-
Если можешь — пойми!	If you can—understand!

Мы любили тебя — как могли, как умели;	We loved you as we could, as we knew how,
Целый сад в наших душах бы мог расцвести,	A whole garden could have bloomed in our
Мы бы рай увидали воочью! . . .	soul.
Но, испуганы зимнею ночью,	We could have seen paradise for ourselves.
Мы из детской уйти не посмели. . .	But, frightened by the winter night
Если можешь — прости!	We didn't dare leave the nursery—
	If you can—forgive!
	(I, 41)

Simply yet eloquently, Tsvetaeva makes the actual setting of the girls'
night-long conversation with Nilender (their former nursery) into a metaphor for the childhood they were afraid of leaving. Given all we know
about Tsvetaeva's respect for the child's freshness and truth of perception,
her reluctance to "leave the nursery" not only as a woman, but even more
as a poet, is perfectly understandable. Her poems of the next few years
revolve around that fear of adulthood.

In the summer of 1910, Professor Tsvetaev had to travel to Germany on
museum business, and offered to take his daughters along "so they would
not forget their German." They would board with the family of a German
pastor in a small town above Dresden, and the pastor's wife would teach
them home economy. But Tsvetaev's attempt to remove his daughters from
dangerous influences and prepare them for marriage was both misguided
and belated. Tsvetaeva spent her time in Weisser Hirsch not learning
domestic science, but writing poems and preparing the manuscript of *Evening Album*. The collection, luxuriously printed and bound, appeared in
October 1910. Marina had it published at her own expense.

Tsvetaeva's "literary notoriety" began that fall, her last year in *gymnasium*. Under Ellis' auspices, she began attending meetings and lectures at
Mussagetes, the new publishing house intended as a center for the younger
generation of symbolists. Their mystical and mythological interests were
not hers at all, and she reacted to the alien simply by ignoring it—a technique we often find in her art.

> I only heard: gnoseology and the Gnostics, the meanings of which I did not
> understand and, repulsed by the words' nasal sound, never asked about.
> Geometry in high school, gnoseology at *Mussagetes*.[7]

With her rapidly developing satiric gift, she parodied the symbolist rhetoric
of the Mussagetians in a poem titled: "Aesthetes:"

Наши встречи, — только ими дышим все мы,	Our meetings—only by them do we breathe
Их предчувствие лелея в каждом миге, —	Cherishing their premonitions in each
Вы узнаете, разрезав наши книги.	moment—
Все, что любим мы и верим — только темы.	As you will discover, cutting the pages of our
	books.
	All that we love and believe in— Are only
	themes.

Сновидение друг другу подарив, мы
Расстаемся, в жажде новых сновидений,
Для себя и для другого — только тени,
Для читающих об этом — только рифмы.

Having bestowed our dreams upon each other,
We part, craving newer dreams,
For ourselves and for the other— only
  shadows,
For those who read about this—only rhymes.
(I, 117)

At its outset, her career crossed the path of Valery Briusov, the erudite, somewhat pedantic "maitre" of the Russian Symbolist movement's older generation. Briusov was almost unique among major Russian poets in arousing Tsvetaeva's hatred rather than her adulation. She admits that beneath her youthful impertinence lay a great admiration which the senior poet should have sensed, but did not. Her taunts reflected her disappointment that Briusov was not acting in a manner worthy of himself. Their first encounter (or rather non-encounter) had taken place the previous spring in a Moscow bookstore. Marina was looking for Rostand's new play *Chanteclair*. Another customer appeared asking for it as well, although, he added gratuitously, "I am not an admirer of Rostand." Tsvetaeva immediately recognized Briusov, but rather than take up the challenge on the spot, she went home to write him a letter:

Moscow, March 15, 1910

Dear Valery Jakovlevich:

Just now at Wolf's you said, ". . .although I am not an admirer of Rostand."

I wanted right then to ask you, "Why?" But I thought that you would take my question as idle curiosity or the ambitious desire to "speak with Briusov." When the door closed behind you, I was sad, and began to regret my silence, but I finally consoled myself with the thought that I could raise this question in writing.

Why do you not like Rostand? Is it that you see in him only a "brilliant phrase-maker?" Can it be that his infinite nobility, his love of exploit and purity escape you?

This is not an idle question.

For me Rostand is part of my soul, a very large part.

He consoles me, he gives me the strength to live in loneliness. I think that no one, no one knows him, loves him, and values him as I do.

Your passing phrase deeply grieved me.

I began to think: all my favorite poets should feel akin to Rostand. Heine, Victor Hugo, Lamartine, Lermontov—they would all have loved him.

He and Heine share a mutual love for the King of Rome, for Melissande, the princess of Tripoli. Lamartine could not help but love this "Amant du Reve." The Lermontov who wrote *Mtsiry* would have immediately recognized a brother in the author of *l'Aiglon*, Victor Hugo would have been proud of such a pupil.

Why then is Briusov, who loves Heine and Lermontov, who values Victor Hugo, so indifferent to Rostand?

If you, respected Valery Jakovlevich, find my question worthy of an answer, write me about it. . . .

Yours truly,
M. Tsvetaeva[8]

What makes this bit of adolescent fanaticism particularly interesting is that it was not available to Tsvetaeva in 1925, when she was writing "A Hero of Labor," her memoir-obituary of Briusov. In retelling the incident, she reconstructed the letter from memory—and that "memory," aided by fifteen years of maturity and her own poetic imagination, created a rather more sophisticated missive:

Dear Valery Jakovlevich,

Today, in Wolf's shop, ordering *Chanteclair*, you added to the clerk, "although I am not an admirer of Rostand." And you asserted this not once, but twice. Three questions:

How could you, a poet, announce your non-love for another poet to a shop clerk?

Second: How could you, who wrote *Renata*, not love Rostand, who wrote *Melissande*?

Third: And how could you prefer Marcel Proust to Rostand?

I didn't approach you then, in the store, for fear you would take that as an ambitious desire to "speak with Briusov." You are free not to answer this letter.[9]

Tsvetaeva's reconstruction is only a third as long as the original, rhetorically much stronger, and offensive rather than defensive in tone. Its major striking point (How could a poet denigrate to a mere clerk the work of another poet?) partakes of one of Tsvetaeva's fundamental premises—only an artist is fit to judge another artist—but it is totally absent from the original. The original implies a great deal of admiration for Briusov himself, putting him in the company of Heine, Hugo, Lamartine, and Lermontov. It is also much more personal, with its declaration of Rostand's meaning for Tsvetaeva ("He is part of my soul. . . ."), a passage Tsvetaeva's mature memory understandably suppressed. These two letters provide a vivid example of the way Tsvetaeva transformed reality in her lyrics and "auto-biographical" prose.

Another such mythification is her account, also in "Hero of Labor" of how she deposited all five hundred copies of her first book in one "God-forsaken" bookstore, sending none for review. How miraculous, then, and what a tribute to her talent that three major poet-critics (Briusov, Gumilev, and Voloshin) would notice the book and review it. For years, Tsvetaeva scholars took her at her word. But recent research has turned up inscribed copies of the book dedicated to Briusov, Voloshin, and others, which pre-date their reviews.[10]

In his review of *Evening Album*, Briusov, ultimately more important to Russian literature as a critic than a poet, was astute enough to note some of Tsvetaeva's essential qualities:

> Marina Tsvetaeva's poems always take as their starting-point some fact of reality, something actually experienced. Unafraid of introducing the everyday into poetry, she takes the characteristics of life spontaneously, and that gives her poems an eerie intimacy. When you read her book, at moments you feel awkward, as if you have indiscreetly gazed through a half-open window into someone else's apartment and seen a scene not for the eyes of outsiders. However this spontaneity, which is attractive in the more successful pieces, becomes on many pages of the thick collection a kind of "homeyness."

> What results is no longer poetic creativity (bad or good is another question) but simply pages of a personal diary and, at that, rather insipid.[11]

Throughout her career, Tsvetaeva's lyrics would continue the form of a personal diary. Even when she later assumed the masks of literary and mythical heroines (Princess Yaroslavna, Phaedra, the sibyl, Ariadna) her persona's emotions were always her own, transformed by her art. The achievement of the mature Tsvetaeva, of course, was in making these lyrics both confessionally immediate and universal at the same time. Briusov was broad-minded enough to allow for the possibility of a "genuine poetry of intimate life" so different from the often portentous mysticism of Symbolism. He was also correct in warning her that intimacy alone is not enough:

> We will expect that the poet will find in her soul feelings somewhat keener than those sweet nothings which occupy so much space in *Evening Album*, and thoughts more necessary than the repetition of the old truism "the arro-

gance of the Pharisee is hateful." Undoubtedly talented, Marina Tsvetaeva
can give us a genuine poetry of intimate life and can also, given the ease with
which, it appears, she writes verse, waste all of her gift on unnecessary, though
elegant, trifles . . ."[12]

It was not the intimacy of Tsvetaeva's verse *per se* which discomforted
Briusov. As a pioneer of Russian "decadence" Briusov himself had introduced into his work intimacies of a different sort—primarily sexual—previously taboo in Russian poetry. In his condescension to the "homeyness"
and "elegant trifles" of her subjects, there is the clear disdain of the traditional "poet-seer" for the *feminine* intimate life. Significantly, the book's
only female reviewer, Marietta Shaginian, noted and applauded the book's
essential femininity, its themes of sympathy, maternity, and caring. "Marina
Tsvetaeva broaches the question of gender," wrote Shaginian, "not with
macho [muzhchinstvuiushchii] self-assertion, . . . but from her own position
. . . her instinct is a hostile repulsion from the masculine." It was a rather
radical statement for 1911, and Shaginian, who later became a successful
Soviet novelist, conveniently forgot it, indeed, "forgot" she had ever heard
of Tsvetaeva.[13]

Tsvetaeva's friends regarded Briusov's review as a great triumph, but her
pride was wounded. She was further offended when, at a reading of young
Moscow poets, Briusov avoided shaking Tsvetaeva's hand with the lame
excuse, "We are all friends in the family of poets." Later, she submitted a
poem[14] to a competition judged by Briusov, who pompously announced,
"No one received first prize. The first of two second prizes goes to M.
Tsvetaeva."[15] When Tsvetaeva's second collection, *Magic Lantern*, appeared
in early 1912, it contained her answer to Briusov's review. Its second stanza
again parodies the commonplaces of symbolism, then rejects them:

Улыбнись в мое «окно»,   Smile in my "window"
Иль к шутам меня причисли, —   Or rank me among the buffoons—
Не изменишь, все равно!   You won't change me anyhow!
«Острых чувств» и «нужных мыслей»   God did not grant me "keen emotions"
Мне от Бога не дано.   Or "necessary thoughts."

Нужно петь, что все темно,   One must sing that all is dark,
Что над миром сны нависли. . .   That dreams hover above the earth. . .
— Так теперь заведено. —   That's what is now prescribed—
Этих чувств и этих мыслей   God did not grant me
Мне от Бога не дано!   These emotions or these thoughts.
                                                      (I, 120)

Briusov took up the gauntlet:

True to herself is Miss Tsvetaeva, who stubbornly continues to take her
themes from the realm of narrowly-intimate personal life, even somehow
reveling in it. ("God did not grant me keen emotions and necessary thoughts.")

In the final analysis we could reconcile ourselves to this, since everyone writes about what is closest, dearest, and most familiar to him, but it is impossible to reconcile oneself to that carelessness of technique which Miss Tsvetaeva more and more frequently flaunts. Five or six genuinely poetic, beautiful poems drown in her book in a wave of purely "album" verselets, which are interesting only to her good friends, if at all.[16]

Briusov, ignoring the quotation marks, did not seem to recognize the irony of her line about "keen emotions" and "necessary thoughts," or to have noticed it as a direct quote from his own review. Tsvetaeva, never one to retreat from a battle, again defended her lyric diary in a preface to *From Two Books* (1913), a slim selection of poems from her first two collections.

All of this existed. My poems are a diary, my poetry a poetry of proper names.

All of us will pass. In fifty years we will all be in the earth. There will be new faces beneath the eternal heaven. And I want to cry out to all those who are still alive:

Write, write more! Fix every moment, every gesture, every sigh! Not only the gesture, also the form of the hand which made it; not only the sigh but the cut of the lips from which it lightly flew.

Do not disdain the "external." The color of your eyes is as important as their expression; the upholstery of the divan is no less than the words spoken on it. Note things down more carefully! There is nothing unimportant! Talk about your room: is it high or low, how many windows does it have, and what kind of curtains, is there a carpet, and what kind of flowers are on it?

The color of your eyes and your lamp shade, the letter opener and the pattern on the wallpaper, the precious stone in your favorite ring—all this will be the body of your poor, poor soul which will remain behind in the huge world.

Moscow, January 16, 1913, Wednesday (I, 289)

The piece is embarrassing for its naivete, particularly if we compare it to Mandel'stam's essays "The Morning of Acmeism" and "On the Addressee," written that same year. Tsvetaeva's cult of proper names and physical detail has some superficial resemblance to the emerging tenets of Acmeism, a largely Petersburg movement of which Tsvetaeva may have been dimly aware by late 1912. Yet it totally lacks Acmeism's sense of the importance of high culture and its artifacts (the young Tsvetaeva seems to prefer interior decoration to the architecture which fascinated the young Mandel'stam). The manifesto's stress on *realia*—the windows of a room, the curtains, the carpet—seems to reveal a contradiction in her poetics between a "poetry of real life" and her often-declared preference for imagination and fantasy. The key to her ultimate solution emerged from the last line, the desire to "fix in memory the body of her poor, poor soul." At first blush (and we do!) this seems Romanticism at its worst. But it points toward the essence of Tsvetaeva's mature art, subsuming both halves of the *byt/byt'ie*, reality/ fantasy dichotomies, capturing the *body* of her *soul*. She learned to do this by rooting her poetry in the actual events of her own life, transmuting them so they emerged, in Trediakovsky's phrase, "as they *could* and *should* be."

Tsvetaeva would never again produce such a manifesto, and it is well that she didn't. But the piece does point out an essential trait of Tsvetaeva's art—it was always the events of her *own* life which directly provided the material for her poetry. Tsvetaeva was never a philosophical or narrative poet in any conventional sense, nor did she ever attempt to write fiction (the few minor, disastrous exceptions prove the rule). Her art is predicated on the importance of the events of *her* inner life, the life and emotions of *one* individual, and a woman at that. These simple, seemingly self-evident facts bear recalling, for in 1913 Russia was preoccupied with grand apocalyptic philosophies of either the religious or political sort. Tsvetaeva always offered her reader a *point* of view, not a world view. Her greatness was that she managed to turn the one into the other.

In the only new poem in *From two Books*, Tsvetaeva once more addressed Briusov directly, mixing insult with back-handed tribute as she recalled her early admiration for him:

В. Я. БРЮСОВУ	TO V. JA. BRIUSOV
Я забыла, что сердце в вас — только ночник,	I forgot that your heart is only a night-light,
Не звезда! Я забыла об этом!	Not a star! I forgot
Что поэзия ваша из книг	That your poetry comes from books
И из зависти — критика. Ранний старик,	And your criticism from envy. Early old man,
Вы опять мне на миг	You again, for a moment,
Показались великим поэтом. . .	Seemed to me a great poet. . .
	(I, 252)

Tsvetaeva, temporarily, had the last word. But she would pay a heavy price for the victory. After the Revolution, Briusov was the only poet of the older symbolist generation to support the Bolsheviks; he even joined the Communist party. In those years, his word would determine what poetry the State Publishing House would print, and he was personally responsible for rejecting Tsvetaeva's third collection, *Juvenilia*.

CHAPTER THREE

Max and Seryozha

The publication of *Evening Album* brought an even more important figure into Marina's life—Maximilian Voloshin. Poet, translator, and watercolorist, a rotund, hirsute giant of a man, Voloshin played a crucial role in Russian poetry of the 1910's and 1920's, less through his own writing than through his genius at bringing people together. His house in Koktebel', in the Crimea, was a meeting-place and resort for Russian writers and artists. It was a circle, perhaps the only one in Russia, in which women's intellect was taken for granted—Tsvetaeva was not the only woman poet Max championed—and in which the ideal of androgyny flourished. Tsvetaeva claims, for instance, that Max once urged her to publish some poems pseudonymously—as the work of brother and sister twins! Max himself, despite his great bulk and flowing beard, was the least "macho" of men, and his formidable mother, always dressed in flowing Turkish pantaloons, was the androgynous genie dominating the household. She was universally called "Pra," the Russian prefix in "*great*grandmother" and other analagous forms. Stories from her biography rightly play an important role in Tsvetaeva's memoir of Max ("Something Alive about the Living"), stories which always return to the androgynous theme: how, for instance, a caller on her considerably older husband once encountered the young woman standing in trousers on a ladder whitewashing the ceiling, and took her to be his friend's son, not his wife.[1] These passages on Pra were precisely those excised from the memoir in its original publication by an emigre editor who, failing to understand either the piece or Tsvetaeva, could not see their relevance. Tsvetaeva, furious, threatened to withdraw the piece but could not—she needed the honorarium.

The fun-loving, sun-drenched Koktebel' circle was leagues away in spirit from the mystic solemnity of the Mussagetes "aesthetes;" summers in Koktebel' were the happiest times in Tsvetaeva's life. Max introduced her to a whole new circle of friends, including Sergei Efron, her future husband. But Max's role in her life was much more than that of a matchmaker, intellectual or otherwise. He was the mentor she needed, the first of Tsvetaeva's new friends to give her confidence in herself as a poet. Voloshin had a good ear and understood what she was doing in her lyric diary:

> This is a young and inexperienced book. Many of the poems, if you open to them by chance in the middle of the book, can evoke a smile. You must read it straight through, like a diary, and then every line will be understood and appropriate.[2]

Tsvetaeva's early letters to Voloshin record her voluminous reading, as indefatigably, though without success, he tried to interest her in contemporary French literature (she found it too "licentious" for her taste).[3] Her reading and writing left little time for school-work, and in the spring of 1911, she announced that she intended to abandon school for good. The eighth and final year of *gymnasium* was "strictly pedagogical," and since she had no intention of teaching, she saw no reason to continue. Russian universities, of course, were closed to women, though there were separate "higher courses for women" (Akhmatova attended some of them). Tsvetaeva, rebellious professor's daughter that she was, had never had scholarly aspirations.

Leaving school before the end of the term, she travelled alone to Gurzuf, in the Crimea, where Pushkin had lived in exile. Tanned and lonesome in a dacha high above the edge of the sea, she was not happy. The books through which she had lived for so long began to seem a fraud. "Every book is a theft from life itself. The more you read, the less you want and know how to live yourself."[4] But she hesitated to give them up. "Books have given me more than people. Remembrance of a person always fades before remembrance of a book—I'm not speaking of my childhood memories, no—only my grown-up ones." She was unsatisfied both with "reality" and imagination: "Life is a butterfly without powder on its wings. Dream is the powder without the butterfly. What, then, is a butterfly with powder?" Characteristically, she sought to subsume both elements of the dichotomy. She felt herself tortured, aimless, restless—she had already begun to smoke, and was smoking more than ever as she lay alone, day after day, in the sun, reading. From Gurzuf she sent Voloshin a cry for help, though she begged him, "Don't be wise in your answer—if you answer. For wisdom also comes from books, and I need a human, not a bookish answer."[5]

Voloshin soon provided that answer, though not intentionally, and to his own dismay. On May 5, Tsvetaeva arrived in Koktebel', and both the ambience of the house and its inhabitants immediately began to work changes on her. When Anastasia arrived two weeks later, she found Marina looking like a boy, tanned, wearing sandals, her hair glinting gold from the sun. After her depression of the winter and spring, Marina's animation seemed forced and unreal. Among the celebrities of the house, Marina informed Anastasia, was the famous decadent poet (a matinee-idol in his day) Igor' Severyanin. Soon "Severyanin" appeared:

> A tall youth, very well-proportioned, with a long, dark face, a fine-boned hand with long fingers, came out onto the path, brushing aside a branch of wild grape with a deer-like motion of his head, and with intentional slowness brushed a lock of hair from his brow . . .[6]

When Anastasia came down to breakfast the next day, Marina was deep in conversation with "Severyanin," but for some reason kept calling him

"Seryozha." Anastasia had fallen victim to a typical Koktebel' hoax. "Seryozha" was a seventeen-year-old schoolboy named Sergei Efron, and Marina hastened to tell her sister all about him: "Seryozha is marvelous. . . . You'll see. . . .He is ill—tuberculosis. We, perhaps, will leave here soon. He can't take the heat . . ."[7] In this intentionally offhand "we" was the revelation of a momentous change in Tsvetaeva's life. She had joined her fate with that of this handsome, delicate youth, and their strange marriage would last, in various metamorphoses, till they met their separate, though equally horrifying, deaths in 1941.

An aura of tragedy hung over Sergei's family. Efron lost his father at fifteen, his mother and younger brother in a single day, one year later: fourteen-year-old Kostya Efron committed suicide, and his mother hanged herself from the same hook on hearing the news. After his mother's death, Sergei, like Marina, was left with minimal adult supervision. His two older sisters, Lilya (1885–1976) and Vera (1888–1945) were with him in Koktebel'. The Efron family, in which there were originally nine children, had a long revolutionary history. Sergei's mother, Elizaveta Petrovna Durnovo, daughter of an adjutant to Nicholas I, was a disciple of the anarchist Kropotkin. Like the Kropotkins, the Durnovos were of the high aristocracy. She met Yakov Konstantinovich Efron, grandson of a rabbi, through her revolutionary activity—they were both members of Socialist-Revolutionary radical-terrorist groups. Arrested in 1880, Elizaveta Petrovna was freed through her father's influence and fled abroad, where her first three children were born. She eventually returned to Russia, and in the late 1890's again became involved with revolutionary work, now with the help of her older children. After 1905, she was arrested again. Released on bail, she again escaped abroad, with her youngest son Konstantin. It was there that the double suicide occurred.[8]

Sergei Efron was handsome, intelligent, and a neophyte writer, though not in a league with the considerably older and more sophisticated company Tsvetaeva had been keeping. This was precisely the secret of his attraction. Seryozha was not threatening, he was vulnerable. He needed care, and Marina needed to be needed. Three years later she wrote about her young husband:

> Sergei is very sickly. At 16 he contracted tuberculosis. Now the disease is in abeyance, but the general state of his health is below average. If you only knew what an ardent, magnanimous, profound young man he is. I constantly tremble over him. At the least excitement his temperature rises—he is all a fevered desire for everything. In three, or almost three years of life together, not one shadow of a doubt in one another. Our marriage is so unlike a usual marriage that I don't feel married at all, and I haven't changed at all—I love and live just as I did at seventeen.[9]

In marrying Sergei, Tsvetaeva tried to marry childhood, in a Peter Pan-like refusal to grow up. Nilender and Ellis had offered her an unwanted adult-

hood; Sergei seemed to promise perpetual childhood. Marina's first poem
to him was titled, "Grandmother's Grandson," a phrase from the poem in
which she and Asya awaited their childlike enchanted prince. Two more
poems dedicated to "Serezha" immediately followed:[10] in both, the hero
again appeared as a small boy at play, with romantic dreams of gypsies,
smugglers, and bandits. Tsvetaeva easily convinced herself that fate had
chosen this gentle, childlike young man for her. There was his tragic yet
exotic family history: Elizaveta Durnovo's life certainly suited her childhood
fantasies better than did Maria Mein's. There was his consumption, the
same disease which had claimed her mother and the Duke of Reichstadt.
And there was the coincidence of his name and initial with those of her
mother's tragic love, "Seryozha E." He even shared her birthday—Sergei
was a year, to the day, younger than Marina.[11]

In early July, Marina and Sergei left Koktebel' and headed for the Urals,
where he planned to take the "kumiss" (fermented mares' milk) cure. Filled
with the spirit of adventure, she addressed her young lover in a poem which
compared them to both gods and children:

Ждут нас пыльные дороги,	Dusty roads await us,
Шалаши на час	Cabins for an hour
И звериные берлоги	And the dens of animals
И старинные чертоги. . .	And ancient mansions. . . .
Милый, милый, мы, как боги:	Darling, darling, we're like gods!
Целый мир для нас!	The whole world is ours!
Всюду дома мы на свете,	Everywhere we are at home,
Всё зовя своим.	Calling all our own.
В шалаше, где чинят сети,	In a hut where nets are mended,
На сияющем паркете. . .	On a shining parquet floor . . .
Милый, милый, мы, как дети:	Darling, darling, we're like children:
Целый мир двоим!	We'll divide the world!
	(I, 127)

In her letters to Voloshin from the Urals, Marina was already savoring the
thought of appearing at Mussagetes "the three of us, and on intimate terms.
Of course you'll take Seryozha there? Because I really don't want to ask
Ellis to do it."[12]

In September, they were back in Moscow, living, in her father's absence,
at Three Ponds, along with the seventeen-year-old Anastasia and her
"fiance" Boris Trukhachev: "Papa will probably return in five days. We all
(Sergei, Boris, Asya and I) expect a grandiose scene because of our not
entirely cautious behavior."[13] Undoubtedly. Though she hoped to set up
house alone with Sergei, at the beginning of October they set up a "menage
a quatre" with his two sisters. "Papa and I talked a lot yesterday about my
moving away; he agrees to it all. The presence of Lilya and Vera (in general
very unnecessary) proved useful."[14] In the space of a few months, her life

had totally changed. "It's strange," she wrote to Max, "to find oneself suddenly completely independent. For me this is a surprise—it always seemed to me that someone else would manage my life. Now I will act in everything as I did in printing my collection. I'll go ahead and do it. Do you approve?"[15]

Max, unfortunately, did not approve of her decision to formalize her relationship with Sergei, nor, it would seem, did many of their friends and relatives. In early November she wrote him in Paris with the news: "In January I'm marrying Sergei. Come! You'll be best man." Despite the nuptial excitement of the letter, there is a hint at the end that she suspected Max's doubts. "Maksin'ka, write me. Only not about 'the seriousness of such a step, youth, inexperience, etc.'"[16] Max's answer has not survived (Tsvetaeva probably tore it up or burned it), but he wrote his mother on the same theme: "Marina and Sergei's wedding seems to me simply an 'episode' and a very short lived one. But it seems to me that it's rather good for them, since it will immediately make them both into adults. And that, it seems to me, is what they need."[17] Tsvetaeva later recalled: "Instead of approval or at least encouragement, Max sent me from Paris his most sincere condolences, regarding us both as too genuine for such a false form of common life as marriage."[18] Marina was furious. She answered Max with a brief note—addressing him pointedly in the formal "vy" they had abandoned months ago:

> Your letter is a great mistake. There are realms in which a joke is out of place, and things about which one must speak with respect or be silent entirely . . .[19]

But she could not stay mad at Max for long.

The wedding took place on January 27 in Moscow, though neither Tsvetaeva nor her daughter ever mentioned the date in print.[20] The family reticence is due to the fact that Ariadna Sergeevna Efron entered the world little more than seven months later, on September 5, 1912. Marina's pregnancy certainly expedited the wedding. Since her lonely stay at Gurzuf, she had committed herself, in rapid succession, to both marriage and motherhood—the two things, if we believe her early poetry, she dreaded the most. But, stubbornly, she believed she could have it both ways, "remain a little girl, though a wife," as she wrote, perhaps on her wedding night, to her new husband:

ИЗ СКАЗКИ — В СКАЗКУ	FROM FAIRY-TALE—TO FAIRY-TALE
Все твое: тоска по чуду,	All is thine: longing for a miracle
Все тоска апрельских дней,	All the longing of April days.
Все, что так тянулось к небу, —	All which so strove toward heaven—
Но разумности не требуй.	But don't demand reasonableness.
Я до самой смерти буду	Till death I will remain
Девочкой, хотя твоей.	A little girl, though thine.

Милый, в этот вечер зимний	Darling, on this winter evening,
Будь, как маленький, со мной.	Be like a little boy with me
Удивляться не мешай мне,	Don't keep me from being surprised,
Будь, как мальчик, в страшной тайне	Be like a little boy, in a terrible mystery,
И остаться помоги мне	And help me remain
Девочкой, хотя женой.	A little girl, though a wife.

(I, 134)

In March, the newlyweds left on their long-postponed honeymoon trip to Italy. They were back in Moscow by May 18, the day of the ceremonial opening of her father's museum.

Sergei and Marina founded their own private publishing house, to which they gave the name Ole-Lukoe (Ole Shut-Eye, the wise old gnome in the fairy tales of Hans Christian Andersen). Its first two imprints were books by the newlyweds in which childhood was the central concern. Sergei's *Childhood* was a book of short stories. Childhood remained a dominant theme of Marina's second, velvet-bound, book of verse, *Magic Lantern*: its three sections were titled, "Little Children," "Children Grow Up," and "Not for Happiness." The book, not surprisingly, was dedicated to Sergei Efron. Its opening poem tells the reader how to approach it:

Милый читатель! Смеясь, как ребенок,	Dear reader! Laughing, like a child,
Весело встреть мой волшебный фонарь.	Gaily encounter my magic lantern.
Искренний смех твой, да будет он звонок	Your candid laughter, let it be ringing,
И безотчетен, как встарь.	And instinctive, as of old.
Все промелькнут в продолжение мига:	All will flash by in the course of a moment:
Рыцарь, и паж, и волшебник, и царь. . .	Knight and page, magician and Tsar . . .
Прочь размышленья! Ведь женская книга —	Away with reflection! Of course a woman's book—
Только волшебный фонарь!	Is only a magic lantern!

(I, 75)

Tsvetaeva's sarcasm, which in her mature years was a devastating weapon, is here directed at her critics—most likely Briusov above all. The ironically attributed "Of course, a woman's book / Is only a magic lantern!" Is one of the few explicitly "feminist" moments in Tsvetaeva's poetry—that is, assuming we are to read it ironically, and I, after some hesitation, think we can. But it cuts both ways, for the magic lantern, of course, was a device for projecting fantastic images. She still had not worked out the conflict in her poetics between "a poetry of real life" and the valorization of imagination.

Magic Lantern represented no great advance over *Evening Album*. Many of the poems, particularly in the section "Little Children," are thematically similar, and, judging from the conventionality of their metrics, were undoubtedly written at the same time. Certain poems, because of the events they describe or their addressee (those addressed to Max and Seryozha, for example) can definitely be dated after 1910. But they, too, represent little that is new. The third section, "Not for Happiness," is a mixed bag of various traditional themes: reminiscence, parting, even the knights and ladies of the early Blok. Tsvetaeva had trouble moving beyond childhood as a poetic theme.

The year and a half following her marriage is a puzzling blank in Tsvetaeva's creative chronicle: only two of her known poems[21] are dated 1912, none in early 1913. The gap may represent a lost collection of poems: on the back cover of *From Two Books*, Tsvetaeva announced that her third collection, to be titled, "Maria Bashkirtseva," was "in preparation." Bashkirtseva was a talented painter from a wealthy Russian family who lived most of her life in Paris, where she died at the age of 23; her posthumously-published diaries had a great vogue at the end of the century, particularly among female readers. Both Bashkirtseva and her diaries promised Tsvetaeva models of female creativity. Tsvetaeva was still promising to publish "Maria Bashkirtseva" in the spring of 1914,[22] but never did (ostensibly because of the outbreak of the war) and she never mentioned the book again.[23] There are three possibilities: 1) these eighteen months account for a sizeable collection of poems, whose manuscript has been lost; 2) there simply were no poems from this period; 3) at some later date, Tsvetaeva destroyed the poems because she realized their immaturity. Each explanation has its drawbacks. Tsvetaeva was meticulous about the preservation of her archive—it was, after all, the record of her life—and took considerable pains to preserve it in each step of her wandering. We have no evidence that she ever willingly destroyed any of her own work. Her next collection, "Juvenilia" (1913-1915) remained unpublished throughout Tsvetaeva's life, but she kept the manuscript intact, and published many individual poems from it both before and after her emigration. She even republished a few poems from her first two books as late as 1925, but no poems from the "Maria Bashkirtseva" years have ever emerged. My best guess is that there were poems, perhaps not too many, and that they were roughly on the level of the later poems in *Magic Lantern*. When the possibility of publishing poetry returned a few years after the revolution, Tsvetaeva had many more recent and much better poems to offer her readers. Perhaps she left that volume of her notebook in Russia when she emigrated, and it was lost. Whatever the reason, this unprecedented silence in the lyric diary at precisely the moment of her marriage and entry into motherhood raises tantalizing questions about the interaction of creativity and biography in her life. Can it be coincidental that these are precisely the years which her daughter Ariadna later described as "the only period of carefree happiness" in her parents' lives?[24] Even with a new husband and baby, it is unlikely that Tsvetaeva was simply "too busy" in her new life; no matter what the difficulties of *byt* in her later life, she nearly always managed to find time each day to write. It is more likely that she had exhausted and outgrown the old themes of her first two volumes, and these years were a creative breathing space in which her development proceeded internally, rather than on the pages of her notebook.

Another clue that she was writing little is the publication, in 1913, of *From Two Books*, the only book she ever published composed entirely of selections from already-published books. Despite its immaturity, *From Two Books* received a favorable review from Vladimir Narbut in *The Messenger of Europe*, one of the oldest and most respected of the Russian "thick journals." Though he criticized the excessive "sweetness" and use of diminutives in many of the poems, he saw that Tsvetaeva gave promise of becoming "a great poetess in the future."[25] For almost nine years, the Russian reading public would hear little of her. A few new poems appeared in a Petersburg journal in 1915 and 1916, a few more in post-Revolutionary almanacs and anthologies. Her next book was published only at the end of 1921, nearly ten years after the publication of *Magic Lantern*. By the time she reappeared on the literary scene, Tsvetaeva had fulfilled that promise and become not a great Russian poetess, but a great Russian poet.

CHAPTER FOUR

Poems of a Female Youth: Marriage and Motherhood

The years 1912–1914 pushed a very unwilling Tsvetaeva into adulthood, while she struggled in her poetry to hold on, if not to childhood, at least to adolescence. Life would not let her remain "a little girl, though a wife," the marriage which she had entered so young and so hastily could not remain a fairy tale. Her young husband, impractical as she, was sickly, and still had to finish school. In the spring of 1913, they took the baby Alya to Feodosia in the Crimea, and remained for a year while Sergei nursed his weak lungs and studied for his baccalaureate. This Crimean idyll was a return to the hospitable and protective Koktebel' circle of Max Voloshin and his mother. It coincided with Tsvetaeva's return to her lyric diary: the first poems in its next volume, *Juvenilia*, were written that spring. The death of Tsvetaeva's father in August, 1913, briefly brought her back to Moscow, though, except for nearly two months of silence, it left no mark in her lyric diary. The outbreak of World War in July, 1914, brought their idyll, and that of their whole generation, to a sudden end. Within the family circle, the outbreak of war coincided symbolically with the death of Sergei's only surviving brother Pyotr from tuberculosis.

The near-total absence of poems from 1912 and early 1913 intensifies the contrast between *Juvenilia*,[1] (literally, "Poems of Youth") and Tsvetaeva's *real* juvenilia, the poems of her first two books. Her major achievement in *Juvenilia* was the discovery of her own unique poetic persona and poetic voice. Her concentration on her self, and the way in which others perceived that self, is not surprising in a collection titled "Poems of Youth." Adolescence, after all, is the time for identity crises, for trying on masks, for asking, "Who am I, really?" All these adolescent qualities are there in *Juvenilia*. But Tsvetaeva, when she wrote them, was no longer an adolescent. By 1913, she was twenty-one and a mother. The persona of the early poems in *Juvenilia* seems younger than Tsvetaeva herself, uttering, without evident embarassment, lines like:

Я одна с моей большой любовью	I am alone with my great love
К собственной моей душе.	For my very own soul.
	May 13, 1913
	(I, 140)

In *Juvenilia*, Tsvetaeva idealized and glorified adolescence as she had glorified childhood in her first two collections. Yet the unembarrassed focus on the self in these poems should not necessarily be taken as Tsvetaeva's unmediated authorial voice. There is an element of stylization here, and some self-awareness, though at times, admittedly, it is slight.

These are the poems of a young woman who recognized in herself a large poetic gift. The questions of self-image and identity which her persona raises were the questions of, as it were, a *poetic* adolescence: not only "Who am I?" in a creative sense, but "What does it mean to be a woman and a poet? A mother and a poet? A wife and a poet?" These were questions few women, particularly in Russia, had asked, and none had yet answered satisfactorily. One of the first poems in the collection not only declares, but demonstrates, Tsvetaeva's new self-confidence and poetic maturity. She sees her poems as an explosive force, rudely challenging the tired mysticism ("dream and incense") of Symbolism. And so they were:

Моим стихам, написанным так рано,
Что и не знала я, что я — поэт,
Сорвавшимся, как брызги из фонтана,
Как искры из ракет,

To my poems, written so early
That I didn't even know I was a poet,
Poems which broke away, like drops from a
    fountain
Or sparks from a rocket,

Ворвавшимся, как маленькие черти,
В святилище, где сон и фимиам,
Моим стихам о юности и смерти,
— Нечитанным стихам!

Which burst, like little demons
Into the sanctuary of dream and incense,
To my poems about youth and death,
Unread poems!—

Разбросанным в пыли по магазинам,
Где из никто не брал и не берет,
Моим стихам, как драгоценным винам,
Настанет свой черед.

Scattered in the dust of bookstores
(Where no one bought or buys them!)
To my poems, as to rare wines,
Will come their time.
                    Koktebel', May 1913
                           (I, 140)

Written when Tsvetaeva was only 20, this poem is a small *tour de force*.[2] Its twelve lines are, in fact, one sentence, whose verb and grammatical subject form the concluding line. The first words, "To my poems," are the dative (and logical) subject of that verb; the rest of the poem is a series of modifying clauses describing them. Throughout the first eleven lines, the reader assumes that the dative is dedicatory: "To my verses" (in the eighteenth-century fashion of, for instance, Kantemir). Only in the last abrupt line does the syntax of the poem reveal itself: to them "Will come their time." This grammatical leap leaves the reader with a montaged superimposition of both meanings—dedicatory dative and subject dative. Though his expectation has been upset, he has been given a far more interesting meaning than the one he expected.

In these poems of 1913, Tsvetaeva's persona is preoccupied with the way others see her, with whether they see through her defensive masks to her "real" self:

Мальчиком, бегущим резво,	Like a boy, running playfully,
Я предстала Вам.	I appeared before you.
Вы посмеивались трезво	You laughed softly, soberly,
Злым моим словам:	At my angry words:
«Шалость — жизнь мне, имя — шалость.	"Mischief is life to me—my name is mischief!
Смейся, кто не глуп!»	Laugh, if you're not stupid!"
И не видели усталость	And you didn't see the weariness
Побледневших губ.	Of my whitened lips.
Вас притягивали луны	You were attracted by the moons
Двух огромных глаз.	Of two enormous eyes.
— Слишком розовой и юной	—Too rosy and young
Я была для Вас!	Was I for you!
Тающая легче снега,	Melting faster than snow
Я была — как сталь.	I was—like steel.
Мячик, прыгнувший с разбега	A ball, bouncing on the run
Прямо на рояль,	Straight at the piano,
Скрип песка под зубом, или	The grit of sand beneath the tooth
Стали по стеклу. . .	Or steel across the glass . . .
— Только Вы не уловили	—But you didn't catch
Грозную стрелу	The terrible arrow
Легких слов моих, и нежность	Of my frivolous words, the tenderness
Гнева напоказ. . .	Of anger for show . . .
— Каменную безнадежность	The stony hopelessness
Всех моих проказ!	Of all my pranks!
	May 19, 1913
	(I, 142)

This self-image remained constant through her life: an outer shell of boyish wit, mockery, and rebellion against the accepted ("The grit of sand under the tooth") hiding an inner self of angry vulnerability and "stony hopelessness." Tsvetaeva always sought the understanding few who would see through the protective mask to the hidden soul, just as, later on, she valued the reader willing and able to penetrate the surface difficulty of her poems to their real meaning. This poem is about poetry as well as personality. Tsvetaeva's early poems are seldom "difficult" to read on their first, most obvious level. But, as with the introduction to *Magic Lantern* or the preface to *From Two Books*, it is sometimes difficult to know *how* to read them— ironically, or straight-faced—to know whether Tsvetaeva is being "mischievous" or deadly serious.

Her persona in these 1913 poems often wondered, as poets are wont to do, how she would be thought of after her death—another way of asking whether her poetry would be understood. In a manner which echoes the worst of Symbolist decadence, she dedicated the collection "to those who will arrange my burial," drawing a picture of herself, still rebellious, in the coffin. But her attitude toward death was now very different from that of the suicide-enamored teenager who wrote *Evening Album*. After she met Sergei, Tsvetaeva's poems became death-defying and life-affirming. She now had someone who needed her, who gave purpose to her life.

> I do not believe at all in the existence of God and of life beyond the grave. From this comes my hopelessness, my horror of old age and death. The utter inability of my nature to pray and repent. A mad love for life, a spasmodic, feverish desire to live. (March 7, 1914)[3]

This "feverish desire to live" arose from Tsvetaeva's fear that she, like her mother, grandmother, and so many other women in her family, would die young. Before she was twenty-one, she had lost both parents, her only surviving grandparent, and several close friends and relatives. Her intimate acquaintance with death is one explanation for her impatience to marry and become a mother—even more, to write and publish—at an age when some of her contemporaries were still in school. The chance of early death was a threat—or an incentive—to live life to the fullest as soon as possible, and to give that life a permanence in her verse. She addressed a poem (I, 176) to her maternal grandmother, the beautiful Polish aristocrat who died giving birth to her only child. Tsvetaeva saw in her grandmother's portrait unfulfilled possibilities, and in the premature wisdom on that twenty-year-old face sought her own heritage.[4]

Tsvetaeva's preoccupation with her "foremothers" was a seeking of artistic roots. The male poet, with generations of tradition of male personae to draw on, enters more easily into that tradition. Tsvetaeva was creating her poetic "I" in a Russian tradition which until the twentieth century knew only one female poet of any renown—Karolina Pavlova (1807–1893). Pavlova was hardly an appealing role model. Scorned by her contemporaries as a cold and heartless bluestocking because she dared to write like a man, and even worse, to sue her husband for squandering her fortune, Pavlova died alone and in poverty in Dresden, one year after Tsvetaeva's birth, after four decades of voluntary exile from her homeland. Besides Pavlova's "emigration," there are other curious biographical parallels. Born Karolina Karlovna Jaenisch, Pavlova was also a professor's daughter; her German-born father taught physics and chemistry at the Moscow institute of medicine and surgery. Like Tsvetaeva, Jaenisch married a minor litterateur of far inferior talent, a marriage which proved as disastrous as Tsvetaeva's (at least Sergei's intentions were more honorable than those of the fortune-hunter Pavlov). Pavlova, too, was initiated into the literary world by a sympathetic older poet who admired her talent—the great Polish poet Adam Mickiewicz, who served as her tutor during his Russian exile.[5] Pavlova was so scorned by her contemporaries that it is not certain the young Tsvetaeva had even heard of her. She was rediscovered in 1915 when the first post-humous edition of her poetry appeared, edited, ironically, by Briusov, who liked to fancy himself as something of a patron of women poets. Tsvetaeva certainly knew Pavlova's work by 1921, when she chose two lines from Pavlova as her subtext in titling her collection *Craft* (*Remeslo*).

According to Harold Bloom's Freudian model, the poet's relation to his great predecessors resembles the oedipal struggle of father and son, with the younger poet tormented by "anxiety of influence." Yet Bloom's archetypal poet is male, as are his predecessors. Tsvetaeva, breaking new ground, needed models to identify with as well as authority to rebel against. She found the latter in ample measure in the staid world of her father and in her *gymnasia*, less in the poetic tradition. (Her quarrel with Briusov, after all, resulted from disappointed idealization.) Since women poets were very few, in Europe as well as in Russia, she sought out women artists in other fields. This explains her veneration of Maria Bashkirtseva and Sarah Bernhardt, and her emphasis on the "frustrated talents" of her mother and grandmother. (Conveniently dead, they could be mythologized to her liking.)

In these female forbears, she sought the roots of her own "melancholy" (*grust'*) and rebellion (*miatezh*), words straight out of the lexicon of 19th-century romanticism. It is not surprising, then, that a pair of 1913 poems addressed to Pushkin and Byron, the giants of that generation, like so many other poems in *Juvenilia*, really focused on the persona herself. An imaginary "Encounter with Pushkin," inspired by the Crimean places of his exile, evokes little of Pushkin but the traditional portrait in school anthologies: "the curly-haired magician," "with his swarthy hand to his brow." The weight of the poem is in the conversation which the two poets *would* have had, which is essentially Tsvetaeva's monologue about what *she* loves and hates:

Не опираясь о смуглую руку,	Not leaning on his swarthy arm,
Я говорила б, идя,	I would say, as we walked,
Как глубоко презираю науку	How deeply I despise science
И отвергаю вождя,	And reject the leader,
Как я люблю имена и знамена,	How I love names and banners,
Волосы и голоса,	Hair and voices,
Старые вина и старые троны,	Old wines and old thrones
— Каждого встречного пса! —	And every dog I meet!

October 1, 1913

(I, 147-8)

Carried along by its sing-song dactylic meter (Tsvetaeva hardly ever wrote in such regular ternary meters any more) the catalog runs on for eight of the poem's sixteen stanzas, and is more than slightly self-indulgent, if not at times downright silly: "Play-actors and the sound of the tambourine/ Gold and silver/ The unrepeatable name: "Marina"/ Byron and the bolero." Yet Tsvetaeva expected from Pushkin, as a brother poet, instant understanding. He would know better than to offer his arm on the steep slope to this independent young woman, he would hear out her tirade and respond with tolerant silence. In a poem written only a week earlier, she imagined a meeting with Byron and the poems which each poet would read to the other. These imagined conversations of equal with equal are the beginning of Tsvetaeva's search for a place in the world of poetry, in the "brotherhood" of poets.

Her search for female models extended not only back along the maternal line, but forward as well. Ariadna Efron first appeared in her mother's poetry when she was scarcely a year old. Throughout her childhood, Alya was for Marina a second self, a kindred spirit, the reincarnation of her own childhood. In 1918, Tsvetaeva would write:

Не знаю, где ты и где я.	I don't know where you leave off and I begin.
Те ж песни и те же заботы.	The same songs and the same cares.
Такие с тобою друзья,	We are such friends together
Такие с тобою сироты.	And such orphans together.
	Aug. 24, 1918
	(II, 29)

Tsvetaeva sought in Ariadna the traits of her own independent character, and, even more, of those fearless Amazons whose life she had contrasted with "captivity to the cradle." Like her mother before her, she hoped that her first-born would not only follow in her footsteps, but outdo her:

Ты будешь невинной, тонкой,	You will be innocent, slim,
Прелестной — и всем чужой.	Charming—and a stranger to all.
Пленительной амазонкой,	An impetuous amazon,
Стремительной госпожой.	A captivating miss.
И косы свои, пожалуй,	And you'll wear your braids, perhaps,
Ты будешь носить, как шлем,	Like a helmet.
Ты будешь царицей бала —	You'll be the queen of the ball
И всех молодых поэм.	And of all youthful poems.
. . . .	. . . .
Всё будет тебе покорно,	All will be submissive to you
И все при тебе — тихи.	And all quiet in your presence.
Ты будешь, как я — бесспорно —	You'll be like me—indisputably—
И лучше писать стихи. . .	And you'll write better poems. . .
	June 5, 1914
	(I, 166)

Before Alya turned two, Tsvetaeva was quoting her verbal precocity in her own verse:

Ты с няньками в какой-то ссоре —	You've some sort of quarrel with your nannies—
Все делать хочется самой.	You want to do everything yourself.
И вдруг отчаянье, что «море	And suddenly, despair that
Ушло домой».	"The ocean went home."
Не передашь тебя — как гордо	Impossible to convey what you're like—
Я о тебе ни повествуй! —	No matter how proudly I recount it—
Когда ты просишь: «Мама, морду	When you ask: "Mama,
Мне поцелуй».	Kiss my mug!"

June 6, 1914

(I, 167)

Yet, at the same time, she feared she saw in Alya the same innate sadness ("*grust'*") that was her own maternal legacy.

What was she like as a mother, this young woman so reluctant to give up her own childhood? Tsvetaeva did not in fact spend a great deal of time with her daughter when Ariadna was very young; Alya had a wet-nurse (five of them, in fact), and full-time nannies. In her demanding, pedagogical bent, Tsvetaeva consciously or unconsciously imitated her own mother:

> In the child I was, Marina tried to develop, right from the cradle, the qualities she herself possessed: the ability to overcome difficulty, and originality of thought and deed. . . .She taught me to express, coherently and comprehensibly, what I had seen, heard, experienced, or imagined. She never descended to the child's level, but instead raised him up slightly, to meet him at that point where adult wisdom borders on the childish primoridal.

> My reward for good behavior, for something achieved or overcome, was not sweets or gifts, but a story read aloud, an excursion together, or an invitation to "visit" in her room.[6]

Tsvetaeva's diary jottings from Alya's infancy are those of a proud young mother,[7] but in her lyric diary she often treated Alya in a "spartan" manner. In the terrible revolutionary year of 1919, she wrote:

Упадешь — перстом не двину.	If you fall—I'll not move a finger.
Я люблю тебя как сына.	I love you like a son.

(II, 31)

Her more conventionally maternal feelings were reserved for Sergei. Two 1913 poems titled "To Sergei Efron-Durnovo" (the only time she ever used the hyphenated form of his last name) stressed his artistocratic lineage: ". . . The weariness/ of blue, of ancient blood. . . ." He is "Of a class with the Decembrists and the habitues of Versailles," but still so young that "You don't yet know/ Whether those fingers seek/ The brush, the sword, or the strings." Sergei, in Marina's mind, had unlimited promise, though as yet little achievement. Her portrait of him matches the Koktebel' photos of 1913, where he is usually reclining languidly in a chaise lounge, often with Marina kneeling watchfully beside him:[8]

Как водоросли Ваши члены,	Your limbs like sea-weed
Как ветви мальмэзонских ив. . .	Like the branches of the Malmaison willows. . .
Так Вы лежали в брызгах пены,	Thus you lay in the spray of foam
Рассеянно остановив	Absent-mindedly resting
На светло-золотистых дынях	On the shining-gold melons
Аквамарин и хризопраз	The aquamarine and chrysoprase
Сине-зеленых, серо-синих,	Of your blue-green, grey-blue,
Всегда полузакрытых глаз.	Always half-closed eyes.
Летели солнечные стрелы	Arrows of sunshine flew
И волны — бешеные львы.	And crazed lions of waves.
Так Вы лежали, слишком белый	Thus you lay, too white
От нестерпимой синевы. . .	From this intolerable blue. . .
А за спиной была пустыня	Behind your back arose the desert
А где-то станция Джанкой. . .	And somewhere the Dzhankoi station. . .
И тихо золотилась дыня	And quietly, the melon shone golden
Под Вашей длинною рукой.	Beneath your elongated hand.
Так, драгоценный и спокойный,	Thus, precious and tranquil
Лежите, взглядом не даря,	You lie, not bestowing a gaze
Но взглянете — и вспыхнут войны,	But should you glance—wars will blaze up
И горы двинутся в моря,	And mountains fall into the sea,
И новые зажгутся луны,	And new moons will shine
И лягут радостные львы —	And the joyful lions will lie down
По наклоненью Вашей юной,	At a nod of your youthful
Великолепной головы.	Magnificent head.
	Koktebel', July 1, 1913
	(I, 145)

Sergei is indeed strikingly beautiful in those 1913 photos (Russian, by the way, does not distinguish between "beautiful" and "handsome"), in contrast to the nearsighted Tsvetaeva who did not always remove her owlish spectacles for the photographer. Tsvetaeva's celebration of that beauty is curiously androgynous: besides the dedication, only one adjectival ending reveals the gender of the addressee. Throughout her career, this androgynous tendency is particularly noticeable in her poems to Sergei, as is the stress on his youth. Tsvetaeva's attitude toward Efron continued to be maternal throughout their marriage. All who knew them stress that she was by far his superior in intellect and talent. Perhaps because she sensed this, her poems asserted her loyalty even more vehemently, and wildly exaggerated Sergei's virtues beyond the bounds of human possibility. Her loyalty to Sergei would last until the end of their lives; her fidelity, in a narrower sense, would not last much longer.

It is hard to know what Sergei's feelings were. The "silence" so often mentioned in her poetic portraits of him applies to his documentary legacy as well. All we have from this period is the barely fictionalized portrait of Marina in his short story, "The Enchantress." The narrator, Kira, is a small boy of about ten. (The name is itself androgynously odd, for Russian "Kira"'s are usually female.) The story's title character and heroine is the seventeen-year-old Mara, a school friend of Kira's older sister. Mara arrives for a visit, preceded by her reputation as a "madwoman:" "She never settled into any *gymnasium*, and dropped out of the final year" proclaims Kira's father disapprovingly. The eccentric Mara drinks her tea black as coffee, smokes one cigarette after another, and refuses breakfast and lunch. To adult cautions about damaging her health she replies, "Animation (excitation) is essential to me—only in excitement am I myself." Like the Marina we know from her poems, she "does not want to live long, and cannot." "People who worry too much about their own health I find distasteful. A too healthy body is always to the detriment of the soul." (Was this the way a rosily healthy Marina consoled the sickly Sergei?). The quality she values most highly, not surprisingly, is imagination. "I was not given much: I don't know how to prove things, I don't know how to live, but my imagination has never betrayed me, and never will." As Kira and his brother are dozing off in the nursery, Mara appears in their room. She treats their childhood fantasies seriously, encourages them to compose a "totally silly" tale for her, and recites a poem she has written. (It is conscientiously footnoted, "Marina Tsvetaeva. Magic Lantern.") Mara confesses her horror of growing old:

> They'll demand rational behavior of me, a calm view of life, knowledge of it. But in the depths of me I'm still the same tomboy, the same seventeen-year-old, with the same heart and the same soul: I know perfectly well that for old people to slide across the floor is forbidden, impossible, absurd, ridiculous."[9]

She muses: "Life is so boring that you always have to imagine various things. But imagination is also life. Where is the border? What is 'reality'?"

It is a vivid portrait of Tsvetaeva as she must have been when Sergei first met her. The questions are precisely those she posed to Voloshin just before she met Efron. But how much of this is to his credit? So many of the details are straight out of Tsvetaeva's self-portraits that he seems more the faithful reporter than a creator. Efron's authorial viewpoint is identical with that of his ten-year-old narrator; the reader is expected to share the boys' unquestioning worship of Mara. Does the story give us a psychologically accurate version of the relationship: Marina, the unconventional tomboy, capturing the imagination of a frail, malleable young man and captivating him? From what little evidence we have about the early years of the marriage, Tsvetaeva certainly seems to have played the traditionally masculine role of aggressor in the relationship, with the gentle, languid and sickly Sergei swept up by the force of her will. Enchanted he certainly was, and so, it seems, he remained for a long time. A Civil War comrade of Sergei's recalled how he would talk about Marina during their long evacuation journey from Constantinople to Prague in 1921:

> When he spoke of his wife, there was quiet rapture in his voice. In fact, these speeches were not about a wife. Marina, as Efron saw her. . .was a crystal goblet of wisdom and literary talent. In his stories there was neither stilted rapture nor the least indication of philistine braggadocio. Secretly, and without reservation, he acknowledged Marina's superiority over himself, over all contemporary poets, over all that surrounded her.[10]

In the spring of 1914, Sergei finally passed his baccalaureate; in the fall, a few years behind schedule, he would enter Moscow University. Marina's praise of her young husband reached fever pitch. Of her marriage, she wrote:

Да, я, пожалуй, странный человек,	Yes, I, perhaps, am a strange one
Другим — на диво!	For others to wonder at!
Быть, несмотря на наш двадцатый век,	To be, despite our twentieth century
Такой счастливой!	So happy!
Не слушая о тайном сходстве душ,	Deaf to "the secret likeness of souls"
Ни всех тому подобных басен,	And all such old wives' tales,
Всем говорить, что у меня есть муж,	To say to all, "I have a husband
Что он прекрасен! . .	And he is beautiful. . .!"
Я с вызовом ношу его кольцо	In defiance I wear his ring!
— Да, в Вечности — жена, не на бумаге. —	—Yes, his wife in Eternity, not on paper—
Его чрезмерно узкое лицо	His too-narrow face
Подобно шпаге.	Is like a rapier.
Безмолвен рот его, углами вниз,	His mouth is silent, its corners down,
Мучительно-великолепны брови.	His brows excruciatingly magnificent.
В его лице трагически слились	In his face are tragically blended
Две древних крови.	Two ancient bloods.
Он тонок первой тонкостью ветвей.	He's slender with the first slenderness of
Его глаза — прекрасно-бесполезны! —	branches.
Под крыльями распахнутых бровей —	His eyes are marvelously helpless!—
Две бездны.	Beneath the wings of wide-open brows—
	Two abysses.
В его лице я рыцарству верна.	In his person, I am faithful to knighthood
— Всем вам, кто жил и умирал без страху. —	—To all of you who lived and died without
Такие — в роковые времена —	fear!
Слагают стансы — и идут на плаху.	It is such—in fatal times
	Who write stanzas—and go to the block!

Koktebel', June 3, 1914
(I, 166)

The first two stanzas were too fulsome even for Tsvetaeva, who cut them out at some point before 1919.[11] The poem is much better without them: the truncation of the initial introductory material gives a greater intimacy to the poetic "conversation." The reader is addressed as if she/he of course knew who "I" and "he" were, and even, perhaps, why the persona wears his ring "in defiance." Such an *in medias res* opening became increasingly characteristic, and was often achieved by the elimination of initial draft stanzas.

The shrill insistence of both letter and lyric are forced, as if Tsvetaeva sensed that her loyalty was unsteady, and some ominous hints appear in the poetic diary. Between June 19 and July 16, 1914, Tsvetaeva addressed four poems to Pyotr Efron, (1881–1914), Sergei's elder brother. An actor by profession, who lived most of his life in European emigration, he had returned home, dying of tuberculosis. Physical beauty and approaching death, so often twinned in her early poems, made Pyotr dangerously attractive. She sent him a poem describing her confusion:

Не думаю, не жалуюсь, не спорю.	I don't think, don't complain, don't argue.
Не сплю.	I don't sleep.
Не рвусь ни к солнцу, ни к луне, ни к морю,	I don't strain toward the sun, nor moon, nor sea,
Ни к кораблю.	Nor ship.
Не чувствую, как в этих стенах жарко,	I don't feel how hot it is within these walls,
Как зелено в саду.	How green the garden.
Давно желанного и жданного подарка	I don't expect the long-desired and-awaited
Не жду.	Gift.
Не радуют ни утро, ни трамвая	Neither morning, nor the ringing tram
Звенящий бег.	Delight me.
Живу, не видя дня, позабывая	I live without seeing the day
Число и век.	Forgetting date and century.
На, кажется, надрезанном канате	I'm a small tightrope-walker
Я — маленький плясун.	On a rope that seems about to give.
Я — тень от чьей-то тени. Я — лунатик	I'm the shade from someone's shadow.
Двух темных лун.	I'm the sleepwalker of two dark moons.

July 13, 1914

(1980 I, 43-44)

Tsvetaeva here uses a favorite technique—alternating lines of different length—to mimic her persona's ambivalence. We can hear her arguing with herself as she constructs long five- or six-foot iambic lines, countered by a very short one-, two-, or three-foot line. The irregularities in line length convey the persona's agitation; her repeated anaphoric denials ("I don't, I don't . . .")—her obsession. Pyotr's death freed her both from conflicting feelings and from constraints in addressing him—the three poems she wrote after his death are even more outspoken in expressing her devotion. Post-humous adoration became a Tsvetaeva specialty.

Her infatuation with Pyotr Efron was a foretaste of infidelities to come. But it was not the only thunder in the blue sky of summer, 1914. The war which brought all of Europe into what Akhmatova would call "The real, not calendar 20th century" was declared on July 16(O.S.)/29. Tsvetaeva greeted the news, and the wave of Russian patriotism it evoked, with the disdain she held for most political events:

Война, война! — Кажденья у киотов	War, war!—Incense by the icons
И стрекот шпор.	And the rattle of spurs.
Но нету дела мне до царских счетов,	But I've no use for kings' calculations,
Народных ссор.	For nations' quarrels.
	July 16, 1914 (I, 172)[12]

Ever the dissenter, Tsvetaeva penned a defense of the Germany of her grandfather's forbears, the Germany of her childhood and her mother's music-stand, the Germany of Goethe and Kant:

ГЕРМАНИИ	TO GERMANY
Ты миру отдана на травлю,	You're rendered to the world for torment
И счета нет твоим врагам.	Your enemies are legion.
Ну, как же я тебя оставлю.	Then how can *I* abandon you?
Ну, как же я тебя предам.	How can *I* betray you?
И где возьму благоразумье:	And where will I find such prudence:
«За око — око, кровь — за кровь», —	"An eye for an eye, blood for blood,"
Германия — мое безумье!	Germany—my folly!
Германия — моя любовь!	Germany—my love!
	Moscow, December 1, 1914
	(I, 175)

The beginning of the war marked the end of the mock-childhood in which Sergei and Marina had been living. But it was not, in itself, the immediate cause of disruption in their lives. Sergei's poor health exempted him from military service, and he began his studies at Moscow University in the fall of 1914. Only later, sometime before March, 1915, did he volunteer as a front-line medic. The cloud which came over their marriage that first autumn of the war came from Marina's first serious infidelity—her lesbian love affair with Sofia Parnok.

CHAPTER FIVE

Marina and Sonia

Tsvetaeva's affair with Sofia Parnok dominated her life and lyric diary from their meeting in the fall of 1914 till their final break in early February, 1916. Strong, conflicting emotions always nourished Tsvetaeva's art—the poems which emerged from the romance are among the best in *Juvenilia*. Emotionally, the affair made Tsvetaeva confront the empty myth of her "child-marriage." Creatively, Parnok's complex personality and Tsvetaeva's own conflicting feelings about the affair provided her with psychologically richer material than had her paeans of praise to herself, Sergei, Asya, Ellis, Alya, and other near and dear ones.

Sofia Yakovlevna Parnok (1885–1933) was a minor poet who by 1914 had already published a few poems in the Petersburg journal *Northern Notes*. Though she had briefly been married to the writer V.M. Volkenstein, Parnok was a lesbian and unabashedly frank about it in both her poetry and her life-style. She dressed mannishly and wrote love poems to female amours. The seventeen poems in Tsvetaeva's cycle "The Girl Friend" ("Podruga") (October 16, 1914–July, 1915) are addressed to Parnok. "Podruga," like its English equivalent "girl friend" has two meanings—when used by a woman about a woman, it simply means a close female friend; when used by a man about a woman, it implies romantic involvement. In Tsvetaeva's cycle the two meanings overlap with an intentional, and playful, ambiguity. Tsvetaeva was fascinated by the novelty of the relationship, by what she called in the very first poem, "The ironic fascination/ That you are not he." (I, 177) Her poems capitalize on this: by various canny manipulations of syntax, she managed in many poems to leave the addressee's gender ambiguous throughout, or almost to the end. Tsvetaeva usually addresses Parnok in the polite plural "vy:" Russian does not distinguish gender in the plural as it must do, particularly in past tense verbs, in the singular. This is how Tsvetaeva recalled their first meeting in a Moscow drawing-room:

Мы были: я — в пышном платье
Из чуть золотого фая,
Вы — в вязаной черной куртке
С крылатым воротником.

Я помню, с каким вошли Вы
Лицом — без малейшей краски,
Как встали, кусая пальчик,
Чуть голову наклоня.

We were: I—in a magnificent dress
Of almost golden faille,
You—in a black knitted man's jacket
With a wing collar.

I remember your face as you walked in
Without a bit of make-up,
How you stood, biting your finger
With your head slightly inclined.

И лоб Ваш властолюбивый	And your power-loving brow
Под тяжестью рыжей каски,	Beneath your heavy helmet of reddish hair,
Не женщина и не мальчик, —	Not a woman and not a boy,
Но что-то сильней меня!	But something stronger than I.
Движением беспричинным	With an unmotivated movement
Я встала, нас окружили.	I rose, others surrounded us.
И кто-то в шутливом тоне:	And someone said, jokingly,
«Знакомьтесь же, господа».	"Gentlemen, let me introduce you!"

January 1915
(I, 183)

Parnok's Amazonian "helmet" of reddish hair and her "power-loving brow" recall the "braids like a helmet" Tsvetaeva had foreseen on her own "impetuous Amazon" daughter, ultimately sending the attentive reader back to that early poem written in the Jardin de Luxembourg: "I love those women who did not fear battle,/ Who knew how to hold both sword and spear . . ." (I, 11) It is clear that the romance, often stormy, was itself a kind of battle—a clash of strong wills. The weaker, often younger, men whom Tsvetaeva usually chose as the objects of her passion either submitted to her dominance or (more often) took fright and fled. Parnok, though evidently much smitten by Tsvetaeva, stood her ground. Seven years older, Parnok was evidently the dominant personality in the relationship, or at least the romantic aggressor. Tsvetaeva was both fascinated by her and resentful of her power. The poem above reenacts that struggle of personalities in its unusual rhyme scheme: (*abcd/abcd*). Its paired stanzas, in effect, rhyme with each other, giving it the structure of a poetic duel.

Marina, or at least her persona, was somewhat uncomfortable with a lesbian attachment. That persona retains an almost childlike innocence through the cycle, while she associates the darker, "sinful" aspects of the romance with Parnok. It is Parnok who has "kissed too many" in her romantic career, over whom hangs "sin" and "dark fate." Parnok is the Snow Queen, the icy enchantress of Hans Christian Andersen's fairy tale, who whisks the young boy Kai off to her icy kingdom when he foolishly hitches his sled behind hers. Tsvetaeva is her little Kai. She tries to link Parnok's dominating personality to her "thrice-damned passion," and blames her for her own loss of innocence:

Взгляд — до взгляда — смел и светел,	My gaze—till your gaze—was bold and bright,
Сердце — лет пяти. . .	My heart was five years old. . .
Счастлив, кто тебя не встретил	Happy the one who has not met you
На своем пути.	On his path!

April 28, 1915
(I, 185)

The affair was evidently conducted with some discretion at first, though Efron's sister (and presumably Efron himself) knew of it. Pra wrote about them with concern to a mutual friend:

As for Marina that's rather scary: that affair has taken a rather serious turn. She went off with Sonya somewhere for several days, and kept it a big secret. That Sonia has already quarreled with the girl friend she was living with and taken herself a separate apartment on the Arbat. This has me and Lilya very embarrassed and anxious, but we're not strong enough to break these spells . . .[1]

Sergei's attitude throughout the affair has been described as "Tolerant. He was always trying to get out of the way."[2] Indeed, he himself was involved in another romance in the fall of 1914:

Seryozha's romance has ended safely; Marina's continues to develop with intensity, and with such irrepressible force that nothing can stop it. She'll have to burn out in it, and Allah knows how this will end . . ."[3]

This disapproval by even the unconventional Pra can be taken as representative of those close to Tsvetaeva, and it is reflected in the way Marina's persona steadfastly retains the pose of innocence seduced. In fact, she originally titled the cycle "The Mistake" (*oshibka*), the same word she had used to describe Ellis' proposal.

The destination of Tsvetaeva's secret trip with Parnok was Rostov Velikii, an ancient Russian town near Vladimir. There, according to a poem of Tsvetaeva's, the lovers visited a colorful Christmas market and the ancient cathedral. This is one of the poems in which Tsvetaeva speaks most openly about her own affection: "In your honor, I admired all the reddish hobby-horses" (Parnok had chestnut hair). When Parnok, standing before an icon of the madonna, exclaims "Oh, I want it!," Tsvetaeva impetuously promises to steal it for her that very night. The poem ends with a frankly erotic scene in, of all places, their room in a nunnery guest-house:

Как голову мою сжимали Вы,	How you embraced my head
Лаская каждый завиток,	Fondling every curl,
Как Вашей брошечки эмалевой	How the flower on your enameled brooch
Мне губы холодил цветок.	Chilled my lips.
Как я по Вашим узким пальчикам	How I nuzzled my drowsy cheek
Водила сонною щекой,	Against your slender fingers,
Как Вы меня дразнили мальчиком,	How you teased me for my boyishness,
Как я Вам нравилась такой. . .	How you loved me that way. . .

December, 1914
(II, 181)

Tsvetaeva, with her bobbed hair, had always affected boyishness in dress (see the sailor blouses in the Koktebel' photos) and manner, as well as in her poetic persona. But Sofia Poliakova[4] points out the ways in which this poem particularly stresses her childishness—her admiration of the hobby-horses, her indulgent overeating of "six pink waffles," her impulsive promise to steal the icon, the way in which, as she falls asleep, she cuddles her cheek against Parnok. Tsvetaeva, the maternal protector of Sergei, now found herself in quite the opposite role. It is not unlikely that she sought in Parnok some of the motherly affection of which she was deprived by her mother's death. Several traits of Parnok's character, as Tsvetaeva paints them in her poems, recall Maria Mein-Tsvetaeva: a strong-willed, artistic personality with an aura of "tragic fate" hanging over her. In a poem written a few months after their final break, Tsvetaeva stylized the mother-daughter aspect of the relationship while addressing Parnok in a language so archaic and liturgical that it seems intentionally to recall that night in the nunnery:

В оны дни ты мне была, как мать,	In those days you were like a mother to me,
Я в ночи тебя могла позвать,	I could call to you in the night,
Свет горячечный, свет бессонный,	Fevered light, sleepless light,
Свет очей моих в ночи оны.	Light of my eyes in those nights.
	. . .
Не смущать тебя пришла, прощай,	I've not come to embarrass you, farewell,
Только платья поцелую край,	I'll only kiss the hem of your dress
Да взгляну тебе очами в очи,	And glance straight into your eyes,
Зацелованные в оны ночи.	Eyes kissed in those nights.

April 26, 1916
(I, 225)

The two women spent most of June and July together in Koktebel', then visited friends of Parnok's in the Ukraine till mid-August. From there, Tsvetaeva wrote her sister-in-law:

> I love Seryozha for all my life—he is near and dear to me (rodnoi), I will never leave him. I write to him every day, or every other day, he knows my whole life, I only try to write less frequently about the saddest thing. There's an eternal weight on my heart. I fall asleep with it and awake with it.
>
> Sonia loves me very much and I love her, and that is eternal, and I can't leave her. The sense of being torn to pieces by days which it is necessary to divide—the heart combines it all.
>
> Simple gaiety, it seems, I don't have and never will, and, in general, that's not characteristic of me. And deep joy I also don't have. I cannot cause hurt, and I cannot not cause it . . .[5]
>
> (August 5, 1915)

Tsvetaeva wanted to have the love of both Sergei and Sonia, without hurting anyone: "I cannot cause hurt, and I cannot not cause it. . ." We can interpret this either as a childish reluctance to confront reality, or as an early instance of a "dichotomous" attempt to subsume seemingly self-contradictory opposites. What she could bring off in her art, however, would not work in life.

When Marina and Sonia returned to Moscow, they lived together quite openly; Sergei moved in with his sister. But the situation was clearly untenable; a September, 1915 poem suggests Tsvetaeva already had a rival for Sonia's affections. In several lyrics of late September and early October,

1915, Tsvetaeva tried to "settle her scores with the world." The theme of death, absent since the opening pages of *Juvenilia*, returned to its final poems. Death was now an incentive to set her philosophical, emotional, and even literal house in order. She wonders to whom she should bequeath beloved objects (a wolfskin coat, the plaid plush blanket her father bought her just before his death, her trademark silver bracelets) as well as her literary and emotional capital: "My last rhyme, and you—my last night!" She called for a spirit of reconciliation,

Я знаю правду! Все прежние правды — прочь!	I know the truth! Away with all earlier truths!
Не надо людям с людьми на земле бороться.	People should not quarrel together on earth. . .

October 3, 1915

(I,194)

But Sonia was not interested. She viciously teased Sergei in a poem stylized as a translation from Alcaeus' poem to Sappho:

АЛКЕЕВЫ СТРОФЫ	ALCAEAN STANZAS
И впрямь прекрасен, юноша стройный, ты:	Indeed you are beautiful, well-proportioned youth:
Два синих солнца под бахромой ресниц,	Two deep blue suns beneath the velvet of your lashes,
И кудри темноструйным вихрем	And curls, crowning your tender face
Лавра славней, нежный лик венчают.	With a dark-flowing whirlwind more glorious than laurel.
Адонис сам предшественник юный мой!	My young predecessor is Adonis himself!
Ты начал кубок, ныне врученный мне, —	You began the goblet, now entrusted to me,—
К устам любимой приникая,	As I press the lips of my beloved
Мыслью себя веселю печальной:	I gladden myself with this sad thought:
Не ты, о юный, расколдовал ее.	Not you, O youth, freed her from her spell.
Дивясь на пламень этих любовных уст,	Wondering at the flame of these loving lips,
О, первый, не твое ревниво, —	O first one, not your name, but mine
Имя мое помянет любовник.	Will her lover jealously remember.

October 3, 1915[6]

Parnok wrote about Tsvetaeva both during and after the romance. In May, 1915, she drew a picture of a headstrong, tomboyish young woman of genius essentially identical to Tsvetaeva's self-portraits. More interesting both as a poem itself (Parnok's late poetry is often rather good), and as a psychological characterization, is a poem she wrote in 1928 to a subsequent beloved also, coincidentally, named Marina:

Я помню мрак таких же светлых глаз.	I recall the darkness of just such bright eyes,
Как при тебе, все голоса стихали,	As in your presence, all voices would fall silent,
когда она, безумствуя стихами,	When she, raving with verses,
своим беспамятством воспламеняла нас.	Set us aflame with her own delirium.

Как странно мне ее напоминаешь ты!	How strangely you remind me of her!
Такая ж розоватость, золотистость,	The same rosiness, goldenness,
и перламутровость лица, и шелковистость,	And mother-of-pearl-ness of your face, and
такое же биенье теплоты.	Silkiness, the same throb of warmth.
И тот же холод хитрости змеиной	And the same cold of snake-like guile
И скользкости. . . Но я простила ей,	And slipperiness. . .But I forgave her,
и я люблю тебя, и сквозь тебя, Марина,	And I love you, and through you, Marina,
виденье соименницы твоей.	The ghost of your namesake.[7]

Parnok's straightforward recollection of "cold. . .snake-like guile and slipperiness" is unique among memoirs of Tsvetaeva, which tend toward the hagiographic. But it rings true. It was at the height of their relationship that Tsvetaeva confessed to being "A virtuoso of virtuosi at the art of lying."

Безумье — и благоразумье,	Madness—and prudence,
Позор — и честь,	Disgrace—and honor,
Всё, что наводит на раздумье,	All that leads to meditation,
Всё слишком есть —	There's too much of all
Во мне. — Все каторжные страсти	In me.—All the hard-labor passions
Свились в одну! —	Knotted into one!
Так в волосах моих — все масти	Thus in my hair—all colors
Ведут войну!	Conduct a battle.
Я знаю весь любовный шепот,	I know all the lovemaking whispers,
— Ах, наизусть! —	Oh, by heart!
— Мой двадцатидвухлетний опыт —	My twenty-two-year-old experience—
Сплошная грусть!	Is sheer sadness!
Но облик мой — невинно розов,	But my appearance is innocently rosy,
— Что ни скажи! —	—No matter what you say!
Я виртуоз из виртуозов	I'm a virtuoso of virtuosi
В искусстве лжи.	At the art of lying.
В ней, запускаемой как мячик	In a lie, flung like a ball—
— Ловимый вновь! —	—Caught once again!—
Моих прабабушек-полячек	The blood of my Polish great-grandmothers
Сказалась кровь.	Proclaims itself.
Лгу оттого, что по кладбищам	I lie because in graveyards
Трава растет,	Grass grows,
Лгу оттого, что по кладбищам	I lie because in graveyards
Метель метет. . .	The snowstorm blows . . .
От скрипки — от автомобиля —	I lie from a violin, from a motorcar—
Шелков, огня. . .	From silks, from fire . . .
От пытки, что не все любили	From the torment that not everyone
Одну меня!	Loves only me!

От боли, что не я — невеста
У жениха. . .
От жеста и стиха — для жеста
И для стиха!

От нежного боа не шее. . .
И как могу
Не лгать, — раз голос мой нежнее, —
Когда я лгу. . .

From the pain that it's not I
Who is the bridegroom's bride . . .
From gesture and from verse—for gesture
And for verse!

From the delicate boa on my neck. . . .
And how can I
Not lie—when my voice is more tender
When I lie.
                                    January 3, 1915
                                    (I, 189)

This poem invites comparison with the May, 1913 poem, "Like a boy, . . . I appeared before you," discussed earlier. There, she questioned her address-ee's ability to see through to the "real" self hidden under her mask, her real-life "persona." Now, after the self-examination and experience recorded in *Juvenilia*, she has come to realize that the dichotomy is not a question of "real self" versus "mask," but that such simultaneous containment of two contradictory truths is in fact her essence. The real world, the world of "*byt*" cannot handle contradictory truths, and must see them as "lying." But, as Tsvetaeva acknowledges in the last two stanzas, "lying"—the sub-suming of seemingly contradictory opposites—is the essence of her art. She lies "for the sake of verse," and her voice is "more tender"—i.e. is creating poetry—when she "lies."

Between the spring of 1913 and the end of 1915, the period covered in *Juvenilia*, Tsvetaeva developed from a young poet of promise to one of real achievement. She also worked out the conflict in her poetics between diary-like "poetry of real life" and the primacy of imagination. Though her poems of late 1915 are uneven in quality, (prolific as she was, there would always be unevenness in Tsvetaeva's work) there are far more that can be taken seriously, as the work of a mature poet, than there are among the poems of 1913. One of the best-known and more frequently anthologized poems of the book, and one of my particular favorites, will serve as a closing example. It was set to music by the Soviet composer M. Tariverdiev, appeared in a popular movie, and became a "hit" in the Soviet Union. It is a playfully flirtatious poem about "non-love" addressed to A.A. Mints, who was soon to become the common-law husband of Tsvetaeva's sister Anastasia (Ana-stasia and Boris Trukhachev separated not long after the birth of their son Andrei in 1912):

Мне нравится, что Вы больны не мной,
Мне нравится, что я больна не Вами,
Что никогда тяжелый шар земной
Не уплывет под нашими ногами.
Мне нравится, что можно быть смешной —
Распущенной — и не играть словами,
И не краснеть удушливой волной,
Слегка соприкоснувшись рукавами.

I like the fact that you ache not for me,
I like the fact that I ache not for you,
That never will the heavy sphere of earth
Swim out from underneath our feet.
I like the fact that I can be absurd,
Undisciplined—and not play games with words,
And need not blush with stifling wave
When our sleeves happen to brush.

Мне нравится еще, что Вы при мне	I like it, too, that in my presence
Спокойно обнимаете другую,	You calmly embrace another,
Не прочите мне в адовом огне	You don't destine me to burn in hell fire
Гореть за то, что я не Вас целую.	Because it's not you I'm kissing.
Что имя нежное мое, мой нежный, не	That my pet name, my pet, you don't
Упоминаете ни днем ни ночью — всуе. . .	Mention, day or night—at all—
Что никогда в церковной тишине	That never in the silence of a church
Не пропоют над нами: аллилуйя!	Will they sing "Halleluia" over us!
Спасибо Вам и сердцем и рукой	I thank you with my hand and heart
За то, что Вы меня — не зная сами! —	For loving me—without knowing it!
Так любите: за мой ночной покой,	For my nocturnal peace,
За редкость встреч закатными часами,	For the rarity of meetings at sunrise,
За наши не-гулянья под луной,	For our non-strolls beneath the moon,
За солнце не у нас над головами, —	For the sun, above not *our* heads—
За то, что Вы больны — увы! — не мной,	Because you ache—alas—not for me,
За то, что я больна — увы! — не Вами.	Because I ache—alas—not for you!

May 3, 1915
(I, 188)

This is not simply the poem of a young wife flirting with her future brother-in-law. As the "alas" in the final line reveals to the reader with knowledge of Tsvetaeva's lyric diary, she still "aches" for Sonia—a heterosexual attraction for Mints, she implies, would be preferable. Yet what is new in Tsvetaeva's work is that the reader needs none of this background information to appreciate the poem, as was the case with so much of her previous work. She has managed to turn the intimate diary entry into a poem of universal appeal, for which the reader can find echoes in his own life. She/he, meanwhile, can appreciate Tsvetaeva's mastery of poetic technique: her play with Russian syntax—the crucial importance of the placement of the negative ("vy bol'ny *ne mnoi*: you ache *not for me*"), the deft manipulation of the eight-line double quatrain stanzas, which require not two but *four* lines for each rhyme.

There is a sense of closure at the end of *Juvenilia*, as at the end of all Tsvetaeva's collections from this point on. Though the exact dating and generally chronological order of the poems are a device to give the *illusion* of diary verisimilitude, there is indeed a structure and dynamic to each of the volumes which Tsvetaeva subtly sculpted in preparing them for publication. It is not simply that the new year 1916 puts a convenient end to the collection (the last poem is dated December 31, 1915). All the last poems of *Juvenilia* are retrospective and self-judgmental. Tsvetaeva was at a turning-point in her life, both emotionally and creatively; the new year brought major changes.

CHAPTER SIX

Petersburg

A *verst* is an old Russian unit of distance (about 2/3 mile); "versts" were also the mileposts which marked off those distances along the road. Tsvetaeva chose "Versts" as the title for two collections of poems written between 1916 and 1920: *Versts I* is her lyric diary for the year 1916. Tsvetaeva's personal life in 1916 was full of mileposts: a January trip to Petersburg, where she met a whole new circle of poets, the end of her romance with Sofia Parnok, a brief romance with Osip Mandel'stam and another, simultaneously, with the minor (and half-mad) poet Tikhon Churilin, still another later that year with an enigmatic figure named Nikodim Plutser-Sarna of whom we know almost nothing. Her second child, Irina, was conceived sometime that summer. We have no evidence that Sergei Efron was not the father, nor do we have any assurance that he was.

While the poems of *Juvenilia* were largely concerned with the poet's self, her family and close friends, and with the development of her poetic persona, in *Versts I* Tsvetaeva turned outward to address three major poetic contemporaries—Mandel'stam, Blok, and Akhmatova—with worshipful admiration. Fully a third of the poems in the book are addressed to them, and her praise is often so fulsome as to seem embarrassing. Yet, paradoxically, these very poems are Tsvetaeva's declaration of poetic maturity. The act of praise itself defines her role: Tsvetaeva believed that only a poet is qualified to judge another poet. Reassured by her reception in Petersburg, she asserted her right as a poet to praise her peers. At the same time, in a fine stroke of poetic irony, the very form of that praise—some of the best poems she had yet written—glorified its author.

By linking her tributes with the theme of Moscow, Tsvetaeva stakes out her poetic place. What did she, a young, barely recognized poetess, have to offer in homage to these poetic luminaries of Petersburg? Nothing more or less than Moscow itself. In March she presented it to Mandel'stam:

Из рук моих — нерукотворный град	Take from my hands, my strange, my beautiful brother,
Прими, мой странный, мой прекрасный брат.	This city not built by human hands.
	March 31, 1916
	(I, 215)

In May, she stood beside *her* river, the Moskva, addressing Blok, who stood by *his* Neva:

И проходишь ты над своей Невой	And you pass by, above your Neva
О ту пору, как над рекой-Москвой	While I stand, with head bent,
Я стою с опущенной головой. . .	above the Moscow River.
	May 7, 1916
	(I, 229)

And in June, she gave both Moscow and herself to Akhmatova:

И я дарю тебе свой колокольный град,	I give you my city of bells
— Ахматова! — и сердце свое в придачу.	Akhmatova, and my heart in the bargain.
	June 19, 1916
	(I, 232)

These two major themes of *Versts I*—the poet and Moscow—emerged from the pivotal event which marks the boundary between *Juvenilia* and *Versts I*: Tsvetaeva's trip to Petersburg (by then renamed Petrograd) over New Year's, 1916. Tsvetaeva's childhood and youth, we recall, were spent in Moscow, Tarusa, Europe, and the Crimea. There is no mention of Petersburg in her early poetry; if she went there at all, except to meet her future sister-in-law, it was not often. When she first began to make contacts in the literary world, it was definitely a *Moscow* world, commanded by Briusov, brightened by Bely. But Petersburg, the imperial capital, had so far played a more important role than Moscow in the turn-of-the-century revival of Russian poetry. Though Bal'mont and Briusov, the pathbreakers of Russian symbolism, were Muscovites—as was Bely—Blok, Vyacheslav Ivanov, Kuzmin, Merezhkovsky and Gippius all lived in Petersburg, and it was there, in literary salons and in editorial offices of new journals that the polemics of literary schools swirled and poetic debuts were made. It was there, too, that a younger generation of poets began to differentiate themselves from the symbolists, and the neo-classical school called Acmeism was born. Moscow seemed a somewhat old-fashioned academic backwater.

The highpoint of Tsvetaeva's trip to Petersburg was an evening gathering at which she met almost all of literary Petersburg, or at least its younger set. Kuzmin, Mandel'stam, Esenin, and many other poets were there; all recited their poems. Tsvetaeva was received with enthusiasm: "I read all of my 1915 verse—and still it was too little—and still they wanted more."[1] Her warm reception by this elegant, affected, and often eccentric society was important in assuring Tsvetaeva that she was their equal. Yet at the same time, she recalls, she was conscious of belonging not to the Northern Capital and its society, but to Moscow, of which, by force of circumstances, she became the representative. "*All* Petersburg read, and *one* Moscow." ("Petersburg" in Russian is a masculine noun; Moscow is feminine.)

These descriptions of the evening are from Tsvetaeva's essay-memoir "An Otherworldly Evening" (1936), a posthumous tribute to Mikhail Kuzmin, whom she met for the first and only time that evening. The title pays tribute to Kuzmin's collection, "Otherworldly Evenings," while the word "otherworldly," literally "not-of-here," emphasizes her Moscow viewpoint. In the essay, she claims her description of the evening is simply copied from a letter she wrote Kuzmin in 1921. But that letter has recently come to light. The texts, like the two versions of Tsvetaeva's 1910 letter to Briusov, provide a glimpse of Tsvetaeva "tenderly lying," as she transforms "reality" into art.

Mikhail Aleksandrovich Kuzmin (1872?–1936)[2] was a major figure in Russia's Silver Age. A prose writer as well as a poet, he was also a musician who began his career by writing romances to which he then composed his own lyrics. Like Tsvetaeva, he belonged to no poetic school, though he was personally and professionally close to both the symbolists and to the younger acmeist poets, who saw him as something of a mentor. Kuzmin was openly homosexual; his 1908 novel *Wings* caused a sensation as Russia's first novel on a homosexual theme.

Tsvetaeva, according to both her 1936 memoir and the 1921 letter, had to leave the party early, after Kuzmin had read only one poem, and before he began to sing, because the friend with whom she was staying was ill at home, waiting impatiently for her return. At this point, her two versions diverge. According to "An Otherworldly Evening," the friend in question was Sofia Chatskina, editor of *Northern Notes*, which had recently published several of Tsvetaeva's *Juvenilia* poems, and would soon publish more. Chatskina, Tsvetaeva carefully explained, had invited her to Petersburg as a gift in lieu of payment, since the financially independent Tsvetaeva would not accept honoraria. Her determination to leave early, depriving herself of the pleasure of hearing Kuzmin sing, is in this version of a piece with Tsvetaeva's ideals of gratitude, loyalty, and self-denial.

Her letter to Kuzmin, however, reveals that the Sofia in question was not Chatskina at all, but Parnok, with whom Tsvetaeva had travelled to Petersburg. I take the liberty of quoting it at some length:

> I had just arrived. I was with someone, i.e. with a woman.—Lord, how I cried!—But that's not important. Well, in a word, she absolutely didn't want me to go to that party, and for that reason was urging me to go with particular fervor. She herself couldn't go—she had a headache—and when she has a headache—and her head always aches—she is unbearable (A dark room—a blue lamp—my tears. . .) But my head didn't ache (it never does!)—and I was terribly unwilling to stay home: (1) because of Sonya, in the second place because K[uzmin] would be there and he would sing.
>
> —Sonya, I'm not going!—
>
> —Why? After all, I'm no one.
>
> —But I'm sorry for you.

—There'll be lots of people there, you'll find it diverting.

—No, I feel very sorry for you.

—I can't stand pity. Go, go! Think, Marina, Kuzmin will be there, he will sing.

—Yes, he will sing, and when I come back, you will nag me, and I will cry. I won't go for anything.

"Marina!" The voice of Leonid [Kannesinger, the host of the party—JT] "Marina Ivanovna, are you ready?"

I, without hesitation, "This minute!"

Tsvetaeva's account reads like an excerpt from a nineteenth-century psychological novel. She continued:

I had to leave almost immediately. I had only just arrived, and to leave immediately! (As in childhood, you know?)

Characteristically, Tsvetaeva exaggerated the brevity of her stay for her own rhetorical purposes. After all, if *all* the poets she mentions in "An Otherworldly Evening" got their chance to read, and she herself read *all* of her 1915 poems (there are over 30 of them) she must have been there for quite a while! She goes on:

Everyone: "But Mikhail Aleksandrovich will read some more. . ."

I, in a businesslike way: "But I have a friend at home!"

"But M.A. will sing some more!"

I, complainingly: "But I have a girlfriend (?) at home."

Light laughter, and someone couldn't resist adding: "You sound as if it's 'I have a child at home.' A girl friend will wait."

I, to myself: "Like hell she will!"

The letter to Kuzmin leaves no doubt that the friend in question was Parnok, while, in the bargain, it gives us Tsvetaeva's only account of the end of the romance:

And the girlfriend?[3]

My girlfriend? When I returned, she was sleeping.

Where is she now?

Somewhere in the Crimea. I don't know. In February, 1916, that is little more than a month later, we separated. Almost because of Kuzmin, that is, because of Mandel'stam, who, not having finished our conversation in Petersburg, came to Moscow to finish it. When I came to see her after two Mandel'stam days of absence—the first such absence in years—on her bed sat another: very big, fat, dark . . .

We were friends for a year and a half. I don't remember her at all, that is, I never think of her. I only know that I'll never forgive her for the fact I didn't stay . . .[4]

Writing to the homosexual Kuzmin in 1921, Tsvetaeva felt perfectly comfortable discussing the affair. But in 1936, in Paris, she shifted Parnok's function in the narrative ("sick friend at home") to *another* Sofia, Sofia Chatskina. Poliakova, to whom we are indebted for the publication of the Kuzmin letter and much other information about the Tsvetaeva-Parnok relationship, explains the substitution as follows: "Tsvetaeva could not resist an onomastic game; there was no other "Sofia" in her circle besides Chatskina, and *she couldn't bring herself to introduce a fictitious character.*"[5] [Emphasis mine—JT] It was characteristic of Tsvetaeva's "tender lying" that it always stayed within certain bounds.

Writing at a time when she clearly foresaw her own eventual return to the USSR, Tsvetaeva was not about to raise the dual specters of Parnok or her own bisexuality, nor did she more than hint discreetly at what was well-known about Kuzmin. There is, however, a curious and otherwise unmotivated episode in "An Otherworldly Evening" which may be the locus of these displaced issues. As Tsvetaeva tells the story, the father of her two young hosts jokingly announced to her that he had just returned home, walked into the hall where the party was in progress, and saw, from behind, his son sitting on a bench embracing a figure whom he took to be Tsvetaeva:

I:

"Wha-a-at?!"

He, unperturbedly:

"Yes, arms around each others' shoulders, heads together: Lenya's black nape and your blond curly one. I've seen a lot of poets—and poetesses—but still, I must confess, I was amazed . . ."

"That was Esenin!"

"Yes, it was Esenin, as I discovered the moment I walked around to the other side of the bench. You have perfectly identical napes."

"Yes, but Esenin is wearing a light blue shirt, and I'm. . ."

"That, I must admit, I hadn't noticed; due to all the hair and arms nothing was visible."

Lenya. Esenin. Thick as thieves, inseparable friends. In those two, in their so strikingly different faces, converged, merged two races, two classes, two worlds. But for all their differences, **across** all their differences, they were poets—and fast friends.[6]

The passage can be read on several levels. First, it reasserts Tsvetaeva's lifelong ideal of a higher brotherhood among poets (*"across* all their differences, they were poets—and fast friends.") This blends into Tsvetaeva's related ideal of androgyny and ambivalent gender: Esenin and Tsvetaeva, two blond, curly-headed young poets, not only look much alike but, the passage implies, are *more alike* than different. The embrace of Lenya and Esenin, finally, discreetly introduces the homosexual theme (this is, after all, a tribute to Kuzmin) displaced from her self-censored account of her relations with Sonia.[7]

Two more of Tsvetaeva's "tender lies," tiny though they may be, remind us that her memoirs and letters are subject to the same law as her poetry: "how a thing *could* and *should* be." To Kuzmin she wrote: "It was the winter of 1916. I was in Petersburg for the first time in my life." But a pre-nuptial letter to Voloshin was dated, "Petersburg, January 10, 1912," and began, "Now we are at Sergei's relatives' in Petersburg."[8] This stay with Sergei's older sister, who was trying to forestall the marriage, may have been so unpleasant that Tsvetaeva's memory suppressed it. Nevertheless, she had indubitably been to Petersburg at least once before. But that fact is irrelevant to the essence of her tale, in fact, it blurred her major theme. So it "tenderly" disappeared.

In "An Otherworldly Evening," Kuzmin tells Tsvetaeva: "We all read your poems in *Northern Notes* . . . 'I know the truth! Away with all earlier truths!'" Kuzmin might well have seen an autograph copy of the poem (written only three months earlier) but he certainly could not have read it in *Northern Notes*, for it appeared there in No. 7/8 for 1916, that is, no earlier than July. In fact, the five poems which had already appeared in *Northern Notes* were all from 1913—fresh and promising, certainly, but still full of Tsvetaeva's adolescent excesses. "I know the truth!" like the other 1915 poems Tsvetaeva read that evening, is a poem which could justly have won her the approval of that sophisticated Petersburg crowd.

CHAPTER SEVEN

Mandel'stam and Moscow

The "otherworldly evening" marked Tsvetaeva's second encounter with Osip Mandel'stam. They had first met in the summer of 1915 on the beach at Koktebel', the same beach where, four years earlier, Tsvetaeva met Sergei Efron. The qualities that drew her to Sergei must have attracted her to Mandel'stam as well. Apart from Mandel'stam's incomparably greater talent, and the fact that Sergei was considerably more handsome, there were outward similarities between the two young men, as photographs of both reveal.[1] To Tsvetaeva, they were both vulnerable, childlike, and in need of her protection. But in the summer of 1915, Tsvetaeva was at Koktebel' with Parnok, and Mandel'stam made little impression on her. Many years later, she recalled laconically, "I was on my way to the ocean, he from the ocean. At the gate of Voloshin's garden, we passed each other by."[2] (The word she used here, "razminulis'," with its connotation of "missed meeting" had by the time she wrote become associated in her poetry with another "brother poet," Boris Pasternak.)

After their January meeting in Petersburg, Mandel'stam became infatuated by Tsvetaeva, began making trips to Moscow to visit her. The archetypal Petersburg poet, he knew Moscow as little as Tsvetaeva knew Petersburg; Tsvetaeva gave him tourist excursions that left an invaluable legacy to Russian poetry. We know of this friendship little more than what its participants chose to tell us, Mandel'stam in three dense, puzzling poems "belonging" to Tsvetaeva, she in nine hardly less cryptic poems,[3] one vivid—though seldom explicit—memoir, "The History of a Dedication" (1931), and a recently-published letter to her sister-in-law which gives a more concrete and less mythic account of his final visit.

Their friendship raises the possibility of an uncommon instance: the simultaneous influence of two major poets on each other. Nadezhda Mandel'stam recalls that "In M's verse after his romance with Marina Tsvetaeva, there suddenly appeared a new voice." "His friendship with Tsvetaeva, I think, played a tremendous role in Mandel'stam's life and work (for him life and work were equally meaningful). It was a bridge which he crossed from one period to another. Mande'lstam's poems to Tsvetaeva open *The Second Book* or *Tristia*."[4] Nadezhda Mandel'stam summarized Tsvetaeva's importance for her husband: "In giving him her friendship and Moscow, she somehow released him from a spell. It was a wonderful gift, for with Petersburg alone, without Moscow, there's no freedom of breath, no feeling of Russia, no moral freedom. . .She unfettered in him a love of life and a talent for spontaneous and unbridled love."[5]

It is striking that, for both poets, the romance occurred precisely at a moment of transition between two collections, two periods—a moment which represented a major leap forward for both. Though less than two years older than Tsvetaeva, Mandel'stam was in 1916 considerably more mature as a poet, and better known, at least among those Russians who cared about poetry. He had been publishing since 1910 in the widely-read journal *Apollon*. The first edition of his collection *Stone* appeared in 1913. Major poems in the Mandel'stam canon, such as "Hagia Sophia" or "Notre Dame" date as far back as 1912; nothing Tsevtaeva had produced by 1914 or 1915 could rival them. But her best poems of 1916, beginning with the period of their friendship, attain that level of mastery. How much of the leap from *Juvenilia* to *Versts I* can we attribute to Mandel'stam's influence? How accurate is Nadezhda Mandel'stam's judgement about Tsvetaeva's role in the transition from *Stone* to *Tristia*?

There is little clear "influence," as such, visible in the work of either poet. Before as after their brief romance, Tsvetaeva and Mandel'stam were in most respects antipodes on the Russian poetic landscape, if not figures in two entirely different landscapes. Most striking is the contrast of poetic voice and persona. As Lydia Ginzburg put it succinctly, "The personality of the poet is not the focal point of the early Mandel'stam's poetic world."[6] She quotes Mandel'stam himself from *The Noise of Time*: "My desire is to speak not about myself, but to track down the age, the noise, and the germination of time. My memory is inimical to all that is personal." Though the last sentence is a polemical overstatement, nevertheless, Kiril Taranovsky can justly interpret Blok's cryptic words about Mandel'stam ("His poems arise out of dreams—very idiosyncratic, lying in the realms of art alone") as meaning either that "The main concern of Mandel'stam's poetry is art itself, or that art is the main source of his inspiration."[7] Nowhere is this more evident than in *Stone*, whose ostensible subjects are largely the artifacts of world culture, be it architecture (Hagia Sophia, Notre Dame, Petersburg's Admiralty spire) music (Bach, Beethoven) or classical literature (Homer, Racine's *Phaedre*).

If the subject of Mandel'stam's early poetry could be summed up (as of course it cannot) as "art," then Tsvetaeva's, in an equally oversimplified fashion, could be summed up as "life." "My specialty is Life!" she once declared.[8] To Mandel'stam's denial of the personal we can counterpose Tsvetaeva's 1913 manifesto: "My poems are a diary, my poetry a poetry of proper names." This was as true of *Juvenilia* as it was of her first two collections. Such artifacts of culture and history as flash through the pages of *Juvenilia* are there because of Marina's subjective preference alone. Contrast this with the balanced weight of European and Classical culture in Mandel'stam: how clearly this contrast reflects the difference in their educations! Marina was educated by a haphazard string of European boarding schools, private tutors, three different *gymnasiums* and much self-directed reading. Mandel'stam was educated at Petersburg's Tenishev school, which provided both the finest classical and at the same time the most westernized education then available in Russia. Its other most illustrious alumnus, several years Mandel'stam's junior, was Vladimir Nabokov. They were indeed an odd couple, the rebellious daughter of a Moscow professor and the semi-dandified son of a Jewish leather merchant.

Tsvetaeva's poetry, in contrast to Mandel'stam's, represents the apotheosis of the lyric persona. To sense the magnitude of the difference we have only to contrast the first lines of the opening lyrics in *Juvenilia* with those in *Stone*. Tsvetaeva: "*I* dedicate these lines," "Pass by, you who are like *me*," "To *my* poems, written so early," "You, who pass *me* by," "*I* appeared to you as a boy," "*I* am now lying face up," "Go then! *My* voice is dumb!" [emphasis mine—JT]. Mandel'stam: "A sound tentative and hollow," "Like gold tinsel burn," "From the half-dark hall, suddenly," "To read only childish books," "More tender than tender your face," "On the pale-blue enamel," "There are austere spells," "Inexpressible sorrow," "On the mother-of-pearl shuttle." The only one of Mandel'stam's first twenty-five poems to have a first-person singular pronoun in the first line begins, "I am given a body— What am I to do with it?" (#8)[9] When Mandel'stam's lyrical "I" is present in a poem, it seldom makes its presence known in the first line or even in the first stanza. Even then, the "I" is more often a perceiver than a subject of inquiry or a participant in the action.

Tsvetaeva's concentration on her "I" diminished somewhat as her poetry matured, and her concerns expanded to a wider world beyond her friends and family. In *Versts I*, for the first time, she experimented with a persona who was self-evidently *not* Tsvetaeva. In *Tristia*, on the other hand, Mandel'stam's "I" more often becomes a participant, as, for example, in his much-analyzed "Tsvetaeva" poem, "On a sledge overlaid with straw." Was this the result of mutual influence or simply natural development?

Mandel'stam's first Tsvetaeva poem (#83) is much like the poems of *Stone* in its suppression of the persona:

В разноголосице девического хора	In the discordance of the maiden choir
Все церкви нежные поют на голос свой,	All the tender churches sing in their own voice,
И в дугах каменных Успенского собора	And in the stone arches of the Uspensky cathedral
Мне брови чудятся, высокие, дугой.	I see high, arched brows.
И с укрепленного архангелами вала	And from the wall, fortified by archangels
Я город озирал на чудной высоте.	I beheld the city at a miraculous height.
В стенах Акрополя печаль меня снедала	In the walls of the Acropolis sorrow consumed me
По русском имени и русской красоте.	For a Russian name and Russian beauty.

Не диво ль дивной, что вертоград нам снится,	Is it not a marvelous marvel, that we dream of a vineyard,
Где реют голуби в горячей синеве,	Where doves soar in a burning blue,
Что православные крюки поет черница:	That a nun sings Orthodox notes:
Успенье нежное — Флоренция в Москве.	A tender Assumption—Florence in Moscow.
И пятиглавые московские соборы	And the five-headed Moscow cathedrals
С их итальянскою и русскою душой	With their Italian and Russian soul
Напоминают мне явление Авроры,	Recall for me Aurora's appearance
Но с русским именем и в шубе меховой.	But with a Russian name, and in a fur coat.
	Moscow, February 1916

In the whole poem, there is only one verb with "I" as its subject, and that, characteristically, is "I beheld." The other two first person pronouns (lines 4 and 15) are gramatically distanced from the action, which also involves perception (literally: "Brows seemed to me," "cathedrals . . . recall for me.") The actual grammatical subject here is not the perceiver but the perceived. What Mandel'stam perceives is the cathedral of the Assumption (the coronation cathedral for Russia's Tsars), one of the five cathedrals which enclose the Cathedral square in the Kremlin, where "All the tender churches sing each in its own voice."

Though Mandel'stam's central image here is again architectural, this marks the first appearance of *Moscow's* architecture in his work; under Tsvetaeva's aegis, the poet who had created verbal portraits of Notre Dame and Hagia Sophia now turned his eye to the Kremlin cathedrals. His theme, however, is vintage Mandel'stam: in the heart of the Kremlin his cultural memory rejoices in Russia's links with Europe. The Assumption cathedral (1475–1479), like its neighbors, was built by an Italian architect. This "Florence in Moscow" reminds Mandel'stam of Italian hillside vineyards, with doves soaring in the hot blue sky.

But where is Tsvetaeva? It was she who brought Mandel'stam to the Kremlin, but what remains of her in his poem is, at most, the "arched brows" of line 4, the "Russian name" (lines 5 and 16) and "Russian beauty" (line 5), and the "fur coat" of line 16, reputedly a tiger-fur coat she then affected. The Assumption cathedral is, by the way, the most rotundly "feminine" of the Kremlin churches in the shape of its cupolas and of the arches which crown its outer walls. The poem is a love poem only at some remove: what Mandel'stam loves here is the architecture of the cathedral which reminds him both of the Italy which is far away and the Marina who is beside him. The poem moves toward something more intimate, however, in an elegeantly artful, yet shy and tender fashion. The phrase, "sorrow consumed me" is a conscious echo of Pushkin's 1824 "You fade and are silent; sorrow consumes you" itself a free translation from Andre Chenier. The Pushkin/Chenier poem is addressed to a maiden by a gentleman presumably older and wiser, who has read in her sorrow the evidence of her love for a certain young man. For our purposes, the most important lines of the poem are:

Любви не утаишь: мы любим, и как нас,	You can't hide love, and, *tender girls,*
Девицы нежные, любовь волнует вас.	Love agitates you as us.[10]

Here is the source of Mandel'stam's "tender maiden churches;" here also is a lovely example of the way in which a subtext works to add an entire new layer of meaning to a Mandel'stam poem.

In their poems to each other, we have a shared experience, separately transmuted into poetry by two poets of genius. They may or may not have recited their poems to each other—I suspect they did. There are a good many echoes between the two sets of poems, probably even a ciphered conversation. Many of the phrases which mystify the reader in Mandel'-stam's poems echo—or are echoed in—Tsvetaeva's. The Tsvetaeva poem dated February 18, 1916, for example, is either another source for "In the discordance" or, more likely, an answer to it. Tsvetaeva reacts with bemusement to her new suitor's "tenderness" and her own response:

Откуда такая нежность?	Whence cometh such tenderness?
Не первые — эти кудри	It's not the first time
Разглаживаю, и губы	I stroke these curls, and I have known
Знавала темней твоих.	Lips darker than thine.
Всходили и гасли звезды,	Stars have risen and faded,
Откуда такая нежность? —	Whence cometh such tenderness?
Всходили и гасли очи	Eyes have risen and faded
У самых моих очей.	Next to my very eyes.
Еще не такие гимны	I have not yet listened to such hymns
Я слушала ночью темной,	In the dark of night,
Венчаемая — о нежность! —	Crowned—O tenderness!—
На самой груди певца.	On the very breast of the singer.
Откуда такая нежность,	Whence cometh this tenderness?
И что с нею делать, отрок	And what's to be done with it, crafty lad,
Лукавый, певец захожий,	Newcomer, singer,
С ресницами — нет длинней?	With eyelashes that couldn't be longer?
	February 18, 1916
	(I, 204)

Here for the first time in Tsvetaeva is a note of ironic distance from her own emotions, perhaps a lesson learned from Mandel'stam. In line 14, she playfully turns back on him his own: "I am given a body—what am I to do with it?" Her persona is an experienced woman of the world: lines 2–4 could refer either to Sergei, or to Sonia, or to both. Her "crafty lad," by the way, had just turned twenty-five, and though his behavior as a suitor may well have been awkward, Tsvetaeva exaggerates his boyishness.[11]

The same distancing irony is evident in Tsvetaeva's other poem dated the same day, which captures Mandel'stam's characteristic way of holding his head:

Ты запрокидываешь голову
Затем, что ты гордец и враль.
Какого спутника веселого
Привел мне нынешний февраль!

Преследуемы оборванцами
И медленно пуская дым,
Торжественными чужестранцами
Проходим городом родным.

Чьи руки бережные нежили
Твои ресницы, красота,
И по каким терновалежиям
Лавровая тебя верста. . . —

Не спрашиваю. Дух мой алчущий
Переборол уже мечту.
В тебе божественного мальчика, —
Десятилетнего я чту.

Помедлим у реки, полощущей
Цветные бусы фонарей.
Я доведу тебя до площади,
Видавшей отроков-царей. . .

Мальчишескую боль высвистывай,
И сердце зажимай в горсти. . .
Мой хладнокровный, мой неистовый
Вольноотпущенник — прости!

You throw back your head
Because you're a liar, and proud.
A fine gay companion
This February has brought me!

Pursued by ragamuffins
And slowly exhaling smoke,
Like ceremonial foreigners
We walk our native city.

Whose hands have tenderly caressed
Your eyelashes, my beauty,
And across what fallen thorn-branches
Lies your laurel path . . . —

I do not ask. My thirsting spirit
Has mastered that dream.
In you I sense a divine boy
Ten years old.

Let us linger by the river, which washes
The colored beads of street-lamps.
I will lead you to the square
Which has seen adolescent tsars . . .

Whistle out your boyish pain,
And squeeze your heart in your hand . . .
My coldblooded, frenzied one
Now set free—farewell!

(I, 203-4)

This poem is less playful in tone than its twin, as Tsvetaeva hints that her "divine boy" will face a less than carefree future. In the poem's lexicon ("adolescent Tsars") and the common experience which underlies it, we find the origins of Mandel'stam's second Tsvetaeva poem.

While the tone of "In the discordance . . ." reflected the happy, early period in their friendship, a period of mutual discovery, "On a sledge overlaid with straw . . ." (March, 1916) is ominous rather than joyous: Mandel'stam the perceiver is now the passive victim of someone else's action.

На розвальнях, уложенных соломой,
Едва прикрытые рогожей роковой,
От Воробьевых гор до церковки знакомой
Мы ехали огромною Московой.

On a sledge overlaid with straw,
Ourselves but partly covered by the fateful blast,
We rode through immense Moscow
From the Sparrow Hills as far as the familiar little church.

А в Угличе играют дети в бабки,
И пахнет хлеб, оставленный в печи.
По улицам меня везут без шапки,
И теплятся в часовне три свечи.

Не три свечи горели, а три встречи —
Одну из них сам Бог благословил,
Четвертой не бывать, а Рим далече, —
И никогда он Рима не любил.

Ныряли сани в черные ухабы,
И возвращался с гульбища народ.
Худые мужики и злые бабы
Переминались у ворот.

Сырая даль от птичьих стай чернела,
И связанные руки затекли;
Царевича везут, немеет страшно тело —
И рыжую солому подожгли.

But in Uglich children play at knucklebones,
And there's a smell of bread left in the oven.
I am conveyed about the streets bareheaded,
And in the chapel three candles glimmer.

Not three candles burning, but three meetings—
And one of them had God's own blessing on it,
There is to be no fourth, and Rome is far away—
And Rome He never loved.

The sledge dove into the black ruts,
And people were returning from the open place
   for strolling.
Thin mouzhiks and cross old women
Shifted at the gate from foot to foot.

Raw distance seemed to blacken with the flight
   of birds,
And bound hands went numb.
They're bringing the Tsarevich, the body numbs
   with terror—
And now the amber straw's been set on fire.
   (#85) Trans. Clarence Brown.[12]

It is an opaque poem, but the first stanza at least is clear about its basic occasion. The second stanza introduces an historical subtext—the murder of Ivan the Terrible's young son, the Tsarevich Dmitry, in the town of Uglich (Boris Godunov, as all who have seen the opera will know, was popularly believed to be responsible). The years of interregnum and civil war which followed are known in Russian history as the Time of Troubles. Both Tsvetaeva and Mandel'stam recall this period in their poems of March and April, 1916. Clarence Brown has given a detailed and imaginative reading of "On a sledge".[13] For our purposes, his most important conclusion is that the entire "Uglich" level of the poem, which eventually merges with the first so that Mandel'stam himself becomes identified with the innocent martyred Tsarevich, is evoked by the name Marina. As Brown convincingly argues, any Russian free-associates the name Marina with the historical Marina Mniszek, a Polish adventuress who managed to become the wife of all three usurpers who pretended to be the surviving Dmitry. Tsvetaeva, one-quarter Polish herself, was named after Mniszek (or so she believed) and was proud of her namesake.[14] Khardzhiev, by the way, points out another historical reference for the last stanza:[15] on the orders of his father, Peter the Great's son and heir Alexei was transported from Moscow to Petersburg, where he was executed in 1718. The addition of another murdered Tsarevich to the background of the poem in no way conflicts with Brown's thesis that *legitimacy* is an underlying, "perhaps *the* underlying theme of the poem," opposed within the poem by the theme of violence.

This is clearly a poem with something to say about Russian history. Whether it is also a premonition of Mandel'stam's own final exile and death, as his widow claims, is not our concern here.

It is also true that in March of 1916 Mandel'stam was pursuing a woman who, "emancipated" and unfaithful though she may have been, was in fact *legitimately* married to someone else. That someone else, moreover, was an acquaintance of Mandel'stam's, probably even a friend.[16] They would have met at Koktebel' in the summer of 1915; Sergei arrived just after Marina and Parnok left. For all the attention that has been given to the third stanza of "On a Sledge" in terms of the "Moscow as the third Rome" ideology,[17] ("Not three candles burning, but three meetings— . . .") it is quite likely that Mandel'stam was referring, at the same time, to his meetings with Tsvetaeva (one in January in Petersburg, and two in Moscow in late January and late February,[18] at which, perhaps, she told him "there would not be a fourth."

Mandel'stam was not the only contender for Tsvetaeva's affections after her break with Parnok. Two March, 1916 poems, radically different in tone from the gently ironic Mandel'stam poems, were addressed to Tikhon Churilin. In one, the persona asks a young man "Did not Rogozhin [the passionately jealous murderer in Dostoevsky's *The Idiot*] clutch the garden knife in just such fingers?" The adressee's dominant characteristic in the other poem is "blueish-black plumage," of "a hard, greedy, hot color," and he is addressed as "my pitiable young raven." After the Churilin poems, Tsvetaeva returned to address Mandel'stam, reading portents of disaster on his palm:

Гибель от женщины. Вòт знàк
На ладони твоей, юноша.
Долу глаза! Молись! Берегись! Враг
Бдит в полуночи.

Ruin because of a woman. That is the sign
On your palm, youth.
Lower your eyes! Pray! Take care! The enemy
Keeps watch at midnight.

Не спасет ни песен
Небесный дар, ни надменнейший вырез губ.
Тем ты и люб,
Что небесен.

Neither the heavenly gift of your songs
Nor the haughty cut of your lips will save you.
You are dear,
Just because you are heavenly.

Ах, запрокинута твоя голова,
Полузакрыты глаза — что? — пряча.
Ах, запрокинется твоя голова —
Иначе.

Oh, your head is thrown back,
Your eyes half-closed—what are they hiding?
Oh, your head will be thrown back
In a different way.

Голыми руками возьмут — ретив! упрям!
Криком твоим всю ночь будет крй звонок!
Растреплют крылья твои по всем четырем
                                              ветрам,
Серафим! — Орленок! —

They will seize you with their bare hands—
       zealous! stubborn!
The whole night will ring with your cries!
They'll tear your wings and scatter them to the
       four winds,
Seraphim!—Eaglet!—
                              March 17, 1916
                                    (I, 207)

Tsvetaeva had earlier identified Mandel'stam, in his tenderness and vulnerability, with young swans and eagles, birds which grow up to be powerful and majestic, despite their awkwardness in youth. Her next Mandel'stam poem tells of a youth who will be threatened by "loud-winged eagles." One of them, "the master of the cliff," will "dishevel his curls with his beak," but the youth will sleep on, unaware of the danger. What are we to make of this avian combat? Did Tsvetaeva fear a confrontation between the jealous young raven Churilin and the baby swan Mandel'stam? Is Efron—it seems unlikely—the eagle-like "master of the cliff," swooping down to defend his nest? Or is this all private symbolism, and the product of Tsvetaeva's imagination? Whatever the case, these poems certainly resonate with Mandel'stam's "Raw distance seemed to blacken with the flight of birds." And it is difficult to resist the suspicion that the phonetic similarity of Tsvetaeva's "Rogozhin" and Mandel'stam's "fatal bast mat" ("rogozha") is not entirely accidental.

Tsvetaeva's flirtation with Mandel'stam was growing too serious for her comfort. More than any other poet of her generation, she was aware of belonging to a close, fatally linked, brotherhood of poets, and at one time or another, in one sense or another, she was "in love" with Mandel'stam, Akhmatova, Pasternak, and Blok. But we know from her relationship with Pasternak that she saw this as a higher love, a non-physical marriage of souls in the higher world of *byt'ie*, which had little or nothing to do with real bodies in the world of *byt*. Seven years later, she recalled saying to Mandel'stam, "What is Marina when there's Moscow? Marina when there's spring? Oh, you don't *really* love me!" She elaborated, "I was always stifled by this narrowness. Love the *world* in me, not me in the world—so that 'Marina' means the world and not the world Marina."[19]

Beginning in mid-March, the lyric diary sounded notes of guilt: "To the clanging of bells/ Archangels will lead me to the block." Seeking the strength to free herself from romantic entanglements, Tsvetaeva's persona turned to the church, as Moscow's churches and traditional burgher life became a dominant presence in her poems. Though Tsvetaeva often used the imagery and language of the Orthodox liturgy in her poetry, she was not a regular church-goer:

> All my life I have not been tied to the church. I am non-, extra-ecclesiastical, that is, I feel comfortable next to a church, in the churchyard, in the entryway, around and about, passing by it, and I feel uncomfortable, out of place, *in* the church, particularly during the service . . . alienation, a sense of differentness." (1914)[20]

But her favorite church holiday, Annunciation (March 25) was approaching. It was a popular Russian custom to release caged birds on that day,[21] and she took advantage of the holiday to vow that, "I have no need of tame doves, cygnets, eagles." "On Annunciation day, I smile until evening/ Having parted from my feathered guests!" "Annunciation Eve" describes a visit to the services in the Kremlin's Annunciation cathedral. She prays to the Virgin Mother not for her sinful self, but for her daughter, who had vanished from her poems two years earlier when Sofia Parnok entered:

К Солнцу-Матери,	To the Sun-Mother,
Затерянная в тени,	Lost in shadow,
Воззываю и я, радуясь:	I, too, appeal, rejoicing:
Матерь — матери	Mother—preserve for a mother
Сохрани	Her blue-eyed daughter!
Дочку голубоглазую!	Enlighten her
В светлой мудрости	With radiant wisdom,
Просвети, направь	Set her on the lost path
По утерянному пути —	Of blessing.
Блага.	
	Give her health,
Дай здоровья ей,	Place by the head of her bed
К изголовью ей	The Angel who has
Отлетевшего от меня	Flown away from me.
Приставь — Ангела.	Protect her from verbal splendor,
От словесной храни — пышности,	Lest she turn out like me—
Чтоб не вышла как я — хищницей,	A bird of prey,
Чернокнижницей.	Worker of black magic.

March 24–25, 1916
(I, 210–11)

At the end of the service, she runs "gaily" to the river, to watch the ice breaking up, as if, having sought in vain for consolation and redemption within the church, she craves the fresh, cold air of pagan nature.

"Going-on-four" continues the story. Alya, "like a little god," watches the ice breaking up from the Kremlin parapet. Well aware of her mother's emotional conflicts, she sees in the breaking ice a sign of change, and fears that the foundations of her own life may be breaking up as well. Alya could have been jealous of the strange "uncles" who were taking up so much of her mother's time:

Синий	The blue-eyed gaze
Взор — озабочен	Is worried
— Ты меня любишь, Марина?	—Do you love me, Marina?
— Очень.	—Very much.
— Навсегда?	—For always?
— Да.	—Yes.

March 24, 1916
(I, 211–212)

Just at this point (March 29–30) Tsvetaeva wrote a poem about the False Dmitry and Marina Mniszek which resonates with Mandel'stam's "On a sledge." Here is the Time of Troubles, the pretender and his Marina, even, in the last stanza, one of Mandel'stam's "three candles burning:"

Марина! Димитрий! С миром,	Marina! Dmitri! Go in peace
Мятежники, спите, милые.	Rebels, sleep, dear ones.
Над нежной гробницей ангельской	Above the tender angel's coffin
За вас в соборе Архангельском	In the Archangel cathedral
Большая свеча горит.	A large candle burns for you.

(I, 214)

We should beware of the temptation simply to read "Mandel'stam" for "Dmitry"—the situation is more complex. First, the initial conceit of the poem, that Dmitry and Marina were born "under one ambivalent star" is a recurrent motif in Tsvetaeva's poems to Sergei, who (theoretically) shared her birthday.[22] Nor is this poem one of the nine which Tsvetaeva identified as "Mandel'stam's." It seems, rather, to be about her confusion of Sergei and Mandel'stam. Her abortive romance with Mandel'stam, by precipitating her final break with Parnok, may have facilitated a reconciliation with Sergei.

Immediately following the Dmitry/Marina poem come Tsvetaeva's "Poems about Moscow." In the first, she presents her "wonderful city" to her daughter as a heritage, but at the same time urges on her the kind of traditional, church-going woman's role she had depicted in other late March poems. "Moscow" 2 and 3, however, are dedicated to Mandel'stam. The city which she has just promised to her daughter she now presents to her "strange, marvelous brother:"

Из рук моих — нерукотворный град	Take from my hands, my strange, my beautiful
Прими, мой странный, мой прекрасный брат.	brother, This city not made by hands.
По церковке — всё сорок сороков,	One church at a time—all forty times forty,
И реющих над ними голубков.	And the doves who soar above them.
И Спасские — с цветами — воротà,	And the Spassky gates with flowers,
Где шапка православного снята.	Where the cap of the Orthodox is doffed.
Часовню звездную — приют от зол —	The starry chapel, refuge from evils,
Где вытертый от поцелуев — пол.	Where the floor is worn from kisses.
Пятисоборный несравненный круг	Take, my ancient, inspired friend,
Прими, мой древний, вдохновенный друг.	The five-cathedral incomparable circle.
К Нечаянныя Радости в саду	I will lead my foreign guest
Я гостя чужеземного сведу.	To Unexpected Joys in the garden.
Червонные возблещут купола,	The golden cupolas will blaze,
Бессонные взгремят колокола,	The sleepless bells will thunder,
И на тебя с багряных облаков	And the Mother of God will let fall on you
Уронит Богородица покров,	Her protection from the crimson clouds,
И встанешь ты, исполнен дивных сил. . .	And you will rise, filled with miraculous strength . . .
Ты не раскаешься, что ты меня любил.	You won't repent that you loved me.

March 31, 1916

(I, 215-216)

"Where the hat of the Orthodox is doffed" (line 6) must have emerged from the same material as Mandel'stam's "I am conveyed through the streets without a hat." There might be a playful reference here to Mandel'stam's Jewishness.[23] (Orthodox Jewish men cover their head at all times.)

Tsvetaeva often addressed her fellow poets in imitations of their own voice. Imitation is the sincerest form of flattery, yet for Tsvetaeva it was also a demonstration of her own genius. "Take from My Hands" is, in part, just such an imitation of Mandel'stam. What is there about the poem which makes us hear his voice? First, the meter, a regular iambic pentameter, is the one he used in "On a sledge," in so many ways a sister poem to this. This most common English meter is a comparatively long line for Russian verse, but Mandel'stam used it often. Tsvetaeva did not. Not only the length, but the regularity of the meter is unusual for Tsvetaeva at this period. Then there is the elevated, almost eighteenth-century diction, common both to Mandel'stam and Derzhavin, whom he admired. The formula, "Iz ruk moix . . . Primi" ("Take from my hands . . .") strikes us as typically Mandel'stamian. But Tsvetaeva's "imitation" here actually anticipated the original. Her gesture of gift was answered two months later in Mandel'stam's third and final Tsvetaeva poem, where, in return for Moscow, he gave her a handful of Koktebel' sand:

Прими ж ладонями моими	Take the sand poured out
Пересыпаемый песок.	By my hands.

The last of Tsvetaeva's Mandel'stam poems, "Past Nocturnal Towers" ("Moscow 3") is very different from the elevated "Take from my hands," though written the same day. The otherworldliness and innocence of her February poems has been displaced by a passion which the persona knows is unacceptable. Once again, she turns to the church:

Мимо ночных башен	The squares rush us
Площади нас мчат.	Past nocturnal towers.
Ох, как в ночй страшен	Oh, how frightening is
Рев молодых солдат!	The roar of young soldiers in the night!
Греми, громкое сердце!	Ring out, loud heart!
Жарко целуй, любовь!	Kiss passionately, love!
Ох, этот рев зверский!	Oh, this beastly roar!
Дерзкая — ох — кровь!	Oh, this insolent blood!
Мòй ро́т разгарчив,	My mouth is inflamed,
Даром, что свят — вид.	In vain is my aspect holy.
Как золотой ларчик	The Iverskaya chapel
Иверская горит.	Shines like a golden chest.

Ты озорство прикончи,
Да засвети свечу,
Чтобы с тобой нонче
Не было — как хочу.

Finish up your mischief
And light a candle,
So it will not be for you now
As I want.

March 31, 1916
(I, 216)

This poem is a sister to Mandel'stam's #107, which begins:

О, этот воздух, смутой пьяный,
На черной площади Кремля
Качают шаткий «мир» смутьяны,
Тревожно пахнут тополя.

Oh, this air, drunk with sedition,
On the black Kremlin square
Troublemakers shake the unsteady "world,"
The poplars smell in alarm.

April, 1916

An even clearer picture of the "realia" underlying these poems emerges from an earlier draft of Mandel'stam's poem: "How the poplars smell! We are drunk."[24]

Such goings-on made Tsvetaeva's persona uncomfortable. A cluster of six poems written in imitation of folk diction tells the story of a young wife ostracized for her practice of black magic (writing poetry?) and her illicit love for a young man. An old crone predicts a dire fate:

Говорила мне бабка лютая,
Коромыслом от злости гнутая:
Не дремить тебе в люльке дитятка,
Не белить тебе пряжи вытканной, —
Царевать тебе — под заборами!
Целовать тебе, внучка — ворона!

A cruel old woman,
Bent like a yoke from malice, said to me:
Not for you to lull a wee one in a cradle,
Not for you to bleach woven worsted—
It's for you to reign under fences!
For you to kiss, granddaughter, the raven!

April 1, 1916
(I, 220)

The persona asks to be buried as an apostate, either "under the apple tree, without prayers, without incense" or "at the crossroads," with a signpost as her grave marker.[25] Yet despite the retribution she knows awaits her, she defiantly declares the strength of her love for her "darling boy." She has a multitude of admirers, all seeking to "christen her" with new endearing names. "I have a whole monastery of godfathers for my soul." But estranged from her husband, she is "neither wife, nor widow, nor fiancee."

Коль похожа на жену — где повойник мой?
Коль похожа на вдову — где покойник мой?
Коли суженого жду — где бессонница?
Царь-Девицею живу — беззаконницей!

If I'm like a wife, where's my [married woman's] kerchief?
If I'm like a widow—where's my dear deceased?
If I'm waiting for my promised one—where's my insomnia?
I live like the Tsar-maiden—an outlaw!

April 6, 1916
(I, 223)

The persona's moral dilemma was causing insomnia. This theme, which dominated the last months of 1916, made its first appearance here. The absolution she had unsuccessfully sought in the church is, paradoxically, given by insomnia herself (the word is gramatically feminine in Russian, and Tsvetaeva personifies it):

Обвела мне глаза кольцом	Insomnia passed her shadowy ring
Теневым — бессонница.	Over my eyes.
Оплела мне глаза бессонница	Insomnia twined round my eyes
Теневым венцом.	Her shadowy crown.
	April 8, 1916
	(I, 224)

But the shadowy ring and shadowy crown are symbols of a marriage with death, and the sleep into which she finally falls is deathlike, with people bowing at her bier while insomnia serves as the deacon reading prayers.

Just when she needed him most, Max Voloshin, Tsvetaeva's mentor and "spiritual father," passed through Moscow in mid-April on his way home from Europe. She must have sought his help in putting her life in order, for suddenly, on two successive days in late April, appear twin poems in which she makes abject apology to those she has loved and wronged: Sofia Parnok (see Chapt.5) and Sergei. The poem to her husband partakes of the now-familiar "Time of Troubles" imagery: Tsvetaeva is a kingdom during an interregnum, where the legitimate order has been flagrantly violated by "pretenders." Reduced to spiritual and moral beggary, she stands in repentance before her "true Tsar:"

С. Э.	S. E.
Я пришла к тебе черной полночью,	I have come to you in the black of midnight,
За последней помощью.	For my last help.
Я — бродяга, родства не помнящий,	I am a tramp, of unknown ancestry,
Корабль тонущий.	A sinking ship.
В слободах моих — междуцарствие,	In my villages there is interregnum,
Чернецы коварствуют.	The monks are perfidious.
Всяк рядится в одежды царские,	Everyone dons the tsar's vestments,
Псари царствуют.	Kennelmen reign.
Кто земель моих не оспаривал,	Who has not contended for my lands,
Сторожей не спаивал?	Who has not made drunkards of the watchmen?
Кто в ночи не варил — варева,	Who, in the night, has not brewed slop,
Не жег — зарева?	Who has not lit fires?
Самозванцами, псами хищными,	I am totally plundered by pretenders
Я до тла расхищена.	By predatory dogs.
У палат твоих, царь истинный,	In your chambers, my true tsar,
Стою — нищая!	I stand—a beggar!
	April 27, 1916
	(I, 226)

The poem seems to signal a reconciliation with Sergei. At least the theme of errant wife vanished from the lyric diary as Tsvetaeva turned to concentrate on worshipful praise of Alexander Blok, a poet whom she had never met, who was probably unaware of her existence, and who was, unlike Mandel'-stam, far away in Petrograd and likely to remain so.

But there was one more meeting with Mandel'stam, an abortive visit in early June which inspired his third and last poem to her:

Не веря воскресенья чуду,	Not believing in the miracle of resurrection,
На кладбище гуляли мы.	We strolled in the graveyard.
— Ты знаешь, мне земля повсюду	—You know, the earth everywhere
Напоминает те холмы	Reminds me of those hills
. . . .	. . . .
. . . .	. . . .
Где обрывается Россия	Where Russia breaks off
Над морем черным и глухим.	Above an ocean black and remote.
От монастырских косогоров	From the monastery slopes
Широкий убегает луг.	A wide meadow runs away.
Мне от владимирских просторов	I so did not want to go south
Так не хотелося на юг,	Away from those Vladimir expanses,
Но в этой темной, деревянной	But in this dark, wooden
И юродивой слободе	Village of holy fools
С такой монашкою туманной	To remain with such a misty nun—
Остаться — значит быть беде.	Means only trouble.
Целую локоть загорелый	I kiss the sunburned elbow
И лба кусочек восковой.	And a bit of the waxen brow.
Я знаю — он остался белый	I know, it remained white
Под смуглой прядью золотой.	Beneath the swarthy golden curl.
Целую кисть, где от браслета	I kiss the wrist, where from the bracelet
Еще белеет полоса.	A white strip still remains.
Тавриды пламенное лето	Tavrida's flaming summer
Творит такие чудеса.	Works such wonders.
Как скоро ты смуглянкой стала	How quickly you grew swarthy
И к Спасу бедному пришла,	And went up to the poor Savior
Не отрываясь целовала,	You kissed without tearing yourself away,
А гордою в Москве была.	But you were proud in Moscow.
Нам остается только имя —	For us remains only a name—
Чудесный звук, на долгий срок.	A wonderful sound, for a long, long span.
Прими ж ладонями моими	Take the sand poured out
Пересыпаемый песок.	By my hands.

(Mandel'stam, #94)

Tsvetaeva described that visit and glossed the poem in her 1931 memoir, "The History of a Dedication." She was staying at her sister's house in Aleksandrov, with Alya, Asya's son Andriusha, and his nanny, Nadia (she recalled, "That very Aleksandrovskaya Sloboda where Ivan the Terrible killed his son.") The nearby graveyard was a favorite destination for her strolls with the children. She found it picturesque, but the proximity of death made Mandel'stam distinctly uncomfortable:

> Mandel'stam, after the first ecstasies, couldn't take Alexandrov. Man of Petersburg and the Crimea, he could not get used to my hillsides. Too many cows (walking past, mooing past, twice a day), too many crosses (too eternally standing). A cow could butt you. A corpse could rise, go mad, haunt your dreams. In the cemetery, I was, he said, "somehow abstracted," I forgot about him, and thought about the dead, read the epitaphs (instead of poems!). . .in a word, I looked either up or down, but always away—I was distracted.[26]

Mandel'stam's childish desire for attention and care is a leitmotif of Tsvetaeva's memoir. The nanny Nadya evidently found Mandel'stam as puzzling as he found her inscrutable:

> Miss Marina! What a strange one this Osip Emilevich of ours is! I'm just now feeding Andriusha his kasha, and he says to me, "Your Andriusha is fortunate, Nadya, his kasha is always ready for him and his socks are always darned. But no one feeds me kasha and no one darns my socks," and he sighs so deep, poor bitter orphan![27]

With a poet's insight, Tsvetaeva theorizes that the "misty nun" of Mandel'stam's poem is an amalgam of Nadya ("a tame she-wolf,") a swarthy nun who brought the laundry, and Tsvetaeva herself. She explains that the white strip beneath her bracelet remained from the burning Koktebel' sun of the previous summer, when they had first met. Her parsing of the last stanza seems to substantiate the temporary warming in her attitude toward the church which we can feel in her other Alexandrov poems. It was not, she makes clear, Mandel'stam whom she kissed "without tearing herself away," but the icon of Christ. In Moscow, she had been "too proud" to do so.

As in all Tsvetaeva's memoir-portraits of her poetic contemporaries, she distilled Mandel'stam's personality to unforgettable images. The art involved is all the more evident when we compare "History of a Dedication" with a June, 1916 letter to Lilya Efron in which she described the Aleksandrov visit quite differently, in ironic and impatient tones.[28] Mandel'stam's stay, it turns out, was less than a day, and he suddenly fled to Koktebel' on a midnight train. Except for occasional uneventful meetings, he played no role in Tsvetaeva's life thereafter. When *Versts I* was finally published in 1922, their romance belonged to the distant past, and Mandel'stam had a new (and jealous) wife, Nadezhda Yakovlevna Khazina. Tsvetaeva saw no need to create trouble for him by revealing the dedications of "his" poems. Nadezhda Mandel'stam recalls how she and Osip stopped by to visit Tsvetaeva shortly before her emigration. Tsvetaeva greeted Mandel'stam warmly as an old friend and invited him into the apartment, leaving his new wife to cool her heels in the hall. In the same year, perhaps as a gesture of loyalty to Nadezhda, Mandel'stam dismissed Tsvetaeva's poetry—precisely those poems which she wrote during their friendship—in a passage which Clarence Brown labels "dismaying and quite indefensible:"

> The tastelessness and historical false notes of Marina Tsvetaeva's poems about Russia—pseudo-folk and pseudo-Muscovite—are immeasurably lower than the verse of Adalis, whose voice from time to time attains masculine force and truth.[29]

Whatever else is to be said of Mandel'stam, it cannot be said he was sympathetic to "women's liberation" (see Nadezhda's memoirs) and, except for his close friend Akhmatova, he had little patience for women poets. The kindest thing to do with such a judgment would be to let it pass swiftly into oblivion. It is evident from Tsvetaeva's memoir that she bore him no grudge.

In "giving Moscow" to Mandel'stam, Tsvetaeva found it truly more blessed to give than receive. For the "Mandel'stam" poems mark the entry into her work of Russia and its history. *Juvenilia*, much of it written in the Crimea, focused on the persona and her intimates, hardly ever on the wider society which surrounded them. Mandel'stam's gift to her was her new consciousness of Moscow's churches, and of the Russian history of which they were an essential part. A turning point in that history was fast approaching, and, when it came, she would be mature enough to meet its challenges.

CHAPTER EIGHT

Blok

Blok was the only poet in Tsvetaeva's life whom she revered not only as a colleague in the "stringed craft," but as a deity whom she worshipped. All the others whom she loved she felt to be her peers—rather, she considered herself their colleague and peer."[1] —Ariadna Efron

Only eleven years Tsvetaeva's senior, Alexander Blok in 1916 was already a figure of legend, as much for his sensual, brooding good looks and troubled marriage to Liubov' Mendeleeva, inspiration for his "Poems about the Beautiful Lady," as for his mystical, occasionally demonic and often pro- phetic poems, which answered the mood of his pre-revolutionary generation.

"Blok and Tsvetaeva:" The juxtaposition seems an odd one at first. The enigmatic figure of Blok, surrounded by the mists of Petersburg and Sym- bolism, Tsvetaeva brassy and outspoken, her voice clarion-clear and asser- tive. Yet Blok was a major influence, perhaps *the* only influence on Tsve- taeva from within the Russian tradition. Blok and Tsvetaeva are most alike in the romantic tendency to blur poet and persona, to work toward a con- fessional poetry through a lyric diary.[2] "A Poet usually gives his works to the public; Blok gives his very self" wrote Gumilev in 1912.[3] The Russian reader has always demanded of the writer (particularly of the poet) more than just his work, he asks a life in some way exemplary as well.[4] Blok played this role for Tsvetaeva's generation, and she is now playing it for a broad circle of Russian readers. For them, her biography is the object of as much intense interest as her poetry. Joseph Brodsky has recently hypothe- sized that, at the beginning of the twentieth century, just as the church lost its legitimacy, the Russian intelligentsia turned to the lives of its modern poets in same way that generations of Russians had sought moral exemplars in saints' lives.[5]

The dualism of Blok's persona was important for Tsvetaeva. He, too, embraced contradictory opposites (mystical, quasi-religious purity and drunken dissipation), he, too, was guilty of impossible idealization (The memoir of his wife, recently translated, could be called "The Beautiful Lady's Complaint.")[6] Blok provided a formal model for Tsvetaeva as well: while the diction and meters of her first two collections were borrowed straight from nineteenth-century and early Symbolist practice, her explora- tion of new metrical forms and rhymes paralleled such strivings in the later Blok—her achievements can be seen as a continuation of his.[7] Blok's influ- ence on Tsvetaeva is most obvious in her earliest verse dramas, written in

1918–19.[8] Finally, his groundbreaking achievement in "The Twelve," a *poema* originally conceived as a lyric cycle, pointed the way for Tsvetaeva's masterpieces, "The Poem of the Mountain" and "The Poem of the End."

Tsvetaeva never met Blok, nor did she ever mention him in her early work. But just after Easter, 1916, he suddenly appeared as the new hero of her lyric diary. Altogether, she would write him 21 poems. The last 12, written after his death in 1921, comprise a lyric requiem; it is the first eight, written between April 15 and May 18, 1916 which interest us at the moment. They appear in the lyric diary as a counterweight to the February and March poems of dalliance and infidelity. Developing the ecclesiastical diction and imagery of the Moscow and Aleksandrov poems, Tsvetaeva turned religiosity on its head to glorify not God or His son, but a mortal poet. She began by literally praising his name—not his person or his poetry, but his name alone:

Имя твое — птица в руке,	Thy name is a bird in the hand,
Имя твое — льдинка на языке,	Thy name is a snowflake on the tongue.
Одно единственное движенье губ,	One single movement of the lips.
Имя твое — пять букв.	Thy name is five letters.[9]
Мячик, пойманный на лету,	A ball caught in flight,
Серебряный бубенец во рту,	A silver bell in the mouth.
Камень, кинутый в тихий пруд,	A stone dropped in a quiet pond
Всхлипнет та̀к, как тебя зовут.	Will sob your name.
В легком щелканье ночных копыт	In the light flicker of nighttime hooves
Громкое имя твое гремит.	Thy thunderous name resounds.
И назовет его нам в висок	And the loud click of the trigger cocking
Звонко щелкающий курок.	Aims it at our temples.
Имя твое — ах, нельзя! —	Thy name—Ah! impossible!
Имя твое — поцелуй в глаза,	Thy name—a kiss on the eyes,
В нежную стужу недвижных век,	On the tender immobility of frozen lids,
Имя твое — поцелуй в снег.	Thy name—a kiss on the snow.
Ключевой, ледяной, голубой глоток. . .	A swallow of spring water, icy, pale-blue . . .
С именем твоим — сон глубок.	With thy name—sleep is deep.

April 15, 1916
(I, 227)

The images are icily pure: "a bird in the hand," "a snowflake on the tongue," "a kiss on the eyelids," "a kiss on the snow," "a swallow of spring water." Tsvetaeva sees Blok as a "pure angel" (albeit, perhaps, an angel of death—the cocked pistol is ominous) much as he himself had seen his "Beautiful Lady."

The poem, in Russian, has a feeling of tight organization and metallic precision due, not as we have come to expect in Tsvetaeva, to its rhythm and meter, but to the rhymes. The meter is a *dol'nik*, an accentual meter organized only by the number of stresses in the line, with no regard for the number of syllables between them. It was a meter revived in the twentieth-century by Blok and popularized by Akhmatova, who used it frequently. Tsvetaeva used it rarely, preferring the more hightly structured *logaed*. The rhymes are arranged in couplets (aabbcc), one rhymed line hitting immediately after the the first, but, of prime importance, they are *all masculine* (stressed on the final syllable of the line). Masculine rhymes are harder to find in Russian, with its profusion of multi-syllable declensional endings. End-stressed words are likely to be of only one syllable (like "Blok") or two. Tsvetaeva has used eight such rhymes, repeating herself only once—in the final rhymes of the second and third stanzas: "—OK." This emphasized rhyme, repeated at two of the poem's most structurally significant spots, is of course the talisman of that name, never uttered—held sacred, like the names of ancient deities—that is the poem's subject.

Several of Tsvetaeva's poems intentionally mimic those in Blok's first collection, "Poems about the Beautiful Lady" (published in 1905.) Their recurring cold and snow reflect not the early May weather during which she was writing, but Blok's early poetry, which she was probably re-reading. More than once she consciously echoes him:[10]

Blok:

Ты отходишь в сумрак алый,	You *depart* into a scarlet dusk,
В бесконечные круги.	Into endless circles.
Я послышал отзвук малый,	I heard a small echo,
Отдаленные шаги.	Distant steps.
	March 6, 1901[11]

Blok's subtext, as F. Scholz has pointed out, is the Orthodox vesper hymn. Tsvetaeva echoes both:

Ты проходишь на Запад Солнца,	You *pass by* to the West of the Sun,
Ты увидишь вечерний свет,	You will see the evening light,
Ты проходишь на Запад Солнца,	You pass by to the West of the Sun,
И метель заметает след.	And a snowstorm covers your trace.
Мимо окон моих — бесстрастный —	Past my windows—passionless one—
Ты пройдешь в снеговой тиши.	You will go in snowy silence,
Божий праведник мой прекрасный,	My wonderful righteous man of God,
Свете тихий моей души.	Quiet light of my soul.
Я на душу твою — не зарюсь!	I'll not hanker after your soul!
Нерушима твоя стезя.	Inviolable is your path.
В руку, бледную от лобзаний,	I'll not drive my nail
Не вобью своего гвоздя.	Through your hand, pale from kisses.
И по имени не окликну,	And I'll not hail you by name,
И руками не потянусь.	And I'll not stretch out my hands.
Восковому святому лику	Only from afar will I worship
Только издали поклонюсь.	The holy, waxen face.

И, под медленным снегом стоя,
Опущусь на колени в снег,
И во имя твое святое,
Поцелую вечерний снег. —

Там, где поступью величавой
Ты прошел в гробовой тиши,
Свете тихий — святыя славы —
Вседержитель моей души.

Standing in snow slowly falling,
I will fall on my knees in the snow,
And in your holy name,
I will kiss the evening snow.

Where with stately, magnificent tread,
You passed by in deathly silence,
Quiet light—holy glory—
Almighty of my soul.

May 2, 1916
(I, 228-229)

The liturgical Slavonicisms of Tsvetaeva's diction implicitly substitute Blok for Christ (her refusal, for instance, to drive the "nail" of her kiss into Blok's hand).[12]

The real-life Blok of 1916 was, however, hardly the "pure angel" of Tsvetaeva's poems. His life was marked by constant drinking bouts and a series of love affairs. His health was beginning to break; he suffered from chronic syphilis. His marriage to Liubov' Mendeleeva had long ago broken down, though they continued to share the same apartment. Blok's own lyric diary had reflected the emergence of the "demonic" Blok as early as 1904, but Tsvetaeva steadfastly refused to acknowledge the "other" Blok in her panegyrics. Blok would always remain for her a disembodied spirit, and she reaffirmed that pledge in a poem which pointedly re-evoked the Moscow images of her Mandel'stam poems: the Kremlin cathedrals, the street-lamps reflected in the river. In the capitalized "Joy" she linked the Moscow church "Unexpected Joys," mentioned earlier in a poem to Mandel'stam, with the title of Blok's 1907 collection, "Unexpected Joy."

У меня в Москве — купола горят!
У меня в Москве — колокола звонят!
И гробницы в ряд у меня стоят, —
В них царицы спят, и цари.

И не знаешь ты, что зарей в Кремле
Легче дышится — чем на всей земле!
И не знаешь ты, что зарей в Кремле
Я молюсь тебе — до зари!

И проходишь ты над своей Невой
О ту пору, как над рекой-Москвой
Я стою с опущенной головой,
И слипаются фонари.

Всей бессонницей я тебя люблю,
Всей бессонницей я тебе внемлю —
О ту пору, как по всему Кремлю
Просыпаются звонари. . .

In my Moscow—cupolas flame!
In my Moscow—bell-towers chime!
Here sepulchres stand in a row—
Tsarinas sleep there, and their tsars.

You don't know that at dawn in the Kremlin
Breathing's easier than anywhere on earth!
You don't know that at dawn in the Kremlin
I will pray to you—till sunset.

And you pass by above your Neva
While here above the Moscow River
I stand with head inclined
And the street-lamps flow together.

With all my insomnia I love you
With all my insomnia I heed you
At the hour when, through the whole Kremlin
The bell-ringers awaken . . .

Но моя река — да с твоей рекой,	But my river—with your river,
Но моя рука — да с твоей рукой	But my hand—with your hand
Не сойдутся, Радость моя, доколь	Will not merge, my Joy, until
Не догонит заря — зари.	The sunrise overtakes the sunset.

May 7, 1916
(I, 229-230)

Here, quite possibly in reaction to Mandel'stam's infatuation, is the first instance of a characteristic pattern in Tsvetaeva's relations with her poetic contemporaries: she saw poetic dialogue as a "conversation of souls" which could be endangered or destroyed by face-to-face meetings. Tsvetaeva had a chance to meet Blok in 1920, when he gave his last readings in Moscow, but she intentionally let it pass:

> In life, by the will of a verse, I missed a great meeting with Blok (had we met, he wouldn't have died)—I myself, at the age of twenty,[13] had frivolously conjured: "And I shall never reach out to him with my hands." And there was, in fact, a second when I stood *right next* to him, in the crowd, shoulder to shoulder (seven years later!) and I looked at his sunken temples, his reddish, so unattractive (cut short, he was ill) thin hair, at the dusty collar of his worn jacket. I had my poems in my pocket [the poems to Blok—JT]—I had only to stretch out my hand—I didn't move. (Letter to Pasternak, February 11-14, 1923) [14]

By actually meeting Blok and performing the symbolic contact of hands, she risked taking him out of the world of *byt'ie* and imprisoning him in the world of *byt*. Even their momentary proximity was enough, for a moment, to eclipse Blok's god-like nimbus with "sunken temples . . . and reddish, so unattractive . . . thin hair." Instead, she sent the seven-year-old Alya backstage to present a copy of "his" poems. According to one story, a mutual friend later described to Tsvetaeva how "he read them—silently—read them for a long time, and then such a lo—ong smile."[15] We will have to posit our own interpretation of that smile. Blok left the manuscript in Moscow with friends, and never replied.

Blok's death in August, 1921 at the age of 40 inspired a return to panegyrics. Trying to cope with the loss, Tsvetaeva toyed with the notion that, like Christ or the Dalai Lama, he had been reincarnated in a newborn babe, and her persona set off on a pilgrimage to find him. Willfully confusing myth and reality, she let herself believe that the infant son of their mutual friend Nadezhda Nolle-Kagan was in fact Blok's. She persisted in this belief for several years, and it lies behind the subcycle of Blok poems titled "Bethlehem," dedicated "To Blok's son Sasha."

Blok returned to Tsvetaeva's work in a 1935 essay titled "My Meeting with Blok," which she read at one of her Paris fund-raising evenings. Unlike her other critical/memoir essays on her poetic contemporaries, it never found its way into print, and Ariadna Efron simply notes cryptically, "the manuscript has been lost." She recalls that it was "just as much a poetic genuflection, an unreserved "Alleluia!" as her poems to him."[16] Its loss is both frustrating and tantalizing. Tsvetaeva was conscientious about preserving her archive. Was the Blok piece perhaps not lost at all, but destroyed by Tsvetaeva because she was dissatisfied with it? Or did she, perhaps, finally "overcome" Blok as, much earlier, she "overcame" Akhmatova?

CHAPTER NINE

Akhmatova

Just as readers of my generation say "Pasternak and Tsvetaeva," so her generation pronounced "Blok and Akhmatova." But for Tsvetaeva herself, the conjunction between these two names was pure convention—she put no equal sign between them, her lyrical glorifications of Akhmatova were expression of *sisterly* feelings, carried to their apogee, nothing more. They were sisters in poetry, but by no means twins; the absolute harmony, the spiritual plasticity of Akhmatova, which so captivated Tsvetaeva at first, later began to seem qualities which limited Akhmatova's creativity and the development of her poetic personality. "She is perfection, and in that, alas, is her limitation," Tsvetaeva said about Akhmatova.[1] (A. Efron)

While Blok was for Tsvetaeva an otherworldly angel whom she could only worship, Akhmatova was an elder sister, the object of both affection and rivalry. Akhmatova's *Rosary* (1914) her second collection of poems, brought her acclaim, even celebrity beyond the usual circles of poetry readers. Her admirers would "say the *Rosary*," one beginning a poem by heart and the next continuing it. Akhmatova's success presented Tsvetaeva with a thorny problem. With the possible exception of Gippius, the Russian poetic tradition had never had a major female voice. Now it had one, and Akhmatova's presence both defined and usurped the "female territory" in Russian poetry. Nadezhda Mandel'stam, who can be taken as an example of the "common reader" of that period, recalls, "I granted the existence of several male poets, but for women my criterion was more severe. There was one slot and that was all. And the slot was solidly filled."[2] Tsvetaeva knew she would inevitably be read not only in comparison with Akhmatova, but in the *context* of Akhmatova. Was there room for her radically different, though no less female, voice?

The labels most often applied to the art of the early Akhmatova are "classical" and "realist." Mandel'stam observed that Akhmatova's roots were in nineteenth-century psychological prose.[3] Tsvetaeva's sources, such as they were, are in French and German romanticism, certainly not in Turgenev, Goncharov, and Tolstoy. Akhmatova's poems give such an illusion of intimacy that most of her readers relished them as voyeuristic glimpses into the poet's intimate biography and that of her ill-starred husband, Nikolai Gumilev. Akhmatova's secretiveness about the real details of her personal life did nothing to destroy the illusion, but illusion it most often was. Tsvetaeva's lyric diary, for all its hyperbole and "tender lies," is closer to biographic reality than is Akhmatova's.

Sam Driver pointed out the way in which Akhmatova's use of detail—in the depiction of female dress, or domestic interiors, adds "an extremely feminine intimacy to a poetry which, in its form and syntax, generally strives toward the impersonal."[4] Akhmatova, after all, did share many values with her fellow-Acmeist Mandel'stam. Precise realistic detail, for example Akhmatova's endlessly-quoted "I put my left glove on my right hand" signalling intense agitation, was not Tsvetaeva's *metier*—she painted in far broader strokes. Rather than letting the physical detail obliquely convey the persona's emotion, Tsvetaeva's persona simply declared herself straight out.

Two characteristic verbal tics are illustrative. Akhmatova's is "I know" (*znaiu*)—the classical consciousness of self and immutable reality. Tsvetaeva's is "I love" (*liubliu*)—the romantic glorification of the individual and her feelings. Driver notes that "Akhmatova often observes herself suffering, often in a mirror, or from another corner of the room."[5] Tsvetaeva seldom distances herself in this way, still less often does she simply suffer. Rather, she fights, be it against fate, the opinion of society, or the beloved himself/ (herself). Both poets occasionally adopted the persona of the simple Russian village woman. Akhmatova's peasant women endure in silence; Tsvetaeva's are outcasts or sorceresses.

Tsvetaeva claimed that she first read Akhmatova in the summer of 1916, but that is the way she *wished* it had been. It is possible she had not noticed Akhmatova's first book, *Evening*, published in a tiny edition in the spring of 1912 while Tsvetaeva was abroad on her wedding trip. But she could hardly have been unaware of *Rosary*. Her first known poem to Akhmatova dates from February, 1915:

Узкий, нерусский стан —	A slender, un-Russian waist—
Над фолиантами.	Above the folios.
Шаль из турецких стран	A shawl from Turkish lands
Пала, как мантия.	Fell like a mantle.
Вас передашь одной	You could be drawn
Ломаной черной линией.	With one broken black line
Холод — в весельи, зной —	Coldness in gaiety, heat—
В Вашем унынии.	In your despondency.
Вся Ваша жизнь — озноб,	All of your life is a fever
И завершится — чем она?	And how will it culminate?
Облачный — темен — лоб	The clouded dark brow
Юного демона.	Of a young demon.
Каждого из земных	To wear out every earthly creature
Вам заиграть — безделица!	Is a trifle for you!
И безоружный стих	And a defenseless verse
В сердце нам целится.	Aims at your heart.

<table>
<tr><td>

В утренний сонный час,
— Кажется, четверть пятого, —
Я полюбила Вас,
Анна Ахматова.

</td><td>

At a sleepy morning hour,
—I think quarter past four—
I fell in love with you,
Anna Akhmatova.
</td></tr>
</table>

February 11, 1915
(I, 191)

With this uneven and somewhat naive poem, Tsvetaeva added her name to the growing list of poets, artists, and photographers who tried to capture Akhmatova's elusive beauty. The most famous of these images was then Blok's, which Tsvetaeva could not but have known:

<table>
<tr><td align="center">

АННЕ АХМАТОВОЙ

</td><td align="center">

TO ANNA AKHMATOVA

</td></tr>
<tr><td>

«Красота страшна» — Вам скажут, —
Вы накинете лениво
Шаль испанскую на плечи,
Красный розан — в волосах.

</td><td>

"Beauty is terrifying" They'll tell you—
You'll lazily throw
Your Spanish shawl on your shoulders,
A red rose in your hair.

</td></tr>
<tr><td>

«Красота проста» — Вам скажут, —
Пестрой шалью неумело
Вы укроете ребенка,
Красный розан — на полу.

</td><td>

"Beauty is simple" They'll tell you—
Awkwardly you'll cover the child
With the many-colored shawl,
The red rose on the floor.

</td></tr>
<tr><td>

Но, рассеянно внимая
Всем словам, кругом звучащим,
Вы задумаетесь грустно
И твердите про себя:

</td><td>

But, half-hearing
All these words ringing about you,
You'll grow sadly pensive
And say to yourself:

</td></tr>
<tr><td>

«Не страшна и не проста я;
Я не так страшна, чтоб просто
Убивать; не так проста я,
Чтоб не знать, как жизнь страшна».

</td><td>

"I'm neither terrifying nor simple;
I'm not so terrifying as simply
To kill; not so simple
As not to know the terror of life."
</td></tr>
</table>

December 16, 1913[6]

Blok has captured not only Akhmatova's dark beauty and her trademark shawl, but also the awesome majesty of her self-knowledge. Tsvetaeva has the shawl and the famous profile. (Could she have known the now-famous Modigliani sketch of Akhmatova, done in Paris in 1911, which essentially does "convey her in one broken black line?") But there is no sense of the poet, or at least *that* poet. The "clouded dark brow of the young demon" is straight out of Parnok's iconography in "The Girl Friend," not at all surprising since the Akhmatova poem was written at the height of that romance. The Parnok context adds an important overtone to Tsvetaeva's unembarrassed declaration of love in the final two lines, and in fact to Tsvetaeva's attitude toward Akhmatova throughout her life. The poem's last two lines are its best and most characteristic. In declaring her love, Tsvetaeva simultaneously showed her own ingenuity: by choosing an unusual logaoedic meter for the poem she managed to make Akhmatova's name, the pseudonym which Joseph Brodsky called "Akhmatova's first successful line"[7] into the entire final line of her own poem. These twin strategies—frank adoration combined with poetic pyrotechnics—laid the groundwork of Tsvetaeva's strategy for "overcoming" Akhmatova. The third element, Moscow, was added in 1916.

At the time of the "Otherworldly Evening" in Petersburg, Akhmatova, to Tsvetaeva's great disappointment, was in the Crimea. Yet *absent* poets and *non*-meetings were always more important for her poetry. In that society overwhelmingly Petersburg and male, Tsvetaeva was "marked" for two qualities, "Moscow" and "female." Since being a female poet inevitably involved comparison with Akhmatova, Tsvetaeva stressed the element which made her different, her "Moscowness."

> I clearly sense that I am reading in the name of Moscow and that I am showing myself honorably, that I am elevating the name of Moscow to the level of the name of Akhmatova, Akhmatova!—I've said it. With all my being I sense a tense, unavoidable—in each of my lines—comparison between us (and a playing-off of one against the other): not only between Akhmatova and me but between Petersburg poetry and Moscow poetry, between Petersburg and Moscow.

In both her 1936 reminiscence and her 1916 cycle of eleven "Poems to Akhmatova," Tsvetaeva denies competition as a motive, admitting only love and admiration, though any psychologist would accuse the lady of protesting too much:

> But even if some of the Akhmatova zealots were listening **to** me in order to listen **against** me, I wasn't reciting against Akhmatova but for her, to her. I read as if Akhmatova were the only person in the room. I read for the absent Akhmatova. I need this success as a direct line to Akhmatova. And if in that moment I wanted to present in myself Moscow—I couldn't do better, not with the goal of conquering Petersburg but of giving Moscow **to** Petersburg—as a gift, to give Akhmatova that Moscow in myself, in my love, to present it to her and to pay homage.
>
> .   .   .
>
> To say it all: for the poems I wrote about Moscow after my visit to Petersburg I am indebted to Akhmatova, to my love for her, to my desire to give her something more enduring than love. If I could simply have given her—the Kremlin, I would probably never have written those poems. So that in some sense there was competition between Akhmatova and me, but not "to do better than she"—it would be impossible to do better—but to place that impossibility—at her feet. Competition? Ardor.[8]

(Trans. J. M. King)

Obviously—both.

Tsvetaeva's eleven "Poems to Akhmatova" (June 19–July 2, 1916) emerged in a rapid stream after Mandel'stam's Aleksandrov visit. Their immediate inspiration must have been an intensive re-reading of Akhmatova, inspired by Mandel'stam's enthusiasm. Like the poems to Blok, they are panegyrics, but very idiosyncratic ones, which foreground the praise-giver rather than the praised. These cycles could be called "*My* Blok" or "*My* Akhmatova" just as Tsvetaeva later titled a prose memoir "My Pushkin." Tsvetaeva's Akhmatova is a larger-than life "Muse of lamentation," hovering over Russia like an ancient pagan goddess:

О, Муза плача, прекраснейшая из муз!	Oh, Muse of lamentation, most beautiful of
О ты, шальное исчадие ночи белой!	muses!
Ты черную насылаешь метель на Русь,	Oh, you mad progeny of the white night!
И вопли твои вонзаются в нас, как стрелы.	You send down a black blizzard on Rus,
	And your cries pierce us like arrows.

И мы шарахаемся и глухое: ох! —	And we are startled, and a deep "ОКН!"
Стотысячное — тебе присягает: Анна	A hundred thousand strong swears homage to
Ахматова! Это имя — огромный вздох,	you: Anna
И в глубь он падает, которая безымянна.	Akhmatova! that name is a huge sigh,
	And it falls into a nameless deep.

Мы коронованы тем, что одну с тобой	We are crowned by the fact that we tread the
Мы землю топчем, что небо над нами —	same
то же!	Earth with you, that the heaven above us is the
И тот, кто ранен смертельной твоей	same!
судьбой,	And he who is wounded by your mortal fate,
Уже бессмертным на смертное сходит ложе.	Descends immortal to his death bed.

В певучем граде моем купола горят,	In my singing city the cupolas blaze,
И Спаса светлого славит слепец бродячий. . .	And a blind tramp glorifies the bright Saviour.
И я дарю тебе свой колокольный град,	And I give you my city of bells,
— Ахматова! — и сердце свое в придачу.	Akhmatova! And my own heart in the bargain.
	June 19, 1916
	(I, 232)

Tsvetaeva's rhetoric in several of these poems is ornate—very long lines encrusted with archaisms, recalling both Muscovite church ornamentation and the medieval stylistic tradition called "word-weaving." She has transported the Petersburg Anna into the alien setting of her own Moscow, placing, almost by force, the classical portrait of the "Muse of Tsarskoe Selo" behind the ornate frame of a Muscovite icon-case. In the poems of the cycle, Akhmatova's face acquires the features of the narrow-faced, solemn Byzantine madonna until:

И всё *твоими* очами глядят иконы!	All the icons gaze with *your* eyes.
	July 1, 1916
	(I, 237)

One poem is an icon-like portrait of mother (Akhmatova) and child (Lev, her son by Gumilev):

Имя ребенка — Лев,   The name of the child is Lev
Матери — Анна.   The name of the mother is Anna.
В имени его — гнев,   In his name—anger,
В материнском — тишь.   In hers—quiet.
                                              June 24, 1916
                                                 (I, 234)

Its spare verbal strokes mimic the severe stylization and simplification of
icon painting. In proper iconographic tradition, the infant holds in his hand
the representation of his mother's collection *Rosary* and his father's *Pearls*
(1910):

И нить жемчужных   In your fist a string
Черных четок — в твоей горсти!   Of pearly black rosary beads.
                                                 (I, 234)

   It is not only Akhmatova's portrait which Tsvetaeva has turned to her
own uses. Like a sorceress, she conjures with her very name:

                   Анна   . . . Anna
Ахматова! Это имя — огромный вздох,   Akhmatova! That name is a huge sigh
И в глубь он падает, которая безымянна.   And it falls into a nameless abyss.
                                                 (I, 232)

This deep sigh echoes throughout the cycle, in the "okh" and "akh" which
begin five different lines of Akhmatova 2, in the first rhyme (*vzmakh/prakh*)
of Akhmatova 3, and we cannot but suspect that the "*gorech i gordost'*"
(pride and bitterness) of Akhmatova 5 echo the real name of the pseudony-
mous Akhmatova, Anna Andreevna *Gore*nko.
   Tsvetaeva's posture seems to be one of humble reverence before this awe-
inspiring "most beautiful of muses." Yet the humble worshipper is herself
the central focus: she takes pride in the very quality of her adoration: "Oh,
I am happy . . . That . . . It was I who first called . . . you The Muse of
Tsarskoe Selo." Adoration is a form of possession—the adored cannot
escape her worshipper:

Не отстать тебе! Я — острожник,   You cannot fall back! I am a convict.
Ты — конвойный. Судьба одна.   You are my escort. Our fate is one.
                                              June 26, 1916
                                                 (I, 235)

   Tsvetaeva's emotional hyperbole often frightened not only her critics but
even those to whom she addressed her poems. But to react to her poetry in
this way is to confuse art and reality. Mayakovsky could proclaim:

Мама!   Mama!
Ваш сын прекрасно болен!   Your son is marvelously ill!
Мама!   Mama!
У него пожар сердца.   His heart is on fire!

and have the firemen arrive to put it out. Or relate how the sun came to join him for tea. This is simply "hyperbole." But Tsvetaeva's poetic exaggeration is seen not as a device, but as "hysterics." Has this anything to do with what we expect of the female and by extension the female artist? Would we admire Akhmatova as much for her "self-control" if she were a man?

We can see the sharp difference between the two women poets in something as simple as punctuation. The "hysterical" Tsvetaeva was addicted to the breathless hyphen and the exclamation point. Simon Karlinsky, in analyzing the "approximation of Akhmatova's voice"[9] in Akhmatova 8 ("People were Shouting at the Market Place"), did not mention that this is the only poem in the cycle in which Tsvetaeva's ubiquitous exclamation point is totally absent, suppressed in an effort to imitate Akhmatova's blank tone. There are only forty-five exclamation points in all the eighty-two poems of Akhmatova's first collection, *Evening*. Of them, nine are in quotations where another, usually male, voice is addressing the female persona. (This works out, for those who love statistics, to an average of less than 0.5 per poem.) But in Tsvetaeva's eleven "Poems to Akhmatova" alone, there are thirty-three exclamation points, an average of three per poem! To the exclamation point, Akhmatova far preferred the question mark, sign of the tentative, gentle feminine mode. Tsvetaeva hardly ever used it. And while Tsvetaeva usually avoided the past tense, which compels the speaker of Russian to reveal his or her gender, Akhmatova uses it intentionally, to emphasize the femininity of her voice.

Self-assertion through praise-giving was an element in Tsvetaeva's cycles to Blok and Mandel'stam as well. Yet Akhmatova, alone of the three, stood squarely in Tsvetaeva's creative path. Mandel'stam, with his boyish infatuation, presented Tsvetaeva with more of a personal than a creative dilemma. His poetry simply operated on such different terms that he could neither influence her nor stand in her way. Blok, too, presented no real obstacle. He was a poet of an earlier generation (how quickly generations changed in those hectic days!). By canonizing him, (indeed, in one 1916 poem, already mourning his untimely death) she implicitly fixed him in time past. By standing across Tsvetaeva's creative path, Akhmatova ultimately did her a great service. With the genre of the female love poem "Akhmatovized," Tsvetaeva was given the impetus to develop the magnificent chorus of different voices which characterizes her mature poetry.

Tsvetaeva's poems from the latter part of 1916 illustrate the way in which Akhmatova stood in her way. Tsvetaeva once noted that all the poems in *Versts I* after the last Akhmatova poem (July 2) are addressed to Nikodim Plutser-Sarna, "The only one who knew how to love me. . .and it's a very complicated thing to love such a complex creature as I."[10] We know nothing more of the mysterious Plutser-Sarna besides this note, nothing else of the relationship but what we can surmise from reading the lyric diary (always a risky undertaking). If indeed Tsvetaeva was involved at just this time in an ill-fated love affair, then she found herself, thematically, square in the territory which Akhmatova had made her own. This may explain the sense of creative floundering near the end of *Versts I*. There is not the structure and dynamic we find in the first two-thirds of the book; there are some strong poems, but few that equal the best, written earlier in the year. These months were a breathing space after the intense productivity of February through June, a time, too, for artistic experiments, awkward at first, which would bear fruit later.

One step in that direction was Tsvetaeva's first use of a literary mask— writing her poem, that is, in the person of a character from world literature or myth. This was an important element in the 1920's, when she rewrote Greek myth, Biblical tradition, and Russian folk tales. But from 1916 through about 1919, her favorite literary source was the eighteenth century, particularly as seen through the eyes of her adolescent favorites, the nineteenth-century French romantics. A pair of poems from July, 1916 is based on Mme. deStael's novel *Corinne*. Corinne is a poetess whose future lover, Lord Neville, notices her and is smitten at the moment when she is being crowned with laurel for her poetic accomplishments. Neville, obedient to his family, eventually abandons his romantic questing and Corinne to marry her younger sister. Is there something in this situation which echoed Tsvetaeva's relations with Plutser-Sarna?[11]

Another new direction of late 1916, more immediately successful, was an intensification of rhythmic innovations clearly Tsvetaeva's own. One of the most striking is in a poem from the "Insomnia" cycle:

В огромном городе моем — ночь.
Из дома сонного иду — прочь,
И люди думают: жена, дочь.
А я запомнила одно: ночь.

In my enormous city it is night.
Out of my sleeping house I walk
And people think: a wife, a daughter.
And I remembered only one thing: night.

Июльский ветер мне метет путь,
И где-то музыка в окне — чуть.
Ах, нынче ветру до зари — дуть
Сквозь стенки тонкие груди — в грудь.

The July wind sweeps my path,
And somewhere there's music in a window—faintly.
Oh, now the wind will blow till dawn
Through the thin walls of my breast—into my chest.

Есть черный тополь, и в окне — свет,
И звон на башне, и в руке — цвет,
И шаг вот этот — никому вслед,
И тень вот эта, а меня — нет.

There's a black poplar, and light in the window,
And a peal from the tower, and a flower in my hand,
And this step—following no one,
And this shadow, and I'm not here.

Огни, как нити золотых бус,
Ночного листика во рту — вкус.
Освободите от дневных уз,
Друзья поймите, что я вам — снюсь.

Lights, like strings of gold beads,
The taste of a nocturnal leaf in the mouth,
Free me from the shackles of day.
Friends, understand that you're dreaming of me.

July 17, 1916
(I, 238)

Russian poetry had never heard anything quite like the hypnotic rhythm of this poem, the perfect meter for its theme of sleepwalking. Every line of the poem has the compulsively regular pattern: $-/-/---/ /$, a classic example of Tsvetaeva's *logaed*.

Versts I contains nearly all Tsvetaeva's known poems of 1916. The few she left out were written in the summer and fall; her reasons for suppressing them were evidently personal rather than aesthetic, for they speak clearly of a passionate extra-marital affair. When *Versts I* was finally published in 1922, Tsvetaeva was about to leave Russia for her reunion with Sergei. It was not the moment to remind him of her pre-Revolutionary infidelities. One such poem, written in early August, presents Tsvetaeva in a most uncharacteristic situation: a passive figure totally consumed by the force and passion of her new lover. The persona's emotions, and even her diction, remind us of Akhmatova rather than Tsvetaeva:

И взглянул как в первые раза	And you gazed at me as men don't gaze
Не глядят.	The first time.
Черные глаза глотнули взгляд.	Black eyes swallowed my gaze.
Вскинула ресницы и стою	Lashes cast up, I stand—
— Что, — светла? —	How?—Radiant?
Не скажу, что выпита до тла.	I won't admit I'm drunk up, utterly.
Всё до капли поглотил зрачок.	Your pupil has swallowed me—to the last drop.
И стою.	And I stand.
И течет твоя душа в мою.	And your soul flows into mine.
	August 7, 1916
	(II, 190)

The persona of another poem persists in an illicit love in defiance of God, His church, and the marriage bond:

Чтоб дойти до уст и ложа—	To reach [your] lips and couch
Мимо страшной церкви Божьей	I have to pass
Мне идти.	The terrible church of God.
	August 15, 1916
	(I, 257)

Neither of these is a particularly strong poem, and it could be argued that in omitting them, Tsvetaeva was simply cleaning out some "Akhmatova imitations." But a third poem is clearly her own, and such a strong poem that she could have had no *artistic* reason for suppressing it. It shows the emergence of the characteristic Tsvetaeva love heroine—not the sufferer, but the fighter, the precursor of her martial Tsar-maiden.

Я тебя отвоюю у всех земель, у всех небес,
Оттого что лес — моя колыбель, и могила
                                                    — лес,
Оттого что я на земле стою — лишь
                                    одной ногой,
Оттого что я о тебе спою — как никто другой.

Я тебя отвоюю у всех времен, у всех ночей,
У всех золотых знамен, у всех мечей,
Я ключи закину и псов прогоню с
                                        крыльца —
Оттого что в земной ночй я вернее пса.

Я тебя отвоюю у всех других — у той, одной,
Ты не будешь ничей жених, я — ничьей женой,
И в последнем споре возьму тебя —
                                    замолчи! —
У того, с которым Иаков стоял в ночи.

Но покà тебе не скрещу на груди персты —
О проклятие! — у тебя останешься — ты:
Два крыла твои, нацеленные в эфир, —
Оттого что мир — твоя колыбель, и
                            могила — мир!

I will win you away from every earth, from
    every sky,
For the woods are my place of birth, and the
    place to die,
I'll drive dogs outside, hurl the keys into dark
    and fog,
For in the mortal night I'm a more faithful dog.

I will win you from all my rivals, and from the
    one;
You will never enjoy a bridal, nor I a man.
And in the final struggle I'll take you—don't
    make a sound!—
From him by whom Jacob stood on the
    darkened ground.

But until I cross your fingers upon your breast
You possess—what a curse!—yourself: you are self-possessed;
Both your wings, as they yearn for the ether,
    become unfurled,
For the world's your cradle, and your grave's
    the world.
        August 15, 1916 Trans. Joseph Brodsky[12]
            (I, 257)

Akhmatova's presence remained an essential element of the context in which Tsvetaeva wrote until the end of 1920, when she finally "overcame" her rival. Akhmatova's third collection, *White Flock* (*Belaia staia*), appeared in February, 1917, and an entry in Tsvetaeva's 1917 diary shows her still struggling with Akhmatova's achievement:

> "Always about herself, always about love." Yes, about herself, about love—and yet more—astoundingly—about the silver voice of the deer, about the subdued color of the Ryzan expanses, about a red maple leaf pressed into the Song of Songs, about the air, "the gift of God." What a difficult and seductive gift for *poets*—Anna Akhmatova!"[13]

Both the collections Tsvetaeva prepared from her poems of 1917-1920 evoke Akhmatova: *Versts* (sometimes called *Versts* II) was dedicated to her in its entirety, and echoes the duality of Akhmatova's personae in its division into gypsy-pagan and religious-Biblical halves. The title of Tsvetaeva's *Swans' Encampment* is a clear echo of *White Flock*, whether ironic or not we can only guess.

Tsvetaeva's final "overcoming" of Akhmatova in her own work coincided with the sea-change in her poetics that preceeded her collection *Craft*. But comparison with Akhmatova haunted her until her death. Only days before her suicide, Tsvetaeva was slogging through the mud of Chistopol' with

Lidia Chukovskaia, who was trying to help her find a room. Chukovskaia spoke of Akhmatova: "The conditions here would kill her. Of course she can't do anything practical, she's completely helpless. She'd die here." "And you think I can cope?" Tsvetaeva cut in, sharply. It's no easier here for me than it would have been for her."[14]

CHAPTER TEN

1917: Gypsies and Stenka Razin

Tsvetaeva's dominant themes in this epochal year were "gypsy lyricism" (Mayakovsky's phrase) and, inevitably, the revolution. These seemingly disparate themes were in fact twinned: Tsvetaeva's gypsy poems were not an escape from the revolution but her expression of its spirit. Gypsy life has always symbolized freedom and independence, particularly to the fettered Russian. The gypsy woman represents a specifically sexual independence. Russian literature's most familiar example is Mariula, in Pushkin's narrative poem "The Gypsies," who ran off with her lover, abandoning her husband and small daughter; her own mother had done the same. Tsvetaeva's life in 1915 and 1916 was not dissimilar. To make the parallel explicit, she chose as her epigraph to the first, "gypsy" half of *Versts* the last two lines of a poem by the seven-year-old Alya:

Волны спят и несутся далече,	The waves sleep and drift away,
А цыгане поют и крадут.	While the gypsies sing and thieve.
В их телегах походных заря:	In their caravans a dawn:
Мариулы, Марины.	Of Mariula, of Marina.
	(II, 321)

Tsvetaeva introduced both the gypsy and revolutionary themes, indirectly, in the first poem of *Versts*:

Мировое началось во мгле кочевье:	A worldwide migration has begun in the mist:
Это бродят по ночной земле — деревья,	Trees wander the night earth,
Это бродят золотым вином — грозди,	Clusters of grapes ferment like golden wine,
Это странствуют из дома в дом — звезды,	Stars travel from house to house,
Это реки начинают путь — вспять!	Rivers begin to flow backwards!
И мне хочется к тебе на грудь — спать.	And I want to sleep on your breast.
	January 14, 1917
	(II, 9)

The gypsies enter through the back door of lexicon: Tsvetaeva applies the vocabulary of gypsy life ("migration," "wander," "travel") to the phenomena of nature. As for the revolution, the poem's date inevitably links these disorders in nature with the waves of unrest that preceded the February Revolution. The first five lines set up the expectation that the sixth, too, will describe an unnatural phenomenon. But the reader's expectations are disappointed—this is the most natural of desires, "to sleep on your breast!" How are we to read the poem? "All the world is in turmoil, but . . .?" But the conjunction is not "*a*" (while, whereas) but "*i*" (and). That conjunction gives the poem an evocative ambiguity. Is this poem, like those which concluded *Versts I*, addressed to Plutser-Sarna?

Tsvetaeva soon introduced the gypsy theme explicitly:

Милые спутники, делившие с нами ночлег!
Версты, и версты, и версты, и черствый хлеб. . .

Dear fellow-travellers, who shared our resting place!
Versts, and versts, and versts and stale bread . . .

Рокот цыганских телег,
Вспять убегающих рек —
Рокот. . .

The rumble of gypsy wagons
The rumble of rivers
Flowing upstream.

Ах, на цыганской, на райской, на ранней
                                        заре —
Помните жаркое ржанье и степь в серебре?
Синий дымок на горе,
И о цыганском царе —
Песню. . .

Oh, at the gypsy, paradisical, early dawn—
Do you remember the morning wind, and the steppe in silver?
The deep blue haze on the hill
And the song
About a gypsy king . . .

В черную полночь, под пологом древних ветвей,
Мы вам дарили прекрасных — как ночь
                                        — сыновей,
Нищих — как ночь — сыновей. . .
И рокотал соловей —
Славу. . .

At black midnight, under the cover of ancient branches,
We gave you sons marvelous as the night.
Sons poor as the night . . .
And the nightingale roared—
Glory . . .

Не удержали вас, спутники чудной поры,
Нищие неги и нищие наши пиры.
Жарко пылали костры,
Падали к нам на ковры —
Звезды. . .

Our poor comforts and our poor feasts
Didn't detain you, fellow-travellers of a wondrous time.
The bonfires glowed hot,
And onto our rugs fell stars. . .

                                 January 29, 1917
                                    (II, 10)

With its insistent, galloping rhythm, giving a sense of the irresistible movement of fate, and ringing masculine rhymes (the second line "bowled over" Pasternak when he first read it)[1] "Dear Fellow Travellers" is a vivid evocation of gypsy mores. But in the context of two posthumously published poems, it takes on a clearly personal reference to Tsvetaeva's own pregnancy. In one, written in lullaby rhythm, a mother sits by the fire rocking her infant son, whose "dear father" has forgotten about him:

Дорастешь, царек сердечный,
До отцовской славы,
И поймешь: недолговечны
Царские забавы!

You'll grow up, little Tsar of my heart,
To your father's glory,
And you'll understand: fleeting
Are a Tsar's amusements!

                        February 2, 1917 (Candlemas)
                                    (II, 192)

In 1938, Tsvetaeva penned a note next to the manuscript of this poem: "Through the whole book—the dream of a son." The other poem evokes the ripeness, fruition, and sensuality of late summer:

Август — астры,
Август — звезды,
Август — грозди
Винограда и рябины
Ржавой — август!

Полновесным, благосклонным
Яблоком своим имперским,
Как дитя, играешь, август.
Как ладонью, гладишь сердце
Именем своим имперским:
Август! — Сердце!

Месяц поздних поцелуев,
Поздних роз и молний поздних!
Ливней звездных —
Ауст! — Месяц
Ливней звездных!

August—asters,
August—stars,
August—clusters
Of grapes and rusty
Rowanberry—august!

With your weighty, gracious, imperial apple
Like a child, you play, August.
You caress the heart with
Your imperial name, as with a hand:
August—Heart!

Month of belated kisses,
Late roses and late lightnings!
Of starshowers—
August! Month
Of starshowers!

February 7, 1917
(II, 192)

Why should Tsvetaeva be writing about the fertility of August in a Russian February? Because she was seven months pregnant with a child conceived late in the previous summer. The starshowers and grape clusters in this poem alert the attentive reader to a link with "Dear Fellow-travellers" and "A world-wide migration." Read together, these poems tell us that the addressee of her August love poems fathered the child she was carrying in February. Whether Plutser-Sarna was in fact the father is not our business; the plot of the lyric diary, however, certainly is.

On March 1, 1917, Nicholas II abdicated the Russian throne; Tsvetaeva wrote her first political poem the next day. Though certainly no monarchist, she greeted the February Revolution with reservations. The uniformed masses of revolutionary troops lacked the individuality, flair and daring she admired. This, after all, is the young woman who once worshipped Napoleon:

Над церкòвкой — голубые облака,
Крик вороний. . .
И проходят — цвета пепла и песка —
Рèволюционные войска.
Ох ты барская, ты царская моя тоска!

Нету лиц у них и нет имен —
Песен нету!
Заблудился ты, кремлевский звон,
В это ветреном лесу знамен.
Помолись, Москва, ложись, Москва, на
                                        вечный сон!

Above the chapel, light-blue clouds,
The cry of ravens . . .
And the revolutionary troops, the color of ash
     and sand,
Pass by.
Oh, you aristocratic, regal grief of mine!

They have no faces, they have no names—
They have no songs!
Oh Kremlin peal, you've been lost in this
Windy forest of banners.
Pray, Moscow! Lie down, Moscow, To eternal
     sleep!

March 2, 1917
(II, 60)

Though Tsvetaeva disliked the revolutionary masses, she had no great sympathy for the Tsar:

Пал без славы   The twoheaded eagle fell without glory.
Орел двуглавый.   Tsar! You were unjust!
— Царь! — Вы были неправы.   April 2, 1917
                                                                        (II, 60)

Her sympathy always went out to the underdog, particularly if he were young and innocent. Now, heavy with the child she hoped would be a son, her concern focused on the young Alexei, as if she sensed that Russia would soon have yet another murdered Tsarevich.

The child born to her on April 13 was another daughter. Irina Efron's life, like that of the Provisional Government under which she was born, was brief and ended tragically. She died in February, 1920, in a children's home outside Moscow, of starvation. She was sickly from birth, perhaps even slightly retarded—there is a peculiar silence about her in her mother's lyrics, memoirs, and letters that cannot be explained simply by her early death.[2] Though she was nearly three when she died, she still spoke but a few words, and continually rocked and sang to herself. Tsvetaeva never explicitly mentioned the birth in her poems. But in a poem written three weeks later (II, 198-9), her persona lies near death, "waxen, icy, contorted," reproaching herself for some misdeed or lack of judgment: "You crazy, plague-stricken, ruined woman!" Nuns pray around her, but it is useless: "God won't forgive a lie." We know that Tsvetaeva made slow recoveries from both her other confinements. But there is more at issue here than post-partum weakness or depression. The poem seems to see Irina's birth (sickly and female) as a retribution for the circumstances of her conception.

If bed-ridden, Tsvetaeva was far from silent. Barely a week after Irina's birth, a flood of new poems began and continued until the disruptions (political and domestic) of October. A cycle of ballad-like poems tells of Stenka Razin, leader of an eighteenth-century Russian peasant rebellion, and his love for his captive, a Persian princess. His attentions rejected, Razin drowned the maiden in the Volga, only to have her haunt his dreams. The cycle can be read as a political message about revolution's tendency to destroy what it most values. Razin would reappear later in Tsvetaeva's poetry as a personification of the Bolsheviks.

Russian folklore now became an increasingly important element in Tsvetaeva's art. Her daughter points to the impact of the Revolution:

> It was precisely then, when the streets and squares of Moscow filled with unprecedented, previously unthinkable masters, and began to ring with previously unheard speech, that Marina's notebooks became saturated with conversations, stories, rejoinders, which she'd caught in mid-air, everywhere—at children's ration allocation points, in theaters, at railway stations, on tramcars,

in crowds, on boulevards and in queues. It was precisely then, excited and alarmed by these voices which were new to her that Marina was drawn to the folklore sources of her long poems, as the source of these voices, and in Afanas'ev's collections she discovered what were for her no longer children's fairy tales, but, in their guise, a ciphered chronicle of past fates and past events, of eternal passions and human feats, a chronicle of tragedies and hope for saving miracles.[3]

Ariadna Efron is persistently trying to assure her mother a place in *"Soviet"* literature, but there is still much truth to what she says. The Revolution did thrust Tsvetaeva out of her protected, servant-ordered world into the streets, into a realm of life-and-death realities. But the folk voice had entered her poems well before October. After her Petersburg editors gave her the classic three-volume Afanas'ev collection of Russian folktales in January, 1916, a new folk diction appeared in her poems. On that momentous January night in Petrograd, she recalled, in response to her host's condescending amazement at her Moscow accent, she began to exaggerate it, "Till I was speaking like a Moscow coachman." The folk poems of *Versts I* simply carried the affectation from her speech into her verse, though in that collection it often seemed artificial and contrived.

The gypsy poems of spring, 1917, however, marked a second stage in the development of Tsvetaeva's "Russian" voice. This new diction appeared in mid-May after an encounter with fortune-tellers on Three Ponds Lane.[4] She was fascinated by the whole ritual, even more by its language, which she captured in the three poems of "Fortune-telling." An old gypsy accosts a young woman and her daughter; Tsvetaeva records their negotiations in taut lines with the characteristic economy of colloquial Russian speech:

— Что же нам скажешь?	—What will you tell us?
— Всё без обману.	—All, without falsehood.
— Мне уже поздно,	It's too late for me,
Ей еще рано. . .	Too early for her . . .

The last three lines of the prophecy, including an abrupt request for payment, were stolen directly from the old gypsy, Tsvetaeva confessed:

Линии мало,	The lines are few,
Мало талану. —	There's little good fortune.
Позолоти!	Cross my palm with gold!
	May 19, 1917
	(II, 11)

Tsvetaeva captured the essence of the Russian *zaklinanie*, the rhymed chants of spell-binding or exorcism, which represented *female* wisdom and power, i.e., witchcraft:

От бессонницы, от речи сладкой,   From insomnia, from sweet speeches,
От змеи, от лихорадки,   From the snake, from fever,
От подружкина совета,   From the advice of a girl-friend
От лихого человека,   From an evil man,
От младых друзей,   From young friends,
От чужих князей —   From alien princes—
Заклинаю государыню-княгиню,   I exorcise my young lady-princess
Молодую мою, верную рабыню.   My faithful servant.
                 May 21, 1917
                  (II, 35)

Tsvetaeva's personae soon tried their own hand at spell-binding. She captured the characteristic repetitions and anaphora (repetition at the beginning of a line) of the folk exorcisms, while refining them and making them more literary:

В лоб целовать — заботу стереть.   A kiss on the brow wipes away care.
В лоб целую.   I kiss your forehead.

В глаза целовать — бессонницу снять. A kiss on the eyes takes away insomnia.
В глаза целую.   I kiss your eyes.

В губы целовать — водой напоить.   A kiss on the lips is a drink of water.
В губы целую.   I kiss your lips.

В лоб целовать — память стереть.   A kiss on the brow wipes away memory.
В лоб целую.   I kiss your brow.
                 June 5, 1917
                  (II, 11)

"Gypsy wedding" shows how Tsvetaeva was rapidly learning to manipulate the strong rhythms, short lines, and masculine rhymes which would become her hallmark:

Из-под копыт   From under the hooves
Грязь летит.   Mud flies!
Перед лицом   In front of her face
Шаль — как щит.   A shawl, like a shield.
. . . .
Пьян без вина и без хлеба сыт, —   Drunk without wine and satiated without bread
Это цыганская свадьба мчит!   It's a gypsy wedding rushing by.
                 June 25, 1917
                  (II, 12)

From this point on, a muscular, elliptic diction, much like that of the old gypsy, became more and more characteristic of Tsvetaeva's verse. Patricia Sollner has recently studied the role of these ellipses in establishing Tsvetaeva's relation to her reader:

> The ellipses are part of the strategies Tsvetaeva uses to make direct claims upon her readers' co-creative imagination. . . . By demanding active partici-

pation from readers, the poet creates an intimate bond with these readers on many levels—thematic, logical, aesthetic and emotional.[5]

The phenomenon Sollner describes is essentially identical to the "diaphor" analysed by Kammer in Dickinson, Marianne Moore, and H.D.[6]

The cabinet-shufflings in the summer of 1917 held little interest for the apolitical Tsvetaeva, who was never a political animal. She briefly saw Kerensky as a possible Bonaparte, then lamented the transformation of "freedom" from the treasured ideal of Russian princes and French nobility to "a streetwalker on a crazy soldier's breast." The "Beautiful Lady" image is Blok's, but so is the streetwalker—Tsvetaeva anticipated by several months his use of the prostitute Kat'ka in "The Twelve."

Из строгого, стройного храма	From a stern, orderly temple
Ты вышла на визг площадей. . .	You came out to the scream of the squares . . .
— Свобода! — Прекрасная Дама	Freedom! Beautiful Lady
Маркизов и русских князей.	Of marquises and Russian princes.
Свершается страшная спевка, —	A terrible choir practice is happening—
Обедня еще впереди!	The mass is still ahead!
— Свобода! — Гулящая девка	Freedom! A streetwalker
На шалой солдатской груди!	On a crazy soldier's breast.

May 26, 1917

(II, 62)

A revolution was taking place not only in the streets, but also in the relationships between human beings—even children. One poem describes a walk with Alya by the Moscow river, where a group of boys, imitating their revolutionary older brothers, were fighting and singing. Alya "quietly sneered" at these "lovers of the god Mars" and stared at them "with the icy eyes of a snow leopard." One of them stared back with a look of class hatred "that I will never forget, and you will not remember." (II, 63–4)

As Russia stumbled from one revolution to another during the summer of 1917, Marina grew increasingly alarmed by political developments. The tubercular Sergei had entered an officer-training school that winter (as the war dragged on, the Russian army took what it could get). But the life of an infantry officer was proving too demanding for his fragile health. Marina asked Voloshin to use his connections to get Sergei transferred to the Crimea, and to the artillery. Anastasia, who had just lost her second husband to appendicitis and their infant son to dysentery, was living in Feodosia. In early October 1917, Tsvetaeva arrived in Feodosia alone, leaving the children with Sergei's sister in Moscow. This was evidently to be a brief reconnoitering trip to arrange winter quarters for the family and visit her bereaved sister. While she was there, the Provisional government fell.

Her first poetic response to the Revolution used an image later developed by both Blok and by Eisenstein in his film *October*—the mob raiding and smashing wine-cellars, a universal drunken orgy:

Ночь. — Норд-Ост. — Рев солдат. — Рев волн.   Night. A northeast wind. The roar of soldiers.
Разгромили винный склад. — Вдоль стен   The roar of the waves.
По канавам — драгоценный поток,   They've looted a wine-cellar. Along the walls,
И кровавая в нем пляшет луна.   Through the gutters, a precious flood,
                                           And in it dances a blood-tinged moon.
                                                   Feodosia, last days of October, 1917
                                                                         (II, 65)

Sergei, in Moscow, took part in the last stand against the Bolsheviks. As soon as she could, Tsvetaeva set off for Moscow, determined to find him and bring him back to the relative safety of the Crimea. As she crossed Moscow from the train station, she was understandably agitated, wondering if she would find him alive or dead. But her priorities, as she recalled them some months later, were strange for the mother of two young daughters, even stranger for a wife who had so recently been spectacularly unfaithful:

> Not once do I think about the children. If Sergei doesn't exist any longer, then I do not either, and that means they do not. Alya will not live without me, she won't want to, she won't be able to. As I without Sergei . . .[7]

She found him unharmed and sound asleep in his sister's apartment. They left at once for the Crimea, where Efron, son of two lifelong revolutionaries, intended to join the forces gathering there to oppose the Bolsheviks. Again, Tsvetaeva left the children in Moscow. By the time she returned for them, it was no longer possible to leave—she was trapped in Moscow for the next four and a half years while Sergei, that same tubercular Sergei who in August had not felt strong enough for the everyday duties of an infantry officer in the capital garrison, fought with the White forces on the Don. Somehow, this delicate warrior would survive four years of bitter fighting and be evacuated to Constantinople in 1921 with the sad remnants of that army.

CHAPTER ELEVEN

Duty and Dalliance

Tsvetaeva lost a considerable personal fortune in the revolution—enough to make her independent, if not wealthy. She once defiantly remarked that she never missed it. But with security gone, details of *byt* to which she had never given a thought—food and fuel—became central concerns. The Civil War cut her off from Sergei, from Voloshin, from Anastasia. For the first time in her life, she was alone and on her own in a world where almost everything—from moral values to orthography—had changed.

Amidst all these changes, Tsvetaeva continued to see the world in dichotomies: two disparate groups of themes dominate the lyric diary for 1918. One cluster—the White Army/duty/self-denial—was centered in the poems of *Swans' Encampment* and the second, "Biblical" half of *Versts*; the other cluster—eighteenth-century France/the Theater/romantic intrigue—characterizes a large number of uncollected poems and her first verse dramas. It was an unusually productive year; she wrote well over 100 poems, her first two (perhaps even three) plays and several of her first prose sketches. Though the year brought hardship, it also produced a creative euphoria of extremity similar to that which animated Blok's *The Twelve* and Madel'stam's "Twilight of Freedom" (both 1918).

> But I haven't mentioned the most important thing: the gaiety, the sharpness of thought, the explosions of joy at the smallest success, the passionate intensity of one's whole being—all the walls are scribbled over with stanzas of poems and NB's for my notebook.[1]

"On January 18, 1918, I saw Sergei for the last time" Tsvetaeva wrote in her diary. "How and where, I will say sometime"[2] (but she never did). Is it possible that, in the confusion of that Revolutionary January, Sergei managed to travel from the Crimea to Moscow, see Tsvetaeva, and return to the White army on the Don? If so, why did he not take her and the children with him? Perhaps "seeing" was yet another of Tsvetaeva's keenly-sensed dreams, to which she attributed so much importance. She marked the day by pledging loyalty to her White knight and his cause in a poem which became the epigraph to *Swans' Encampment*. The first poem addressed to Sergei since her abject apology in April, 1916, it signals a new role for him in the lyric diary:

На кортике своем: Марина —
Ты начертал, встав за Отчизну.
Была я первой и единой
В твоей великолепной жизни.

"Marina" you inscribed on your dagger
As you stood to defend your homeland.
I was the first and only one
in your magnificent life.

Я помню ночь и лик пресветлый	I remember the night and the radiant face
В аду солдатского вагона.	In the hell of a transport wagon.
Я волосы гоню по ветру,	I loose my hair to the wind
Я в ларчике храню погоны.	And keep your shoulder-straps in my casket.

January 18, 1918
(II, 59)

Whatever troubles there had been in the Efron marriage were suddenly forgotten, at least in Tsvetaeva's poetry. From the moment of his departure, she began to construct an idealized myth of Sergei and his cause, though this in no way precluded frequent real-life involvements with other men.

She soon began to live a new life, with a new circle of friends, primarily young actors in Vakhtangov's Third Studio of the Moscow Art theater, whom she met through the young poet and actor Pavel Antokolsky (1896-1978). Tsvetaeva's infatuations with the handsome actor Jury Zavadsky (1894-1977), his sister Vera (1895?-1930), and the young actress Sofia Holliday (1896-1935) formed a complex net of hetero-and bi-sexual attachments. These friendships, and the theatrical world into which they drew her, were the major element in her life and work during 1918 and 1919. Soon after she met Zavadsky on a January night in 1918, she addressed the new romantic hero in her life, depicting him in a most unromantic condition—suffering from toothache:

Beau ténébreux! — Вам грустно. — Вы больны.	Beau tenebreux! You're sad. You're sick. The world is unjustified—your tooth aches!
Мир неоправдан, — зуб болит! — Вдоль нежной	Along the tender shell of your cheek—a foulard, like night.
Раковины щеки — фуляр, как ночь.	

January, 1918
(II, 41)

This semi-ironical attitude was her way of defending herself from Zavadsky's attraction. In another poem, he stands "surrounded by 130 Carmens, each with a flower in her teeth, and each begging a role" (in his life, as well as his plays, Tsvetaeva implies). Tsvetaeva's infatuation with Zavadsky paralleled her growing interest in the eighteenth century and its romantic heroes—Casanova, the Duke de Lauzun, Marie Antoinette—out of which grew the plays she later wrote for him. This concern with the eighteenth century was not an escape from the the unpleasant reality of revolutionary Moscow, but an attempt to come to grips with it by exploring the culture which preceded the French Revolution.

The spring and summer of 1918 were among the most creative in Tsvetaeva's life in both the quantity and quality of the poems she produced. Their dominant themes were duty, loyalty, and—an important new theme for Tsvetaeva—the renunciation of the flesh. Though her efforts to resist Zavadsky's charm probably had something to do with these insistent proclamations of chastity and self-denial, it was primarily her distaste for the

Bolsheviks and their militant atheism which pushed her, temporarily, into a defense of the Orthodox church and ascetic values. The first spring cycle of religious holidays under the Bolsheviks gave Tsvetaeva a clear context for her dissent. She made a point of using the church calendar (i.e. "first day of Easter") rather than civil dates for her poems that spring. This was a way to retain contact with the traditional Russian calendar and the hierarchy of values it represented.

On February 1, 1918, the Bolsheviks yanked Russia into Europe and the twentieth century by introducing the Julian calendar to replace the (Old Style) Gregorian, under which Russia had always been thirteen days behind the rest of Europe. They also initiated a reform of Russian orthography, eliminating several letters which no longer had meaning. Tsvetaeva, with her love for the past and her reverence for chronology, refused to accept the changes.[3] Senselessly destroying beauty and history, the revolution had blasphemed the Kremlin cathedrals as well as the calendar:

Кровных коней запрягайте в дровни!	Harness blooded horses to a wood sledge!
Графские вина пейте из луж!	Drink counts' wine from puddles!
Единодержцы штыков и душ!	Autocrats of bayonets and souls!
Распродавайте — на вес — часовни,	Sell off chapels by the pound,
Монастыри — с молотка — на слом.	Auction off monasteries for demolition.
Рвитесь на лошади в Божий дом!	Burst on horseback into the House of God!
Перепивайтесь кровавым пойлом!	Get drunk on bloody swill!
Стойла — в соборы! Соборы — в стойла!	Stables into cathedrals! Cathedrals into stables
В чертову дюжину — календарь!	To the devil with the calendar![4]
Нас под рогожу за слово: царь!	Lay us out for the word "Tsar!" . . .

March 22 1918,
"The first day of spring"
(II, 67)

Against the background of moral and political disorder, Tsvetaeva, the instinctive rebel, turned to traditional authorities. The Tsar whom she had condemned as "unjust" looked much more appealing once she had experienced Bolshevik rule. She tried to justify God *despite* the disorder which reigned, expressing this conservative view in a highly modern style: the poem contains not one verb (except the zero-verb of the present tense of "to be") and is, in essence, a series of parallel adverbial phrases based on instrumental case forms.

Бог — прав	God is right
Тлением трав,	In the rotting of grasses,
Сухостью рек,	The dryness of rivers,
Воплем калек,	The howling of cripples,
Вором и гадом,	Through thief and serpent,
Мором и гладом,	Slaughter and hunger,
Срамом и смрадом,	Shame and stench,
Громом и градом.	Thunder and hail.

Попранным Словом.   By the trampled Word,
Проклятым годом.   Through the cursed year,
Пленом царёвым.   The Tsar's captivity,
Вставшим народом.   The people uprisen.
                                     May 12, 1918
                                         (II, 72)

Yet in the fireworks, meaning almost got sacrificed. Tsvetaeva, perhaps in response to her first readers' puzzlement, felt the need to explain in a footnote that "clearly, one must read it as "God is *nonetheless* right, *despite*. . . ."" To a modern reader, the poem presents few problems. But Tsvetaeva's elliptical style, like Eisenstein's "intellectual montage" to which it was in many ways akin, was too demanding for many of her contemporaries.

The increasingly harsh reality of the Revolution forced Tsvetaeva, for the first time, to question her scale of values, in which poetic creativity and the feelings of the individual held unchallenged priority. One of the best poems in *Swans' Encampment* recalls Andre Chenier, the poet guillotined in the French Revolution. With innocents being slaughtered, Tsvetaeva found it hard to justify her own existence, harder still to justify her poetry:

Андрей Шенье взошел на эшафот.   Andre Chenier has mounted the scaffold.
А я живу — и это страшный грех.   But I'm alive, and that's a deadly sin.
Есть времена — железные — для всех.   There are times—iron ones—for all.
И не певец, кто в порохе — поет.   And he is not a singer who sings amidst the
                                          gunpowder.
                                     April 17, 1918
                                         (II, 70)

Her lengthening separation from Sergei provided a context for her newfound asceticism. She first refers to it in a poem which compared her pain to that of Mary over the body of Christ. Hers, however, is seven times greater. That she could use such a parallel indicates how hyperbolically her myth of the angelic innocent Sergei was developing.

Семь мечей пронзали сердце   Seven swords pierced the heart
Богородицы над Сыном.   Of Mary over the Son.
Семь мечей пронзили сердце,   Seven swords pierced her heart,
А мое — семижды семь.   And mine—seven times seven.

Я не знаю, жив ли, нет ли   I don't know if he's alive or not
Тот, кто мне дороже сердца,   He who's dearer than my heart,
Тот, кто мне дороже Сына. . .   He who's dearer than the Son . . .

Этой песней — утешаюсь.   I console myself with this song.
Если встретится — скажи.   If you chance to meet him, let me know.
                                     May 25, 1918
                                         (II, 73)

The best lines of the poem are the last five, in which Tsvetaeva approaches the heart-rending approximation of every-day diction which Akhmatova used so effectively years later in *Requiem*.

Only as the White forces were suffering their first defeats on the Don did Tsvetaeva, singer of the underdog, address her first poem directly to Sergei's White Army:

Кто уцелел — умрет, кто мертв — воспрянет.	He who survived will die, he who is dead will leap up.
И вот потомки, вспомнив старину: — Где были *вы*? — Вопрос как громом грянет, Ответ как громом грянет: — На Дону!	And thus our descendents, recalling former times, Will ask, "And where were you?—" The question will crash like thunder, The answer come like thunder, "On the Don!"
— Что делали? — Да принимали муки, Потом устали и легли на сон. И в словаре задумчивые внуки За словом: долг напишут слово: Дон.	"What did you do?"—We suffered torments Then tired and lay down to sleep. And in the dictionary, our pensive grandsons Instead of "Duty" will write the word "Don." March 30, 1918 (II, 68)

There is an attention-getting quality to Tsvetaeva's political rhetoric, with its paradoxes ("He who survived will die . . .") ringing alliteration ("crash like thunder" is "kak *gro*mom *gri*anet") and the final line in which, characteristically, she uses a chance coincidence of sound to "prove" the equivalence of "Duty" and "Don" (*dolg* and *Don*). Despite Tsvetaeva's note that it is one of her favorites, this is not a poem which improves on rereading: its rhetorical devices are all on the surface, there are no subtleties hidden in its depths. In this, it is not much different from the political rhetoric being churned out in those years on the other side of the fence.

Many of the directly political poems in *Swans' Encampment* are similarly limited. Tsvetaeva's apologists in the Soviet Union, notably Il'ya Ehrenburg and Ariadna Efron, took great pains to link her decision not to publish *Swans' Encampment* with Sergei's revelations about the White Army:

> Her meeting with her husband was dramatic. He told her of the White Guards' atrocities, the pogroms, the spiritual emptiness. In his accounts the swans resembled crows. Marina was badly shaken. In Berlin I once talked to her all night; at the end of it she said she would not publish the book.[5]

This version, however, fails to explain Tsvetaeva's return to the theme in her long narrative poem *Perekop* (1928–1929). She did, in fact, publish some of the best *Swans' Encampment* poems in the emigre press; several were even published in Moscow before she left. She left most of the the White Army poems unpublished because she realized their artistic as well as their political mistakes.

Far more successful than the political poems are several eloquently simple poems of spring and summer 1918, usually no more that eight lines long, which celebrate the soul and (for Tsvetaeva the two terms were inseparable) the inspiration of the poet. Mortification of the flesh (read: life under the Bolsheviks) only strengthens the soul. Wings are a recurring motif; on one level, they refer to her "winged" soul, but on another, to her fundamental garment of those days, a "winged," capelike overcoat, which became her trademark. She used the image to particularly good effect in a poem which seems to speak of her separation from Sergei. Her soul and his, in this reading, are "like left and right hand," "like right and left wing" of, perhaps, a butterfly at rest. But a whirlwind (read: history) has come and left a gulf between them:

Как правая и левая рука,	Like a right and left hand
Твоя душа моей душе близка.	Your soul is close to mine.
Мы смежены, блаженно и тепло,	We are neighbors blissful and warm,
Как правое и левое крыло.	Like a right and left wing.
Но вихрь встает — и бездна пролегла	But a whirlwind arises—and an abyss has
От правого — до левого крыла!	opened
	Between the right and left wings.

July 10, 1918
(II, 23)

Can we safely assume Sergei is the addressee? A twin poem written the same day is addressed less to him than to God or Tsvetaeva's male "genius:"[6]

Я — страница твоему перу.	I am the page to your pen.
Всё приму. Я белая страница.	I accept all. I am a blank page.
Я — хранитель твоему добру:	I am the respository of thy goods.
Возращу и возвращу сторицей.	I will return them, return them a hundredfold.
Я — деревня, черная земля.	I am the village, black earth,
Ты мне — луч и дождевая влага.	Thou art my light and moisture from the rain.
Ты — Господь и Господин, а я —	Thou art Lord and Master, I—
Чернозем — и белая бумага!	Black earth and white paper.

July 10, 1918
(II, 226)

Discussing this poem many years later, Tsvetaeva implied that it, and others like it, originally had real, human addressees, of whom there were several:

One correction: one must speak this way only to God. For this is a prayer! You don't pray to human beings. Thirteen years ago I still didn't—yes, I did know!—I stubbornly didn't *want* to know this. And once and for all—all such poems of mine are addressed to God. (It was not accidental that I never put their dedications down in writing—not at all from mortal female pride, but from some sort of final purity of conscience.) . . . Above heads—to God. At least to the angels. Even if only because not one of those to whom they were addressed took them as his own, related them to himself, acknowledged receipt.[7]

The offhand reference to other addressees at this period could explain why many of her poems on duty and honor, like the White Army poems of *Swans' Encampment*, are unconvincingly rhetorical.

1918 was the year in which Tsvetaeva often qestioned the rationale for poetry, and gave many answers, ranging from "none" to "self-consolation" to "duty and loyalty." A series of poems written in August explored the nature and genesis of verse, the first time Tsvetaeva raised these meta-poetic questions. Her answers were as varied as her own work had become: "Poems grow, like stars and roses, like a beauty unneeded in the family" (II, 231);[8] poetry is her "refuge from savage hordes" (II, 231). One such poem offers an original, and particularly female conceit, an oblique comment on her own life:

Каждый стих — дитя любви,
Нищий незаконнорожденный.
Первенец — у колеи
На поклон ветрам — положенный.

Сердцу ад и алтарь,
Сердцу — рай и позор.
Кто отец? — Может — царь.
Может — царь, может — вор.

Every verse is a child of love,
A poor illegitimate child.
A firstborn, left at the roadside
To the will of the winds.

For the heart—hell and altar,
For the heart—paradise and shame.
Who is the father? Perhaps the Tsar,
Perhaps the Tsar, perhaps a thief.
August 14, 1918
(II, 231)

The series concluded with Tsvetaeva's determination to turn the deprivation and hardship of her life to the advantage of art: poetic creativity is a purifying fire which turns the simplest things, those which no one else wants, into spiritual treasures.

Что другим не нужно — несите мне:
Всё должно сгореть на моем огне!
Я и жизнь маню, я и смерть маню
В легкий дар моему огню.

What others do not need—bring to me!
All must burn up on my fire!
I beckon even life, even death
As a light gift to my fire.
September 2, 1918
(II, 24)

The fall of 1918 marked a major turning-point in Tsvetaeva's lyric diary. The simple, eloquent lyrics she had written all summer were both a triumph and burden; she could go little further in that direction. So she turned from her stark, compressed lyrics and themes of self-denial to the more expansive romanticism of her plays:

I've begun to write plays—this has come as a necessity—it's simply that my voice has outgrown my verse and there's too much breath in my chest for a flute."[9]

Meanwhile, her living conditions rapidly and steadily deteriorated. Lodgers were moved into the "surplus" rooms of the Boris and Gleb Lane apartment, while she and the girls retreated to the kitchen and two third-floor, semi-attic rooms. Food was procured by bartering possessions (those which weren't stolen by the lodgers), or through the charity of friends. Fuel often meant breaking up the furniture or the railing of the circular staircase in the two-story apartment. In November 1918, for the first and only time in her life, she took a regular job.[10] It was with an obscure division of the rapidly growing Soviet bureaucracy, the "Information Section of the Commissariat of Nationality Affairs" (the Commissariat as a whole was headed by an ambitious Georgian Communist, Joseph Stalin, but Tsvetaeva doesn't mention this fact and probably was unaware of it). Her job was to summarize newspaper articles (primarily about the progress of the Red Army and the defeat of the Whites) and paste the summaries onto large sheets of paper—to what purpose, Tsvetaeva never knew. Her superiors were tolerant of her scandalously late arrivals (she spent hours standing in food lines), early departures, and frequent absences, probably because they knew nothing of importance was being done. She wrote three plays during her "service," often while on the job. Finally she was given a task with which she couldn't—or wouldn't—cope: establishing "classifications," of what and by what standard she could never make out. Forfeiting the paid leave she would have earned by working another two weeks, she quit, giving the excuse that she had found a job which offered "military rations and free dinners for all members of her family." In reality, she found another job in a library card catalogue, where, seeing no hope of meeting the daily norm, she left after lunch the first day and never returned.

Tsvetaeva's diary sketches provide episodic but vivid pictures of her Moscow life that winter. We see her dragging heavy sacks of frozen, half-rotten potatoes (issued at work) across Moscow on Alya's brightly-painted baby sled, or leading a visitor by the hand through the shattered glass (from the broken ceiling) and puddles (from burst pipes) in the ruins of her former dining room. This was a life for which Tsvetaeva was ill-suited by upbringing, ability, or inclination. Her inability to "cope," especially if coping meant making compromises with principle, made her life harder than that of many. That such a refusal might affect the well-being and even the survival of her two daughters is something Tsvetaeva never even considered.

CHAPTER TWELVE

A Farewell to Romanticism:
Tsvetaeva and the Theater (1918–1919)

"Tsvetaeva's theatrical novel"—or "theatrical romance," the Russian is conveniently ambiguous—is Viktoria Schweitzer's term for the whole complex of poems, plays, and friendship which Tsvetaeva bestowed on her young actor friends. The romance reached its climax and rapid denouement in the winter and spring of 1918–1919, but the novel's last chapter was written only in 1937, as Tsvetaeva's "Tale about Sonechka," a loving memoir of her Moscow life nearly twenty years before. Its picture of Tsvetaeva's friends and her relationships with them is more successful in compelling the reader's interest and sympathy than are the poems, plays, and diary prose she wrote at the time, which themselves served as its sources. Tsvetaeva's romance with the theater was her farewell to the unbridled romanticism of youth. Like all of Tsvetaeva's love affairs, it was ultimately disillusioning, personally and artistically. She looked back on it with bitterness in 1921, quoting Heine, "The theater is not propitious for the poet/ And the poet is not propitious for the theater." She continued:

> I don't revere the Theater. I'm not drawn to the Theater, and I don't reckon with the Theater. Theater (to see with the eyes) has always seemed for me a support for the poor in spirit, security for the sly types like doubting Thomas, who believe only what they see, or even more, what they touch. A kind of alphabet for the blind.
>
> While the essence of the poet is to take on trust!
>
> The Poet, by his innate non-seeing of life, gives us the invisible life (*byt'ie*). The theater takes this at-last-seen life and turns it into visible life, that is, into *byt*.[1]

What, then, drew her to the theater if its spirit and essence were so alien? The answer, as almost always for Tsvetaeva, was "people"—her own ability to value—indeed, to overvalue—not only a wide variety of "souls" but also her own love for them. The life-style and ethic of these young actors, and of the plays Tsvetaeva wrote for them, were miles removed from the ascetic ideals of her latest poems. She would be happy, she wistfully declared, to live "A simple, model life—like the sun, like a pendulum, like the calendar/ As God commanded, but my friends don't allow." (II, 25) Instead, the complexity of her emotional life that fall was matched only by the stylistic versatility of her poetry. In the unbelievably productive month of November, 1918, important poems from both the gypsy and Biblical halves of *Versts* alternated in the lyric diary with the first poems of a new cycle, dedicated to Jury Zavadsky and ironically titled, "Komed'iant" ("play-actor" or "hypocrite," from the obsolete Russian term for actor).

Tsvetaeva was infatuated with Zavadsky, but resented the power simple physical attraction had over her. For it was his striking blonde good looks,[2] rather than his soul, which attracted her:

> First: he's divinely good-looking, in the second place, he has a divine voice. Both of these divinities are for the fancier. But there are many such fanciers: all men who don't love women, and all women who don't love men . . .

> All his charm and all his danger is in his deepest innocence. You could die, and he'd not ask about you for months. And then, in dismay, "Oh, how sad! If I had known, but I was so busy . . . I didn't know people died right off like that . . ."

> Of all his temptations for me I would pick out three main ones: the temptation of weakness, the temptation of impassivity, and the temptation of The Alien.[3]

Poetry became her defense against temptation. Here she could maintain ironic distance, even predict that her infatuation's only outcome would be art itself:

Не любовь, а лицемерье,	It's not love, but hypocrisy
Лицедейство — не любовь!	A theater show—not love!
И итогом этих (в скобках —	And the sum of these (in parentheses—
Несодеянных!) грехов —	Uncommitted!) sins—
Будет легонькая стопка	Will be an oh-so-light pile
Восхитительных стихов.	Of entrancing poems.

November 20, 1918
(II, 241)

That was indeed the case. The rather sizeable pile of "Komed'iant" poems, twenty-five altogether, were written with a wit and elegance that recalled eighteenth-century France. Tsvetaeva boldly declared her passion with a forthrightness equally characteristic of that century, but seldom found in women poets, at least until recent years. The frankness with which she admired Zavadsky's physical beauty—and his beauty alone—turned the tables on centuries of male poets who have sung the beauty, but seldom the mind, of their beloved.

The cycle marked an important new direction in Tsvetaeva's work—the move toward longer forms. It is a sketch for a psychological novel in verse, and in this sense lays the groundwork for her "Poem of the Mountain" and "Poem of the End" (both 1924). The realistic details of setting in the first poem—a street-lamp, a winding staircase, rain, fog, wind, and the hero's countenance, "Dickensian as the night," are more reminiscent of the 19th-century novel than of Tsvetaeva's usual lyric of raw and spontaneous emotion. This uncharacteristic pull toward realism continued throughout the cycle, as Tsvetaeva returned again and again to the details of Zavadsky's face and body. Zavadsky never managed to get a word of his own into the cycle, which is not surprising, for he evidently had not much to say. In "A Tale about Sonechka," Tsvetaeva remarked of him, "Nevertheless, it is a tragedy when your face is the best thing you have and your beauty is the main thing about you. . ." The cycle alternates between admiration of that beauty and the realization that her love for him is met, if at all, by mild affection and wry amusement. Tsvetaeva, however, was far from defenseless. She is not simply a woman in love, but a poet, and poetry has a permanence which love does not:

— Младой военнопленный,	. . . Young prisoner-of-war,
Любовь отпустит вас, но —	Love will release you, but—inspired—
вдохновенный —	My winged voice will roar for all to hear
Всем пророкочет голос мой крылатый —	That there once lived upon the earth
О том, что жили на земле когда-то	You—as forgetful as you are unforgettable!
Вы, — столь забывчивый, сколь	November 25, 1918
незабвенный!	(II, 243)

"Komed'iant," all in all, was a successful first step in extending the single lyrical voice—the "flute song" she now found too limited. But it was still a monologue, as was the relationship it immortalized. For a poet in love with an actor the logical next step was to write verse drama. Tsvetaeva's first plays were, to paraphrase Clausewitz, "a continuation of the lyric diary by other means," which largely explains their weaknesses as theater. Tsvetaeva not only wrote them *for* her actor friends, she wrote *about* them—the plots embodied her own private myths about their relationships. In three of the plays the central female characters are versions of Tsvetaeva herself. About "The Snowstorm's" Lady in the Cape, she once remarked: "She is my soul, how can anyone play her?"

Both Karlinsky and Saakiants have pointed out the clear influence of Blok on Tsvetaeva's earliest verse dramas. Saakiants sees a tribute to Blok's "Puppet Theater" (*Balaganchik*) in the playing-card heroes and heroines of her earliest play, "The Jack of Hearts" (*Chervonnii valet*).[4] In Karlinsky's view, "The Snowstorm" (*Metel'*) is most clearly influenced by the symbolist verse dramas so popular in Tsevtaeva's adolescence. He rightly sees its plot as simply a variation, with the sexes reversed, of the basic situation in Blok's "The Stranger" (*Neznakomka*): "A mysterious bond between an astral being and a chosen, unique mortal, depicted against a background of vulgarity and incomprehension."[5] The emotional "plot" of the play had an immediacy for Tsvetaeva—a young woman (Tsvetaeva was 19 when she married) who realizes she does not love her husband and turns to a wiser, otherworldly man who bids her forget him and vanishes. The Gentleman in a Cape, however, is a more authoritative figure than Zavadsky, for whom it was written. He represents Tsvetaeva's ideal mentor/lover/genius—an impossible ideal which she always sought and never found. In such a reading, the very strong aura of Blok noted by Karlinsky would be less a sign of his influence than an intentional tribute.[6]

In "Fortuna," Tsvetaeva achieved the freedom, strength, and—in part—the forgetfulness promised by the Gentleman in the Cape, overcoming Zavadsky's charm with the help of her art. "Fortuna's" hero, the Duc de Lauzun, *is* Zavadsky, a man whom no woman can resist, and each of the three aristocratic ladies who loves him represents an aspect of Tsvetaeva. Princess Izabella Czartoryska (Tsvetaeva, remember, was proud of her Polish blood) is so deeply in love with Lauzun, who has fathered her youngest child, that she says of her older children:

Да я бы высушила их в песок	And I would dry them into dust,
Я-б в снег зарыла их по шею:	Bury them to their necks in snow:
Лишь только-б знать, что станут на часок	Only to know that for but an hour
Вот эти щеки розовее!	These cheeks would blush redder.

These are horrifying words for the reader aware that little Irina Efron died less than a year after they were written. Marie Anoinette, like the Lady in the Cape twenty years old and bored with her husband, is no less susceptible to Lauzun's charm. Yet she has enough wit to throw in his face Tsvetaeva's line from Komed'iant: "You are as forgetful as you are unforgettable!" "Fortuna" is a *Drame a clef* and Tsvetaeva has scattered the keys liberally about: in every act, Lauzun's admirers borrow from the "Komed'iant" poems. Though he conquers their hearts, Lauzun-Zavadsky is ultimately bested, for the women get all the best lines. Until the last act, he never has a speech more than three lines long.

Zavadsky played no role, either literally or figuratively, in Tsvetaeva's two plays based on the life of Casanova. In "The Adventure," the dominant personality is not Casanova but the brilliant, daring, and charming Henriette. Like the Countess Lanska, Henriette (who is—should we be surprised?—20 years old) has fled from her noble family disguised as "Henri," a handsome young Hussar. Karlinsky astutely said of the androgynous Henri-Henriette:

> This ambiguous, almost hermaphroditic character is the frank embodiment of Tsvetaeva's indistinct dream of love and intimacy based on personal worth, which would exceed the limitations of one particular sex.[7]

"Phoenix," about the last days of Casanova, combined Tsvetaeva's continuing investigation of love with an important new theme: the poet who had so idealized childhood was beginning to fall in love with old age, to admire older men who preserved old-fashioned aristocratic values. One of these was Alexei Stakhovich, a former aide-de-camp at the Romanov court who was serving as "technical advisor" in courtly manners at the Moscow Art Theater studios. Although she met him only once, Tsvetaeva valued his adherence to old codes of behavior despite the hunger and chaos which surrounded him. Stakhovich became a model in a more ominous way; in March 1919, seriously ill and feeling himself "an old man needed by no one," he hanged himself. Tsvetaeva was to emulate him in the manner of her own death more than twenty years later.

At Stakhovich's funeral, Tsvetaeva rekindled an acquaintance begun a few months earlier with Sof'ia (Sonechka) Holliday (her father had been a Russified English violinist). The intense but short-lived friendship which bloomed that spring had lesbian overtones which Tsvetaeva scarcely bothered to conceal in her retrospective "Tale about Sonechka." In her relationship with *this* Sof'ia (Parnok was always Sonia, Holliday always Sonechka) the roles were reversed: Sonechka was childlike, Marina maternal. Holliday herself, as Tsvetaeva recalled her, was all theater, her personal life a series of fleeting and unhappy relationships with men. In the winter of 1918–1919, she, too, was hopelessly infatuated with Zavadsky, and their mutual infatuation formed the basis for the friendship of actress and poet. Sonechka was physically very small, "the size of a fourteen-year-old," with enormous black eyes and long dark braids. Her size and appearance limited the number of roles she could play, so Tsvetaeva created roles to suit her.

Holliday was the inspiration for Tsvetaeva's "Poems to Sonechka." Unlike "Komed'iant," the cycle does not speak directly of the relationship, and Tsvetaeva's own persona and familiar voice are largely absent. Instead, she tried out a new voice, stylizing the cheap popular romances to which Sonechka was addicted. The heroines of these ballads present a series of possible roles for Sonechka the actress, while mythologizing her real-life treatment at the hands of men. A young girl educated in a school for noble young ladies, for example, becomes a governess and falls in love with her charges' eldest brother, a hussar home on leave. A familiar story follows— pregnancy, banishment, a visit to the foundling home, prostitution, suicide. These stylizations were moderately successful attempts to step beyond the lyric persona, but far more moving—to this reader, at any rate—is a lyric about the two large poplar trees which stood opposite Tsvetaeva's house on Boris and Gleb lane:

Два дерева хотят друг к другу.	Two trees incline toward one another.
Два дерева. Напротив дом мой.	Two trees. Across from my house.
Деревья старые. Дом старый.	The trees are old. The house is old.
Я молода, а то б, пожалуй,	I'm young, or else, perhaps,
Чужих деревьев не жалела.	I'd not be sorry for someone else's trees.

То, что поменьше, тянет руки,	The younger one extends its arms
Как женщина, из жил последних	Like a woman, stretching out from her
Вытянулось, — смотреть жестоко,	Last torments—it's cruel to watch
Как тянется — к тому, другому,	How it reaches—to that other one,
Что старше, стойче и — кто знает? —	Which is older, steadier and—who knows?
Еще несчастнее, быть может.	Perhaps even more unfortunate.
Два дерева: в пылу заката	Two trees. In the dust of sunset
И под дождем — еще под снегом —	And in the rain—and even in the snow—
Всегда, всегда: одно к другому,	Ever, ever: one toward the other
Таков закон: одно к другому,	Such is the law: one to the other
Закон один: одно к другому.	The law is one: one to the other.

August 1919

(II, 257)

Tsvetaeva manipulates grammatical gender for her own ends. "Tree" in Russian is neuter; "poplar," which has the same stress and number of syllables in the gentive singular, is masculine. Tsvetaeva chose the term unmarked for either species or gender, in part, certainly, so that the crucial metaphor, "extending its hands like a woman . . ." would not jar with a masculine noun. As a result, of course, all the modifiers and pronouns referring to the trees are neuter, which is particularly evident in the last three, parallel, lines. The trees represent not only Sonechka's longing for Marina (more imagined than real, it transpired) but Tsvetaeva's dream of love between soul and soul unconstrained by categories of gender.

Most of the Sonechka poems, like the friendship itself, belong to April, May, and June, 1919. In June, Holliday went off to spend the summer on tour. Tsvetaeva poured her feelings into letters, but got few in return. Sonechka returned for one brief visit, then vanished; she never contacted Tsvetaeva again. Her betrayal must have hurt Tsvetaeva deeply, as she herself once hurt Parnok, but she never admits to pain. In "A Tale About Sonechka," she spoke frankly about the end of the affair:

> I knew we would have to part. If I had been a man, it would have been the luckiest, most fortunate love, but *this* way—we inevitably had to part, for her love for me would inevitably have kept her—and was already keeping her— from loving another.
>
> . . . Her not coming to see me was only her obedience to her female lot: to love a man—in the final analysis, it mattered not which one—and to love him alone till death . . .[8]

This passage recalls one of Tsvetaeva's strangest works, published as *Mon Frere Feminin*[9] in French, the language in which it was evidently originally written in 1932. The Russian title, "A Letter to an Amazon," refers to the work's (unstated) addressee: Natalie Clifford Barney, an American expatriate writer whose *Pensees d'une Amazone* was published in 1918. Barney[10], a leader of the Paris literary lesbians, maintained a celebrated salon at her home on Rue Jacob. Tsvetaeva evidently had met her, but it is unlikely she knew her well. *Mon Frere Feminin* answers Barney's *Pensees* on what Tsvetaeva sees as the weak point of lesbianism—woman's instinctive desire to have a child. Tsvetaeva charts the course of a "typical" love affair, contending the younger woman will inevitably leave the older to marry and have a child. Rather than a repudiation of lesbianism, it is a knowing and sympathetic account of the feelings involved.[11]

Tsvetaeva's theatrical romance was a last fling with the romanticism of her youth, a farewell to Eros in its youthful, impetuous, sensual guise. It was not a final farewell, to be sure, but during the winter of 1919–1920 the balance, in her art at least, tilted away from "the great baseness of love" toward a denial of the flesh and a Platonic "love without bodies." Her new year poem for 1919 marked her first mention of the sibyl, a centrally important image in her later poetry.

И, упражняясь в старческом искусстве	And, practicing the elder's art
Скрывать себя, как черный бриллиант,	Of camouflage, a black diamond,
Я слушаю вас с нежностью и грустью,	I hear you all with tenderness and sorrow,
Как древняя Сивилла — и Жорж Занд.	Like the ancient sibyl—and George Sand.

December 31, 1918
(II, 240)

The sibyl, in Tsvetaeva's favorite version of the legend, requested immortality (from Apollo) but forgot to ask for eternal youth. Her body dried up to nothing, leaving only her voice. The sibyl, like the aged George Sand, became Tsvetaeva's new ideal—a female sage, freed by old age from the bonds of Eros. After all, she was now all of 27!

CHAPTER THIRTEEN

Tragedy and Guilt (1919–1920)

By the time the terrible winter of 1919–1920 set in, Tsvetaeva's theatrical circle had dispersed. Life itself, the *byt* she so despised, burned away the last remnants of Tsvetaeva's adolescent romanticism and brought not only premature grey hairs, but a new sobriety and depth to her poetic voice. It took a great deal, however, to sober Tsvetaeva. Both bravado and wit were evident as she provided a versified tour of her half-ruined apartment. She now routinely referred to it as a slum—the pipes had burst, there was no running water and often no electricity.

Чердачный дворец мой, дворцовый чердак!	My attic palace, my palace attic!
Взойдите. Гора рукописных бумаг. . .	Come on up. A mountain of manuscripts . . .
Так. — Руку! — Держите направо, —	So. Give me your hand. Keep right—
Здесь лужа от крыши дырявой.	There's a puddle from the leaky roof.
Теперь полюбуйтесь, воссев на сундук,	Now—seat yourself on a trunk,
Какую мне Фландрию вывел паук.	And admire the Flanders my spider has woven.
Не слушайте толков досужих,	Don't heed those idle rumors,
Что женщина — может без кружев!	That woman can do without lace!
Ну-с, перечень наших чердачных чудес:	Well, then, a catalogue of our attic wonders:
Здесь нас посещают и ангел, и бес,	Here we are visited by angel and demon,
И тот, кто обоих превыше.	And he who is higher than both.
Недолго ведь с неба — на крышу!	It's not far from heaven to our roof!
Вам дети мои — два чердачных царька,	My children—two attic princelings,
С веселою музой моею, — пока	With my jolly muse, will show you my empire,
Вам призрачный ужин согрею, —	While I cook you up
Покажут мою эмпирею.	A phantom dinner.
— А что с Вами будет, как выйдут дрова?	"And what will happen when you run out of wood?"
— Дрова? Но на то у поэта — слова	"Wood? But a poet always has
Всегда — огневые — в запасе!	A stock of flaming words!
Нам нынешний год не опасен. . .	This year is no danger to us . . ."
От века поэтовы корки черствы,	For centuries poets have eaten stale crusts,
И дела нам нету до красной Москвы!	And what is Red Moscow to us?
Глядите: от края — до края —	Just look—from one end to the other—
Вот наша Москва — голубая!	Our Moscow is noble sky-blue!
А если уж слишком поэта доймет	And if even a poet is too tired out
Московский, чумной, девятнадцатый год, —	By this plague-stricken Moscow '19,
Что ж, — мы проживем и без хлеба!	Then we'll live even without bread!
Недолго ведь с крыши — на небо.	For it's not far from our roof to heaven.

1919

(II, 263)

The brave concluding lines proved prophetic for poor Irina, nearly so for Alya.

Tsvetaeva's theatrical romance provided no role for her two daughters. Only the childlike Sonechka paid special attention to them. A brief passage in "A Tale about Sonechka" is the only description of Irina in all Tsvetaeva's writing:

> As soon as she entered the apartment, she would take Irina out of her crib. "Well, my little girl? Do you recognize your 'Galli-da?' How is it you sing about me? 'Galli-da, Galli-da! . . .'"

> Irina onto her knees, Alya under her wing—the right arm, which wasn't holding Irina. . . . Thus I see three of them; a group of three heads, frozen in motionless bliss—Irina, with her high brow, with her thick, tight, bright-gold curls, almost like a ram's horns about the rise of her brow. . . .[1]

The reference to Irina's "high brow" and a later allusion to her "slender neck" suggest that perhaps Irina was hydrocephalic. The only two poems dedicated to her during her lifetime, both from the summer of 1918, are oratorical rather than personal—we cannot see the face of the child in the cradle.

In October, 1919, Alya, just turned seven, reappeared in her mother's lyric diary after a year's absence. Left without a nanny, Tsvetaeva seemed to know—or care—only about nurturing Alya's intellect. During their years together in Moscow, and later, during their first year of emigration, Marina was Ariadna's only teacher; she had no formal schooling until she was eleven. Tsvetaeva's method was simple—she required Ariadna to keep a diary, just as she was doing. Alya's diary, written when she was six and seven, is strikingly mature in its lexicon and grammar, though the child's viewpoint remains to give it its unique appeal. Visitors were amazed to hear Alya reciting her mother's poetry; by the fall of 1919, she was writing her own. Twenty of Alya's poems, collectively dated, "spring, 1920," are appended to *Psyche*. Did Tsvetaeva consciously *instruct* Alya in poetry writing? That would explain a rather anomalous set of "Quatrains" dated "Moscow, 1919." Written in a wide variety of meters and rhyme schemes, they may have been intended as models for the beginning poet. Their common theme—Tsvetaeva's "sinful" life style, may seem inappropriate for a seven-year-old, but Alya was witness and confidante to all aspects of her mother's life.

Ты зовешь меня блудницей, —	You call me a loose woman—
Прав, — но малость упустил:	Right,—but you forgot one little thing:
Надо мне, чтоб гость был статен,	I demand that the guest be stately,
Во-вторых — чтоб не платил.	And again—that he not pay.

1919

(II, 267)

We should not be surprised to find echoes of Tsvetaeva's voice in Alya's poetry. Beginning poets are imitative (Tsvetaeva herself certainly was!) and

Alya's model for imitation was her own mother, who read her new work to
an audience of one every evening. Alya's poems reflect the romanticism of
Tsvetaeva's plays:

ВАША КОМНАТА	YOUR ROOM
Пахнет Родиной и Розой, Вечным дымом и стихами. Из тумана сероглазый гений Грустно в комнату глядит.	There is a scent of native land and roses, Of eternal smoke and poems. Out of the mist a grey-eyed genius[2] Sadly gazes into the room.

(II, 318)

There are echoes of Tsvetaeva's gypsy poems:

Спите, Марина, Спите, Морская Богиня. Ваше лицо будет скрыто в небесных морях. Юноши будут давать Вам обеты в церквах. Звери со всех сторон мира Будут реветь под цыганской звездою любви.	Sleep, Marina, Sleep, Goddess of the Sea. Your face will be hidden in the heavenly seas. Youths will make you vows in churches. Beasts from all ends of the earth Will roar beneath the gypsy star of love.

(II, 317)

And the martial poems of *Swans' Encampment*:

Где-то играет старинный марш Кто-то летит на гибель. Где-то вздымается гулкий крик: — Родина не погибла!	Somewhere an old-fashioned march is playing Someone flies to his doom. Somewhere rises the hollow cry: —The motherland has not perished!

(II, 319)

But there are poems, such as the first and briefest, which reveal real
originality:

Корни сплелись. Ветви сплелись. — Лес Любви.	The roots are twined The branches twined— A forest of Love.

(II, 317)

We can certainly wonder whether Tsvetaeva "touched up" her daughter's
poems before publishing them. There is an even more interesting question:
was Alya's poetry a source for some of Tsvetaeva's own phrases, rhymes,
or images? To what extent did the verbal inventiveness of the child, which
Tsvetaeva so often praised as the essence of poetry, provide her mother
with the kernel of a poem? A childishly bold willingness to break rules—
both behavioral and stylistic—was always characteristic of Tsvetaeva, as
was her valorization of the immediate, spontaneous, highly colored. There
is, however, something disturbing about a mother who, while valuing
childhood, allowed her own daughter so little of it.

> My mother is not at all like a mother. Mothers always admire their child, and
> children in general, but Marina doesn't like small children. . . . She is melan-

choly, swift, loves Poetry and Music. She writes poems. She is patient, always patient in the extreme. She gets mad and she loves. She's always hurrying somewhere. She has a big soul. A tender voice. A rapid step. Marina's hands are all in rings. Marina reads at night. Her eyes are almost mocking. She doesn't like it when people bother her with stupid questions—then she gets very mad.[3]

Though she herself had suffered from her mother's efforts to make her a pianist, she unconsciously repeated those efforts in trying to make Alya a poet.

Tsvetaeva's ruminations in 1921, while Alya was spending a month in the country with friends, cast light back on this earlier period and on Tsvetaeva's character in general:

I begin to think—quite seriously—that I am bad for Alya. For me, who never was a child and therefore has always remained one, for me a child—a forgetful creature which avoids pain—is alien. . . . Alya is better with others: they were children, then they forgot it all, they served out their obligation and believed on faith that children have "other laws." That's why, with others, Alya laughs and with me she cries, with others she grows fat, and with me, thin. . . . Without me, of course, she won't write any poems at all—she won't go near her notebook, because poems are me, the notebook is pain.[4]

Tsvetaeva perhaps demanded even more of the talented Alya to make up for what Irina would obviously never achieve.

Alya managed to survive somehow, though she was very small for her age. But Irina was not thriving. Tsvetaeva was persuaded to send her off to the country for the summer of 1919 with the nanny Nadya. But Irina was back by early fall, when Tsvetaeva's living conditions grew even more desperate:

There is no flour, there is no bread. Under the desk are about twelve pounds of potatoes, the remainder of the thirty-six pounds "loaned" by neighbors— our entire store! . . . The anarchist Charles has carried off Sergei's antique gold watch . . .

I get up. The upper window is barely grey. Cold, puddles, sawdust, buckets, pitchers, rags—everywhere children's dresses and shirts. I saw wood. I stoke the fire. I wash some potatoes in icy water and boil them in the samovar. I heat the samovar with burning coals which I take straight from the stove. Day and night I wear the same brown dress . . . It's full of holes from falling coals and cigarettes . . .[5]

She continued her routine, down the back stairs to the neighbors' for water, then the washing, then to four different institutions collecting dinners for the children, and perhaps bread on her ration card. Then, back home to heat up the dinners and, most terrible, the parenthetical remark:

(If Alya was with me, first I untie Irina from the chair. I began to tie her up
when once, when Alya and I were out, she ate half a head of raw cabbage.)[6]

Some time that winter, conditions at her apartment grew so bad that she
put both girls into shelters and moved in with friends. Alya contracted
malaria, and Tsvetaeva took her back, to care for her as best she could.
During Alya's brief absence, Tsvetaeva (or at least her poetic persona)
missed her terribly:

Маленький домашний дух,	Little domestic spirit,
Мой домашний гений!	My domestic genius!
Вот она, разлука двух	There is is, the separation
Сродных вдохновений!	Of two kindred inspirations!
Жалко мне, когда в печи	I'm sorry when there's flame
Жар, — а ты не видишь!	In the stove, and you can't see it!
В дверь — звезда в моей ночи! —	Star in my night, you won't
Не взойдешь, не выйдешь!	Come in the door, or go out!
Платьица твои висят,	Your little dresses hang,
Точно плод запретный.	Like forbidden fruit.
На окне чердачном — сад	On the attic windowsill
Расцветает — тщетно.	The garden blooms—in vain.
Голуби в окно стучат, —	Doves knock at the window—
Скучно с голубями!	I'm bored with doves!
Мне ветра привет кричат, —	The winds call me greeting—
Бог с ними, с ветрами!	What are they to me?
Не сказать ветрам седым,	Not the grey winds,
Стаям голубиным —	Nor the flocks of doves—
Чудодейственным твоим	Will say, in your wonderworking
Голосом: — Марина!	Voice:—"Marina!"

                                                          November, 1919
                                                              (II, 264)

Alya was not only companion and fellow poet, she was consolation, as
angelic as her (now mythologized) father:

Видно с ангелом спала я,	Clearly I slept with an angel,
Бога приняла в объятья.	Took God into my embrace.
Каждый час благословляю	Every hour I bless
Полночь твоего зачатья.	The midnight of your conception.

                                                          October, 1919
                                                              (II, 32)

With her huge grey eyes the physical reminder of her father, Alya was an
incentive to good behavior. Tsvetaeva's renewed attention to Alya in the
poems of late 1919 is part of her rejection of Eros. She undertook a moral
(if not physical) housecleaning:

Времячко мое златое!	Oh, my golden time!
Сонм чудесных прегрешений!	Host of wonderful transgressions!
Всех вас вымела метлою	Consuela—consolation
Консуэла — Утешенье.	Has swept you away with her broom.
А чердак мой чисто мѐтен,	And my attic's cleanly swept—
Сор подобран — на жаровню.	The trash collected for the brazier.
Смерть хоть сим же часом встретим:	We could meet death this very hour:
Ни сориночки любовной!	Not a dust-speck left of love.

October, 1919
(II, 32)

The rejection of Eros did not take place all at once, and art in this respect was somewhat ahead of life. There were still romantic involvements in Tsvetaeva's life, but the theme of debauch is more and more frequently tempered by the voice of conscience:

Дитя разгула и разлуки, —	Child of revelry and separation—
Ко всем протягиваю руки.	I stretch out my arms to all.
Тяну, ресницами плеща,	Fluttering my eyelashes,
Всех юношей за край плаща.	I draw all young men under the edge of my cape.
Но голос: — Мариула, в путь!	But a Voice: "Mariula, move on!"
И всех отталкиваю в грудь.	And I push them all away.

January 1920
(II, 37)

Tsvetaeva left Irina in the shelter at Kuntsevo, concentrating all her maternal care on Alya, intending to take the baby back as soon as Alya was well. But it was not to be. On February 16 (O.S. February 3) Irina died. In two months, she would have been three. There have been, and undoubtedly will continue to be, conflicting assessments of Tsvetaeva's responsiblity. It was not, alas, uncommon for children to starve in those years, particularly in children's homes; in Gladkov's Soviet classic, *Cement* (1925) the heroine's small daughter Nurka dies just such a death. Tsvetaeva preferred to blame the Bolsheviks, who ran the shelter and had brought about the food shortages. Some versions of the story stress her tragic, impossible choice: she had enough food to feed one child, not two. This, however, begs a deeper question, hidden beneath the surface of Tsvetaeva's memoirs and those of her acquaintances: *why* did she have so little? All urban dwellers suffered hunger and cold in those years, but to judge by the comments of her contemporaries and her own memoirs, Tsvetaeva lived worse than most. There was a large element of pride involved. Tsvetaeva was reluctant to abandon her *real* work—writing poetry—for anything which might more reliably bring food into the house. She did have relatives—Sergei's sisters and her half-brother Andrei, who could and did help, but Tsvetaeva found it demeaning to ask. Lilya and Vera Efron evidently offered to take Irina and care for her but only if Tsvetaeva would give her up for good. A passage in the correspondence of two of Tsvetaeva's friends sends chills of horror up the spine:

> Lilya wanted to bring Irina here and now blames herself for her death. I feel terribly sorry for the poor child. . .in two years of earthly life nothing but hunger, cold, and beatings.[7]

Tsvetaeva's reaction, as reflected in two harrowing letters to a friend, was a mixture of guilt, despair, and grief, grief as much for herself as for the little creature who was no longer there. Tsvetaeva had never summoned the courage to visit the orphanage; she did not attend the child's funeral. Irina's death seemed somehow unreal:

> . . . At night I dream about Irina, that, it turns out, she is alive, and I'm so happy, and it's so natural for me that she's alive. I still don't understand that she no longer exists, I don't believe it, I don't understand the words, but I don't feel it. It still seems to me—to such an extent do I not accept the inevitability—that everything will turn out all right, that this is a lesson for me, in my sleep, that I'll wake up and . . .[8]

Tsvetaeva justified herself while ostensibly accepting blame:

> When it's easy for you, you can't believe it's hard for another. And finally—I was so abandoned! Everyone has someone: a husband, a father, a brother. I had only Alya, and Alya was ill, and I totally buried myself in her illness—and here God has punished me.[9]

She sensed (or feared) reproaches from her friends and Efron's sisters and withdrew into herself. Thoughts of suicide were not far from her mind:

> I have no future, no will. I'm afraid of everything. It's better for me, it seems, to die. If Sergei is no longer alive, I won't be able to live anyway. . .and then, Vera, the most terrible thing: I begin to think that without Irina I am of no use to Sergei, that it would have been better for me to die—more worthy—I'm ashamed that I'm alive. How will I tell him?[10]

The crisis was so deep that, for a while, she even turned away from her notebook. One of the first poems she wrote after two months of near-silence is a hauntingly simple poem to Irina's memory, written, perhaps, on the third anniversary of her birth.

Две руки, легко опущенные	Two hands, lightly lowered
На младенческую голову!	On an infant's head!
Были — по одной на каждую —	There was one for each hand—
Две головки мне дарованы.	Two little heads given me.
Но обеими — зажатыми —	But with both hands clutched—
Яростными — как могла! —	Frenzied, as I could!—
Старшую у тьмы выхватывая —	I snatched the elder from the shadows—
Младшей не уберегла.	I didn't save the younger.

Две руки — ласкать-разглаживать	Two hands, to fondle and pat
Нежные головки пышные.	Tender, luxuriant little heads.
Две руки — и вот одна из них	Two hands, and now, overnight,
Зà ночь оказалась лишняя.	One of them has become superfluous.
Светлая — на шейке тоненькой —	Bright little dandelion on a stem—
Одуванчик на стебле!	On a slender little neck!
Мной еще совсем не понято,	I still haven't fully understood
Что дитя мое в земле.	That my baby's in the earth.

First half of April, 1920
(II, 275)

Yet the odd syntax of the penultimate line—literally, "It is not yet understood by me"—signals her continuing alienation from the event, what a psychologist would call "lack of affect." The Easter holidays in early April resurrected Tsvetaeva's muse. One of the first poems, strangely enough, imagined the stern and handsome son who would one day be born to her. (II, 276) The poem seems more than a bit callous, coming so soon after the death of her unloved and unwanted daughter, even a bit blasphemous, given its Easter date and Kremlin setting.

Guilt and judgement were the major themes in a large cycle of 27 poems written that spring, of which she published only six during her lifetime. The cycle's hero and addressee was most likely V.D. Miliotti (1875–1943), an artist who lived and worked at the nearby Palace of the Arts. She once referred to Miliotti as "the one who began the series of my bad behavior after the death of Irina—simply for his resemblance to Boris[11] —as the first thing which made me smile after all that horror."[12] The cycle's tentative title, "Sputnik" (Traveling-companion) refers to their shared love of long walks. We know little else about the relationship, or of Miliotti himself. And it is not an easy cycle to "read," for the emotions it expresses are conflicting and contradictory. Early in the cycle, the persona stands before the challenge of a new involvement "Like a ship's boy on the canvas/ Laughing in the hours of a great storm." The imagery is often military: "Take heart: I am your shield and courage." Courage in Russian literally means "*man*hood" (*muzh*estvo).

This martial, masculine imagery is particularly characteristic of Tsvetaeva's poetry in 1920, which saw a perceptible shift toward androgyny in her personae. After Irina's death, Mariula, the sexually bold gypsy woman, and the eighteenth-century aristocrats and courtesans were replaced by a series of boyish, stoically courageous figures, such as this ship's boy, the *Tsar-Maiden* of her first folk-tale poem, or the persona of the September, 1920 lyric, "There is in my figure an officer's erectness." Tsvetaeva's habitual costume accentuated this image: Pavel Antokolsky is one of several who recalled it:

A dark-blue dress of neither fashionable nor old-fashioned, but of the most simple cut possible, reminiscent of a cassock, tightly belted in at the waist by a wide yellow strap. Across her shoulder was thrown a yellow leather satchel, like an officer's map case or a hunter's ammunition bag, and in this unfeminine purse fit two hundred or so cigarettes and an oilskin notebook with poems. Wherever this woman went, she seemed like a wanderer, a traveller. . . With broad masculine strides she crossed the Arbat and the nearby sidestreets, right shoulder to the wind, rain, blizzard . . .[13]

Linked to this less-feminine persona was the theme of independence and loneliness, which sounded in some of the year's most eloquent poems:

Мой путь не лежит мимо дому — твоего.	My path doesn't lie past your house.
Мой путь не лежит мимо дому — ничьего.	My path doesn't lie past anyone's house.
А всё же с пути сбиваюсь,	But nevertheless, I wander from my path,
(Особо весной!)	(Especially in spring!)
А всё же по людям маюсь,	And keep pining for humans,
Как пес под луной.	Like a dog under the moon.

April 27, 1920
(II, 16)

For Tsvetaeva, independence meant freedom from love, or at least from passion, and she saw poetry as the means to that freedom. In a poem from the "Biblical" half of *Versts*, she calmly anticipated the revenge of "beautiful Eros" because she had preferred art to love:

И не спасут ни стансы, ни созвездья.	And neither stanzas, nor constellations will
А это называется — возмездье	save me.
За то, что каждый раз,	And that is called retribution
	Because, every time,
Стан разгибая над строкой упорной,	Bending over a stubborn line,
Искала я над лбом своим просторным	I sought above my spacious brow
Звезд только, а не глаз.	Only stars, not eyes.
Что самодержцем Вас признав на веру,	Because, acknowledging you on trust as
— Ах, ни единый миг, прекрасный Эрос,	autocrat—
Без Вас мне не был пуст!	Oh, not for one moment, beautiful Eros,
	Was my life not full without you.
Что по ночам, в торжественных туманах,	Because, at night, in ceremonial mists,
Искала я у нежных уст румяных —	I sought from tender rosy lips—
Рифм только, а не уст.	Only rhymes, not lips.

May 20, 1920
(II, 25)

The stream of "Sputnik" poems was interrupted twice by poems addressed to the only two men whose importance in Tsvetaeva's life remained unchallenged: Alexander Blok and Sergei Efron. Blok made his final visit to Moscow for two readings; Tsvetaeva attended both. The May 9th reading, her first glimpse of Blok in the flesh, inspired a poem which captured the image of a saintly, despairing prophet of Russia's fate. On May 18, the "Sputnik" cycle was interrupted again by a major poem to Sergei, marking the ninth anniversary of their first meeting in Koktebel'. It was an important poem for Tsvetaeva—the many surviving variants in her notebook testify to intensive work and revision:

Писала я на аспидной доске,	I wrote on a slate board,
И на листочках вееров поблёклых,	And on the leaves of faded fans,
И на речном, и на морском песке,	On river sand and sea sand,
Коньками пὸ льду и кольцом на стеклах, —	With skates on ice, with ring on glass,—
И на стволах, которым сотни зим,	And on the trunks of hundred-year-old trees,
И, наконец — чтоб было всем известно! —	And finally, so all would know!—
Что ты любим! любим! любим! —	That you are loved! are loved! are loved! are
любим! —	loved!—
Расписывалась — радугой небесной.	I signed it with a rainbow in the sky.

May 5/18, 1920
(II, 283)

It may seem paradoxical that Tsvetaeva asserted her love for Sergei as her persona developed independence from passion. But that is the key to Tsvetaeva's relationships with men: the more separation confined the relationship to her imagination alone, the freer she was to pledge devotion. So it was with Blok, so it was now with Sergei, so it would be, in the 1920's, with Boris Pasternak and Rainer Maria Rilke.

This characteristic pattern lies behind the difficult, occasionally puzzling folk-tale poem the *Tsar-Maiden*, a book-length work of over 3,000 lines which she wrote in just two months in the summer of 1920. The plot, as in all Tsvetaeva's folk-tales, is adapted from Afanas'ev. Characteristically, she left out the happy ending, in which the Tsar-Maiden is finally united with her Tsarevich. Tsvetaeva's most obvious alteration was the reversal of gender stereotypes in the main characters: the young Tsarevich, though tall, is quiet, shy, and musical, uninterested in war or women's wiles, particularly those of his young stepmother, who, Phaedra-like, is hopelessly in love with him. The Tsar-Maiden, on the other hand, is aggressive, active, martial, and loves her horse "like a fiance." It is she who takes the initiative in courting the Tsarevich.[14]

The central idea of the poem, according to Tsvetaeva, is "the tragedy of missed meeting (razminovenie)," a concept that occupied an increasingly important role in her poetics from this point on. Each of the three meetings at sea between the Tsarevich and Tsar-Maiden is thwarted by the Tsarevich's tutor, in the service of the stepmother, who pricks his charge with a magic pin that brings on deep sleep. The Amazonian Tsar-Maiden, standing over her sleeping princeling, at first mocks his child-like innocence: "I'll bet he still wets his diapers, still sucks a nipple!" But she is soon overcome by an unaccustomed tenderness. It is unsettling to hear the Tsar-Maiden express the maternal tenderness Tsvetaeva herself denied Irina and, with her Spartan pedagogy, Alya as well. One of the few tender phrases Tsvetaeva ever penned to Irina (albeit posthumously), "dandelion on a stem," has been given over to the Tsar-Maiden, who bestows it on her Tsarevich:

«Спи, копна моя льняная,	Sleep, my shock of flax,
Одуванчик на стебле!	Dandelion on a stem.
Будет грудь моя стальная	Let my breast of steel
Колыбелочкой тебе.	Be your cradle.
	(IV, 30)

Anya Kroth[15] rightly used this odd couple as her prime example for Tsvetaeva's valorization of androgyny, stressing the passage in which the narrator affects inability to distinguish between the two:

— Гляжу, гляжу, и невдомек:	I look and look, and can't make out:
Девица — где, и где дружок?	Where's the maiden, and where her friend?
Ты расплетись, верёвьице!	Unwind yourself, you rope!
Где юноша? Где девица?	Where's the youth? Where's the maiden?
	(IV, 29)

G. S. Smith astutely pointed out that "The Tsar-Maiden decides . . . that the Prince would make an ideal partner for her because, since he is so effeminate, he presents no threat to her identity"[16] citing the following lines:

«Баб не любишь? Драк не любишь?	"Don't like women? Don't like fights?"
Ну, тебя-то мне и надо!	Well, you're just what I need!
Как, к примеру, Дева-Царь я,	So, for instance, I'm Tsar-Maiden,
Так, выходит, — Царь-ты-Дева!	Then, it follows, you're Maiden-Tsar!
Уж с таким-то голосочком	A man with such a tiny voice
Муж за прялку не засадит!»	Won't seat me at a spindle!
	(IV, 20)

Smith's interpretation is as true for Tsvetaeva herself as for her Tsar-Maiden. It provides a key to the puzzle of the Efron marriage, of Tsvetaeva's continued loyalty to Sergei, and to her later penchant for lavishing her affection on male homosexuals (Volkonsky, Anatolii Shteiger). None of them posed a threat to her indentity—they could accept her, as woman and poet, for what she was. This, not coincidentally, is the sort of unqualified acceptance a mother has from her young children.

Meanwhile, the contrapuntal theme of the "Sputnik" cycle was the hero's *failure* to accept the persona as she is. He is charmed by her blonde curls, rather than by her soul. Each poem is argumentative: she and her addressee are opposites, but opposites which clash rather than attract:

Ты — каменный, а я пою,	You're made of stone—while I sing,
Ты — памятник, а я летаю.	You're a statue—while I soar.
	May 16, 1920
	(II, 281)

If *The Tsar-Maiden* was about the fatal inability of two complementary souls to connect, "Sputnik," on the other hand, is about the less-than-happy meeting of two opposed natures. From his position as "other," the addressee passes judgment on her actions, seeing her as a "black sheep," whose "laugh rings like a leper's bell." But Tsvetaeva's persona warns him (and her reader) against hasty judgment.

"Nailed to the Pillory" is her most emphatic self-defence. A three-part poem written, not coincidentally, the day after her anniversary declaration of love for Sergei, it is evidently also addressed to him:

Пригвождена к позорному столбу,	Nailed to the pillory
Я все ж скажу, что я тебя люблю.	I'll say, all the same, that I love you.
Что ни одна до самых недр — мать	That not a single mother-to-the-heart
Так на ребенка своего не взглянет.	Will ever gaze thus at her child.
Что за тебя который делом занят,	That for your sake, while you advance your
Не умереть хочу, а умирать.	cause,
Ты не поймешь, — малы мои слова! —	I seek not death but dying.
Как мало мне позорного столба!	You'll not understand—too little are my words—
	How little is the pillory to me.
	May 19, 1920
	(II, 284)

This explosion of a passion maternal yet not maternal could be voiced not only by the Tsar-Maiden but by her rival, the stepmother. Indeed, there is much of Tsvetaeva herself in *both* these female figures contending for the gentle Tsarevich. They represent the two contending forces in Tsvetaeva's poetics of 1917-1920: the Spartan/Amazonian (soul, duty) and the passionate (Eros, the flesh).

Contention between soul and body continued to characterize Tsvetaeva's relationships with men. Her friend Vera Zviagintseva gave a candid recollection of Tsvetaeva's romance with Valery M. Bebutov (1885–1961), an assistant to the theatrical director Meyerhold. Bebutov was then paying court to Zviagintseva (who was happily married, but the mores of that circle were exceedingly "liberated"). Shortly after they met, both stayed the night after an evening at Zviagintseva's, camping out in the dining room:

> When I went out into the dining room during the night for matches, they were already lying "in position." She was lying on top of him and casting a spell with words. She often said that her chief passion was conversation. But physical romances were essential, for only in that way could you penetrate a man's soul."[17]

At roughly the same time (summer and fall of 1920) Tsvetaeva was, according to Zviagintseva, also involved with Vladimir M. Volkenstein (1882–1974),[18] a playwright and theoretician of drama. The ironies here were manifold, for in 1908, Volkenstein had briefly been married to Sofia Parnok. Volkenstein played a role in one of the stranger episodes of Tsvetaeva's biography, which occured a year later, in November, 1921. As Tsvetaeva tells the story, she had gone with him to the Kremlin to ask Lunacharsky to help the writers in the Crimea near starvation after the Bolshevik takeover. Tsvetaeva was particularly concerned about Max, Volkenstein about his former wife. As Tsvetaeva wrote out their petition, Volkenstein watched over her shoulder and prompted, "Sonya! Don't forget Sonya!" Tsvetaeva replied, "Damn it! For me, Max is more important." "But Sof'ia Yakovlevna is a woman and my former wife." "But Max is also a woman and my real (indicatif present) friend."[19] Tsvetaeva's "Max is a woman" was half-playful, half ideological.

Tsvetaeva had met Anatolii Lunacharsky (1875–1933), the People's Commisar of Enlightenment (i.e. the cultural commisar) when they both read their plays at the Palace of Arts in the summer of 1919. She liked and respected him, though their politics differed radically. Lunacharsky, to his credit, used his position to help Tsvetaeva whenever he could. She showed her gratitude in a poem which began, "Your banners are not mine:"

Твои победы — не мои!	Your victories are not mine!
Иные грезились.	I dreamed of others.
Мы не на двух концах земли —	We're not at two ends of the earth—
На двух созвездиях!	But in different constellations!

November 26, 1920

(II, 294)

In early November, 1920, the Red Army took the Crimea, the last refuge of the Whites. With Lunacharsky's help, Tsvetaeva sent a telegram to Voloshin in Koktebel' with one burning question: was Sergei still alive? All the Voloshins knew was that he had been alive as late as early fall. Tsvetaeva continued in a state of fearful uncertainty until she had definite news in July, 1921.

The occupation of the Crimea ended the Civil War and the White campaign, while it brought a last breath of life to *Swans' Encampment*. Tsvetaeva lamented the defeat in several poems whose diction consciously imitated that of Russia's first epic, the Igor' Tale. Despite her sympathy for the Whites, Tsvetaeva saw the senselessness of slaughter, and imagined the field of battle, where white and red were indistinguishable in death:

Все рядком лежат —	All lie side by side—
Не развесть межой.	You can't divorce them with a boundary.
Поглядеть: солдат.	You look: a soldier.
Где свой, где чужой?	Where's yours, where's theirs?
Белый был — красным стал:	He was white, he's turned red:
Кровь обагрила.	Blood turned him crimson.
Красным был — белый стал:	He was red—he's turned white:
Смерть побелила.	Death has made him pale.

December 1920

(II, 89)

Her New Year poem for 1921 saluted the White Army in its new metamorphosis—the White emigration.

С Новым Годом, Лебединый стан!	Happy New Year, Swans' Encampment!
Славные обломки!	Glorious remnants!
С Новым Годом — по чужим местам —	Happy New Year, in alien lands,
Воины с котомкой!	Warriors with a knapsack.

January 13, 1921
(II, 91)

She was more and more certain that she would soon join them. But meanwhile, she was afraid to leave Moscow, for it was the only place Sergei, if he were still alive, would know where to look for her.

CHAPTER FOURTEEN

Retreat from Eros: (1921–1922)

In terms of *byt*, Tsvetaeva's life changed little between the end of 1920 and her emigration in May, 1922. The major change was the end of the Civil War: Soviet power was there to stay, at least for the immediately foreseeable future, and it was a world Tsvetaeva could write neither for nor about. In this psychological limbo, she wrote *Craft*, (in the sense of "vocation") a book whose focus is often the historical Russia of the distant past. Like her fascination with eighteenth-century France in 1918–1919, it was not an attempt to escape the present, but rather to come to terms with it through history.

There is a greater difference between the poems of 1917–1920 and the poems of *Craft* than between any other two stages of her poetic development. This is not to say there are no continuities, for there are many. But there is a new complexity, a new elliptic ambiguity that Margaret Troupin called "a condensation of imagery."[1] Viktoria Schweitzer pointed out the strengthened influence of the Russian folk tradition on her rhythms, syntax, and lexicon.[2] Tsvetaeva pared down her syntax to the essentials—or beyond. One new characteristic was the avoidance of verbs, which she replaced with verbal nouns or instrumental case phrases. Verblessness reflected a distancing of the "I" as her poetic persona became more abstract, sometimes vanishing altogether.

Tsvetaeva herself was well aware of the change in her poetics, though she preferred to stress continuity:

> *Craft*, of course, marks a break, no, not a break, but a bend in the river, or perhaps the *unbending* of my poetic vein. There were never any breaks in my life. The process was that of forests and rivers: growth, perhaps? (June 4, 1934)[3]

It was at this point that many of Tsvetaeva's contemporaries who admired her earlier work began to find her new poetry difficult or inaccessible. This meant most of the reading public of the emigration. Ironically, Tsvetaeva emigrated just as her 1916–1920 poems were becoming widely available in both Moscow and Berlin editions, and she arrived in the West much-lionized. But *Craft* was received coldly by the emigre public when it appeared in Berlin in early 1923. Tsvetaeva was bitter about their desertion:

> No one who knew me at twenty will say to me, at thirty: "How much prettier you've become." At thirty I may have become more defined, more striking, more distinctive, even more beautiful, perhaps. But prettier—no. It's the same

with poetry as it is with facial features. Poems don't become prettier with time. Freshness, spontaneity, accessibility, the *beaute du diable* of the poetic personality—all yield to clearly defined features. "You used to write better"— how often I've heard that! It means only that the reader prefers my *beaute du diable* to my essence. . . .[4]

The title, which seems more appropriate for a craftsmanlike Acmeist than for the spontaneous Tsvetaeva, was bestowed with a touch of irony, as its sub-text (a poem by Karolina Pavlova) reveals:

Ты, уцелевший в сердце нищем,	Thou who survived intact in a beggared heart,
Привет тебе, мой грустный стих!	Greeting to thee, my mournful verse!
Мой светлый луч над пепелищем	My bright ray above the ashheap
Блаженств и радостей моих!	Of all my happiness and bliss.
Одно, чего и святотатство	The one thing in the temple
Коснуться в храме не могло;	Which sacrilege could never touch;
Моя напасть! мое богатство!	My misfortune! My wealth!
Мое святое ремесло!	My holy craft![5]

Yet this volume does mark the beginning of a more disciplined, less personal poetics. The emphasis shifted from the ongoing diary to lyric cycles, which tend to be organized thematically rather than simply by the unity of addressee.

As significant as the new poetics was the shift in the persona's self-image. The renunciation of Eros and femininity, the martial, spartan, Amazonian themes which began to appear in the poems of 1920 now became dominant. The powerful, yet puzzling *poema* "On a Red Steed" is both a declaration and demonstration of Tsvetaeva's new bend in the river, written in the first four days of the new year (by the old calendar, of course!) in her new elliptic style. Tsvetaeva now identified as her guiding spirit not the feminine muse, but a stern male figure in armor, mounted on a red steed—both the winged Pegasus, ancient symbol of poetic inspiration, and the red steed of Russian icons. Her Genius is a harsh mentor, who demands that the persona "liberate love" first by sacrificing her doll, then by renouncing her beloved, her son, and even Christ.[6] She is finally claimed by her genius who *desires her for what she is*, with an androgynous fraternal passion:

И шепот: Такой я тебя желал!	And a whisper: It is thus I desired you!
И рокот: Такой я тебя избрал,	And a roar: It is thus that I chose you,
Дитя моей страсти — сестра — брат —	Child of my passion—sister—brother—
Невеста во льду — лат!	Bride in the ice of the armor.

(IV, 159)

She gives him her vow to be "No one else's," in other words, she renounces Love for the sake of Poetry.

Tsvetaeva broke new ground in this unconventional relationship with her masculine Genius. The classical image of inspiration as a beautiful, ladylike (and, in Russian, grammatically feminine) Muse who visits the (invariably male) poet and somehow merges with his beloved was understandably problematic for a woman poet. Akhmatova adapted the muse to her own uses by making her into a *"muza-sestra,"* a second self often glimpsed in a mirror. Tsvetaeva rejected her entirely:

Не Муза, не Муза	Not the muse, not the muse
Над бедною люлькой	Sang over my poor cradle
Мне пела, за ручку водила.	And led me the hand.
Не Муза холодные руки мне грела,	Not the muse warmed my cold hands,
Горячие веки студила.	And cooled my burning cheeks.
Вихор ото лба отводила — не Муза,	Not the muse brushed a lock off my forehead,
В большие поля уводила — не Муза.	And led me to the wide fields.
Не Муза, не черные косы, не бусы,	Not the muse, not black braids, not beads.
Не басни, — всего два крыла светлорусых	Not fables, just two short light-brown wings—
— Коротких — над бровью крылатой.	Above a winged brow.
Стан в латах.	A figure in armor.
Султан.	A sultan.
К устам не клонился,	He did not bend over to my lips
На сон не крестил.	Nor bless my dreams.
О сломанной кукле	Nor mourn with me
Со мной не грустил.	For my broken doll.
Всех птиц моих — на свободу	He set free all my birds—
Пускал — и потом — не жалея шпор,	And then—not sparing the spurs
На красном коне — промеж синих гор	He took me on a red steed—between the blue mountains
Гремящего ледохода!	Of a thundering ice flow.

(IV, 155)

Many of the images in this passage, as in the *poema* as a whole, remain to be decoded. But I agree with Karlinsky that she clearly refers here to Akhmatova.[7] "Black braids and beads" suggest Akhmatova's dark beauty; in fact, the passage polemicizes with a specific subtext, a 1914 Akhmatova poem, "It Was my Blessed Cradle"[8] which concentrates all the elements from which Tsvetaeva asserted her difference: Petersburg as "blessed cradle," "marriage bed," cathedral, place of first meeting with the "fiance," and, most important, the place where her "sad muse" leads her by the hand. The repudiation of the female Muse signaled Tsvetaeva's abandonment of "female lyricism" and her final overcoming of its supreme Russian practitioner, Anna Akhmatova. "Muse," not accidentally, was the title Tsvetaeva gave her Akhmatova cycle when she published it for the second time in *Psyche* (1923), a collection which also included "On a Red Steed" ("Not the Muse, not the Muse . . .")

Margaret Troupin assumed that so sudden a stylistic change must result from a new literary influence, as she attributed the leap between *Juvenilia* and *Versts I* to Tsvetaeva's discovery of Afanas'ev's folk tale collection or that between *Craft* and *After Russia* to Pasternak's *My Sister Life*. There is certainly much to be said for such an hypothesis, but Troupin then goes on to identify this influence as Mayakovsky, basing her claim largely on the passage in "On a Red Steed" in which Tsvetaeva obviously (and, I think, largely playfully) uses Mayakovsky's famous cardiac conflagration (see Chapter 9 above) as subtext:

Пожарные! — Широкий крик!	Firemen!—a Large-scale cry!
Как зарево широкий — крик!	Like a large-scale glow—the cry!
Пожарные! — Душа горит!	Firemen! A soul's on fire!
Не наш ли дом горит?!	Is it not our house on fire?

(IV, 155)

It is true that Tsvetaeva admired and respected Mayakovsky, despite their political and artistic differences, and their mutual influence does deserve further study.[9] But it is difficult to equate the loud-mouthed Mayakovsky of Tsvetaeva's other poems with the stern icy genius of "On a Red Steed." A far more likely candidate, Ariadna Efron claimed, is the Alexander Blok of Tsvetaeva's myth.

> In the *poema* "On a Red Steed," encoded with a dedication to Anna Akhmatova, later removed, appears the complex image, dynamic in its iconography, of Blok, the creator of "The Twelve," the St. George of the Revolution, the purest and most intrepid genius of poetry, inhabitant of those creative heights which Tsvetaeva considered unattainable for her.[10]

Blok's "The Twelve" did make a profound impact on Tsvetaeva. He had moved beyond the lyric to capture the "music of the Revolution" and become a prophet of Russia's fate, an achievement that was a model for her own efforts to move out beyond the intimate lyric diary. I prefer to see the immediate impetus, however, as a negative one, and the dedication to Akhmatova not as an encoded dedication to Blok, but as an impudent declaration of victory over the vanquished Akhmatova and her feminine muse. In December, 1920, Tsvetaeva was given a copy of Akhmatova's 1917 *White Flock* by her new friend, Evgeny Lann. Though we know she had read the book soon after it appeared, his gift and her gratitude for it imply that she had not owned it, and had not looked at it for some time.[11] A re-reading of *White Flock* in 1920 could only have confirmed Tsvetaeva's first impression that Akhmatova's voice, this "difficult and seductive gift for poets," perfect as it was, had developed little since its first appearance. Akhmatova (or so it looked in 1921) was proving herself to be a "poet without a history," while Tsvetaeva was well aware of her own rapid and many-sided development.

There was one more important event in late 1920: Tsvetaeva's brief but intense friendship with Evgeny Lann (pseudonym of E.L. Lozman, 1896–1958). Trained as a lawyer, Lann was then an aspiring poet; he later became a successful novelist, critic, and translator of English literature.[12] None of

Lann's poetry was ever published, so we cannot assess the possibility of his influence on Tsvetaeva. But it is doubtful that a poet of her maturity could have been so strongly influenced by such an unlikely source. Tsvetaeva told Lann frankly that she found his gift alien, and later regretted that he had read her so few of his poems. But the man himself did have profound importance for her, she claimed:

> About one thing I've managed neither to write nor tell you—and this is important! About the huge creative uplift from my meeting with you. I don't promise anything—for you need nothing—but I simply tell you: that which came down to me from you (I speak as if of a mountain!) will proclaim itself as something different, and in a different way than all that came before. Thank you! Creatively![13]

This less than three weeks before she wrote "On a Red Steed." Tsvetaeva later wrote Lann that the poem was a way of overcoming *him* (not as poet, but as man). Her letters imply that she had fallen in love, a love which Lann, happily married to another, answered only with friendship and admiration. This could well explain the puzzling passage in "On a Red Steed" in which Tsvetaeva fights on a symbolic battlefield (representing love?). It begins:

Не любит! — Не надо мне женских кос!	He doesn't love me! I don't need woman's
Не любит! — Не надо мне красных бус!	braids!
Не любит! — Так я на коня вздымусь!	He doesn't love me! I don't need red beads!
Не любит! — Вздымусь — до неба!	He doesn't love me! Then I'll rise onto my steed
	He doesn't love me! I'll rise—to heaven!
	(IV, 158)

It is immediately after the battle that, wounded, she is claimed by her Genius. It is perfectly consistent to read "On a Red Steed" as an overcoming of *both* Lann and Akhmatova: Tsvetaeva renounced both the traditional formal love lyric and the passive role of Akhmatova's personae, abandoned by men who do not love them. Instead, Tsvetaeva will "leap onto Pegasus" to follow her martial, non-erotic Genius.

Tsvetaeva's infatuation with Lann in no way prevented her from sharing with him her hopes and concerns about Sergei's fate. Nor did it prevent her from giving him, in that very same letter, an amazingly detailed and candid account of her next romantic involvement, an affair in which both her predilection for younger men and her disdain for politics reached new heights. Its hero was Boris Bessarabov (1903–1970?), a strapping young Communist, eighteen years old and fresh from the Crimean front, where he had, perhaps, faced her own Sergei across a battlefield. Tsvetaeva was attracted by his innocence, glowing health, and fondness for her poetry. She depicted him as a kind of Communist saint or holy fool, meekly and willingly chopping wood and hauling water for a whole circle of her acquaintances among the intelligentsia. She declared him "the perfect match for my Tsar-Maiden" and made him the prototype for her next folk-tale *poema*, "Egorushka," based on folk motifs about the life of Egory the Brave (a.k.a. St. George),[14] well as a poem titled "Bolshevik:"

От Ильменя — до вод Каспийских	From the Ilmen' to the Caspian waters
Плеча рванулись в ширь.	His shoulders stretch out wide.
	January 31, 1921
	(II, 297)

They spent long nights together copying over the *The Tsar-Maiden*, clearly an emblematic work for their relationship:

> "I'm sorry for the Tsarevich. Why did he keep sleeping?"
> "And the stepmother—are you sorry for her?"
> "No. The stepmother is a bad woman."[15]

Tsvetaeva's sympathies were obviously with the stepmother. The relationship never went beyond an adolescent level of semi-innocent sexuality thanks, evidently, more to Bessarabov's fortitude than Tsvetaeva's restraint. She described, in a tone at once witty and detached and teasingly erotic, the first night Bessarabov spent at her apartment (their third meeting). It progressed from a reading of *Tsar-Maiden* to his timidly respectful request to stroke her head, to her invitation to join her on the bed:

> "If you were a little boy, a child, I would simply-simply take you in to me—under my wing, and we would lie and amuse ourselves innocently."
>
> "Marina Ivanovna, believe me, I want that so much."
>
> "But you are a grown-up!"
>
> "Marina Ivanovna, I'm only so grown-up in size. I give you my word of honor as a party member. . . ."[16]

Tsvetaeva's account, though undoubtedly autobiographical, could be published as a short story. She deftly captures Bessarabov's combination of naivete and Soviet jargon:

> . . . For how many nights now,—the youth is steadfast, my bones crunch—lips touch lightly—we amuse ourselves, babble nonsense, talk about Russia, and it is all just as both he and I need it to be.
>
> Sometimes, growing weary from tenderness, I say, "Boris! Perhaps . . . ?"
>
> "No. Marina Ivanovna!—Marinochka! We mustn't!—I respect women so much, particularly you—you are a woman with professional qualification (*kvalifitsirovannaia zhenshchina*)—I've come to love you very very much—you remind me of my mom—and most of all, you'll soon be leaving, you have such a hard life—and I want you to remember me *fondly*!"[17]

But this Bolshevik innocent was a rare exception; her alienation to the new order intensified. She took little part in the public readings which, in these years of paper shortage, constituted literary life, for her old nemesis, Briusov, was in charge of most. She did reluctantly agree to take part in an "Evening of Poetesses" he organized. Such a sideshow would never have been to her liking; now it was even more inappropriate given the current tenor of her art. But Briusov, who loved to divide poets into schools and rubrics, would have it this way. She later gave a devastating description of her fellow poetesses, all of them gussied up as best they could manage in these first months of return to "normality." Tsvetaeva, in stark contrast, was dressed in her usual outfit, adorned with remnants of Sergei's ensign's uniform. Briusov gave an introduction: "Woman, Love. Passion. Woman, from the beginning of the ages, has known how to sing only about love and passion."[18] Tsvetaeva responded by reading seven poems from *Swans' Encampment*, "seven female poems without love or the pronoun I." Somehow, she got away with it—either because of Briusov's sponsorship ("le pavillon couvre la marchandise") or because, as she suspected, the public really didn't understand a word of the pro-White poems they applauded.

In her increasing spiritual isolation, she grew close to Prince Sergei Volkonsky, who shared both her disdain for the new Soviet values and her plans for emigration. Volkonsky, a courtly, elegant gentleman of sixty, was the grandson of a Decembrist (those aristocrat-rebels against the Tsar who were exiled to Siberia after their abortive rebellion in 1825). Like Tsvetaeva, he was a staunch defender of principle.[19] Volkonsky was also homosexual, though very discreet about it in his aristocratic fashion.

They met in the fall of 1920 at Zviagintseva's.

> He asked, 'Who is that lady with such an interesting expressive mouth?' She left, and then she went off her head about him. If she stayed the night at my house, she'd wake me up in the middle of the night and say, 'Verochka, wake up. I want to talk about Volkonsky . . .' She just died for the fact that he was a prince. Well, a Decembrist, and a prince—she adored that business . . ."[20]

As he awaited permission to emigrate, Volkonsky wrote his memoirs, in three volumes.[21] Tsvetaeva spent much of her time that winter copying over the text for him in longhand, an act of both friendship and humility. Having declared her independence of the feminine muse, and though herself now a master poet, Tsvetaeva chose to sit, symbolically, at the feet of a new mentor. "The Disciple," the first of the thirteen cycles which give shape to *Craft*, was privately (she did not want to embarrass him) dedicated to Volkonsky, who exemplified for her what was finest in the Russia of the past. Her imagery and diction in the cycle intentionally suggest the ultimate mentor, Christ himself. Themes of martyrdom run through the poems: it is surely no coincidence that the cycle was written during the Easter season.

Tsvetaeva's loyalty to her mentor transcends sex-roles or physical gender, as she seeks to protect him from the insults and attacks of the mob:

Быть мальчиком твоим светлоголовым,	To be your bright-haired boy,
— О, через все века! —	Oh, through all the ages!—
За пыльным пурпуром твоим брести в	To wander behind your dusty purple
суровом	In the severe cape of the disciple.
Плаще ученика.	

Быть между спящими учениками	To be among the sleeping disciples
Тем, кто во сне — не спит.	He who in his sleep—does not slumber.
При первом чернью занесенном камне	At the first stone cast by the mob
Уже не плащ — а щит!	No longer a cape, but a shield.

April 15, 1921
(II, 95)

Given Volkonsky's sexual preference, as well as her own gender, the first line is doubly ironic. Secure in the knowledge of her own poetic mastery, Tsvetaeva praises the moment of discipleship as a Dostoevskian triumph of humility (a traditional theme in Russian Orthodoxy):

Есть некий час — как сброшенная клажа:	There is a certain hour—like a burden cast off:
Когда в себе гордыню укротим.	When we humble the arrogance in ourselves.
Час ученичества, он в жизни каждой	The hour of discipleship—in every life
Торжественно-неотвратим.	It is solemnly inevitable.

April 15, 1921
(II, 96)

The three central poems of the cycle are different views—in the second, third, and first person—of the same symbolic scene: mentor and disciple, covered by a single cloak, stand on a hill watching the sunset and rejoicing in the coming of the night. On one level, of course, this is "Russia's night" in historical terms. The poems should also be read in the context of the Orthodox Easter service, in which the alternation of dark and light play such a central role. The sixth poem is a psalm of praise. With its capitalized "Thou," the reader is not clear whether the adored one is Volkonsky or God himself. Tsvetaeva's ambiguity was intentional:

Все великолепье	All the splendor of trumpets
Труб — лишь только лепет	Is but a babble
Трав — перед Тобой.	of grasses—Before Thee.

Все великолепье	All the splendor of tempests
Бурь — лишь только щебет	Is but a twitter
Птиц — перед Тобой.	of birds—before Thee.

Все великолепье	All the splendor of wings
Крыл — лишь только трепет	Is but a quiver
Век — перед Тобой.	of eyelids—before Thee.

April 23, 1921
(II, 98)

"The Disciple" represents in her poetic biography the overcoming of Romanticism and introduces the new asceticism of *Craft* and *After Russia*.

Just as she was deifying a new mentor, Tsvetaeva finally entered into a (tenuous) real-world contact with the idol she had just overcome, Anna Akhmatova. Sometime after their composition in 1916, we do not know exactly when, Tsvetaeva had sent her a manuscript copy of the "Poems to Akhmatova" (they were not published until 1922). Akhmatova, Tsvetaeva claims, carried that manuscript around in her purse until it disintegrated,[22] but she responded either briefly or not at all. Letters were not for Akhmatova the literary genre they were for Tsvetaeva.

In the early spring of 1921, Akhmatova's fourth book of poetry, *Plantain* (*Podorozhnik*) appeared, a slender collection of poems, some written since 1917, some from earlier periods. Tsvetaeva wrote Akhmatova that it was "the latest joy in my life," and sent her copies of *White Flock* and *Rosary* for inscriptions. Yet some of her exclamations could be read as left-handed praise, an accusation of creative barrenness: "How glad I am for all three of them, so defenseless and small: *Rosary—White Flock—Plantain*. What a light burden to carry with one! Almost a handful of ash."[23] Her letter also contained a seemingly collegial request: would Akhmatova be willing to proofread "On a Red Steed," which a Petrograd publisher was considering, in case the galleys appeared after Tsvetaeva emigrated? In fact, it never came to that—"On a Red Steed" was first published in Berlin—but Tsvetaeva's very idea, to have Akhmatova proofread the work which, though dedicated to her, explicitly rejected her as a muse, is bizarre indeed. Perhaps it was her way of making sure Akhmatova read it.

Suddenly, Tsvetaeva's letter became a flood of adulation and praise:

> Oh, how I love you, how I rejoice in you, how much pain I feel for you, and how uplifted I feel on account of you. . .You are my favorite poet—once, six years ago, I dreamed of you. . . .It grieves me that this is only words—"love" —I cannot have it this way—I would rather a real bonfire, in which I would be burned at the stake.[24]
>
> May 9, 1921

The bonfire was an important motif in Tsvetaeva's writing at this period. We know she was planning a major work on Joan of Arc, who suited her preoccupation with female warriors. She had recently ended the first poem of "The Disciple" with the lines:

| И — вдохновенно улыбнувшись — первым | And, smiling insolently, to be the first |
| Взойти на твой костр. | To mount your bonfire. |

April 15
(II, 95)

The same bonfire pointedly links the letter to Akhmatova with a poem written the very next day:

Душа, не знающая меры,
Душа хлыста и изувера,
Тоскующая по бичу.
Душа — навстречу палачу,
Как бабочка из хризалиды!
Душа, не съевшая обиды,
Что больше колдунов не жгут.
Как смоляной высокий жгут
Дымящая под власняницей. . .
Скрежещущая еретица,
— Саванароловой сестра —
Душа, достойная костра!

A soul which knows no moderation,
A flagellant, fanatic soul,
Craving the whip.
Rushing headlong to meet its executioner,
Like a butterfly from its chrysalis.
A soul which cannot swallow its offense
That wizards are no longer burned.
Like a tall, resinous wick
Smoking beneath a hairshirt . . .
A heretic, gritting her teeth,
—Savonarola's sister—
A soul worthy of the bonfire![25]

May 10

(II, 101)

It is a revealing self-flagellation, in which Tsvetaeva berates herself for the emotional excesses and contradictory emotions of her letter, a mixture of praise and back-biting.

In late May, 1921, Anastasia Tsvetaeva, toothless from scurvy, returned to Moscow from the Crimea. Anastasia's memoirs barely conceal the disillusionment this reunion brought to both sisters. After the first ecstatic days and nights of conversation, it became clear that the two could not live and raise their children in one household. If Marina cared only for *byt'ie*, Anastasia had become adept at attending to *byt*. Tsvetaeva's apparent neglect of Alya and the apartment annoyed her, and she annoyed Marina, who soon found her another place to live. The sisters' lack of rapport after years of separation could only have reminded her of the problems that might arise from her reunion with Sergei—if it ever came to be.

The next three cycles of *Craft*, "Separation," "Georgii," and "Annunciation," form a poetic triptych dedicated to Efron. "Separation" (*Razulka*) begins on a contradictory note—the cry of a longing wife couched in a strong, muscular, "masculine" verse form.

Башенный бой
Где-то в Кремле.
Где на земле,
Где —

Крепость моя,
Кротость моя,
Доблесть моя,
Святость моя.

Башенный бой.
Брошенный бой.
Где на земле —
Мой
Дом,
Мой — сон,
Мой — смех,

The peal of towers
Somewhere in the Kremlin.
Where on earth,
Where is—
My fortress,
My meekness,
My valor,
My saintliness.

A peal of towers.
An abandoned peal.
Where on earth—
Is my
Home,
My—dream,

Мой — свет,	My—light,
Узких подошв — след.	The trace of narrow soles.
Точно рукой	A peal—as if cast
Сброшенный в ночь —	By a hand into
Бой.	The night.
— Брошенный мой!	—My abandoned one!

May/June 1921

(II, 105-106)

Sergei combines three traditional qualities of a saint in a medieval icon: meekness, valor, saintliness. She yearns to leap out of the "black, empty" window into space, to go "home," "head first from the tower." But this leap, she hastens to explain, will not be suicide, "crashing down against the cobblestones of the square." No: "A certain young Warrior/Will cushion me with his wing." Sergei, as a winged angel, will appear from his other world to save her as she falls, and presumably carry her off "home" to "that other world" for which she so often yearned. Tsvetaeva's predicament is the more maddening, for she does not know if their separation is temporal or eternal. In seeking to cope with the second possibility, she argues that the gods are jealous of too-perfect earthly love, and of the beauty of her beloved, so they have stolen him away, as Zeus stole Gaynemede. The cycle's final poem is both a cry of despair at human powerlessness and a rebellious attack on heaven:

Я знаю, я знаю,	I know, I know,
Что прелесть земная,	That earthly delight,
Что эта резная,	This carved
Прелестная чаша —	And charming cup—
Не более наша,	Is no more ours
Чем воздух,	Than the air,
Чем звезды,	Than the stars,
Чем гнезда,	Than nests
Повисшие в зорях.	Which hang in the sunrise.
Я знаю, я знаю	I know, I know
Кто чаше — хозяин!	That the cup has a master!
Но легкую ногу вперед — башней	But with a light foot forward—like a tower
В орлиную высь!	Into the eagle height!
И крылом — чашу	And with a wing—sweep
От грозных и розовых уст —	The cup from the threatening and rosy lips
Бога!	Of God!

June 30, 1921

(II, 110)

Tsvetaeva's challenge to the gods was not merely metaphorical. With the Civil War over, travel to some parts of Europe was easier for those with Soviet passports. The writer Ilya Ehrenburg, habitue of pre-war Paris cafes, was one of the first to go (on assignment as a Soviet journalist) and Tsvetaeva asked him to look for Sergei. She gave him letters from herself and Alya, photographs, and her latest poems. While Ehrenburg searched, Tsvetaeva continued her idealization of Sergei in the cycle "Georgii," which equates her innocent knight with St. George. The first poem has the static, descriptive quality of a verbal icon.

Ресницы, ресницы,	Eyelashes, eyelashes,
Склоненные ниц.	Cast down.
Стыдливостию ресниц	Eclipsed by the bashfulness of lashes—
Затменные — солнца в венце стрел!	Suns in a crown of arrows!
— Сколь грозен и сколь ясен! —	How menacing and how clear!
И плащ его — был — красен,	And his cape was red,
И конь его — был — бел.	And his steed was white.

July 9, 1921
(II, 112)

Her St. George is a hero who cannot bear the burden of his victory, the paradoxical figure of a gentle, humble, shy warrior, who "pales like a beautiful maiden" at the sight of the dragon he has slain, and is embarrassed by the "premarital passion" of his prize—the Tsar's daughter; he has much in common with the shy hero of *Tsar-Maiden*. The final poem of the cycle is nothing less than a prayer to her iconic saint by the sinning wife he has redeemed:

О лотос мой!	Oh, my lotus!
Лебедь мой!	My swan!
Лебедь! Олень мой!	Swan! My deer!
Ты — все мои бденья	Thou art all my vigils
И все сновиденья!	And all my dreams!
Пасхальный тропарь мой!	My Easter anthem!
Последний алтын мой!	My last penny!
Ты, больше чем Царь мой,	Thou art more than my Tsar,
И больше, чем сын мой!	And more than my son!
Лазурное око мое —	My azure eye—
В вышину!	To the heights!
Ты, блудную снова	Thou hast again
Вознесший жену.	Uplifted thy prodigal wife.
— Так слушай же! . .	—So heed! . . .

July 14, 1921
(II, 118-119)

The poem breaks off and is followed by the note, "(not finished because of the letter)." Ehrenburg had found Sergei in Prague, where he was preparing to enroll in the Russian university in exile set up with the help of the Masaryk government.

Efron's letter is that of a man deeply shaken by the ordeal of the last four years, whose only links to life were his wife and daughter:

> What shall I write to you? Where shall I begin? There is much that needs to be said, but I have forgotten not only how to write, but how to speak. I live by faith in our meeting.
>
> There will be no life for me without you—you must live! I will ask nothing of you, I need nothing, except the fact that you are alive.
>
> Our meeting was a great miracle, and an even greater miracle will be our coming meeting . . .[26]

Marina answered:

> My Seryozhenka! If people don't die of happiness, then at least they turn to stone. . . .I don't know how to begin—I know how to begin, with that with which I will end: my love for you . . .[27]

and began the third cycle of the triptych, "Annunciation."

Жив и здоров!	Alive and well!
Громче громов —	Louder than thunder—
Как топором —	As with an axe—
Радость!	Joy!
Нет, топором	No, with an axe
Мало: быком	Is too little: like a bull,
Под обухом	Under the axe head
Счастья!	Of happiness.

July 16, 1921
(II, 120)

Strangely, the very image of her joy is mixed with pain (the axe): she feared that "they," the Greek gods of "Separation," would extract some terrible price in return for his salvation. On August 7, hardly a month after she received the letter from Sergei, Alexander Blok died in Petrograd. Tsvetaeva may have seen his death as the retribution she expected for Sergei's "resurrection."

One by one her ties with contemporary Russia were breaking, even as she continued to live within it. Her cycle "In the Khan's Captivity" compared Russia's captivity by the Bolsheviks to the darkest period in Russian history, the Mongol yoke. The persona of the first two poems is a maiden—both Russia and Tsvetaeva herself—fleeing from Tartar captivity. The cycle's language is the highly rhythmic, short-lined style of Tsvetaeva's folk-tale poems:

Ханский полон	Having tasted my fill
Вò сласть изведав,	Of the Khan's captivity,
Бью крылом	I pay homage
Богу побегов.	To the god of escapes.

Спорый бог,	Successful god,
Скорый бог,	Rapid god,
Шпоры в бок-бог!	Spurs-in-the-flank-god!

October 1, 1922
(II, 127)

She flees, of course, on her by now familiar swift steed. The "God of flight"—her imagination and her art—is the only escape open to her at the moment, though she would join Sergei in emigration as soon as she could. There is surely a political statement in the lines, "I've had enough/ Of gnawing horses' bones/ With the Tartars!" She has had enough, that is, of the Bolshevik decimation of poetry. Rejecting the amorous advances of the Khan himself, her persona asks her magic carpet to carry her "to the camp of the angels"—that is, to the remnants of the White Army in emigration.

All Tsvetaeva's October 1921 poems deal in one way or another with transition. A week after her 29th birthday, she wrote of a snake throwing off its old skin and lying in wait for the new, cleaner, purer one to harden. (II, 135). In the cycle "Praise to Aphrodite," the title is bitterly ironic:

Блаженны дочерей твоих, Земля,	Blessed are those, O Earth who have
Бросавшие для боя и для бега.	Renounced your daughters for battle and flight.
Блаженны в Елисейские поля	Blessed they who have entered the Elysian fields,
Вступившие, не обольстившись негой.	Not seduced by voluptuousness.

Так лавр растет, — жестоколист и трезв,	Thus grows the laurel, sharp-leaved and sober—
Лавр-летописец, горячитель боя.	The laurel—chronicler, instigator of battle.
— Содружества заоблачный отвес	I will not exchange concord's slope beyond the clouds
Не променяю на юдоль любови.	For the valley of love.

October 17, 1921
(II, 132)

Personifying her youth as a swarthy dancer with a raspberry-colored skirt—the sensual, female muse of her gypsy poems—she haughtily bid her farewell: "My Youth! I'll not call you back,/ You were only a burden to me." (II, 135)

These poems were a psychological preparation for her reunion with Sergei, to whom her attitude was one of loyalty rather than passion. She confided her thoughts about emigration to Voloshin:

It's my last gamble. If I still want to live here [evidently, on this earth—JT], then it's because of S. and Alya. . . .But I must see Sergei, simply to enter the room, so he sees me, so I see him. "Instead of a son"—That's how I would call it.[28]

She wondered how Sergei would react to the changes in her over these five eventful years. In summing them up, she spoke as much of her poetic voice as of her physical appearance:

С. Э.   S.E.

Не похорошела за годы разлуки!
Не будешь сердиться на грубые руки,
Хватающиеся за хлеб и за соль?
— Товарищества трудовая мозоль!

I've not grown prettier in the years of
  separation!
You won't be angry at my coarse hands,
Grasping for bread and salt?
—The hard-earned callous of comradeship!

О, не прихорашивается для встречи
Любовь. — Не прогневайся на просторечье
Речей — не советовала б пренебречь:
То летописи огнестрельная речь.

Oh, you can't spruce up love for reunion!—
Don't be angry at the commonness of my
  speech,—
I'd advise you not to scorn it:
It's the chronicle's firearm speech.

Разочаровался? Скажи без боязни!
То — выкорчеванный от дружб и приязней
Дух. — В путаницу якорей и надежд
Прозрения непоправимая брешь!

Disillusioned? Don't be afraid to say!
That's my spirit, purged of friendships and
  hatreds
In the muddle of anchors and hopes
The incorrigible flaw of insight!
January 23, 1922
(II, 152)

Tatiana Scriabina, widow of the composer, was one of Tsvetaeva's few close female friends in the last two Moscow years. Her funeral in April, 1922 symbolized the final burial of Tsvetaeva's Moscow life. A month later, on May 24, 1922, Tsvetaeva boarded a train for Berlin with Alya and a few carefully-packed bags. She hardly suspected that a casual acquaintance she encountered at Scriabina's graveside would become the dominant presence (dominant *absence* is more accurate) in her life and art for the next ten years. That acquaintance was a former composition student of Scriabin's just beginning to receive wide recognition for his poetry. His name was Boris Pasternak.

CHAPTER FIFTEEN

Berlin (May–July, 1922)

The Berlin Tsvetaeva found in May 1922, a city glittering with the brilliance of Weimar culture, was very different from the wounded and hungry Moscow she had just left. It was the center of emigre literary life. Germany was then one of the few European countries to recognize Soviet Russia, one of the few places to which Russians with Soviet passports could travel and return fairly freely. Many Russian writers who later decided to return home, such as Ehrenburg, Viktor Shklovsky, Alexey Tolstoy, and Andrey Bely, were there in the early twenties. Soviet authors routinely published their works in Berlin as well as Moscow to establish international copyright. Russian publishers and booksellers flourished for a few brief years until chaotic inflation of the mark shifted the emigre literary center to Paris.

One of Tsvetaeva's first encounters in Berlin was with the mercurial and impractical Bely. She had known him slightly, through Ellis, in 1910. Now, reeling from his separation from his wife Asya, Bely was agonizing over whether to return to Russia. The day after her arrival, Tsvetaeva and Bely found themselves together at a table in the Praegerdeile cafe, a favorite meeting-place of Russian literati. Bely, the son of Professor Bugaev, saw a kindred soul in the daughter of Professor Tsvetaev, and sought her advice about life in Moscow. That night, someone lent him a copy of *Separation*, the little volume containing that cycle and "On a Red Steed," which had been published in Berlin, under Ehrenburg's aegis, in January. The next morning, Tsvetaeva received an ecstatic letter:

> Allow me to express my deep exhilaration at the completely winged melody of your book *Separation*.
>
> I have been reading it all evening—almost aloud, and—I am almost singing (it). I have not had such aesthetic enjoyment for a long time. . . .[1]

Bely's next book of verse was titled *After the Separation* (*Posle razluki*), with a double meaning: it was written after his separation from his wife Asya, and after reading Tsvetaeva's *Separation*. Its final poem is a tribute to her:

Тихо пою стих	I quietly sing a verse
В неосязаемые угодия	To the intangible realm
Ваших образов.	Of your images.
Ваши молитвы —	Your prayers are ringing melodies
Малиновые мелодии	And
И —	Inconquerable
Непобедимые	Rhythms.
Ритмы.	(1922)

A few years earlier, such praise from a major Symbolist would have meant a great deal to her. But Symbolism's day had passed, as had Bely's, and Tsvetaeva, now fully aware of her own strength and maturity, took his tribute more or less for granted. Bely left no trace in her Berlin poems, and Tsvetaeva's account of their friendship, "A Captive Spirit," gives no indication that for her he was any more than a suffering fellow-poet and fellow-Russian.

A more important Berlin friendship was with Abram Grigorevich Vishniak, owner of the small emigre publishing house *Gelikon*, which had published *Separation* and was preparing to bring out *Craft*. Vishniak was infatuated with Tsvetaeva, and she with him, or, perhaps more accurately, with her own attraction to him. The literary results, as with most of Tsvetaeva's loves, were far more substantial than the romance itself: it lay behind a large number of Tsvetaeva's Berlin poems, and a series of letters she wrote to Vishniak. The ease with which, ten years later, she transformed those letters into a novel in letters titled *Florentine Nights* (primarily by translating them into French)[2] indicates how close her letters always were to artistic prose in the first place.

Ariadna, not yet ten, described their relationship in her notebook:

> When Marina enters his office, she is like that soul which disturbs and takes away peace and raises you to itself, not lowering itself to you. In Marina's friendship there's no singing of lullabies or shoving into a cradle. She shoves *out* of the cradle even a child she's talking to, while divinely certain that she's babying him. Such babying sometimes leaves permanent scars. Marina speaks with Gelikon like a Titan, and she's incomprehensible to him, like the North Pole to an oriental, and just as enticing. From her words he senses that among his burdensome everyday affairs there is a shaft of light and something extraordinary. I've seen how he's drawn to Marina, as to the sun, with all his rumpled little stalk. But meanwhile the sun is far away, for all of Marina's being is reserve and compressed lips, and he himself is soft and flexible, like the sprout of a sweet pea.[3]

The Vishniak poems are addressed to a young man by an older and wiser woman, whose tone is colloquial and attitude playfully ironic. She seems anxious to avoid the relationship he offers, drawing an ironic portrait of herself and his affections:

Так, в скудном труженичестве дней,	Thus, in the meager toil of days,
Так, в трудной судорожности к ней,	Thus, in difficult convulsiveness toward her,
Забудешь дружественный хорей	You will forget the amicable trochee
Подруги мужественной своей.	Of your courageous lady friend.

Ее суровости горький дар,	Her bitter gift of severity
И легкой робостью скрытый жар,	And ardor hidden by slight shyness,
И тот беспроволочный удар,	And that wireless blow
Которому имя — даль.	Whose name is distance.

June 15, 1922
(III, 12)

Tsvetaeva revels in a pun on the title of the book Vishniak is about to publish:

Ищи себе доверчивых подруг,	Find yourself credulous lady friends
Не выправивших чуда на число.	Who haven't corrected a miracle to a cipher.
Я знаю, что Венера — дело рук,	I know that Venus is the work of hands,
Ремесленник, — и знаю ремесло. . .	I'm a craftsman, and know my craft.

June 18, 1922
(III, 14)

As she was preparing the manuscript of *Craft* for Vishniak, she "gave" him (by a dedication in the manuscript) a four-poem cycle ("The Youth," 1921) written before she had ever met him. To do so, she had to take it back from its original addressee,[4] but this bothered her not at all; it was something she did fairly often. Those poems, with their Old Testament imagery, emphasize the Jewishness of the addressee, as do the letters of *Florentine Nights*:

> I know you, I know your race, you are greater in depth than in height . . .
> You dimly remind me of a friend of several years ago, author of a whole race of my poems, in which no one recognizes me, except all of his race which recognizes itself there in its entirety.[5]

The title of *Florentine Nights* is taken from a prose work by one of Tsvetaeva's favorite German poets, Heinrich Heine, remembered as much for his Jewish origin as for his romantic idealism and long years of political exile in Paris. Surely it is more than mere coincidence that so many of the young men who passed through Tsvetaeva's life and poetry had Jewish blood in their veins—beginning with Sergei Efron and continuing with Mandel'stam, Plutser-Sarna, Lann, Vishniak, Bachrach, and Pasternak. In a Russian milieu which knew more than its share of anti-semitism, Tsvetaeva's partiality for Jewish men was an aspect of her life-long sympathy for the underdog, a sign of her oft-proclaimed defiance for Philistine prejudices.

A striking pattern of lexical repetition runs through all of the Berlin poems, both those addressed to Vishniak and the others as well.[6] Some rather uncommon words occur with unusual frequency;[7] more common words occur with a frequency that sets them off as marked:[8] Each poem contains at least one or two of these words, creating an intricate linkage in which one poem thus becomes a subtext for the others. Such lexical linkage or "drift" can be found in Tsvetaeva's poetry of all periods, but it is particularly pronounced in her later work, where it accompanies the evolution of the lyric diary into larger forms. Some of the repetitions have plausible explanations: honeysuckle blooms in June, and has a pervasive, if not oppressive, scent. Jet-black was the color of Vishniak's hair. Early-morning bird calls must have been a familiar sound to Tsvetaeva, who often stayed up writing until the early June dawn. But each of the repeated elements carries with it Tsvetaeva's own special meaning. Though the reader senses the interrelation of these poems, the conflation of private meanings makes this group of poems perhaps the most obscure and difficult part of the entire poetic diary. Full understanding of such poetry requires a diligent, perceptive reader, willing to read her work "from beginning to end" as Tsvetaeva asked. But such readers were fewer and fewer in the 1920's, especially in the emigration.

The Berlin poems indicate that at the beginning of her emigration she was moving in the direction of an ever more hermetic, self-referent and basically private poetry. But that tendency suddenly reversed itself when she discovered "her greatest contemporary"—Boris Pasternak. That momentous event came in the last days of June 1922, when she unexpectedly received a letter from Moscow:

Moscow, June 14, 1922

Dear Marina Ivanovna!

Just now, with a tremble in my voice, I began to read to my brother your, "I know, I will die at the dawn . . ." and I was like someone else, interrupted by a wave of sobbing which rose in my throat and finally burst, and when I transferred my efforts from that poem to "I will tell you about a great deception," I was bowled over by you in exactly the same way, and when I carried them over to "Versts, and versts, and stale bread" the same thing happened.

You are not a child, my dear, golden, incomparable poet, and I hope you understand *what* that means in our day, with the *abundance* of talents never discredited, like Mayakovsky and Akhmatova.

Forgive me, forgive me, forgive me!

How could it happen that, trudging together with you behind the coffin of Tatiana Feodorovna [Scriabina] I didn't know with whom I walked?

. . . How strangely and stupidly life is cut out! A month ago I could have reached you only a hundred paces away, and your *Versts* already existed, . . . And I'm not ashamed to admit my attachment to the nastiest fault of Philistinism—you don't buy a book because it is *possible* to buy it. . . .[9]

Tsvetaeva's reply contained a detailed recounting of their five previous encounters, at each of which, she would have him believe, she had sensed something special about him.[10] Tsvetaeva confessed that she still, on receiving his letter, knew only five or six of his poems, and had not even seen his latest book, *My Sister Life*. But within a week she had found a copy, devoured it, and written in response "A Downpour of Light: Poetry of Eternal Courage," an essay that has become a foundation of the Pasternak critical canon. It was, by the way, the first prose Tsvetaeva ever published.

None of Tsvetaeva's critical prose can be called objective—it usually says as much about its author as about her ostensible subjects, who are seen through her transforming and idiosyncratic perception. "A Downpour of Light" is no exception. Its tone is panegyric, and it devotes as much attention to Tsvetaeva's discovery of *My Sister Life* as to the book itself. But no matter. "This is not a review. It is an attempt at release, so I don't choke. I've discovered the only contemporary for whom my lungs are inadequate."[11] She introduces both the book and its author not as they are in some objective sense, not even as she saw them as she wrote, but as she saw them first, when she initially dismissed them both out of hand. She recalls her first mistaken judgment of the book by its cover: "like a catalog of coffin accessories, or the last gasp of some expiring publishing house."[12] She had been equally misled by Pasternak's awkward manner when she first heard him read in Moscow: "He spoke in a monotone and forgot almost all of his poems. . . .I thought impatiently, 'Lord, why torture oneself and others this way?'"[13] In her letter to Pasternak, Tsvetaeva indicated considerably more original sympathy. The essay exaggerates her initial incomprehension as a rhetorical strategy to make her discovery seem the more dramatic.

Pasternak's achievement, which she admired and probably envied, was the overcoming and transformation of her old nemesis, *byt*. He used the most mundane details in his verse, but never lost control of them. His prosaic details were "almost always in motion—a mill, a railway coach . . . even sleep is in motion in his poetry: a pulsating temple."[14] Tsvetaeva wrote two later essays about Pasternak in the 1930's, "Epic and Lyric of Contemporary Russia" (in which she contrasted him to Mayakovsky) and "Poets with a History and Poets without a History" (in which she compared him to Mandel'stam, among others). But her image of him as a poet changed little from this first impression. Central was her view of his unique relationship to nature:

Who of our poets has depicted nature?. . .They have written, both much and well, . . . about themselves in nature. . . . They have written about nature in themselves (comparing, comparing themselves). They have written about events in nature, her individual aspects and hours. But none has written so amazingly [as in *My Sister Life*]. They have all written "about"—no one has given us nature herself—point blank.[15]

Her analysis of his achievement recalls Shklovsky's concept of defamiliarization, or "making strange" (*ostranenie*), though Tsvetaeva, who had only scorn for formalist criticism, would have been loath to admit it:

> We humanize nature too much—that is why, at first, before we wake up, we don't recognize a thing in Pasternak. Between the thing and ourselves stands our (or rather someone else's) idea of it, our habit, which hides the object itself. . . . Between the object and us is our blindness, our faulty, corrupted eye.

> Between Pasternak and the object there is nothing—that is why his rain is too close—it beats upon us harder than the rain from the clouds, which we are used to . . .[16]

Pasternak himself seems so much a part of the nature in his poetry that Tsvetaeva sometimes suspected, "You are a phenomenon of nature. . . .God conceived you as an oak, but created you a man." Of all creatures and aspects of nature, Tsvetaeva most frequently associated Pasternak with trees. "Every poet can identify himself with a tree. But Pasternak *feels* like a tree."[17]

Tsvetaeva concluded "A Downpour of Light" in frustration: "I have said nothing. Nothing about anything—for before me is Life, and I do not know the words for that."[18] But she tried to find them. A poem dated the day after she finished her essay is orchestrated around the word "*zhizn'*" (life).[19] As with all her brother poets, Tsvetaeva was immediately "*na ty*" with Pasternak addressing him in the intimate second-person singular in her poetry, while she used the formal second person plural in their correspondence for at least a year.

Неподражаемо лжет жизнь:	Life lies inimitably:
Сверх ожидания, сверх лжи. . .	Beyond expectations, beyond lies . . .
Но по дрожанию всех жил	But by the trembling of all your veins
Можешь узнать: жизнь!	You can recognize it: life!
Словно во ржи лежишь: звон, синь. . .	As if you're lying in the rye: ringing, blue . . .
(Что ж, что во лжи лежишь!) — жар, вал. . .	(As if you're lying in a lie!)—heat, wave . . .
Бормот — сквозь жимолость — ста жал. . .	A muttering—through the honey-suckle—of a
Радуйся же! — Звал!	hundred stings . . .
	Rejoice! He has beckoned!
	July 8, 1922
	(III, 19)

She later described the poem's genesis to Pasternak, calling it "The Words to a Dream:"

It was then summer, and I had my own balcony in Berlin. Stone, heat, your green book on my knees (I sat on the floor). I lived it for ten days, as if on the crest of a wave. I gave myself to it (I listened) and I didn't choke—I had only enough breath for those eight lines which—I am so happy—you liked.[20]

Tsvetaeva was tempted to dedicate *Craft* to Pasternak on the spot, but she restrained herself for fear of offending Vishniak:

> . . . My first gesture, on turning the last page of *My Sister Life* was to throw open my own *Craft* and there on its first page, in black and white, to write your name. But here begins baseness; I was then friendly with Gelikon, who was in love (I shrug my shoulders) with my poetry. He was a black velvet nonentity, touching, all "sh" (Good God, "cat" in French is "chat!" Now I understand). Well. To dedicate *Craft* under his suede catty nose, to another, and to a demigod at that (which, modestly and for all to hear, I consider you to be)—my heart sank: . . .[21]

Vishniak was quickly eclipsed by Pasternak in Tsvetaeva's thoughts, poetry, and correspondence. Her letters to him were only a rough sketch for the great epistolary romance with Pasternak.

Tsvetaeva's discovery of Pasternak was prefigured in the lexicon and imagery of several Berlin poems written before his letter arrived. "Eternal Courage," the sub-title of her Pasternak essay, appears in a poem dated June 24. The word "*zhizn'*" ("life") appears in no less than eight of the twenty-two Berlin poems, all of them, it so happens, *pre*-dating her acquaintance with *My Sister Life*. "*Svet*" (light) and its variant "*rassvet*" (dawn) are also important elements of the Berlin "drift." "Downpour" seems to emerge as much from Tsvetaeva's own poems of those weeks as from her reading of Pasternak. It is as if he and his poetry provided something that Tsvetaeva particularly needed at just that moment, and her image of him, as she formed it in June 1922, was colored by concerns and themes she was already exploring in her own work. Pasternak's influence can most clearly be felt in the sudden appearance of nature, particularly the forest, in Tsvetaeva's poetry. Before Pasternak, Tsvetaeva was a poet of abstract emotions in mythical, historical, or Biblical, and largely urban settings. The turn to nature coincided with her move to Czechoslovakia, where she lived mostly in small villages outside of Prague, and spent much of her free time hiking in the surrounding hills. The setting, however, only provided the material; Pasternak provided the inspiration.

But where in the Berlin diary is the husband with whom she was to be reunited in Berlin? His arrival was delayed until she could scrape up enough money to pay for his trip from Prague. It is significant that though she several times mentioned the date of their last meeting, nowhere did she record the date of their reunion. Her daughter "doesn't remember exactly." Even at its beginning, it was a missed meeting. Ariadna recalled:

Either the telegram about his arrival was delayed, or Marina was absent when it arrived—I only remember that the news we had awaited from day to day caught Marina unawares, and we didn't just go to meet Seryozha, but raced there at breakneck speed, in a hurry, losing our sense of direction. Someone offered to come with us and was about to make a big fuss, but Marina didn't want any company: she had to meet Seryozha alone, without outsiders.

When we dashed into the railway station, our legs quaking with agitation, excitement and haste, it was empty and echoing uselessly, like a cathedral after the end of a mass. Seryozha's train had left long ago. No one remained of the passengers, or those meeting them. Cooling down from our run, and freezing with horror, we painstakingly and futilely investigated the platforms and waiting rooms, the baggage room and the restaurant—Marina in her new blue dress, I in my new sailor collar. So dressed up! And so miserable, lost and confused, as can happen only in dreams. . . .

We went out onto the empty square, white in the sun, and the sunlight reflected off all its flat surfaces struck us painfully in the eyes. We felt the burning city heat, the weakness in our knees, and a huge emptiness inside from this missed meeting. Marina began blindly and absent-mindedly to fumble in her purse for cigarettes and jingle her matches. Her face grew wan. And then we heard Seryozha's voice: "Marina! Marinochka!" From somewhere on the other side of the square, waving at us, came running a tall, thin man. . . . With a face distorted by happiness, he embraced Marina, who slowly opened her arms to meet him, as if rooted to the spot. . . .[22]

Sergei, recalled Ariadna, was "silently affectionate" with her, but spent most of his time with Marina. The Ehrenburgs "welcomed Sergei like a relative" and busied themselves making plans for the reunited couple. Berlin, despite its surface glitter, offered no prospects for education or work to emigre Russians like Sergei. Czechoslovakia at least offered the modest student stipend he was already receiving, the opportunity to finish his education, and the promise of a writer's stipend for Marina. Eventually, it was decided that Marina and Alya would come to join him in Prague, though they had originally thought they might stay in Berlin.

Tsvetaeva's carefully constructed myth of Sergei and their relationship finally had to confront reality. After their long separation, the differences between husband and wife were even more evident:

Seryozha, who would be 29 in the fall, still looked like a boy who had just suffered a serious illness—he was that thin and big-eyed, and still so orphaned, despite Marina sitting next to him. She seemed grown-up, once and for all: right to the threads of premature grey already glinting here and there in her hair. (Ariadna Efron)[23]

Sergei probably came to Berlin at the end of June. Some readers assume that a poem dated June 25 is addressed to him:

Здравствуй! Не стрела, не камень:	Hello! Not an arrow, not a stone:
Я! — Живейшая из жен:	I! The most lively of wives:
Жизнь. Обеими руками	Life. I come with both arms
В твой невыспавшийся сон.	Into your un-slept-out dream.
Дай! (На языке двуостром:	Give! (On a two-edged tongue:
Нà! — Двуострота змеи!)	There!—The two-edgedness of a snake!)
Всю меня в простоволосой	Take me in all of my
Радости моей прими!	Bareheaded joy!
Льни! — Сегодня день на шхуне,	Cling! Today is a day on a schooner,
— Льни! — на лыжах! — Льни! — льняной!	—Cling!—On skis!—Cling!—Flaxen!
Я сегодня в новой шкуре:	Today I'm in a new skin:
Вызолоченной, седьмой!	Gilded, the seventh!
— Мой! — и о каких наградах	My own!—and of what rewards
Рай — когда в руках, у рта:	Paradise—when in my arms, at my lips
Жизнь: распахнутая радость	Is life: the flung-open joy
Поздороваться с утра!	Of greeting in the morning!

(III, 17)

Yet, were the poem dated a few days later, we might read it as a response to Pasternak and his "sister life." Efron's arrival in late June would have come smack in the middle of the Vishniak romance and a few days before the first letter from Pasternak—certainly not an opportune moment. Aside from this poem (whose inspiration is at best hypothetical) Efron left no other trace in the Berlin lyric diary. His stay there, in any case, was brief. He soon returned to Prague to prepare for his entrance into the university in the fall, and arrange housing for Marina and Alya.

Tsvetaeva's attitude to Berlin and its literary marketplace soured considerably by midsummer. Rejection of that world was a major theme of the poems she wrote that autumn in Czechoslovakia. When *After Russia* was finally published in 1928, Tsvetaeva carefully separated her Berlin poems from those written later. Yet the last of them, written on the eve of her departure, seems rather to belong with the Czech poems:

Леты слепотекущий всхлип.	Blindly-flowing sob of Lethe.
Долг твой тебе отпущен: слит	Thy duty is absolved: merged
С Летою, — еле-еле жив	With Lethe—barely alive
В лепете сребротекущих ив.	In the murmur of silverflowing willows.
Ивовый сребролетейский плеск	Weeping silverlethean splash of willows,
Плачущий. . . В слепотекущий склеп	Hide in the blindflowing crypt of memories—
Памятей — перетомилась — спрячь	I'm exhausted—
В ивовый сребролетейский плач.	In the willows' silverlethean lament.
Нà плечи — сребро-седым плащом	Lie on my shoulders, like a silver-grey old man's cape
Старческим, сребро-сухим плющом	Like silver-dry ivy
Нà плечи — перетомилась — ляг,	Lie on my shoulders—I'm exhausted—
Ладанный слеполетейский мрак	Incenselike blindlethean gloom of poppies . . .

Маковый. . .
            — ибо красный цвет
Старится, ибо пурпур — сед
В памяти, ибо выпив всю —
Сухостями теку.

For the red grows old
For the purple is grey in memory
For having drunk it all
I flow in drynesses.

Тусклостями: ущербленных жил
Скупостями, молодых сивилл
Слепостями, головных истом
Седостями: свинцом.

In dullnesses: The miserliness of injured
Veins, the blindnesses of young sibyls,
The greynesses of mental lassitude
Like lead.
                                Berlin, July 31, 1922
                                        (III, 23)

A poem without energy or hope, its main image the river Lethe, underground river of forgetfulness and death, it is one of the most pessimistic poems Tsvetaeva ever wrote. "Blindly-flowing sob of Lethe" serves as a lexical and thematic overture to an entirely new "drift" whose most important elements are silver (*srebro-*), grey (*sed-*), dry (*sukx/sh-*), and the related flow (*tek-*) and river (*reka*). In "Lethe," Tsvetaeva combines all of these elements with the roots "blind" (*slep-*) and "Lethean" (Letei-) to create ingenious neologisms whose very length slows down the tempo of the poem, giving the effect of a weed-clogged river. These five-syllable compounds enable the poem to maintain its unusual meter: the concentration of unstressed syllables in the middle of the line (/uuuuu/u/) intensifies the effect of stagnation. The last line of the fourth stanza combines two elements of the "drift" for the poem's basic paradox: "I flow in drynesses." All Tsvetaeva's usual fight is gone, and the silver of the first stanzas is finally replaced by the more ominous lead. Yet these same stanzas contain the lexical germs of the poems which will record her spiritual rejuvenation among the trees of the Czech forest.

Water had never been an important symbolic element in Tsvetaeva's work. The life-giving rain of Pasternak's "Downpour" ("Pasternak loves the rain, more passionately than grasses, sunrises, or snowstorms. And how it drenched the poet—the whole book swims!")[24] started to seep into her poetry right after she read *My Sister Life*. First, it was a consolation for the emotional pains of Berlin:

БЕРЛИНУ

TO BERLIN

Дождь убаюкивает боль.
Под ливни опускающихся ставень
Сплю. Вздрагивающих асфальтов вдоль
Копыта — как рукоплесканья.

The rain lulls the pain.
Beneath downpours of lowering shutters
I sleep. Along the shuddering asphalt
Hooves—like applause.

Поздравствовалось — и слилось.
В оставленности златозарной
Над сказочнейшим из сиротств
Вы смилостивились, казармы!

It has greeted—and merged.
In gold-dawned abandonment
You have taken pity, O barracks,
On the most fantastic of orphanhoods!
                                July 10, 1923
                                        (III, 21)

As she prepared to leave Berlin, the stagnant waters of Lethe mirrored the emotional exhaustion of her psyche. Nina Gove[25] has suggested that Marina and Sergei, as "survivors" of Civil War and famine, may then have suffered from the emotional numbness documented in Holocaust victims. Exhausted physically and emotionally by her years alone in Moscow and by her frenetic summer in Berlin, Tsvetaeva, revived by both Czech nature and the Russian nature of Pasternak's poems, found new strength in the countryside outside Prague. In her lyric diary, the stagnant waters of Lethe were gradually replaced by clear-running mountain brooks.

CHAPTER SIXTEEN

The Czech Forest (August–September, 1922)

On August 1, Marina and Alya arrived in Czechoslovakia, to settle in a village with the unpromising name of Dolni Mokropsy ("Lower Wet Dogs"). Their meager resources required that mother and daughter rent rooms in suburban villages while Sergei commuted to his studies in Prague, often sleeping in the dormitory. Tsvetaeva needed time and solitude in which to write, and her housekeeping burdens in the primitive conditions of the Czech village were not much of an improvement over life in Moscow. But life in Mokropsy, among the Russian students who rented rooms in almost every house, had its virtues: "Life is not social (all are very busy) but friendly. They help each other in times of trouble—no scandals or gossip, a great feeling of purity."[1] This was just what she wanted. Her poems of the period sound a note of abstinence, purification—a rejection of sensuality in the name of a higher spiritual life—and for Tsvetaeva that of course meant poetry. She would seek this purification in the nature which now lay at her doorstep. "Right behind us is the forest. To the right, the high crest of a cliff. The village is full of brooks."[2] Tsvetaeva had always been an avid hiker, her greatest pleasure long walks in the woods; now she used her honoraria to order hiking boots from Berlin.

The Czech poems begin with the cycle "Sibyl," in which Tsvetaeva compares the prophetess to a huge, scorched tree, standing majestically amidst a burned-out forest. Though life has departed, spiritual and prophetic powers have entered, just as the physical dessication of the sibyl's body opened the way for the voice of Apollo:

Сивилла: выжжена, сивилла: ствол.	Sibyl: burned out, sibyl: a trunk.
Все птицы вымерли, но бог вошел.	All the birds have died off, but the god has entered.
Сивилла: выпита, сивилла: сушь.	Sibyl: drunk up, sibyl: dryness.
Все жилы высохли: ревностен муж!	All her veins dried up: a zealous husband!
Сивилла: выбыла, сивилла: зев	Sibyl: she's gone, sibyl: jaws
Доли и гибели! — Древо меж дев.	Of fate and destruction! Tree amidst maidens.

August 5, 1922
(III, 24)

Tsvetaeva had long been fascinated by the Sibyl myth, and planned to develop it into a large work. In a 1919 notebook entry, she outlined her version of the story, taken largely from Ovid's *Metamorphosis*:

SIBYL (some time!) Sibyl, once the favorite of Phoebus, forgot to request eternal youth. And so—she grows older. Her love for Phoebus abides. Sibyl is the voice of Phoebus. Sibyl has not heard people for a long time. . . . The meeting of the sibyl with the son of Phoebus, *their recognition*. The son of Phoebus does not see the sibyl, he only hears her voice: it is the rock cliff speaking! But, as he cries out, the voice of the sibyl softens: it is the grass speaking! it is the brook: The youth falls in love, wishes to see her, insists, finally breaks his way into the cave and smashes his chest against the rock (sibyl), Sibyl over the body of the youth.[3]

As woman and poet she identified with the sibyl, the voice of Phoebus (Apollo), possessor of knowledge far beyond that granted ordinary mortals. But it was another element in the myth which particularly appealed to her. The sibyl, who asked Apollo for immortality but forgot to request eternal youth, dried up until she was literally a disembodied spirit—only her voice remained. Tsvetaeva thought of herself as a poet, but knew that most others thought of her first as a woman, or, at best, "a woman poet." The sibyl myth represented her new ideal of the artist, and explains why correspondence-friendships became so important to her in emigration. "The son of Phoebus does not see the Sibyl, he only hears her voice." Tsvetaeva, as she tried to renounce Aphrodite, needed a situation where she would be for friends and readers only a soul, a disembodied voice without a mortal coil to distract and complicate the relationship. In a poem of August 8, the mountain river whispers a pessimistic message for the artist who hopes to balance creativity and personal relationships: "Beware of earthly entanglements." (III, 26) The artist must distance her/himself from the everyday life of mankind (from *byt*), for human achievements are attained only by lone individuals.[4]

The nine-poem cycle "Trees" is one of Tsvetaeva's greatest achievements. The first seven poems describe the changes wrought by autumn in the Czech hillside forest. The drying up of vegetation, the transient brilliance of the leaves followed by death and decay, all provided her poetic imagination with fitting material for the questions of expiation and renunciation which were occupying her:

В смертных изверясь,	Losing faith in mortals,
Зачароваться не тщусь.	I'll not try to bewitch myself.
В старческий вереск,	Into the senile heather,
В среброскользящую сушь,	Into the silver-crawling dryness,
— Пусть моей тени	—Let the trumpeters trumpet the
Славу трубят трубачи! —	Glory of my shade!—
В вереск-потери,	To the heather-losses,
В вереск-сухие ручьи.	To the heather-dry rivers.

Старческий вереск!	Ancient heather!
Голого камня нарост!	Outgrowth of bare rock!
Удостоверясь	Convinced
В тождестве наших сиротств,	Of the identity of our orphanhoods,
Сняв и отринув	I've cast off and rejected
Клочья последней парчи —	The shreds of my last brocade—
В вереск-руины,	Into the heather-ruins,
В вереск-сухие ручьи.	Into the heather-dry brooks.
Жизнь: двоедушье	Life is the duplicity
Дружб и удушье уродств.	Of friendships and the asphyxia of uglinesses.
Седью и сушью,	By greyness and dryness,
(Ибо вожатый — суров),	(Because the leader is stern),
Ввысь, где рябина	Upwards, to where the rowan
Краше Давида-Царя!	Is more beautiful than David the King!
В вереск-седины,	Into the heather-grey hairs,
В вереск-сухие моря.	Into the heather-dry seas.

September 5, 1922
(III, 29)

She turns to nature, rejecting the mortals who bear their own death within their name (the figurative meaning of the Russian *smertnye* (mortals), as of its English equivalent, has come to dominate in normal usage, though the original meaning lies waiting for the poet to evoke). The visual image of death, and the central image of the poem, is the field of dry heather through which the poet walks. She wants its hollow rasping to be the trumpet of her future glory, and uses the word "*veresk* (heather), which seemed to echo that sound, again and again as a refrain. As the heather's blossoms have faded and withered, so she has taken off the "shreds of her last brocade." Those who knew her in this period remark on the studied unfashionability of her dress, which seemed due to more than the very real poverty in which she lived. In her letters, Tsvetaeva often seems to take perverse pleasure in the utter paucity of her wardrobe. The heather field, like the renunciation of feminine vanity, represents a period of scourging before she can rise to the forested foothills, where the rowan-tree stands as a symbol of spiritual beauty.[5] While introducing a new cycle, "Trees 1" evokes the Lethe and Sibyl poems as subtext, by picking up all five elements of the silver/grey/old/dry/river "drift." The bare rock on which the heather grows recalls the sibyl/rock; and it is a sibyl-like wisdom—renunciation of *this* world—which Tsvetaeva seeks in the forest. In "Trees 2" she sees that forest as a cast of mythical heroes, who beckon her, tempting her to throw open her arms and abandon her manuscripts—a measure of her dissatisfaction with literary Berlin, the "marketplace" from whose roar she seeks salvation in the forest. She feels a sense of release in the trees' "upward flight."

Когда обидой — опилась
Душа разгневанная,
Когда семижды зареклась
Сражаться с демонами —

Не с теми, ливнями огней
В бездну нисхлестнутыми:
С земными низостями дней,
С людскими косностями —

Деревья! К вам иду! Спастись
От рёва рыночного!
Вашими вымахами ввысь
Как сердце выдышано!

Дуб богоборческий! В бои
Всем корнем шествующий!
Ивы-провидицы мои!
Березы-девственницы!

Вяз — яростный Авессалом,
На пытке вздыбленная
Сосна — ты, уст моих псалом:
Горечь рябиновая. . .

К вам! В живоплещущую ртуть
Листвы — пусть рушащейся!
Впервые руки распахнуть!
Забросить рукописи!

Зеленых отсветов рои. . .
Как в руки — плещущие. . .
Простоволосые мои,
Мои трепещущие!

When the soul, incensed,
Has drunk its fill of insult,
When it has seven times vowed to cease
Battle with the demons—

Not with those who are cast down into the abyss
By showers of fire:
With the earthly lowlinesses of days,
With human stagnation—

Trees! I come to you! To save myself
From the roar of the marketplace.
How my heart breathes out
Through your flights upward!

Theomachist oak! Striding into battles
With all your roots!
My willow-prophetesses!
Virginal birches!

Elm—fierce Absalom,
Pine—racked
In torture—thou, psalm of my lips:
Bitter taste of rowan.

To you! To the alive-plashing mercury
Of the leaves—what if they are falling!
For the first time to throw open my arms!
To abandon my manuscripts!

A swarm of green reflections
As into applauding hands . . .
My bare-headed ones,
My trembling ones!

September 8, 1922
(III, 29)

As the dry, rasping sound of "*veresk*" dominated "Trees 1," so the sound of wind rushing through dry autumn leaves dominates the last two stanzas of "Trees 2." Tsvetaeva achieves this effect by the concentrated use of sibilants, (particularly *SHCH*) in multi-syllable words which recall the long compound words of "Lethe," but in a new tonality—her soul is beginning to revive. "Trees 3" is a conceit or riddle poem. It describes something "like a ring of bathers, a flock of guardian nymphs" who, alarmed by a sudden intruder, perhaps, break off their dance and try to cover their nakedness with their long "arms." The last two lines provide the answer—it is a clump of birch trees:

Березовое серебро,
Ручьи живые!

Silver of birches,
Living rivulets!

September 9, 1922
(III, 31)

The silver flow of Lethe and the "silver-crawling" dryness of the dead heather are metamorphosed into the "virginal" silver trunks of the birch trees, while the dry rivers of the Lethe, Sibyl and heather poems have become "living rivulets" in their graceful movements. The birch and the rowan are the most archetypically Russian trees, and indeed, Tsvetaeva loved the Czech landscape for its similarity to her native Tarusa. But we should beware the temptation to read all nature, as Russians are wont to do, as a metaphor for Mother Russia.

There is a personal explanation for the silver/dry/grey/old elements in the "drift" we have been following, and for Tsvetaeva's interest in the aging yet immortal sibyl. On September 26 (O.S.)/October 9, 1922, she observed her thirtieth birthday, a milestone apt to inspire reflection on the passage of youth. When her first grey hairs appeared in 1921, she wrote in her notebook:

> I am too young to maintain out of self-love that I find this—[grey hair]—pleasing—I am glad of it as a proof that certain forces are secretly working in me—not age, of course!—but perhaps my head and heart, working tirelessly, all my passionate creative life, hidden under a careless exterior—as proof of the fact that even an iron constitution, such as mine, is covered by the iron laws of the spirit.[6]

She developed the theme in two birthday poems. The grey of her hair, compared in both poems to ashes, signals a ripening of her soul. A result of the trials she has undergone, it is a token not of loss but of victory:

Золото моих волос
Тихо переходит в седость.
— Не жалейте! всё сбылось,
Всё в груди слилось и спелось.

The gold of my hair
Is in quiet transition to silver.
Don't pity me: everything has come to be,
Everything in my breast has merged and
    ripened.

Спелось — как вся даль слилась
В стонущей трубе окрайны.
Господи! Душа сбылась:
Умысел мой самый тайный.

It has ripened—as all the distance
Has merged in the moaning chimney of the
    suburb.
Lord! My soul has come to be,
My most secret design.

Несгорающую соль
Дум моих — ужели пепел
Фениксов отдам за смоль
Временных великолепий?

Would I give up the ashes of Phoenixes,
The incombustible salt of my thoughts
For the pitch
Of temporary splendors?

Да и ты посеребрел,
Спутник мой! К громам и дымам,
К молодым сединам *дел* —
Дум моих причти седины.

And you, too, have grown grey,
My travelling companion!
To the thunders and smokes, to your early grey
    of *deeds*—
Add the grey hairs of my thoughts.

Горделивый златоцвет,
Роскошью своей не чванствуй:
Молодым сединам *бед*
Лавр пристал — и дуб гражданский.

Haughty gold
Don't boast of your splendor:
Laurel—and the civic oak—
Are becoming to premature grey.
                    Between September 17 and 23, 1922
                                   (III, 130)

"The Gold of My Hair" may have been a sketch for her other birthday poem, "Grey Hairs." It is more colloquial, almost conversational in tone, and more personal in reference. When she asks, "Would I give up my Phoenix-ashes for the jet-black of temporary splendor?" and then turns to address her "travelling-companion" whose hair has also begun to silver, she is affirming her rejection of Berlin and Vishniak (he of the jet-black hair) for the austere life of family responsibilities and Sergei. (Since they ostensibly shared the same birthday, it is a birthday poem for Sergei, too.) She and Sergei, poet and warrior, are clearly the referents of the final couplet. Perhaps because it is such a personal, family poem, she left it out of *After Russia*), from which Sergei is totally absent.[7]

"Grey Hairs," like the poems which surround it in *After Russia*), is more abstract and elevated in diction. "The Gold of My Hair," particularly in its first stanzas, had more of an organic sense of ripening and unity—the lines frequently run on one into another. In "Grey Hairs," on the other hand, every other line stands in rhetorical opposition to the one which precedes it.[8]

Это пеплы сокровищ:
Утрат, обид.
Это пеплы, пред коими
В прах — гранит.

These are the ashes of treasures,
Of losses, of injuries.
These are ashes before which
Granite falls to dust.

Голубь голый и светлый,
Не живущий четой.
Соломоновы пеплы
Над великой тщетой.

Bare and bright dove,
Living un-mated.
Ashes of Solomon
Above a great vanity.

Беззакатного времени
Грозный мел.
Значит Бог в мои двери —
Раз дом сгорел!

The threatening chalk
Of an endless time.
It means God's at my door—
Since the house has burned!

Не удушенный в хламе,
Снам и дням господин,
Как отвесное пламя
Дух — из ранних седин!

Not suffocated in rubbish,
Master of dreams and days,
Like a perpendicular flame
The spirit—from early grey hair.

И не вы меня предали,
Годы, в тыл!
Эта седость — победа
Бессмертных сил.

And it's not you, years,
Who've betrayed me behind my back!
This grey is the victory
Of immortal forces.
                                September 27, 1922
                                        (III, 38)

The imagery of ashes and soot links these grey hair poems to the two "Factory" poems, which they bracket chronologically. The Czech forest was only one part of the landscape in Tsvetaeva's new life. She saw the man-made, soot-covered ugliness of Prague's industrial suburbs as a world of "earthly insult," a landscape of hopelessness which even God has abandoned:

А Бог? — По самый лоб закурен,	But God?—He's smoked to his brow,
Не вступится! Напрасно ждем!	He'll not intervene! We wait in vain!
Над койками больниц и тюрем	He's just tacked up
Он гвоздиками пригвожден.	Above the cots of hospitals and prisons.

September 23, 1922
(III, 36)

It is not often that Tsvetaeva's poems venture direct social commentary. But when they do, here and in the related "God Save Us, the Smoke!" (September 30, 1922) and "Praise the Rich," her acid invective can be murderous:

Объявляю: *люблю* богатых!	I proclaim: I *love* the rich!
За их корень, гнилой и щаткий,	For their roots, rotten and unsteady,
С колыбели растящий рану,	Cultivating that wound from the cradle,
За растерянную повадку	For their absent-minded gesture—
Из кармана и вновь к карману.	Hand out of the pocket and back in again.
За тишайшую просьбу уст их,	For the quietest request of their lips,
Исполняемую как окрик.	Carried out like a shout.
И за то, что их в рай не впустят,	And because they won't be admitted to paradise,
И за то, что в глаза не смотрят.	And because they won't look me in the eye.

September 30, 1922
(III, 40)

From these poems, in which she saw the working-class districts as literally "Godforsaken," she turned to a cycle titled simply "God." Tsvetaeva's God hides in the woods from the self-satisfied burghers who tried to capture and imprison him in their luxurious churches:

Нищих и горлиц	The lonely chant
Сирый распев.	Of beggars and turtle-doves.
То не твои ли	Is it not Thy
Ризы простерлись	Raiments stretched out
В беге дерев?	In the flight of trees?
Рощ, перелесков.	Of glades, of copses.
. . . .	. . . .
Нищие пели:	The beggars sang:
— Темен, ох, темен лес!	—Dark, oh, dark is the forest!
Нищие пели:	The beggars sang:
— Сборшен последний крест!	—The last cross is thrown off!
Бог из церквей воскрес!	God has risen from the churches!

October 4, 1922
(III, 42)

After this extended digression on grey hair/factory smoke and God, Tsvetaeva returned to "Trees." While the first four poems in the cycle saw the forest primarily as spiritual refuge, the three poems she now added are more philosophical treatments of the problem of reality and illusion. Tsvetaeva, of course, prefers illusion, or at least freedom for the play of the imagination. The brilliant colors of the autumn leaves are an illusion: though they seem wildly alive, they preface death. Yet they are also a premonition of another world which lies beyond.

CHAPTER SEVENTEEN

Pasternak in Berlin: So Near and Yet So Far (October, 1922–February, 1923)

Imagination was the means by which Tsvetaeva escaped from a reality with which she could not, or would not, cope. In "Dawn on the Rails," she pretends that the pre-dawn countryside outside the window of her commuter train is not Czech, but Russian:

Покамест день не встал
С его страстями стравленными,
Из сырости и шпал
Россию восстанавливаю.

While day has not yet risen
With its conflicting passions,
From dampness and railroad sleepers
I restore Russia.

Из сырости — и свай,
Из сырости — и серости.
Покамест день не встал
И не вмешался стрелочник.

From dampness—and pilings,
From dampness—and greyness.
While day has not yet risen
And the switchman doesn't interfere.

(October 12, 1922)
(III, 43)

The poem's dactylic and hyperdactylic endings imitate the incessant "clickety-clack" of the train, lulling its early-morning riders into a dream-filled half-sleep.

It was not just the absent Russia that Tsvetaeva conjured up on her occasional trips into Prague—it was one particular Russian. Pasternak was becoming more and more a part of her life, whether he knew it or not. She later wrote him:

> The last months of this fall I spent constantly with you. . . .At one time I often travelled back and forth to Prague, and there, waiting for the train at our damp little station, I would arrive early, in the half-light, before they turned on the lamps. I would walk back and forth along the dark platform—a long way! And there was one place—a lamp post without a light. There I would summon you, "Pasternak!" And we would have long conversations, wandering side by side. . . .[1]

Pasternak was much closer than he had been in June. Shortly after Tsvetaeva left Berlin, he arrived, bringing his new wife Zhenya to meet his parents, who were living there in emigration. From Berlin, he wrote Tsvetaeva that he was "disappointed and disheartened" to learn she was no longer there. Ariadna Efron indicates that this "missed meeting" was intentional on Tsvetaeva's part: though circumstances dictated that the family settle into their Czech village before autumn, she could have remained in Berlin a bit longer:

> In her departure from Berlin on the eve of Pasternak's arrival there was something like the nymph's flight from Apollo, something mythological and 'not of this world.'[2]

Tsvetaeva's answering letter to Pasternak set out the conditions of their future correspondence:

> My favorite kind of relationship is otherworldly: to see someone in a dream.
>
> And the second is correspondence. A letter, as a kind of otherworldly relationship, is less perfect than a dream, but its laws are the same. Neither the one nor the other comes on command: we dream and write not when *we* want to, but when *they* want to—when the letter wants to be written, the dream to be dreamed. (My letters always want to be written.)
>
> Therefore, right from the beginning: don't reproach yourself, even the slightest bit, if you don't answer, and don't speak of gratitude: every great feeling is an end in itself.[3]

Tsvetaeva revealed the most important truth about her epistolary friendships, and that with Pasternak in particular: "I don't like meetings in life: a knocking of heads—two walls. You won't get through to someone that way."[4] Indeed, a face-to-face meeting with Pasternak in Berlin, now that she had discovered their spiritual kinship, could hardly have helped in her struggle with Aphrodite. A seemingly dispassionate question was the first hint of the drama which would unfold the following spring:

> . . . Nowadays people part for too long—that's why I ask, clearly and soberly: how long have you come for, when are you leaving? I won't hide the fact that I'd be happy to sit with you somewhere in a God-forsaken (or remembered) cafe, in the rain.[5]

Of course, this directly contradicted what she had just said about disliking meetings in life. The meeting in Berlin would never take place—as perhaps Tsvetaeva foresaw even then. But their *non*-meeting was to inspire some of her most powerful poetry.

For the moment, she sent Pasternak "Grey Hairs," which she described as a favorite, and asked for recent poems of his. But she didn't mention her current project, of which she wrote to her Berlin friend Roman Gul' some weeks later:

> I am finishing a large work (in verse) which I love passionately and without which I feel orphaned. I have been writing it for three months. . . . I will not write you its name, out of pure (lover's) superstition, until the last period is in place.[6]

This was the folk-tale *poema The Swain (Molodets)*, which she was to finish on Christmas Eve, 1922, and dedicate:

> To Boris Pasternak:
>   For your magnificent play
>   For your tender consolation.

The Swain was not published until 1924, and the dedication, as well as the consolation to which it refers, date from that later stage of the friendship. But in the plot, Tsvetaeva already outlined the myth she was creating about herself and Pasternak.

In substance, *The Swain* is a reworking and expansion of the Russian folk-tale "The Vampire." Tsvetaeva's version follows Afanas'ev until the conclusion. A maiden, Marusia (one diminutive of Marina), is approached by a handsome stranger who asks her to marry him. She discovers he is a vampire, but refuses to betray him as he kills her brother, mother, and then Marusia herself. Anticipating her death, she asks to be buried at the crossroads, traditional resting-place of witches. A gentleman sees a red flower growing there and takes it home, where it turns into the maiden. She marries him on condition that they have no guests and absent themselves from church for five years. When a son is born to them, the husband breaks his vow and invites in a group of revellers, who chide him that his wife and son are apostates. Shamed, the husband orders Marusia to church. At this point, in Afanas'ev's version, the vampire appears and kills the husband and son. On the advice of her grandmother, Marusia sprinkles holy water on the vampire, who promptly dissolves into dust. Then she sprinkles her husband and son who immediately come to life."[7]

This sudden happy ending to what had been a tale of ever-increasing horror struck Tsvetaeva as unmotivated.

> I . . . began to wonder why Marusia, fearing the vampire, so steadfastedly refused to admit what she had seen, knowing that to name him was to be saved. . . .
>
> When I am told: do such and such and you are free and I don't do it, that means I do not want freedom very much—that "unfreedom" is dearer to me. And what is that dear unfreedom between people? Love. Marusia loved the vampire, and for that reason did not name him, and lost, one after another, her mother—her brother—her life. Passion and crime, passion and sacrifice. . . .[8]

In her version, Marusia flies off with the vampire, deserting her husband and son:

Та — ввысь,	She—upwards,
Тот — вблизь:	He—nearby:
Свились,	Twisting,
Взвились:	Soaring:

Зной — в зной,	Heat to heat,
Хлынь — в хлынь!	Surge to surge!
До—мой	Home—wards
В огнь синь.	Into blue fire.

(IV, 151)

She explained: "My task was to discover the essence of the folk tale . . . to release the thing from its spell."[9] The essence she saw was a tale of predestined unity which predated and transcended mortal marriage. These last lines, describing the heroine's escape with her beloved to "that other world" echoed a few months later in a poem dedicated to Pasternak. (III, 62) Pasternak remained on Tsvetaeva's mind during the winter of 1922-1923, but there seem to have been no more letters—he was, after all, in Berlin on his honeymoon. When the Berlin edition of *The Tsar-Maiden* appeared in January, she sent him a copy and asked for news.

She had written no short poems since October. Suddenly, in early February, there was a flood of them—five in five days, ten within two weeks. Their inspiration was a renewed contact with Pasternak, who had sent her his just-published *Themes and Variations*. Tsvetaeva praised Pasternak as man and poet, but there are some strange and troubled notes in these poems, and in her letters of February and March. First, there is her obsession with Pasternak, her belief in their out-of-the-ordinary relationship, which she later developed into a myth of their "otherworldly marriage." Later, she spoke of it directly in both her poems and letters, for the moment, her ambivalent emotions found expression in her poems. In March, when she learned of Pasternak's imminent departure for Russia, she wrote:

> Pasternak, this began with "Sister." I wrote you. But then, in the summer, I stopped it, severed it by leaving for another country, for another life. But now my life is you and I have nowhere else to go.[10]

There was also her attitude to Pasternak as a poet. By 1923, Tsvetaeva was in the flower of her maturity and strength, a master of her art, breaking her own creative path. But the first of the February poems speaks of "the creative anxiety of intrusion." Tsvetaeva was troubled by something akin to Bloomian anxiety of influence. In her poems to Mandel'stam, Akhmatova, and now Pasternak, there was always an element of self-assertion mixed with her praise. Tsvetaeva took the "brotherly greeting" of Pasternak's book as a challenge, and in her answering poems defended herself from both the enormity of her own emotions and the power of his poetic voice. In defending herself, she opposed her voice to his, raising it to the highest pitch.

When Pasternak had inscribed *Themes and Variations*: "To the incomparable poet Marina Tsvetaeva: Of the Donets, inflammable, infernal,"[11] he was citing a poem in the book which began:

Нас мало. Нас, может быть, трое	We are few. We are perhaps three
Донецких, горючих и адских	Of the Donets, inflammable, infernal
Под серой бегущей корою	Beneath the grey fleeting crust
Дождей, облаков и солдатских	Of rains, clouds and soldierly
Советов, стихов и дискуссий	Advice, poems and discussions
О транспоре и об искусстве.	About transport and about art.

Pasternak's third, by the way, was Mayakovsky.[12] The dedication, of itself, was flattering. But the book? Comparing it to *My Sister Life*, Tsvetaeva wrote: "Your book is a scorch." Here is Tsvetaeva's typical love for contrasts: if the first book was a "Downpour of Light," full of rain, then the new one was "a scorch." The contrast of fire and water. She had written of *Sister*: "My first gesture, having borne it all, from the first blow to the last—was to throw out my arms: so that all my knuckles cracked. I fell under it as under a downpour."[13] Now, in a different way, she "suffered" his new book: "It hurt, but I didn't blow on it. Others would smear it with cold cream or sprinkle it with potato starch. Scoundrels!"[14] Why does she emphasize her *pain* from a book with such a flattering inscription? Giving herself over to pain, even seeking it, was an important trait of Tsvetaeva's romantic poetics. Pain and happiness were often twinned. After Pasternak's departure she wrote:

Ла—донь в ладонь:	Hand into hand:
— За—чем рожден?	Why—was he born?
— Не—жаль: изволь:	Don't pity: allow [me]
Длить — даль — и боль.	To draw out—the distance—and pain.
	(April 23, 1923)
	(III, 69)

She sought pain because it generated poems. But here yet another emotion played a role: the main theme of these poems and letters is that this book is an intrusion, an unwanted invasion of her "serene" creative life. Half in jest, she wrote of her plans on finishing "The Swain":

> . . . and I, liberated, was already rejoicing: now I will write autocratic poems and copy over my Moscow diaries at leisure, and all will go so well. And suddenly—you, "wild, creeping, growing," (a deer? a reed?) with your questions for Pushkin, with your damned nightingale, with your barracks and convoys . . .

Pasternak's greeting had deflected her from her creative path and called forth unexpected (and perhaps unwanted?) poems:

> But you yourself hinder my writing. This broke through like a dam—the poems to you. And I recognize such strange things in them. They hurl you over, like waves.[15]

Just what strange things were they? Images of pain, almost of insult predominate in the first poem:

Не надо ее окликать:
Ей оклик — что охлест. Ей зов
Твой — раною по рукоять.
До самых органных низов

Встревожена — творческий страх
Вторжения — бойся, с высот
— Все крепости на пропастях! —
Пожалуй — органом вспоет.

А справишься? Сталь и базальт —
Гора, но лавиной в лазурь
На твой серафический альт
Вспоет — полногласием бурь.

И сбудется! — Бойся! — Из ста
На сотый срываются. . . Чу!
На оклик гортанный певца
Органною бурею мщу!

You mustn't call to her:
To her a call is a lash.[16] To her your call
Is a wound to the hilt.
To the very organ-like depths.

She is alarmed—the creative fear
Of intrusion—be afraid, from the heights
—All fortresses are over abysses!—
Perhaps, she will sing out like an organ.

But will you cope? Steel and basalt
The mountain, but like an avalanche into the
blue
She will sing out to your seraphic alto—
With a pleophony of storms.

And it will come to pass!—Fear it!—Of a
hundred
They fall through at the hundredth . . . Hark!
I'll avenge myself on the gutteral call of the
singer
With an organ-storm!
                    February 7, 1923
                          (III, 45)

It is peculiar that her answer to her "brother poet" begins with a warning: "You mustn't call to her." This is Tsvetaeva's masculine aggressive tone. But her aggression is also a defense. Answering his challenge, Tsvetaeva "avenges" herself with the "organ-storm" of her poems. This vengeance is nothing less than a poetic competition, to which we could well apply a phrase from one of Tsvetaeva's favorite poems in *Themes and Variations*, "A duel of two nightingales." Tsvetaeva asks if Pasternak can cope with her "pleophony of storms," the eruption of her emotions and poems.

She personifies herself first as an organ, then a mountain. It is not the last time Tsvetaeva would compare herself to a mountain, which in her poetic lexicon represented friendship and a striving for spiritual heights, as opposed to the sea, which symbolized love and passivity. Her poems and feelings are the eruption of a volcano.[17] The organ grows out of another leitmotif in the February poems, which mention the organ, voice, bag-pipe, lute, and guitar as well as the lyre, nightingale, the librettist Metastasio and the composer Schumann. Music played an important role in the childhood of both poets; Pasternak's mother, like Maria Mein, was a gifted pianist who gave up the chance of a concert career for marriage and a family. Not by chance had Pasternak titled the book *Themes and Variations*. Tsvetaeva wrote to him:

> For example I know that most of all you love Beethoven, (even more than Bach), that you are devoted to *Music* more passionately than to poetry . . .

that you are a Catholic (as a spiritual order, a nature) and not orthodox . . .[18]

Where she had gotten this information and to what extent it is true are not our concern here. What is important is that they explain the thematics of *Western* church music in these poems. For the organ is not used in the Orthodox church, and "cathedral alps" (poem of February 8, III, 45) are undoubtedly the image of a Gothic cathedral. She sings out like a powerful organ, while he has a "seraphic alto." In Russia, the alto is a *boy's* voice, yet Pasternak was already thirty-three, and this his fourth collection of verse! He was neither a boy nor a novice poet. But it is not simply a question of relative age. Recall what she wrote of Pasternak in "A Downpour of Light:"

> He doesn't yet know our words; his speech seems to come from a desert-island, from childhood, from the Garden of Eden: it doesn't quite make sense, and it knocks you over. At three this is common and is called, "a child." At twenty-three this is uncommon and is called, "a poet."[19]

The question of the roots of poetic imagination in the child had always fascinated her. It was precisely of this that Pasternak wrote in one of the poems in the new book, which Tsvetaeva liked so much she asked him to "give" it to her:

Так начинают. Года в два	Thus they begin. At about two
От мамки рвутся в тьму мелодий,	They rush from nurse to a swarm of melodies,
Щебечут, свищут, — а слова	They twitter, whistle—while words
Являются о третьем годе.	Appear around three.

According to her poems, Pasternak's' voice was not only "boyish," it was "guttural" and "broken" though she declared that "Your breaking voice is dearer to me than any heights!" She, the senior poet, evaluates and defends him, praising him and by that act underlining her right to judge. But why does she speak of his "breaking" voice? Perhaps, like many readers, she liked *Themes and Variations* less than *My Sister Life*. Perhaps she felt Pasternak's voice had "broken" in the search for too high a note, that his innovations in syntax and sound orchestration were not always successful.

> I'm beginning to guess about a secret of yours . . . Your passion for words is only proof of the extent to which they are for you only a *means to an end.* This passion is the *despair of narrative.* You love the sound more than the word, and (empty) noise more than sound, for in it is *everything.* But you are condemned to words, and you exhaust yourself like a forced laborer. . .You want the *impossible*, that which is outside the realm of words.[20]

Often, when we try to unravel the secrets of others, we rely on our own experience. These words characterize Tsvetaeva's late poetry no less than Pasternak's.

While her first two February poems spoke about Pasternak's *voice*, the poems "Emigrant" and "Soul" spoke about his soul. In praising his voice, she displayed the "boundlessness" of her own emotions; speaking of his soul, she flaunted her own voice. The first two poems were addressed directly to Pasternak; these are addressed to emigre Berlin, chiding it for not valuing its guest:

Здесь, меж вами: домами, деньгами, дымами,	Here among you, among houses, money, smoke, Ladies, Thoughts,
Дамами, Думами,	Not accepting you, not gone astray with you,
Не слюбившись с вами, не сбившись с вами	Like a certain Schumann carrying spring under his coat.
Неким —	Higher! Out of sight!
Шуманом пронося под полой весну:	The weight of a nightingale's tremolo—
Выше! йз виду!	A certain—chosen one.
Соловьиным тремоло на весу —	February 9, 1923
Некий — избранный.	(III, 46)

The nightingale's tremolo—the most traditional image of the poet—consciously answers another of her favorite poems in Pasternak's new book, "Margarita:"

Бился, щелкал, царил и сиял соловей.	The nightingale fought, trilled, reigned, radiated.
Он как запах от трав исходил. Он как ртуть	He emanated like a scent from the grass. He hung
Очумелых дождей меж черемух висел.	Like the mercury of maddened rains amidst
Он кору одурял. Задыхаясь, ко рту	the birdcherry.
Подступал. Оставался висеть на косе.	He stupefied the bark. Suffocating, he
	Came near the mouth. He remained hanging on the scythe.

This is one of the most virtuoso examples of Pasternak's sound orchestration. Tsvetaeva, in this "duel of nightingales," answered in an (untranslatable) orgy of alliteration and assonance (*"Lishnii! Vyshnii! Vykhodets! Vyzov! Vvys'/ Ne otvykshii . . . Viselets . . ."*):

Лишний! Вышний! Выходец! Вызов! Ввысь	Superfluous! Divine! Emigrant! Challenge!
Не отвыкший. . . Виселиц	He's not forgotten how to soar . . .
Не принявший. . . В рвани валют и виз	He refused to accept gallows . . . In the rags of
Веги — выходец.	hard currency and visas
	An emigrant—from Vega.
	February 9, 1923
	(III, 47)

What a difference! Pasternak works with the complex syntax of the written language, breaking it up and reconstructing it, while Tsvetaeva doesn't remake syntax—she simply does without it altogether. Hers is the oral language of exclamations, of unfinished sentences. Sending Pasternak these poems just before his departure, she wrote that "they absolutely must be read aloud, otherwise they'll fall flat."[21]

"The Soul" is also characterized by Tsvetaeva's bravura sound orchestration, adding to it a rhythmical bravado[22] totally absent in Pasternak, whose sound orchestration was couched in the framework of a quite traditional metrics. "Margarita," for example, is written in a classical four-foot anapest (uul/uul/uul/uul). Tsvetaeva was an innovator in rhyme as well as meter. In "Soul," the first three lines of each stanza rhyme, as do the fourth lines of each two stanzas (*aaab, cccb*), giving the poem a dynamic sense of striving and upward flight.

The three poems of "Scythians" (February 11–14) are also linked to Pasternak; they were composed during the same days when Tsvetaeva was—intermittently—writing him a long letter. There is a ciphered reference to their friendship:

Сосед, не спеши! Нечего	Neighbor, don't hurry! No need to hurry
Спешить, коли верст — тысячи.	If there are thousands of versts.
Разменной стрелой встречною	Through the exchange of meeting arrows
Когда-нибудь там — спишемся!	Sometime we will meet in letters—*there*!
	February 11, 1923
	(III, 48)

There is the theme of emotional self-defense as the persona asks protection from the great goddess Ishtar:

От стрел и от чар,	From arrows and charms,
От гнезд и от нор,	From nests and lairs,
Богиня Иштар	Goddess Ishtar
Храни мой шатер:	Protect my tent:
Братьев, сестер.	Of brothers and sisters.
	February 14, 1923
	(III, 49)

She asks the Great Mother goddess to protect her haven of non-sexual friendship from the dual threats of sexual attraction and domesticity. Those threats were strong; she described her obsession in almost sexual terms:

> You are wearisome in my life—my head tires. How many times a day do I lie down, lolling on my bed, capsized by all this cranial, between-the-ribs dissonance of lines, emotions, illuminations—and simply of noises. When you read [my poems] you'll believe it. Something has arisen and spread and doesn't want to stop, and I can't take it away.[23]

She foresaw that "it will be very difficult, very difficult for me to meet you face-to-face," and pointedly told him the story of how she intentionally avoided meeting Blok. She concluded, "I'll send the poems, but not now." The emotional outburst of her letters was serious enough. If Pasternak wasn't frightened off by them, then he could perhaps bear the force of the poems.

CHAPTER EIGHTEEN

A Missed Meeting: Pasternak's Return to Russia (March–June, 1923)

Inconsistency remained Tsvetaeva's hallmark. As she urged Pasternak "not to hurry," and warned about the dangers of face-to-face meetings, she was making plans which would give her an excuse for a trip to Berlin, a trip which depended on the goodwill of those Berlin publishers whom she scorned. She had returned to work on *Signs of Earth*, the book she proposed to make from her Moscow diaries of 1917–1919 (Alya's diaries were to form its second volume). When Vishniak first saw the diaries just after her emigration, he "almost tore the book from my hands," but she had done nothing with them since. She asked Gul' to prepare the ground for negotiations. "If I found a reliable publisher, I would come to Berlin at the beginning of May."[1] Meanwhile she asked Pasternak:

> Don't go back to Russia without seeing me. Russia is for me almost the other world. Were you to go to Guadeloupe, to the snakes, to the lepers, I wouldn't call you back. But go to Russia—I will. And so, Pasternak, I warn you. I will come. Outwardly on business, honestly, to you. To say farewell to your soul . . . I won't ask again, but if you don't fulfill my request (under whatever pretext)—*a wound for life.*[2]

Vishniak offered favorable terms for the book on one condition: that it contain no politics.

> Moscow of 1917–1919, does he think I was rocking in a cradle? . . .

> There is no *politics* in the book, there is a *passionate* truth: the biased truth of cold, hunger, anger, the *year*! My younger daughter died of hunger in a children's home—that is also "politics"—(the home was a Bolshevik one).

> Oh, Gelikon and Co.! Aesthetes! They don't want to dirty their hands. . . .[3]

Tsvetaeva's disdain erupts in two poems in which Ophelia addresses Hamlet. The Hamlet-like Visniak, who had once declared himself "in love with her verse," now was letting her down. Key words from earlier Vishniak poems ("adolescent," "coddle") pop up, and there are several references to a "chronicle," possibly *Signs of Earth*. But "Ophelia in Defense of the Queen" introduces the theme of forbidden passion and the persona of Phaedra, both linked in her later poems with Pasternak:

Принц Гамлет! Довольно царицыны недра	Prince Hamlet! Enough of defaming
Порочить. . . Не девственным — суд	The Queen's womb . . . It's not for the virginal
Над страстью. Тяжеле виновная — Федра:	To judge the passionate. Guiltier far
О ней и поныне поют.	Is Phaedra: Of her they sing to this day.

February 23, 1923
(III, 53)

Then Tsvetaeva heard from Liubov' Ehrenburg that Pasternak was getting ready to return to Russia. She would not have time to arrange her trip before he left. Wounded that he had not told her himself, she sent him a brief, correctly polite note—a slap in the face after the intimacy of her February letters:

> I hear from all sides that you are leaving for Russia . . . Leave your address, so I can send you my poems . . . Thank you again for your attention and memory . . .[4]

From this point on, all notes of poetic rivalry disappeared from her work, dislodged by her feelings for Pasternak the man.

"Phaedra I" (subtitled "Plaint") is one of the most frankly sensual poems ever written by a twentieth-century Russian poet, man or woman. Tormented by impossible passion for her stepson Hippolytus, Phaedra literally writhes with frustrated passion:

ЖАЛОБА   A PLAINT

Ипполит! Ипполит! Болит!	Hippolytus! Hippolytus! It aches!
Опаляет. . . В жару ланиты. . .	It scorches . . . My cheeks are ablaze . . .
Что за ужас жестокий скрыт	What a cruel horror is hidden
В этом имени Ипполита!	In this name of Hippolytus!
Точно длительная волна	Like a protracted wave
О гранитное побережье.	Hitting a granite embankment.
Ипполитом опалена!	I'm scorched by Hippolytus!
Ипполитом клянусь и брежу!	I swear by, rave of Hippolytus!
Руки в землю хотят — от плеч!	My arms want to flee my shoulders for the earth!
Зубы щебень хотят — в опилки! . .	My teeth want to grind stone to shavings! . . .
Вместе плакать и вместе лечь!	To cry together and lie together!
Воспаляется ум мой пылкий. . .	My passionate brain is inflamed!
Точно в ноздри и губы — пыль	As if the dust of Herculaneum has entered my
Геркуланума. . . Вяну. . . Слепну. . .	Nose and lips . . . I'm withering . . . I'll go blind . . .
Ипполит, это хуже пил!	Hippolytus! This is worse than saws!
Это суше песка и пепла!	This is dryer than sand and ashes!

March 7, 1923
(III, 54)

Two days later, she received a letter from Pasternak, asking her to come see him off in Berlin. Somewhat mollified, she explained why she could not come:

> I have a Soviet passport and no evidence of a dying relative in Berlin . . . in the best case, a visa takes two weeks . . . If you had written earlier, and if I had known that you were leaving so soon . . . I kept waiting for your letter, I didn't dare act without your permission, I didn't know whether you needed me or not . . . Now I know, but it's too late.[5]

With her reproaches out of the way, she confessed how much he had come to mean to her in what is, for all practical purposes, a declaration of love, though she studiously avoids the word:

> Now, frankly. What *is* it exactly? I am honest and clear, but, I swear, I don't know the word for it. I'll try them all! (To what extent I don't know you'll see from my February poems.) A meeting with you would have been for me a liberation from you yourself.[6]

Pasternak hoped to return in two years to Weimar. Tsvetaeva fixed her attention on the future, and planned her life till then:

> I will send you poems and everything that I have in life. I will speak to others about you, the poet. I won't disavow a single word, but if this is difficult for you, or unnecessary, I ask nothing but demand this: break it off. Then I'll suppress it, break it off, so it smoulders underground, as the poems did in February.[7]

She was well aware how frightening her intensity could be: "Two passions are contesting within me, two fears: the fear that you won't believe me, and the fear that, believing me, you will recoil." She sought to reassure him: "Don't be afraid. This is the only such letter I'll write . . . I'll control myself. Not in my poems. But you'll forgive it in my poems."[8] Of those poems, she sent him "Emigrant." She promised to send the rest of the February poems in another letter, but asked that he read them only once his train was underway. Was she afraid that if he read them first he might actually decide to stay? Or, more likely, that he would read them as a request to stay and leave anyway?

She returned to her notebook and added a second Phaedra poem, "A Missive," which begins in a somewhat more restrained tone. The "Tsarina" (Phaedra) sends greetings to "the capricious boy who flees from Phaedra." But by the second stanza, her longing surfaces again, and Phaedra declares what Tsvetaeva had nearly confessed to Pasternak: that her spiritual longing is inseparable from physical passion.

Ипполиту от Матери — Федры —
           Царицы — весть.
Прихотливому мальчику, чья красота
           как воск
От державного Феба, от Федры бежит. . .
           Итак,
Ипполиту от Федры: стенание нежных уст.

To Hippolytus from his Mother—from
    Phaedra—The Queen—news.
To the capricious boy, whose beauty,
Like wax from the sovereign Phoebus, flees
    from Phaedra..and so,
To Hippolytus from Phaedra: the moaning of
    tender lips.

Утоли мою душу! (Нельзя, не коснувшись
           уст
Утолить нашу душу!) Нельзя, припадя к
           устам,
Не припасть и к Психее, порхающей гостье
           уст. . .
Утоли мою душу: итак, утоли уста.

Slake my soul! (It's impossible, without touch-
    ing the lips, to
Slake the soul!) Impossible, without pressing
    lips,
To press Psyche, flitting guest of the lips . . .
Slake my soul: thus, slake my lips.

Ипполит, я устала. . . Блудницам и жрицам
           — стыд!
Не простое бесстыдство к тебе вопиет!
           Просты
Только речи и руки. . . За трепетом уст и
           рук
Есть великая тайна, молчанье на ней как
           перст.

Hippolytus, I'm tired . . . Shame to whores
    and priestesses!
It's not simple wantonness cries out to you!
Simple are only my speech and my arms. Behind
    the trembling of lips and arms
There's a great secret—the commanding finger
    of silence stands over it.
        March 11, 1923
        (III, 55)

In reproaching Hippolytus, Phaedra uses some of the same epithets that Tsvetaeva-Ophelia had hurled at Vishniak-Hamlet two weeks earlier: "virginal one," "adolescent."

Tsvetaeva's letters and lyrics often present two very different attitudes to the same event. As she was writing these plaints, she explained her predicament to Gul' in studiedly casual terms:

> My poet—my very favorite—Pasternak, of course—is leaving, and I can't even go to say farewell. I have no dying relative in Berlin, and I can't invent one by the 18th.[9]

She asked him to buy a copy of Eckermann's *Conversations with Goethe* and present it to Pasternak just before he left. She was quite explicit about the edition and the way the book was to be presented; the Eckermann was a talisman of their promised meeting in Goethe's Weimar two years hence. Tsvetaeva's insistence on detail was an attempt to assuage her disappointment by the acting-out of an exact ritual.

Pasternak left Berlin on March 18. Between March 17 and April 11, Tsvetaeva transformed her conflicting emotions into one of her greatest lyric cycles—the ten poems of "Wires" ("*Provoda*"). The cycle's title, major theme, and imagery revolve around a pun, one element of which is "provoda" (initially, the telegraph wires which followed Pasternak's train back to

Russia), the other "provody"—"a leave-taking, seeing off," the ritual of which Tsvetaeva felt cheated. Verbal coincidence (paranomasia) is the link which connects her two central concerns—her inability to see Pasternak off in Berlin (*provody*) and the inadequacy of earthly communications (*provoda*) for the spiritual intercourse of two poets.[10]

| Я прòводы вверяю проводàм | I entrust my farewells to the wires |
| И в телеграфный столб упершись — плачу. | And, leaning against the telegraph pole, I weep. |

March 18, 1923
(III, 58)

Here, as so often in her work, Tsvetaeva chooses the most emotionally charged moment for a seemingly incongruous play on words. This is neither unintentional nor frivolous—to her, the very essence of the poet's craft was just such a revelation of hidden parallels in language, whether or not justified by etymology. Tsvetaeva's devices of word-play—punning, paronomasia, or the reworking of an idiom, have another function as well. Their very incongruity serves to draw the reader's attention to the meaning of the words themselves, while avoiding emotional cliche; they serve as a sort of verbal *ostranenie*.[11]

Genuine as was her grief and disappointment at Pasternak's unexpected departure, Tsvetaeva was also glad to avoid a face-to-face encounter. Their earlier meetings in Moscow had been awkward and inconsequential; what if despite their increasingly intimate correspondence this happened again? That was obviously on Tsvetaeva's mind when she chose the epigraph for the cycle (it is from Hölderlin):

> Des Herzens Woge schaumte nicht so schon empor, und wurde Geist, wenn nicht der alte stumme Fels, das Schicksal, ihr entgegenstande.

> (The Heart's wave would not have foamed up so beautifully, and become spirit, had not the old mute cliff Fate risen in its path.)

The old mute cliff of Fate was the means for transmuting raw emotion (the heart's wave) into spirit (in Tsvetaeva's poetic lexicon, a synonym for the soul and its language—poetry). Satisfied emotion seldom turns to art as an outlet, nor, Tsvetaeva would have said, could friendships which faced no physical barriers in the world of *byt* ever rise into the realm of *byt'ie*.

While "Provoda" is a genuine emotional response to a real situation, it is also an artistic exploration of grief itself. The movement of emotion in the cycle is from despair to a confident promise, almost a threat, of eventual triumph. The first four poems, written during the days immediately surrounding Pasternak's departure, are more immediately concerned with the actual event. Their imagery centers around the telegraph poles which, like an escort, followed his train back to Russia. The last six, written somewhat later, abandon the railway and telegraph images and concentrate on Tsvetaeva's determination to carry on their dialogue along "lyrical wires," no matter what obstacles she may encounter. Telegraph poles are the first image in the opening poem:

Вереницею певчих свай,	Along a row of singing piles,
Подпирающих Эмпиреи,	Supporting the Empyrean,
Посылаю тебе свой пай	I send you my ration
Праха дольнего.	Of earthly dust.
По аллее	Along an avenue
Вздохов — проволокой к столбу —	Of sighs—like a wire to the pole—
Телеграфное: лю—ю—блю. . .	A telegraphic: I lo-ove . . .
Умоляю. . . (печатный бланк	I implore . . . (the printed blank
Не вместит! Проводами проще!)	Won't fit it! It's simpler by wire!)
Это — сваи, на них Атлант	These are the pilings on which Atlantis
Опустил скаковую площадь	Let down the race track
Небожителей. . .	Of the Olympians
Вдоль свай	Along the piles
Телеграфное: про—о—щай. . .	The telegraphic: Fa-are-well!

As if she cannot bear to introduce them in their unvarnished reality, Tsve-taeva has already transformed the poles into "a row of singing piles sup-porting the Empyrean;" the mundane telephone poles make an incongruous underpinning for the games of the gods. On the eve of Pasternak's depar-ture, she tries to send not a message but her mortal body—the "ration of earthly dust" which cannot get to Berlin—along the wires. But her voice grows alien as it travels along this "avenue of sighs," becoming mechanical, telegraphic. The medium is inadequate to her message, and she cannot even be certain she is getting through. "Do you hear?" she asks, desperately. Her cries of hopeless despair rise to blend with their mythical antecedents:

Выше, выше — и сли—лись	Higher, higher—and they're merged
В Ариаднино: ве—ер—нись,	With Ariadna's: re-turn!
Обернись! . .	Turn back!

Like Eurydice, she longs to call the departing traveller back:

Через насыпи — и — рвы	Across the embankments and the ditches
Эвридикино: у—у—вы,	Eurydice's: alas!
Не у—	Don't g—
	March 17, 1923
	(III, 57-58)

But the last line is incomplete, broken off, unheard in the distance (or unspoken?).

The second poem of the cycle asks whether poetry, even the greatest, is adequate to express grief. She questions the ability of generalizing art to express emotions, for all losses are individual and unique:

Чтоб высказать тебе. . . да нет, в ряды
И в рифмы сдавленные. . . Сердце — шире!
Боюсь, что мало для такой беды
Всего Расина и всего Шекспира!

«Всѐ плакали, и если кровь болит. . .
Всѐ плакали, и если в розах — змеи». . .
Но был один — у Федры — Ипполит!
Плач Ариадны — об одном Тезее!

To express to you—But no, not squeezed
Into ranks and rhythms—the heart is broader!
I fear that for such a woe all of Shakespeare,
   all of Racine are inadequate!

"They all cried, and if the blood pains . . .
They all cried, and if there are serpents in the
roses . . ."
But Phaedra had *one* Hippolytus.
Ariadna wept for *one* Theseus!

Her loss is particularly keen, for she has lost not a friend whose potential
was explored, but one whom she had only begun to know:

Что я в тебе утрачиваю всех
Когда-либо и где-либо *небыших*!

. . . I lose in you all who
Have ever *not been*!
                              March 18, 1923
                              (III, 58)

She tries to deny the truth spoken by the calendar, that this is indeed the
day of his departure. But the dimensions of her quest are as boundless as
her grief, and realizing the futility of her situation, she entrusts her farewell
to the hopelessly inadequate telegraph wire.

In the third poem, Tsvetaeva explores the various ways in which she can
"get through," constructing a new myth of her non-terrestrial communication with Pasternak. It is now to be *lyrical* wires which ring with her lofty
yearning. They will run from pole to pole, "across the evil years of the
epoch, across embankments built of lies" (i.e., the political boundaries which
now separated them) and carry Tsvetaeva's "unpublished sighs," her "furious passion" without benefit of earthbound telegraphy. (III, 58) Her heart,
with a magnetic spark, "breaks the meter"—breaks out from the rigid limitations of *byt*, submissive to the power which those telegraph poles represent. Hers is the revenge of the fourth dimension. (III, 60)

With Pasternak gone a week, Tsvetaeva declared her unusual strength of
vision:

Не чернокнижница! В белой книге
Далей донских навострила взгляд!
Где бы ты ни был — тебя настигну,
Выстрадаю — и верну назад.

Ибо с гордыни своей, как с кедра,
Мир озираю: плывут суда,
Зарева рыщут. . . Морские недра
Выворочу — и верну со дна!

No sorceress! In the white book
Of Don distances I sharpened my gaze—
No matter where you are, I'll over-take you,
Win you by suffering, and bring you back.

For from the height of my pride, as from a
   cedar,
I view the world: ships are sailing,
Fire-glows rove . . . I'll turn up
The ocean depth—and bring you back from
   the bottom!

The "White book of the Don distances" is *Swans' Encampment*. Having "sharpened her gaze" across that five-year separation from Sergei, and brought him back alive, she is prepared to tackle the new challenge of her separation from Pasternak. She is omnipresent and eternal, and vows "to attain his lips as God attains the soul." Yet suddenly, she stops in her tracks, powerless, as she remembers that Pasternak is not alone, that his wife occupies a place she cannot pretend to usurp in *this* world. She will wait for her final triumph in the next.[12]

Ибо другая с тобой, и в судный	For another is with you, and on the
День не тягаются. . .	Judgment Day one does not sue . . .
Вьюсь и длюсь.	I'll hover and last.
Есмь я и буду я и добуду	I am and I will be, and I'll win your
Душу — как губы добудет уст-	Soul—as The Peacegiver will attain
Упокоительница. . .	Your lips.

March 25, 1923
(III, 61-62)

At this point in the manuscript Tsvetaeva made a note, later incorporated in a letter to Pasternak, which could serve as an epigraph for the whole cycle:

> Verses are the traces by which I enter your soul. But your soul grows ever more distant, and I, greatly annoyed, run ahead, leap, blindfold, at random, and then, fainting, wait—which way will he turn?[13]

It was only not space and time or the existence of a rival which frustrated Tsvetaeva. Pasternak, as we know from his published letters, could be as maddeningly cryptic in them as he was in his poetry. Clearly her friendship meant a great deal to him, but exactly what and how much was hard for her to know.

Pasternak's departure, transformed by her mythic imagination, has become a symbolic journey in which the landmarks are emotions writ large:

В час, когда мой милый брат	At the hour when my dear brother
Миновал последний вяз	Passed the last elm
(Взмахов, выстроенных в ряд),	(Of waves of the hand, set up in a row),
Были слезы — больше глаз.	There were tears—bigger than my eyes.
В час, когда мой милый друг	At the hour when my dear friend
Огибал последний мыс	Rounded the last promontory
(Вздохов мысленных: вернись!)	(Of unspoken sighs: "turn back!")
Были взмахи — больше рук.	There were waves—larger than my hands.

March 26, 1923
(III, 61)

The pace and tempo of the poem add to the unreal effect—heavy and ponderous, it reads like a dream in slow motion. Tsvetaeva's hyperbolic treatment of herself and her outsize grief recall the early work of Mayakovsky:

Пройду,	I'll pass by
любовищу мою волоча.	Dragging my enormous love
В какой ночи,	In what night
бредовой,	Delirious,
недужной,	Ailing,
какими Голиафами я зачат —	By what Goliaths was I conceived—
такой большой	So big
и такой ненужный?	And so unneeded?

"To His Beloved Self the Author
Dedicates These Lines" (1916)

And, in another tonality entirely, Pasternak himself:

Куда мне радость деть мою?	Where can I fit my joy?
В стихи, в графленую осьмину?	Into poems, onto ruled paper?

"Our Thunderstorm"
(1917)

But the author of the phrase, "tears—bigger than my eyes" was actually Sonechka Holliday. Once, telling Tsvetaeva about some insult, Holliday remarked, "Oh, Marina! My tears were so big—larger than my eyes!" Tsvetaeva promised to steal the phrase and put it into a poem; four years later, she did.[14]

As Tsvetaeva asserts her patience and determination to wait out the separation, her manner harkens back to the incantation-poems of 1917 and 1918:

Терпеливо, как щебень бьют,	Patiently, as one crushes rock
Терпеливо, как смерти ждут,	Patiently, as one waits for death
Терпеливо, как вести зреют,	Patiently, as news ripens
Терпеливо, как месть лелеют —	Patiently, as one nurtures revenge.

March 27, 1923
(III, 62)

Some of her waiting images are painful ("Patiently, as one gnaws one's fingers") or dull ("Patiently, as one strings beads"). Yet two of them are unambiguously erotic: "Thus her lover awaits the Queen" and "Patiently, as one draws out bliss." Or is it the waiting intself which is something close to bliss? It seems clear, as the cycle progresses, that Tsvetaeva is intentionally prolonging her grief, as she acknowledged in the cycle "Words and Meanings":

Ты обо мне не думай никогда!	Don't think about me ever!
(На—вязчива!)	(I'm persistent!)
Ты обо мне подумай: провода:	Think of me only thus: wires
Даль — длящие.	Prolonging the distance.
Ты на меня не жалуйся, что жаль. . .	Don't complain of me, that you're sorry.
Всех слаще мол. . .	That I'm sweetest of all . . .
Лишь об одном пожалуйста: педаль:	I only ask for one thing, please: the pedal
Боль — длящая.	Which prolongs the pain.

April 23, 1923

(III, 68)

Tsvetaeva invites Pasternak to join in her favorite form of communication, the mutual dream. "Sleep rejoins all broken sets: perhaps we'll see each other in our dreams." She bemoans the lot of those, like herself, who "cry without a shoulder" [to cry on]—taking advantage of the opportunity for another play on words: *pechal-, plach-, plech-.*

. . . О, печаль	. . . Oh, the grief
Плачущих без плеча!	Of those who cry without a shoulder!

April 5, 1923

(III, 63)

She cries because "the places are all occupied, the hearts are rented out." The hearts in question are hers and Pasternak's, "rented out" to their respective mismatched spouses and doomed to live out their earthly lives "without bliss," walled up alive in "the archive, the Elysium of cripples."

In the final poem of the cycle she develops more explicitly the notion of a "poetic marriage," to which their worldly marriages would make no difference. She vows to become for him "a treasurehouse of likenesses, sensed at random moments" which are the stuff of the poet's art. More than that, she will present him with a "living offspring, now quickening beneath her skirt." This "miracle of the womb," their "first-born" will be nothing less nor more than "song" itself—the time-honored eponym of poetry. With this firstborn she will "overpower the most certain thicket of the womb with seemings"— overcome reality, that is, with the creatures of her poetic imagination. (III, 63) This may well be her answer to a fact she could have learned from Liubov' Ehrenburg: Pasternak's wife was three months' pregnant when they left Berlin.

"Poets" is a magnificent statement about the ambivalent stature of the poet, particularly in those two Russian worlds (emigration and Moscow) where Tsvetaeva and "her" poet lived. She began the poetic triptych between the ninth and tenth poems of "Wires." Its first poem describes the poet in the third person: his path, "the comet's path," is roundabout and unpredictable, "not foretold by the calendar." He is the one whose place it is to be out of place. Like Pasternak, he is always just beyond reach.

Он тот, кто смешивает карты,
Обманывает вес и счет,
Он тот кто *спрашивает* с парты,
Кто Канта нàголову бьет,

He is the one who mixes up the cards,
Who swindles weight and tally.
He's the one who *questions* from the school
    bench,
Who puts Kant to rout,

Кто в каменном гробу Бастилий
Как дерево в своей красе.
Тот, чьи следы — всегда простыли,
Тот поезд, на который все
Опаздыают. . .
        — ибо путь комет

Who, in the stony grave of the Bastille
Is like a tree in his beauty.
He whose tracks are always cold,
The train which everyone
Misses . . .
            for the comet's path

Поэтов путь: жжя, а не согревая,
Рвя, а не взращивая — взрыв и взлом —
Твоя стезя, гривастая кривая,
Не предугадана календарем!

Is the poet's path, burning, but not warming,
Tearing, but not nurturing—explosion and
    breaking open—
Thy path, long-maned curve,
Is not predicted by the calendar!
            April 8, 1923
            (III, 67)

"Poets 2" uses one of Tsvetaeva's favorite techniques—the sudden, ironic shift of tone. The first three stanzas describe those in the world who are "superfluous appendages." The key here is the seemingly innocuous phrase "in the world"—i.e., in *this*, lower world:

Есть в мире лишние, добавочные,
Невписанные в окоём.
(Нечислящимся в ваших справочниках,
Им свалочная яма — дом).

There are in the world superfluous ones,
    accessory ones
Who can't be grasped with the eye.
They're not mentioned in your guidebooks,
A waste dump is home to them.

Есть в мире полые, затолканные,
Немотствующие — навоз,
Гвоздь — вашему подолу шелковому!
Грязь брезгует из-под колес!

There are in the world hollow ones, jostled ones,
Mute ones: manure,
A nail to your silk skirt!
Even mud from beneath wheels avoids them!

Есть в мире мнимые, невидимые:
(Знак: лепрозариумов крап!)
Есть в мире Иовы, что Иову
Завидовали бы — когда б:

There are in the world imaginary ones, invisible
    ones
(Their sign: the spot of leprosariums!)
There are in the world Jobs, who would
Envy Job—if:

Поэты мы — и в рифму с париями,
Но выступив из берегов
Мы бога у богинь оспариваем
И девственницу у богов!

We are poets—it rhymes with pariahs,
But, overstepping our bounds
We'll contend with goddesses for a god,
And with the gods for a virgin!
            April 22, 1923
            (III, 67)

While the first poem was about *the* poet (Pasternak) and the second about "us" (in the first person plural), the third, in the first person singular, is about Tsvetaeva herself and her predicament in a world where she does not fit:[15]

Что же мне делать, певцу и перевенцу,	What am I to do, singer and firstborn,
В мире, где наичернейший — сер!	In a world where the blackest is grey!
Где вдохновенье хранят, как в термосе!	Where they keep inspiration
С этой безмерностью	As if in a thermos!
В мире мер?!	With this measurelessness
	In a world of measures?!
	April 22, 1923
	(III, 68)

An event in the world of *byt* intensified her alienation:

> Our landlords lodged a complaint, the sheriff came and shouted at us (the pretext: damp walls and an unwashed floor). Tomorrow we have to appear in court in the next hamlet. We lived through the whole winter in this rotten hole, where, despite the fact that we stoked the fire every day, streams flowed down the walls and mushrooms grew in the corners. And now, when summer has come, when everywhere it is paradise, "You've ruined the room—get out on the street!" Seryozha is exasperated and overwrought by the coming trial, and I in general have grown tired of earthly life. You throw up your hands when you think how many washed and unwashed floors lie ahead, boiled and unboiled milk, landlords, saucepans . . .[16]

The affair turned out better than expected. When Sergei arrived in court with a fellow student to serve as translator, the landlord thought him to be a lawyer, got frightened, and simply asked the court to request "Pan Sergei" to wash the floor in the room a bit cleaner. But Tsvetaeva's underlying alienation from *this* world was permanent:

> I don't know how to live in the world!

> Do you believe in another world? I do. But in a dire Retribution. In a world where intentions reign, in a world where the judges will be judged. . . . There they will judge not by my dress (here everyone's is better than mine, for which in life they hate me so) but by my essence, which has kept me from being concerned with dress.[17]

Life looked so bleak that she even looked back on Berlin with envy: "How I felt like a human being there, and here I am worse than the lowliest dog!"

At the beginning of May, Tsvetaeva's poetry temporarily abandoned its preoccupation with Pasternak. Though the lyrics came even faster (fifteen in seventeen days), the emotional intensity of the Pasternak poems is missing. Her concern, instead, is the related one of imagination, the rejection of seeming reality for greater truths. "In Praise of Time" (III, 74) is deeply ironic. Real time is her enemy—it deceives her, cheats her. She, "born outside it" will simply bypass it.[18] The "refugee highway" with which the poem opens, and the date of the poem suggest that this is an anniversary poem: on May 11 it was exactly a year since she left Russia. "Sibyl to the Babe" (III, 25) proclaims that "non-life" is preferable to life in this world: birth is really a fall, while death is a kind of resurrection:

Плачь, маленький, о них и нас:	Cry, little one, about them and us!
Рождение — паденье в час!	Birth is a falling into time!
. . . .	. . . .
Смерть, маленький, не спать, а встать,	Death, little one, is not to sleep, but to rise,
Не спать, а вспять.	Not to sleep, but return.

May 17, 1923
(III, 25)

With this poem, she finished the "Sibyl" cycle, as she had just completed "Trees." She was tying up the loose ends of this notebook, which covered her first year in emigration. In her mind, it was already a complete book of verse, and she wrote of it as such to Roman Gul': she called it *Intentions* (*Umysly*). She tried to turn back to the work of copying her Moscow diaries and finding a publisher for them, but she could not keep the lyrics at bay for long, nor forget her obsession with Pasternak.

The "Second Notebook" of *After Russia* opens with Hamlet's conscience reproaching him for insufficient devotion to Ophelia:

На дне она, где ил:	She's on the bottom where there's silt:
Ил!. . И последний венчик	Silt! And her last crown
Всплыл на приречных бревнах. . .	Has floated onto the riverbank logs . . .
— Но я ее любил	—But I loved her
Как сорок тысяч. . .	Like forty thousand . . .
— Меньше,	—Less
Все ж, чем один любовник.	Though, than one lover.
На дне она, где ил.	She's on the bottom, where there's silt
— Но я ее —	—But I—
(недоуменно)	(perplexed)
— любил??	—*loved* her?

June 5, 1923
(III, 79)

The poem could be read in the light of Tsvetaeva's negotiations with Vishniak, or it could have something to do with the Hamlet-like Pasternak, from whom she might by now have expected a letter (it was almost three months since he returned to Moscow).

Her "lyric wires" were not working as well as she predicted; Pasternak's absence, despite her brave boasts, was distancing him from her. Every day of absence made him harder to reach, she complained in "Crevasse," the first of three poems addressed to Pasternak which commemorate the first

anniversary of their correspondence. Again she is a volcano, which has
dealt with him "as Aetna with Empedocles." His image sleeps within her
"as if in a crystal coffin" (in an ice crevasse, that is), and she bids him tell
his household that their efforts to monopolize his affection are futile. In
"Sahara," she is a desert, which has buried him within herself; she defies
others to find him:

Напрасные поиски,	Your search is in vain,
Красавцы, не лгу!	My beauties, I do not lie!
Пропавший покоится	The lost one is resting
В надёжном гробу.	In a reliable grave.
Стихами как странами	With poems like countries
Чудес и огня,	Of wonder and fire,
Стихами — как странами	With poems like countries
Он въехал в меня:	He rode into me.
Сухую, песчаную,	Dry I am, and sandy,
Без дна и без дня.	Bottomless, timeless.
Стихами — как странами	With poems—like countries
Он канул в меня.	He sank into me.

July 3, 1923
(III, 84)

The incessant rain in Mokropsy recalled the rain-soaked poems of *My
Sister Life*, and seemed to be an unsent letter from Pasternak:

Строительница струн — приструню	Tuner of strings—I'll tune
И эту. Обожди	Even this one. Wait a bit
Расстраиваться! (В сем июне	Before you get upset![19] (This June
Ты плачешь, ты — дожди!)	*You* are crying, you are the rains!)
И если гром у нас — на крышах,	And if we have thunder on the roofs,
Дождь — в доме, ливень — сплошь —	Rain in the house, downpour all over—
Так это ты письмо мне пишешь,	Then that's a letter you're writing me
Которого не шлешь.	Which you do not send.

June 30/July 3, 1923
(III, 84)

A variant of the poem ends with a more direct plea: "Friend! Mail the
Letter!"

CHAPTER NINETEEN

The Search for a Substitute: Bachrach and Rodzevich

Isolated in the Czech countryside, Tsvetaeva particularly needed kindred souls in the outside world. Yet Pasternak had not written since he returned to Russia. She found a temporary substitute in the young emigre critic Alexander Bachrach, who published a sympathetic review of *Craft* in a Berlin newspaper.[1] Tsvetaeva, who usually had no use for critics, wrote to thank him:

> I don't know if it is usual to answer a critic other than with caustic remarks and in print. But poets not only do not observe ceremonies, they create them. Alow me now, in this letter, to establish a rite of gratitude: to the critic by the poet.[2]

It was generous thanks, for in her letter she revealed a good deal about herself and her work. (Her motives, to tell the truth, were not entirely self-less. She thought Bachrach might help in finding a publisher for *Signs of Earth*.) Bachrach answered and almost simultaneously published a review of *Psyche*. Tsvetaeva particularly liked one passage, reminiscent of what she had written of Pasternak:

> Tsvetaeva is dynamic by nature, and the world and existence in her poetry are but a tireless *perpetum mobile* . . . which does not hesitate before any barriers (even before the abundantly-placed sluice-gates of all-conquering love), a tur-bulent and swift stream, ever united and integral, where only the landscape along the banks changes unceasingly . . .[3]

In her next letter, she set forth the fundamental conditions of her corre-spondence friendships, and explained to Bachrach why he was so attractive to her: "An unknown man is all possibilities, the one from whom you keep expecting things . . . He still doesn't exist—he will exist only tomorrow . . ." In an equally frank passage, she explained her reading of the Sibyl myth:

> Your voice is young, I heard that right off. Indifferent, sometimes even hostile to physical youth, I love the youth of voices. Here is an epigraph to one of my future books (words put into the mouth of Sibyl by Ovid, I cite it from memory). "My veins will dry up, my bones dry out, but fate will leave me my VOICE, MY VOICE! . . ."
>
> Your voice is young—that touches me and immediately makes me a thousand years old—a kind of stone maternity—the maternity of a cliff . . .[4]

Of the nine poems she wrote between July 14 and August 14, all but one were addressed and sent to Bachrach during their brief but intense correspondence. Tsvetaeva kept trying to explain and define the relationship she sought:

> I want a miracle from you. A miracle of trust, a miracle of understanding, a miracle of self-denial. I want you, at twenty, to be both a seventy-year-old man and a seven-year-old boy. I want no ages, calculations, battles, barriers.

> I don't know who you are. I know nothing about your life. With you, I am entirely free—I speak with a spirit.[5]

In a poem written on the back of that letter, Tsvetaeva described a nocturnal spiritual encounter:

В глубокий час души и ночи,	In a deep hour of the night and the soul,
Нечислящийся на часах,	Not reckoned on the clock,
Я отроку взглянула в очи,	I gazed into a youth's eyes,
Нечислящиеся в ночах	Not reckoned yet
Ничьих еще, двойной запрудой	In anyone's nights, a double mill-pond
— Без памяти и по края! —	—Without memory and full to the brim!—
Покоящиеся. . .	Reposing . . .
Отсюда	From this
Жизнь начинается твоя.	Your life begins.
Седеющей волчицы римской	The gaze of a greying Roman wolf,
Взгляд, в выкормыше зрящей — Рим!	Who discerns in her fosterling—Rome!
Сновидящее материнство	The dreaming maternity
Скалы. . . Нет имени моим	Of a cliff . . . There is no name for
	My lost-nesses . . . All covers removed—
Потерянностям. . . Всё покровы	Grown up out of losses!
Сняв — выросшая из потерь! —	Thus, once, above a reed basket
Так некогда над тростниковой	Knelt the daughter
Корзиною клонилась дщерь	Of Egypt . . .
	July 14, 1923
Египетская. . .	(III, 87)

Their difference in age allowed her to justify the emotional intensity of her letters as maternal solicitude. Those letters grew longer, more frequent, more intimate.[6] But in response there was suddenly silence. While waiting for his next letter, Tsvetaeva turned to her notebook with poems and rough drafts of the letter she would write when next she heard from him: she eventually titled this diary of growing exasperation her "Medical Certificate." Those poems continued to describe her ideal friendship. In "Sea-Shell" (III, 89) she takes her young protege out of the "leprosarium of lies and evil" (read: Russian Berlin) and cradles him protectively in the shell-like shelter of her palms. The persona will keep her foster son in this womb-like refuge while his soul develops like a pearl.

Five days after Bachrach's last card, she felt him fading away. She began to fear she had scared him off with her emotional excess: "When people who have met me for an hour are horrified by the measure of the emotions which they inspire in me, they make a triple error: not they, not in me, not measure." Her pain culminated in the much-anthologized poem, "The Letter:"

Так писем не ждут,	This isn't the way we wait for mail,
Так ждут — письма́.	This is the way we await—one letter.
Тряпичный лоскут,	A ragged scrap,
Вокруг тесьма	Around it a ribbon
Из клея. Внутри — словцо.	Of glue. Inside—a word.
И счастье. И это — всё.	And happiness. And that's all.
Так счастья не ждут,	This isn't the way we wait for happiness,
Так ждут — конца:	This is the way we await the end:
Солдатский салют	A soldiers' salute
И в грудь — свинца	And three bits of lead
Три дольки. В глазах красно̀.	In the chest. Your eyes see red.
И только. И это — всё.	And only red. And that's all.
Не счастья — стара!	Not happiness—I'm too old!
Цвет — ветер сдул!	The wind's blown away the blossom!
Квадрата двора	The square of a courtyard
И черных дул.	And black muzzles.
(Квадрата письма:	(The square of a letter:
Чернил и чар!)	Ink and magic!)
Для смертного сна	No one is too old
Никто не стар!	For a mortal dream!
	The square of a letter.
Квадрата письма.	August 11, 1923
	(III, 91)

Tsvetaeva describes the torment of waiting, not for mail, but for one *specific* letter, from one *specific* correspondent, on one level, Bachrach. But on another level, it was Pasternak.

Finally, Tsvetaeva could stand the suspense no longer. She wrote Bachrach an icily cold note: "If my letters arrived—all explanations of your silence are superfluous, and your further concern about my worldly affairs is gratefully declined."[7] Two days later, a letter came, and she was "insanely happy." The correspondence resumed, but Tsvetaeva was more cautious. Even though the long silence was due to lost letters (one of hers, one of his), she suspected that the break in the correspondence had affected Bachrach little, if at all. She told him of the "Medical Certificate" and of the poems she had written, which she promised to send—but only after his next letter arrived, as a token of reassurance. She did eventually send them, but was never quite as open and unrestrained again.

The summer of 1923 was a time of major changes. For the first time since 1920, Tsvetaeva thought of writing for the theater. Her later plays, however, are very different from the romantic dramas she wrote in Moscow. Her attraction to dialogue—evident in the Hamlet and Ophelia poems of February and June—and her growing interest in Greek myth eventually coalesced into a grand plan for a trilogy of verse tragedies, to be called "The Wrath of Aphrodite." The hero of the trilogy would be Theseus, cursed by Aphrodite because he abandoned her favorite, Ariadne. She spent much of the summer and early fall of 1923 rereading the Greeks, and the effect on her own work is perceptible in a new monumental simplicity of style.

That fall, she was separated for the first time from her own Ariadna; Alya finally began her formal education in a boarding school for Russian children in Moravia, while Sergei and Marina took a room in Prague. In emigration, Ariadna reverted to the childhood she never had in Moscow: "Alya, who from the age of two to nine was my 'echo in the mountains' now plays with dolls and is profoundly indifferent to me."[8] Still, Tsvetaeva found the parting very difficult.

> I am now at an internal (and external) crossroads; a year of my life—in the woods, with poetry, with trees, without people—is finished. I am on the eve of a big new city (perhaps—a big new grief?) and a big new life in it; on the eve of a new self.[9]

The "big new grief" was a brief, tempestuous love affair, linked in Tsvetaeva's poetry with the urban landscape of Prague. Its hero was Konstantin Rodzevich (1895—), a former White officer now studying in Prague. Rodzevich struck Mark Slonim, who met him only twice, as "rather cunning, not without humor, rather dull, of mediocre caliber."[10] Ariadna was less privy to this romance of her mother's than to many others, since it took place while she was at boarding school. But she knew Rodzevich later on as a friend of the family: soon after his affair with Tsvetaeva, he married the daughter of the emigre theologian Sergei Bulgakov, and by a quirk of fate worthy of a Nabokov plot later became a neighbor of Tsvetaeva's in Paris, where she saw him frequently.[11]

> The hero of the poems was endowed with a rare gift of charm, combining courage with spiritual grace, tenderness with irony, responsiveness with offhandedness, captivation (the ability to be captivated) with fickleness, gentleness with hot temper . . . Charm was in his appearance, manners, and wit, his quick repartee and decisiveness, his youth, even boyishness . . .
>
> And I will add that Seryozha loved him like a brother . . .[12]

Indeed, Sergei was quite complacent about the affair, or at least realized there was little he could do to prevent it. It was probably Rodzevich of whom Tsvetaeva wrote to Bachrach as early as August 16:

My hiking companion is a youngish boy, simple, quiet. He was in the war, and now he's a student. He names for me all the birds in the forest and all the birds in flight. Together we follow animal trails. I don't like natural science, but I listen to him with pleasure. He himself is like a wild little beast—he's wary of everyone. But he trusts me. He doesn't like poems and doesn't read them.[13]

The sensual "Magdalene" cycle of August 26–31, however, describes a very different relationship:

Пеною уст и накипями	With the foam of lips and the scales
Очес и пòтом всех	Of my eyes and the sweat of all
Нег. . . В волоса заматываю	Languor . . . I wind your feet
Ноги твои, как в мех.	In my hair, as in fur.
Некою тканью под ноги	I spread myself like a cloth beneath
Стелюсь. . . Не тот ли (та!)	Your feet . . . Are you not he (I am she!)
Твари с кудрями огненными	Who said to the creature with the flaming curls:
Молвивший: встань, сестра!	Arise, sister!

August 26, 1923
(III, 95)

Almost all the poems in *After Russia* written from late August through October 1923 should be read in light of the affair. Like the "Magdelene" poems, they share a sensuality distinct from the frustrated passion of the Pasternak poems or the strident maternity of the Bachrach poems. Most are set against the background of nighttime Prague, and her sense of guilt is a constant theme:

НОЧНЫЕ МЕСТА	NIGHT PLACES
Темнейшее из ночных	The darkest of night places: a bridge.—
Мест: мост. — Устами в уста!	Lips against lips!
Неужели ж нам свой крест	Are we really deigned to drag our cross
Тащить в дурные места,	To these evil places,
Туда: в веселящий газ	There: to the laughing gas
Глаз, газа. . . В платный Содом?	Of eyes, of gas . . . To a paid Sodom?
На койку, где всё до нас!	To a cot where all have been before us!
На койку, где нè вдвоем	To a cot where no one goes
Никто. . . Никнет ночник.	Except in twos . . . The night light dims.
Авось — совесть уснет!	Perhaps—conscience will slumber!

October 4, 1923
(III, 101)

How long the affair lasted is not completely clear. Ariadna Efron, judging by an entry in her mother's notebook, dates the break December 12, 1923, the date of a poem that seems to record the end of the romance.[14]

Ты, меня любивший фальшью	You who loved me with the falseness
Истины — и правдой лжи,	Of truth—and the truth of lie,
Ты, меня любивший — дальше	You, who loved me—further would
Некуда! — За рубежи!	Be impossible—beyond the borders!
Ты, меня любивший дольше	You, who loved me longer
Времени. — Десницы взмах!	Than time.—The wave of a right hand!—
Ты меня не любишь больше:	You don't love me any longer:
Истина в пяти словах.	Truth in six words.

December 12, 1923
(III, 133)

The episode would deserve but a footnote in Tsvetaeva's biography, except that it provided the material for what many consider her masterpieces: "The Poem of the Mountain" and "The Poem of the End," arguably the most important and influential *poemy* written in Russian between Blok's "The Twelve" (1918) and Akhmatova's "Requiem" (1935–1940) and "Poem without a Hero" (1940–1962).

The mountain was Petrushin Hill in Prague, topped by a park, where the lovers spent their happiest moments. The major tension in the poem is a familiar one—between the mountain's straining upward, like Tsvetaeva's own attempt to make the relationship into a higher, spiritual one, and the downward pull of *byt*, connected with her lover's hunger for domesticity. She is well aware that the mountain itself is unexceptional, that it is her own imagination that has transformed it. Her mountain has a will and a personality of its own. It is she ("mountain" in Russian is feminine) who acts as matchmaker:

Как бы титана лапами	As if with a Titan's paws
Кустарников и хвой —	Of bushes and branches—
Гора хватала зà полы,	The mountain grabbed me by the skirts
Приказывала: стой!	And ordered: Halt!
О, далеко не азбучный	Oh, it's a far from elementary paradise—
Рай — сквознякам сквозняк!	A draft to end all drafts!
Гора валила навзничь нас,	The mountain bowled us over,
Притягивала: ляг!	Pulled us to it: lie down!
Оторопев под натиском,	Struck dumb under her onslaught—
— Как? Не понять и днесь! —	How? I still don't understand!
Гора, как сводня — святости,	The mountain, like a procuress—of sanctity,
Указывала: здесь. . .	Pointed: here . . .

(IV, 162)

The magnificent alliteration and anaphora of parts six and seven ("Gora gorevala") grew out of the spell-binding *zaklinanie* of Tsvetaeva's gypsy poems:

Гора горевала, что только грустью	The mountain grieved, that what now is
Станет — что ныне и кровь и зной.	Blood and heat—will become only sadness.
Гора говорила, что не отпустит	The mountain grieved that she wouldn't let us
Нас, не допустит тебя с другой!	go,
	Wouldn't permit you to be with another!
Гора горевала, что только дымом	The mountain grieved that what now is both
Станет — чтò ныне: и Мир, и Рим.	The world and Rome will become only smoke.
Гора говорила, что быть с другими	The mountain said we must
Нам (не завидую тем, другим!).	Be with others (I don't envy those others!).
Гора горевала о страшном грузе	The mountain grieved of the terrible weight
Клятвы, которую поздно клясть.	Of the vow which it's too late to vow.
Гора говорила, что стар тот узел	The mountain said the Gordian knot
Гордиев: долг и страсть.	Was too ancient: duty and passion.
Гора горевала о нашем горе:	The mountain grieved about our grief:
Завтра! Не сразу! Когда над лбом —	Tomorrow! Not now! When above the brow—
Уж не memento, — а просто — море!	Is no longer *memento*, but simply the sea![15]
Завтра, когда поймем.	Tomorrow, when we will understand!
Звук. . . ну как будто бы кто-то просто,	The sound of . . . as if simply someone
Ну. . . плачет вблизи?	Is . . . well . . . crying nearby?
Гора горевала о том, что врозь нам	The mountain grieved, that we had to
Вниз, по такой грязи —	Go down separately, through such mud—
В жизнь, про которую знаем всё мы:	Into the life which we all know:
Сброд — рынок — барак.	Riff-raff—the market place—a barrack.
Еще говорила, что все поэмы	And it said, too, that all poems
Гор — пишутся — *так*.	Of the mountain—are written—this way.

(IV, 164)

Yet the mountain is at the same time the poet herself. Tsvetaeva looks into the future, when "her" mountain will be covered with summer cottages, broken up into little plots. The mountain is miserable under this burden of *byt*, of Philistine family life. She threatens to erupt—and curses her occupiers (with a fine irony in the final line):

Виноградниками — Везувия	You'll not fetter Vesuvius with
Не сковать! Великана — льном	Vineyards! Nor bind a giant with flax!
Не связать! *Одного* безумия	The madness of lips alone
Уст — достаточно, чтобы львом	Is enough for the vineyards
Виноградники за—ворочались,	To overturn like a lion
Лаву ненависти струя.	Flowing the lava of hate.
Будут девками ваши дочери	Your daughters will be whores
И поэтами — сыновья!	And your sons—poets!

(IV, 166)

With its ten fairly brief sections (none more than 28 lines), "Dedication," and "Afterword," the "Poem of the Mountain" reveals its ancestry in the lyric cycle, from which it is not far removed. The relationship between the sections is contrapuntal rather than narrative and sequential. Tsvetaeva's achievement here was part of a broader trend in modern European and American poetry. M. L. Rosenthal and Sally Gall have written in *The Modern Poetic Sequence*:

> . . . The modern sequence is the decisive form toward which all the developments of modern poetry have tended. It is the genre which best encompasses the shift in sensibility exemplified by starting a long poetic work "I celebrate myself, and sing myself," rather than, "Sing, Goddess, the wrath of Achilles." The modern sequence goes many-sidedly into who and where we are *subjectively*; . . .More successfully than individual short lyrics, however, it fulfills the need for encompassment of disparate and often powerfully opposed tonalities and energies.[16]

Discordant notes marking the genesis of the *poema* began appearing in Tsvetaeva's drafts for the first act of "Ariadna" as early as late September 1923. But it was essentially written in one intense month, January, 1924. Even before she finished, Tsvetaeva wrote in her notebook: "Now—a poem of Parting (another). The whole way of the cross in stages." "The Poem of the End" is a painfully detailed analysis of the emotions of a woman rejected. In the frankness of her self-examination and passion, Tsvetaeva was a generation ahead of her time. The poem recounts the final evening of the romance, beginning with a rendezvous. From her lover's expression alone, the persona begins to suspect something is wrong:

В небе, ржавее жести, Перст столба. Встал на назначенном месте, Как судьба.	In the heavens, rustier than tinplate, The finger of a pillar, He stood at the appointed place, Like fate.
— Бёз четверти. Исправен? — Смерть не ждет. Преувеличенно-плавен Шляпы взлет.	—Quarter to. Am I punctual? —Death doesn't wait. Exaggeratedly smooth Is the flight of his hat.
В каждой реснице — вызов. Рот сведен. Преувеличенно-низок Был поклон.	In every eyelash—a challenge. His mouth is set. Exaggeratedly low Was his bow.
— Бёз четверти. Точен? — Голос лгал. Сердце упало: что с ним? Мозг: сигнал!	—Quarter to. Am I precise? The voice lied. My heart fell: what's wrong with him? My brain: a signal!

                                              (IV, 168)

More than three times as long as the "Poem of the Mountain," the "Poem of the End" is more narrative in structure, though the narrative is difficult to follow, for much of it is carried on through dialogue—or dialogue understood. Tsvetaeva gives us her version of what she and her erstwhile lover mean to say but are not saying:

— Я этого не хотел.	—I didn't want this.
Не этого. (Молча: слушай!	Not this. (Silently: listen!
Хотеть — это дело тел,	Wanting is the business of bodies,
А мы друг для друга — души	And we are for each other — souls
Отныне. . .) — И не сказал.	Henceforth . . .) — And I didn't say it.
(Да, в час, когда поезд подан,	(Yes, at the hour when the train awaits,
Вы женщинам, как бокал,	You hand over to women, like a goblet,
Печальную честь ухода	The sad honor of
Вручаете. . .) — Может, бред?	Leaving . . .) — Perhaps, delirium?
Ослышался? (Лжец учтивый,	Did I hear you wrong? (Courteous liar,
Любовнице как букет	Handing your lover, like a bouquet
Кровавую честь разрыва	The bloody honor of
Вручающий. . .) — Внято: слог	The break . . .) — It's intelligible: syllable
За слогом, итак — простимся,	By syllable, and so — we'll say farewell,
Сказали вы? (Как платок,	You said? (Like a handkerchief
В час сладостного бесчинства	Dropped at the moment of sweet
Уроненный. . .) —	Excess . . .) —

(IV, 173)

Tsvetaeva's demands on her reader's "co-creativity" are extensive. In the process of reading, s/he reexperiences some of Tsvetaeva's difficulty in trying to "read" the text of this last meeting from her lover's—largely unarticulated—meanings. The poem shows influence from the work on her Greek verse tragedies; the dialogue, often a kind of *stichomythea*, makes it a unique blend of lyric and drama. In these two *poemy*, Tsvetaeva had found a successful culmination and extension of the lyric diary, a creative escape from the limitations of the "single flute song" of the lyric melody. Neither the verse drama, nor the folk-tale *poema*, had been able to solve her creative predicament so brilliantly.

At the beginning of her affair with Rodzevich, the lyric diary fell silent for more than a year,[17] signalling a fundamental change in her creative life. Though there would be a brief period in late 1924 when her main energies went into individual lyrics, they now became the exception rather than the rule in her work. Her energies, like Pasternak's, were now devoted to larger forms. During the remainder of the 1920's, she still wrote primarily in verse—verse tragedies and long poems. But increasingly, and in the 1930's almost exclusively, Tsvetaeva turned to prose.

CHAPTER TWENTY

A Marriage of Souls

Neither Bachrach nor Rodzevich could fill the void left by Pasternak's silence. At the height of the Rodzevich affair, Tsvetaeva wrote Bachrach with a surprising request:

> Find me a reliable opportunity [to reach] Boris Pasternak: from hand to hand. I have to send him some poems and a letter. I don't trust the mail and I have no address. Right now many people are going to Moscow—find me a reliable person, who rather likes my poems and therefore won't throw my letter away . . . Don't let it go astray. I have not written him for half a year; after such a period writing is like lifting a mountain—I'll never get myself to do it a second time.[1]

In the midst of a too worldly relationship of the flesh, Tsvetaeva was anxious to renew a friendship still otherworldly and of the spirit. She concluded: "I entrust to you my love (my letter) to Boris Pasternak, like my own soul—do not send it astray." The importance she attached to the letter suggests that it contained "Wires"—a last attempt to evoke a response from Pasternak.

On September 23, 1923, Pasternak's son Evgeny was born in Moscow. Professional responsibilities after his return home, as well as impending fatherhood, perhaps accounted for Pasternak's long silence. He did write Tsvetaeva with news of the birth, and she congratulated him, if idiosyncratically: "A first-born son is always the *only* one, no matter how many brothers he has."[2] Was there an obscure hint here that she intended to mother at least one such brother? In the midst of her work on "Poem of the End," she asked Gul' to have another letter delivered to Pasternak in Moscow "personally—without (female) witnesses—in other words, without his wife." We have neither the text of this letter, nor any indication of the correspondence's frequency that spring. But by June the intensity of Pasternak's letters equalled hers of the previous spring. On the second anniversary of their correspondence, he wrote:

> Marina, my golden friend, my astounding, preternaturally native destiny, my morning billowing soul, Marina . . . What astonishing poems you write. How painful that now you are greater than I. In general, you are a scandalously great poet . . . I won't be allowed to love you as you should be loved, and it's you above all who won't let me. Oh, how I love you, Marina! So freely, so innately, so enrichingly clearly . . . Oh, how I want *life* with you! And, first of all, that part of it which is called work, growth, inspiration, cognition. It's time, it's long been time for it . . . And then there will be the summer of our meeting. I love it because it will be an encounter with a *knowing* force, that

which is closest of all to me, and which I have met only in music, never in life . . . And here again the letter says nothing. Or perhaps it's even retelling your poems in its own words—How superb they are![3]

Equally attentive to the anniversary, Tsvetaeva sent off her answer on the day of *her* first letter. But her response to his desire for life with her was gently but firmly discouraging. Pasternak was proposing the sort of relationship in which she had no interest—all the more so after the pain of her break with Rodzevich:

As for "life with you"—

—My primordial and complete inability to "live with a man," living *through* him, to live *by means of him* while living *with* him.

How can one live with a *soul* in an *apartment?* In the forest, perhaps . . . I think that from stubborness I will never utter *that word* [obviously, "love"—JT] to you. From stubbornness. From superstition.[4]

She was determined that their relationship would be different. At the same time, the letter[5] contained her answer to the birth of Evgeny Borisovich—the news that *she* was pregnant, that she was convinced the child would be a boy and that she intended to name him Boris, in his honor. If Pasternak's real-world son had been named for his mother, *her* son would be named after his spiritual father. Pasternak, for all his understanding, must have found her signals contradictory.

The anniversary, Pasternak's letter and the impending birth together inspired a brief return to the lyric. The three-poem cycle "The Two of Us" (June 30–July 3) was dedicated, in the privacy of her notebook, to "My brother in the fifth season of the year, the sixth sense and the fourth dimension—Boris Pasternak." The cycle sets forth a new variation on her myth about their friendship: she and he are a "fated pair" of poetic equals, doomed forever to be separated in *this* world. The second poem of the cycle began with a blunt declaration:

Не суждено, чтобы сильный с сильным	It is not fated that strong with strong
Соединились бы в мире сем.	Be united in this world.

To illustrate, she cited the legend of Siegfried and Brunhilde. At the exact mid-point of the poem, she abruptly shifted from the legendary to the particular, speaking directly to Pasternak:

Порознь! — даже на ложе брачном —	Apart—even on the marriage bed—
Порознь! — даже сцепясь в кулак —	Apart—even clenched in a fist—
Порознь! — на языке двузначном —	Apart—in a language of double meanings—
Поздно и порознь — вот наш брак!	Too late and apart—that's our marriage!

She returned to myth to recall another missed meeting: Achilles and the Amazon Queen Penthesilea (whom he killed in battle, only to fall in love with her beautiful corpse). To underline Tsvetaeva's point, the lovers are separated not only by fate, but by a stanzaic border:

| Так разминулися: сын Фетиды | So they missed each other: The son of Thetis |
| С дщерью Аресовой: Ахиллес | And the daughter of Ares: Achilles |

| С Пенфезилеей. | And Penthesilea.[6] |

After a suggestive line of dots, she completes the quatrain and the poem by applying her thesis, now developed, to the case at hand:

Не суждено, чтобы равный — с равным. . .	It is not fated that equal—with equal . . .
. . . .	. . . .
Так разминовываемся — мы.	Thus we pass each other by.

July 3, 1924

(III, 108)

This is love poetry of a very unusual sort: the love of one strong poet for her only rival. In the briefest yet most powerful poem of the cycle, Tsvetaeva proclaimed she had only one equal in this world:

В мире, где всяк	In a world
Сгорблен и взмылен,	Where all are hunchbacked and foam-flecked,
Знаю — один	I know—one
Мне равносилен.	Is equal to me in strength.

В мире, где столь	In a world where
Многого хощем,	We want so much,
Знаю — один	I know—one
Мне равномощен.	Is equal to me in power.

В мире, где всё —	In a world where all
Плесень и плющ,	Is mold and ivy,
Знаю: один	I know: only you
Ты — равносущ	Are equal

| Мне. | To me. |

July 3, 1924

(III, 109)

She constructed the poem in the form of a riddle, with the question implicitly posed in the first two stanzas answered in the third. She could have followed the pattern of those first two stanzas and concluded the third "*Mne—ravnosushch*," leaving the final "*Ty*" (thou) as the dramatic, single word of the final incomplete stanza, the answer to the question of the first two. By reversing the two pronouns and upsetting the reader's expectations, Tsvetaeva has given powerful ending to the poem and the cycle, simultaneously illustrating the point she proclaims and engaging in a bit of competition.[7] As she wrote these poems, Tsvetaeva was celebrating the completion of her "Poem of the End." They reflect her pride of achievement and sense of mastery.

Pasternak, too, was turning from individual lyrics or cycles of lyrics to longer narrative *poemy*, but his early attempts were not as successful as hers.[8] Pasternak's breakthrough into longer narrative forms probably owes much to Tsvetaeva's pathbreaking work, even more to her advice. More than a year earlier, she had urged the future author of *Doctor Zhivago*: "You know, Pasternak, you should write a large work."[9] The 1920's, in all fields of Russian art, saw a movement from the impressionistic, momentary works of the Revolutionary years (Mayakovsky's posters and verse, Babel's Red Cavalry sketches) to works of broader scope and more extended narrative. Mandel'stam, for example, was increasingly turning from lyrics to prose, and even in Eisenstein's later silent films there is a strengthening of story line. Tsvetaeva's advice, however, had little to do with general artistic currents but much to do with personal creative psychology: "A large work will be your second life, your first life, your only life. You will no longer need anyone or anything. You will notice no one. You will be frighteningly free." She outlined the difference between writing lyrics and writing longer works:

> Lyric poems (so-called) are separate moments of *one* movement: a movement in segments . . . A lyric is a dotted line. From afar it looks solid, black, but if you look closely, it's all in the gaps between the dots—airless space, death. And you die from poem to poem. (Thus, the "lastness" of every poem.)
>
> In a book (a novel, a *poema*, *even* an article) this is not so—they have their own rules. A book doesn't discard its author, the people—fates—souls about which you write want to live, they want to live further, each day more, they don't want to end.[10]

Following her own advice, Tsvetaeva returned to work on "Ariadna," and finished the five-act play in early October.

In November, six months pregnant, she returned briefly, and for the last time, to her lyric diary. "Under the Shawl" is a rarity in Russian literature, with its Victorian reticence: a poem about pregnancy. Tsvetaeva captures the self-contained haughtiness of the pregnant woman:

Женщиа, в тайнах, как в шалях, ширишься,	Woman, in mysteries, as in shawls, you expand,
В шалях, как в тайнах, длишься.	In shawls, as in mysteries, you persist.
Отъединенная — как счастливица-	Isolated—like the lucky
Ель на вершине мглистой.	Spruce on a misty summit.
Точно усопшую вопрошаю,	I inquire as of a deceased soul,
Душу, к корням пригубившую. . .	A soul which has sipped to the roots.
Женщина, чтò у тебя под шалью?	Woman, what do you have beneath your shawl?
— Будущее!	—The future!

(November 8, 1923)
(III, 110)

Here, as in several poems of the period, Tsvetaeva writes from the viewpoint of an "other," looking at herself from without. Whatever this may signify psychologically, it certainly points away from the lyric diary, whose persona is usually "I."[11]

During the winter of 1923–24, Tsvetaeva became friendly with her Prague neighbor Olga Kolbasina-Chernova, the former wife of Victor Chernov (the

Socialist-Revolutionary leader who was chairman of the short-lived Constituent Assembly in January 1918). In October of 1924, Chernova and her daughters moved to Paris. Tsvetaeva's long letters to her are our best source of information about Tsvetaeva's life during her last year in Czechoslovakia, and provide much information about the parallel correspondence with Pasternak. Tsvetaeva also wrote about her spats and reconciliations with the literary critic Mark Slonim, who recalled this period in his memoir:

> Our personal friendship also passed through a series of changes. It grew firmer in the months after Marina Ivanovna's break with Rodzevich. It was a difficult, tormenting experience for her, and she needed, as she put it, "a friendly shoulder in which to bury herself and forget it all," she needed someone to lean on.

But, characteristically, Tsvetaeva began to idealize Slonim:

> She imagined me as the personification of spirituality and all virtues, completely ignorant of my personal life, inclinations, passions, and short-comings. . . . She was also offended that I offered her neither passion nor insane love, but instead could offer only devotion and affection, as a comrade and close friend . . . [She had the] mistaken idea that I had rejected her—worse, exchanged her for an insignificant woman, preferred, "Plaster trash to Carrara marble" (as she wrote in "An Attempt at Jealousy").[12]

The frequently-anthologized "An Attempt at Jealousy" is dated two days after Tsvetaeva wrote Chernova that Slonim was "vacationing" with "that Russian Czech woman, I forget her name—the one with the terrible voice." Tsvetaeva's poem is a masterpiece of vituperative rhetoric, the more amazing if we realize she was visibly pregnant when she wrote it!

Как живется вам с другою, —
Проще ведь? — Удар весла! —
Линией береговою
Скоро ль память отошла

How do you like life with another—
Is it simpler, then?—A stroke of the oar!—
Along the shoreline
Did memory of me retreat

Обо мне, плавучем острове
(По небу — не по водам!)
Души, души! быть вам сестрами,
Не любовницами — вам!

Soon, like a floating island
(In the heavens—not on the waters!)
Souls! Souls!—you are meant to be sisters,
Not lovers!

Как живется вам с *простою*
Женщиною? *Без* божеств?
Государыню с престола
Свергши (с оного сошед),

How do you like life with a *simple*
Woman? *Without* divinities?
Having overturned the empress from her throne
(Actually, abdicating yourself),

Как живется вам — хлопочется —
Ежится? Встается — как?
С пошлиной бессмертной пошлости
Как справляетесь, бедняк?

How's life—are you harried?
Shivering? What's it like to get up in the morning?
How are you coping, poor man
With the tariff of immortal vulgarity?

Tsvetaeva added a characteristic "surprise" ending, a final ironic turn of the knife:

Как живется, милый? Тяжче ли,	How's your life, dear? Harder
Так же ли как мне с другим?	Then, just like mine with another?

November 19, 1924
(III, 111)

Despite his willingness to accept it, it is unlikely that Slonim deserves full "credit" for inspiring the poem. At roughly the same time, Tsvetaeva had an encounter with Rodzevich and Muna Bulgakova. The former lovers stood for a moment crossing wits while Rodzevich's future wife took a turn around the ballroom with another man. "How simple it all was—if only I could have known beforehand. They have *always* parted with me that way, except B. P. with whom my meeting—and *consequently*, my parting—is still ahead."[13]

The mention of Pasternak was not accidental. "I saw him today in a dream. . .I haven't written since June, and I haven't gotten an answer to my last letter—about my future Boris—I want to check. All the same, I can't live on this earth without love, and all around me are such mediocrities."[14] She asked Chernova to forward a letter, in which she wrote:

> Boris, if word hasn't reached you—I'll repeat briefly: in February I'm expecting a son. . .I dedicate him to you as the ancients dedicated their children to the gods . . .[15]

Except for choosing a name, she had done nothing to prepare for the baby's arrival; she first saw a doctor two weeks before the birth. The burdens of *byt* seemed more overwhelming than ever, and their financial situation was precarious; the Efron's primary source of income was Tsvetaeva's Czech stipend and the meager sums she received as honoraria. She felt trapped by her dependence on the Czech stipend:

> I plan to stay in Czechoslovakia as long as they feed me, that is, probably still another year. Then? Then perhaps Sergei will find a job, or I will "become famous"—now I'm in an airless box, I don't hide it. This is not life, for life (without people) you need nature, a *new* nature with voices that replace human ones. You need freedom. I have neither the first, nor the second, nor the tenth—I have my notebook. And so for another year. (I speak about my soul, about my important, demanding, unsatisfied self.)[16]

Sergei, in addition to his studies, had become involved in an acting studio, which meant that he was home less than ever. Their occasional visitors were small comfort:

> The first moment, joy. (From the change! the break in routine)—but immediately the primus, the stove, dishes to wash—you have no time to cook anything, everything is dirty, everything burns . . . then, in a hurry, to read

some poems—and it's already dark and they're asking about the train. Besides, I don't know how to act "in company." I don't need *people*, but a *person*—one . . .[17]

That **one** was Pasternak, as she confessed to Chernova:

I need Pasternak—Boris—for several "non-evening" evenings—and for all eternity. If that escapes me—*vie et vocation manquees*. It probably will escape me.

And all the same I could never live with him—because I love him too much.[18]

Even the prospect of her much-desired son did not promise immediate relief. "A son. That is a joy after half a year, at first I will be afraid of him." In their financial circumstances, there was, of course, no question of help. "Visions of *terrible* mornings, without poems, with diapers—and again a *cri de coeur*, 'a nanny!'"[19]

This mood was the background for several January, 1925 poems which declare: "The body is a prison for the soul." She is amazed that her muse has managed to survive, for the poet withers and "suffocates in the warmth" of the body, "as in an iron mask." (III, 122-3) She sees herself living out her life like a prisoner at hard labor; her "winter lair is deaf and gravelike" and she "wants no health from God and spring but death." (III, 123) She dreamed of escape—perhaps a brief visit to Paris, leaving the baby with her friend Katya Reitlinger (who seems to have been infatuated with Sergei) or even with Rodzevich's fiancee(!) A letter from Volkonsky increased the temptation. Their correspondence was withering because their lives were now so different: "He's in Rome, or Capri, or Paris—isolated, free, above *byt*—while I . . ."[20] She was toying more seriously with the idea of a permanent move to Paris, with a consequent separation (for how long was not clear) from Sergei. "I think about Paris and ask, 'Do I have the right?' For I came abroad to be with Sergei. He will wither without me—simply from lack of skill at living." (It is ironic to hear the "otherworldly" Tsvetaeva saying this of Sergei—he had, after all, survived the Civil War without her.) "I know that such a life is ruin for my soul—the continual lack of *occasions* for it, a blank, but do I have a right to it (my soul)?"[21]

At this point, she evidently got badly-needed support from her "spiritual brother"—a mid-January poem hints that Pasternak was back in touch.[22] Each of its two-line stanzas ends with an important term from her earlier poems to him: *dvoe, dushi, skifi.*

Не колесо громовое —
Взглядами перекинулись двое.

Не Вавилон обрушен —
Силою переведались души.

Не ураган на Тихом —
Стрелами перекинулись скифы.

Not a wheel of thunder—
The two exchanged glances.

Not Babylon destroyed—
Souls communing by force.

Not a hurricane over the Pacific—
Sythians exchanging arrows.

January 16, 1925
(III, 134)

The three final poems in *After Russia*, all addressed to Pasternak, are far more familiar in tone than the Pasternak poems of 1923 or 1924—their diction is colloquial, conversational, at times almost folksy:

Как на каждый стих —	At every line
Что на тайный свист	As at a secret whistle
Останавливаюсь,	I stop,
Настораживаюсь.	I prick up my ears.
В каждой строчке: стой!	In each line: halt!
В каждой точке — клад.	In every period—a treasure.
— Око! — светом в тебя расслаиваюсь,	—Eye!—Like light I exfoliate in you.
Расхожусь. Тоской	I dissolve. Like melancholy
На гитарный лад	To a guitar chord
Перестраиваюсь,	I retune myself
Перекраиваюсь.	I reshape myself.

Theirs is a union not of the feather-bed but of the swan's quill—she plays ironically on the Russian expression (derived from hunting terminology) "*Ni puxa ni pera!*" (lit.—"[may you bring back] neither down nor feather," on the same principle as the English "break a leg!"):

Не в пуху — в пере	Not in down—in the quill
Лебединым — брак!	Of the swan is our marriage!
Браки розные есть, разные есть!	There are marriages in separation, different marriages!
	January 22, 1925
	(III, 125)

Tsvetaeva's son (and indeed, it was a son!) was born two weeks ahead of time, on February 1, 1925, not, as planned, at a maternity home in Prague but at home in Vsenory. The attending doctor[23] recalled how he was summoned in the night by her landlady's son, and went reluctantly through the forest and a blinding snowstorm to the room where Tsvetaeva waited alone.

> In the pale light of a lonely electric bulb I saw piles of books in one corner of the room; they nearly reached the ceiling. Days of accumulated rubbish was shoveled into another corner of the room. And there was Marina, chainsmoking in bed, baby already on the way. Greeting me gaily: "You're almost late!" I looked around the room for something clean, for a piece of soap. Nothing, not a clean handkerchief, not a piece of anything. She was lying in bed, smoking and smiling, saying, "I told you you'd deliver my baby. You came—and now it's your business, not mine."[24]

Altschuller accepted as fact a matter which was widely surmised among Prague gossips—that Rodzevich, not Efron, was the father of the child. The date Ariadna Efron gives for the end of the romance would make that impossible, but Ariadna had a vested interest in defending her brother's legitimacy. Muna Bulgakova even recalled finding a passionate letter from Tsvetaeva in her husband's pocket after their marriage. It is possible that Tsvetaeva herself was not sure who the father was: Bulgakova, hardly a disinterested source, went so far as to say there were at least three possible fathers.[25] What better way to present Pasternak with an "honorary" son than for the biological father's identity to be uncertain!

For a week after the birth, she could not decide on his name, but finally "accomplished a heroic deed." The baby was named Georgii, for the saint whose guise Sergei had assumed in *Craft*, though she never called him that, however, preferring the pet name "Mur." She explained her decision to Pasternak:

> . . . He was Boris for nine months in me and ten days on earth, but Sergei's desire (not request) was to name him Georgii and I gave in. And after that—relief.
>
> Do you know what feeling was working in me? Confusion, a kind of internal awkwardness: to bring you (love!) into the family, to tame a wild beast (love!)—to render the boar harmless . . .
>
> To take *him* from my family and give *you* over to them. To make you common property . . . Something wild (that is, tame)—like nephew and uncle . . .[26]

Ariadna Efron (understandably) published only excerpts of this letter, but Tsvetaeva described it to Chernova as being:

> . . .about Lilith (before-the-first and not counted—the er-first—me) and Eve. (His wife and all the wives of those whom I "love"—NB! I've never loved anyone but B.P. and that Great Dane)—and my hatred and more often, condescending pity for Eve. And then about Boris and Georgii, that Boris is the divulging of a secret, to tame a wild beast—love. (Barsik would have been his nickname.) To bring *Love into the family*—about jealousy for the sound, which will be pronounced by the indifferent—And further. . .the most important— that by naming this one Georgii, I retain the right to *his* Boris, a Boris from him—madness—no, dreams for the future.
>
> And I asked him to love this one like his own (more, if possible!) because it's not my fault that it's not his son. And not to be jealous, for it is not a child of delight.[27]

She ended the letter to Chernova with another important confession:

> I cannot live with B.P. but I want a son by him, so that he would live in him through me. If this doesn't happen, the design of my life will not be realized . . .

Her next poem "Distance" (its Russian roots mean standing-apart), laments the physical barriers which separate her from Pasternak:

Рас—стояние: версты, мили. . .	Di—stance: versts, miles . . .
Нас рас—ставили, рас—садили,	They've placed us apart, seated us
Чтобы тихо себя вели	So we'd behave ourselves quietly
По двум разным концам земли.	At two different ends of the earth.

But she is carried away by the sheer exuberance of her word-play, and the poem acquires the ambiguous tone of triumphant suffering:

Рас—стояние: версты, дали. . .	Distance: versts, distances. . .
Нас расклеили, распаяли,	They've unglued us, unsoldered us,
В две руки развели, распяв,	Put us at arms' length, crucified us,
И не знали, что это — сплав	And they didn't know that we are an alloy

Вдохновений и сухожилий. . .	Of inspirations and sinews . . .
Не рассо́рили — рассори́ли,	They haven't set us fighting—they've littered
Расслоили. . .	with us,
	Stratified us . . .

February 24, 1925
(III, 126)

Tsvetaeva uses fourteen different verbs with the prefix "*raz/ras-*" (apart, separate) to describe what "they" have done, a repetition with transformation that gives the poem the feeling of a litany.

At first Mur nursed every two hours, and Tsvetaeva got little sleep. It is amazing that she managed to write at all, let alone anything as polished as "Distance." Yet just one month after the birth, she began a big new project, the long poem "The Ratcatcher" (*Krysolov*), based on the story of the Pied Piper of Hamelin. Written in the style and rhythm of her folk-tale poems *Tsar Maiden*, and *The Swain*, it, too, tells of the freeing of a maiden from the everyday world by an otherworldly young man (the Tsarevich, the vampire, the ratcatcher). The poem's original theme was the conflict between the Ratcatcher/poetry and the Burgomeister/*byt*, the object of their conflict the burgomeister's daughter playing the role of the soul.[28] Surely Tsvetaeva's soul, as she worked on "The Ratcatcher" was more than ever an object of contention between *byt*—the care and feeding of her family— and poetry. Tsvetaeva used the battle as the subject for a masterwork. Along with "Poem of the Mountain" and "Poem of the End," "The Ratcatcher" is her best work in the long narrative genre. When we compare it to them, we cannot but be impressed by Tsvetaeva's versatility.

Tsvetaeva added only one more poem to *After Russia*, an *envoi* to her lyrical diary addressed directly to Pasternak:

Русской ржи от меня поклон,	Give my regards to the Russian rye,
Ниве, где баба застится,	To the cornfields tall enough to hide a peasant
Друг! Дожди за моим окном,	woman.
Беды и блажи на́ сердце. . .	Friend! There are rains beyond my window,
	Troubles and joys on my heart . . .

Ты, в погудке дождей и бед	You, who are as at home in the counterpoint
То ж, что Гомер — в гекзаметре,	of rains and troubles
Дай мне руку — на весь тот свет!	As Homer in the hexameter,
Здесь — мои обе заняты.	Give me your hand—to all *that* world!
	Here mine are both occupied.

May 7, 1925
(III, 126)

She sent him the poem along with a copy of *The Swain*, which had finally appeared. The emigre press did not like the book, or pay it much attention.

Julii Aikhen'vald's review in *Rul'* fulminated about the poem's difficulty:

> This tale is written in verse, and written so that it is difficult to understand. It is not the incomprehension of the reader, but the incomprehensibility of the book which is to blame . . .
>
> Not in vain is *The Swain* dedicated to Boris Pasternak, one of the most obscure of contemporary poets.[29]

Tsvetaeva hoped that the one to whom the *poema* was dedicated would understand it better. He evidently did, for in mid-July, she received from him: "[your] first human letter—the others were all *Geistbriefe.*"[30] She contrasted her daily life to his poetry:

> . . .don't think the village is an idyll:. . .
>
> I don't see the trees . . . and the rain is important to me only as it determines whether or not my laundry will dry. . .My day: I cook, wash, fetch water, take care of Georgii—work with Alya on her French (reread Katerina Ivanovna from *Crime and Punishment . . . that's me*). I'm furiously embittered.

Pasternak had complained to her of his life, and written of giving up poetry:

> I don't understand you—giving up poetry. And then what? Throw yourself off a bridge into the Moscow river? But with poetry, my dear friend, it's the same as with love: until it abandons you. . .you are a serf of your lyre.[31]

He had sent her his new book *Stories* (*Rasskazy*) and a *poema*, probably the first version of "A Lofty Malady." Just as she began to talk about his prose, the published copy of the letter tantalizingly breaks off. But she did write shortly thereafter to another correspondent that it was "the most remarkable accomplishment of contemporary Russian prose."

In these last months in Prague, she, too, was turning to prose, writing "A Hero of Labor," the first of her memoir-obituaries for the poets of her generation. Briusov had died the previous fall in Moscow. "Hero" was a bitter attack on one so recently deceased, but the emigres had no love for a man they felt had sold himself to the Bolsheviks, and the piece was printed immediately. Few of her later prose pieces had such an easy time with their editors. She managed to finish five of the six chapters of "The Ratcatcher" before she left for Paris at the end of October. The trip was intended to be temporary, to test the waters in Paris while Sergei finished up his studies in Prague, but she never returned to Czechoslovakia.

Ironically, one tie to the Czech literary community grew closer just as she was about to leave. In 1925 some of her work was translated into Czech under the sponsorship of Anna Antonovna Teskova.[32] As president of the Czech-Russian cultural society (Ceskorusska Jednota), Teskova befriended many of the emigre writers in Prague. She first met Tsvetaeva in 1922, but their contacts were few at first. They grew more frequent and personal only when Tsvetaeva, in an advanced stage of pregnancy, turned to Teskova for advice about maternity hospitals. After Tsvetaeva moved to Paris, a correspondence began between the two women which lasted until Tsvetaeva's return to Russian in 1939. Teskova was instrumental in getting Tsvetaeva's Czech stipend extended through her first few years in Paris, and she helped financially herself.[33] In gratitude, Tsvetaeva "gave" Teskova the cycle "Trees." Like many of Tsvetaeva's dedications, this one considerably postdates the work itself; when she wrote "Trees" in 1922–23, she barely knew Teskova. But Teskova's image, for her, grew confused with that of Czechoslovakia, Prague, and the Czech forest. Like most of her loved objects, she loved Czechoslovakia better from afar, preferring the myth she built of it to the object itself.

Even before she left for Paris, Tsvetaeva began to build that myth:

> You are of that world where only the soul carries weight—the world of dream or fairy-tale. I would like very much to wander with you through Prague, because Prague, in essence, is also such a city—where only the soul has weight
> . . .
>
> Oh, what a marvelous story could be written against the background of Prague. Without plot or bodies—a *novel of souls!*[34]

This disembodied spirituality was to become the dominant theme in Tsvetaeva's myth of the distant Prague and of Czech nature. A constant refrain of the letters to Teskova is her regret that she "hardly knew Prague" while she was there. Yet she must have known it to some extent. The "Poem of the Mountain" and the "Poem of the End" testify to her extensive (if primarily nocturnal) walks about Prague, and Mark Slonim recalled their walks around the Old City. Tsvetaeva exaggerated her ignorance of Prague in order to facilitate her mythification.

She did have reason to remember the Czech years as a comparatively happy interval in her life. The Masaryk government stipend had provided her with a secure, if modest, income. Despite the burden of menial housework (which she had known in Moscow and was to know again in Paris), she wrote much of her finest poetry there. And it was the birthplace of her adored son. The Czech years gave Tsvetaeva a chance to renew her acquaintance with nature. The debris-littered parks of Paris' lower-class suburbs could never take the place of the Czech hillsides: "Not even my shade will remain in Paris—Tarusa, Koktebel' and the Czech villages—these are the places of my soul."[35]

After the Lyric Diary: 1925–1941

Tsvetaeva's lyric diary, as such, came to an end early in 1925. From time to time she wrote individual lyrics and occasional lyric cycles. But lyrics were a creative and financial luxury she could no longer afford. Most of her work through the rest of the 1920's was in longer forms—a second verse tragedy, "Phaedra," and a series of long poems. Though "The Ratcatcher" still had much in common with the book-length folk-tale *poemy* of the early twenties, the six briefer *poemy* she wrote from 1926 to 1928 are abstract, highly personal, and non-narrative—like the two Prague *poemy*, they are much more akin to the lyric diary, which provides us with strategies for reading them. These difficult works were almost universally ignored when they appeared, and still attract little attention; Tsvetaeva was leaving her readers far behind. The general reader, however, was not important to Tsvetaeva—three of the six *poemy* are ciphered letters to her fellow poets Pasternak and Rilke.

As the lyric diary fell silent, Tsvetaeva's correspondence increased, taking over some of its functions. The Paris years saw three new (brief and intense) correspondence-friendships with other poets—with the Prague-born genius of modern German poetry, Rainer Maris Rilke (1926) and with the young Russians Nikolay Gronsky (1928) and Anatoly Shteiger (1936). Her correspondence with Pasternak peaked to a new intensity in 1926 and then ebbed. These correspondences with male poets were, as she said of that with Pasternak—"*ins blaue*," on a highly abstract level. Three lengthy correspondences with women—Anna Teskova, Salomea Halpern, and Vera Muromtseva—were quite different. These women provided her with support both psychological and financial, and her letters to them provide a chronicle of her life during these years.

Paris

Tsvetaeva came to Paris seeking not fame, but money to support her family, though she wasn't averse to some long-delayed recognition and relief from her Czech isolation. She had a large new book of verse, *After Russia*, but the emigre journals and newspapers preferred prose. She cannibalized *Signs of Earth*, placing short excerpts wherever she could. The Paris paper *Poslednie novosti* (*Latest News*), the largest, most prosperous, and best-paying of the emigre newspapers, became the *bete noire* of Tsvetaeva's existence. Its editor Pavel Miliukov, once the leader of the Kadet (Constitutional Democratic) party, was more interested in politics than poetry; his editors would accept only Tsvetaeva's more accessible verse of 1916 and 1917. They claimed their readers couldn't understand her current work at all. But because they paid better than anyone else, she tried to publish as much as she could with them.

The Paris *Sovremennye zapiski* (*Contemporary Annals*) was the major "thick journal," in the nineteenth-century tradition, of the emigration between the wars. Though Tsvetaeva often quarrelled with its editors and felt alien on its pages, they published much of her most important writing.[1] Nearly all the infrequent lyrics she wrote after 1925 eventually appeared on its pages, as did much of her prose.

Tsvetaeva's most difficult and controversial works were published in the Prague *Volia Rossii* (*The Will of Russia*), a journal which was Socialist-Revolutionary in orientation. Its editors were friends from her Prague days. They published "The Ratcatcher" and continued to publish her difficult long poems, often, she felt, even without understanding them, and she was grateful. *The Will of Russia*, like Tsvetaeva herself, was supported by a Czech government subsidy. When it ceased in the depression year of 1932 they were forced to close.

Meanwhile, the young Prince Dmitry Shakhovskoy asked Tsvetaeva to contribute to *Blagonamerennii* (*The Loyal One*). The short-lived journal's second and last issue contained a piece that forever haunted Tsvetaeva's relationship with the Paris literary establishment, the scathing essay "A Poet about Criticism" (or "About the Critic"—the Russian is intentionally ambiguous). Appended to the article was a selection of excerpts from the criticism of Georgii Adamovich, leading critic of the Paris school (he was the regular critic for *Poslednie novosti*), designed to show up his inconsistencies and make him look foolish. The article understandably aroused Adamovich's fury, and his colleagues at the other major Paris publications lept to his defense. Tsvetaeva was seldom given a favorable review again. As with her baiting of Briusov in 1910, Tsvetaeva intentionally began this new stage in her literary career by antagonizing the most powerful critic of the times.[2]

Most of her literary business in Paris was conducted by letter. She seldom went out, particularly in the evening, for not only did she have an infant on her hands, but she had no appropriate clothes. She asked Anna Teskova to find her a cast-off dress among her wealthy friends in Prague, which she could wear at her forthcoming "evening"—a public reading in Paris. It took place on February 6, 1926, and was the first of many Tsvetaeva gave in her Paris years. The preparations—finding a hall, selling tickets through friends —were humiliating and time-consuming, but the evenings were financially essential. This first one was a great success, but the public's interest soon waned.

During Tsvetaeva's first months in Paris, she lived with Olga Chernova, crowded into one room with the two children (and, after Christmas-time, with Sergei as well). She had no place to be alone, not even a writing desk to call her own, as she complained bitterly in one of the very few lyrics dated 1926:

Тише, хвала!	Quiet, praise!
Дверью не хлопать,	Don't slam the door,
Слава!	Glory!
Стола	The corner
Угол — и локоть.	Of a table—and an elbow.
Сутолочь, стоп!	Stop, commotion!
Сердце, уймись!	Heart, calm down!
Локоть — и лоб.	An elbow and brow.
Локоть — и мысль.	An elbow and thought.
Юность — любить,	Youth is for loving
Старость — погреться:	Old age to warm yourself:
Некогда — *быть*,	No time to *be*
Некуда деться.	Nowhere to go.
Хоть бы закут —	Even a pig-sty!
Только без прочих!	Only—without others.
Краны — текут,	Faucets—drip
Стулья — грохочут . . .	Chairs—scrape
. . . .	. . . .
Богом мне — тот	He will be my God
Будет, кто даст мне	Who gives me
— Не времени́!	(Don't tarry!
Дни сочтены! —	The days are numbered!)
Для тишины —	For silence—
Четыре стены.	Four walls.
	January 26, 1926
	(III, 135)

In mid-March 1926, Tsvetaeva took a much-needed vacation and went to London for two weeks to visit Prince Dmitry Sviatopolk-Mirsky. Mirsky was the best literary critic of the emigration, and one of its most enigmatic figures. From 1922 until 1932, when he voluntarily returned to the Soviet Union (he died there in a Siberian transit camp, probably in 1939), he was Reader of Russian Literature at London University.[3] According to one who knew him, Mirsky was at the time infautated with Tsvetaeva,[4] though his first evaluation of her talent as a poet was mixed. He had worse things to say about her early prose: "the prose she has hitherto written is the most pretentious, unkempt, hysterical, and altogether worst prose ever written in Russian."[5] But in a 1926 review of *The Swain*, he changed his mind: "Among post-Revolutionary poets, she is entitled to the first, or one of the two first places . . ."[6] Like Tsvetaeva herself, Mirsky would have given the second, or other first place to Pasternak.

Soon after they were introduced in the winter of 1925–1926, Mirsky in turn introduced her to Salomea Andronikova-Gal'pern, the legendary Petersburg beauty whom, as "Solominka," Mandel'stam had immortalized in a 1916 poem written soon after his infatuation with Tsvetaeva. Now living comfortably in emigration, with houses in both London and Paris, Andronikova-Gal'pern (with the help of Mirsky and a few others) quietly began to provide a monthly stipend which was the Efrons' only regular income during the Paris years.[7]

Mirsky had become involved in a movement known as Eurasianism, a philosophy of Russian history and cultural identity which arose in the early twenties and maintained that Russia was not part of Europe, but had a civilization of her own. The movement shared many of the premises of nineteenth-century Slavophilism, including its view of Orthodox Christianity as an essential element of Russian culture, and its rejection, as Mirsky put it, of the

> . . . *juridical*, Roman, dissecting, and consequently rationalist, individualist, and moralizing spirit of Rome. . .Western man has become incapable of thinking in "wholes;" he can see nothing but logical abstractions.[8]

The Eurasians came to recognize the October revolution as a historical necessity, leading, they hoped, to "the restoration of a Muscovite state of things," and some, like Mirsky, eventually returned to Russia. Eurasianism made a transition from the "right" to a position of support for the Soviet Union philosophically easier for Sergei Efron, who in 1926 became involved with Mirsky in the publication of a journal which they titled *Versts* in honor of Tsvetaeva's two books. *Versts* was almost alone among emigre publications in reprinting the works of Soviet writers. The first issue contained works by Babel, Pasternak, Esenin and Selvinsky, along with Tsvetaeva's "Poem of the Mountain"—she gave this poem about her romance with Rodzevich to be published by her husband Efron and her admirer Mirsky!

Tsvetaeva spent the six months from May through September of 1926 in St.-Gilles, a village on the French Atlantic coast, where she rented a room in a fisherman's cottage. Sergei at first remained in Paris to tend to his fledgling journal. The tone of her letters to other correspondents hints that the lengthy sojurn she planned was something of a trial separation as well. She was theoretically in France only on an extended visit, for she was still receiving her Czech stipend. In late June, she received a letter advising her to return to Czechoslovakia or forfeit it. She toyed with the idea, but had no real intention of returning:[9]

> It's impossible for me to return either now or later: I have **overcome** Czecho-slovakia, all of it is in the Poems of the End and the Mountain (their hero was married on the 13th). Czechoslovakia simply no longer exists. I would return to a buried rough draft.[10]

Tsvetaeva's summer in St.-Gilles was an unreal interlude, suspended between a vanished past and an uncertain future. Like the Czech village in which she took refuge from the literary marketplace of Berlin, St.-Gilles provided a refuge of rural simplicity away from the passions and politics of Paris. Like those first Czech years, it was a very productive period, whose major theme was renunciation. And in St.-Gilles, as in the Czech villages, the major emotional drama centered around her correspondence with Pasternak.

Pasternak and Rilke

While Tsvetaeva was in London, the first chapters were being written in one of the strangest episodes in the history of twentieth-century poetry—the three-way epistolary friendship between Tsvetaeva, Pasternak, and Rainer Maria Rilke. The correspondence took place on three interconnected levels: actual letters entrusted to the French, Soviet, and Swiss postal systems, poems written by each of the poets and addressed to each other, and the "otherworldly correspondence" between poets along what Tsvetaeva had called "lyrical wires"—communication through dreams and intuitive understanding. The poems—dense, cryptic, and difficult—were all published by the end of the 1920's. The letters, which provide important clues for reading the poetry, became available after the opening of the Rilke archive in 1977.[1] But these two sets of texts still present intriguing mysteries for the reader (and that is all of us) who cannot tap in to the "lyrical wires." Rilke's "Elegy to Marina Tsvetaeva-Efron," in the words of Konstantin Azadovsky, is "a classic example of cryptographic writing . . . an intimate conversation of poet with poet, only fully understood by them."[2] He could have said the same about Tsvetaeva's three *poemy* addressed to Pasternak and Rilke[3] and, to a lesser extent, Pasternak's "Lieutenant Schmidt," particularly its acrostic dedication to Tsvetaeva. Nor are the letters themselves without their own complexities. They are at once both a documentary account of a real relationship between three of Europe's greatest poets, and at the same time a novel in letters. Whether or not they consciously thought as they wrote that someday their letters might be available to a wider readership, each of the poets was producing literary texts, if only for his fellow poets. This makes the question of how to read them far from straightforward.[4] For Tsvetaeva, as we have seen, letters had always been an important part of her creative work—the line between poem as letter and letter as poem was often very thin.[5] Tsvetaeva was as adept at maintaining a certain emotional distance between the real, human content of the relationship and the actual texts of her letters—as between the seeming autobiographical immediacy of her lyrics and the "realia" which stood behind them. Rilke seemed to understand and answer her in kind. But for the impetuous Pasternak, spontaneity was a rule of life as well as art. Judging from the torment of his letters to Tsvetaeva, it seems clear that he often lost sight of those boundaries, and was both puzzled and deeply hurt by Tsvetaeva's actions and "tender lies." She, moreover, said rather different things in the letters she sent him and in the poems which, at least for the time being, she did not.[6]

The history of the correspondence goes back to the turn of the century, when the young Rilke, not yet even sure of his vocation as a poet, travelled to Russia twice with his Petersburg-born lover, Lou Andreas-Salome. He later thought of emigrating there, and throughout his life considered Russia his spiritual homeland. Russian culture was an important element in his early poetry.[7] One of his first Moscow acquaintances was the artist Leonid Pasternak; for a while they continued to correspond. When he was seventeen, Boris Pasternak discovered Rilke's poetry through inscribed editions in his father's library. Rilke became for him a poetic deity; at the end of his life he wrote, "I always believed that in my own efforts, in all of my work, I did nothing but translate or write variations on his themes."[8] In 1925, from Berlin, the elder Pasternak took the occasion of Rilke's fiftieth birthday to renew the correspondence and, with paternal pride, to mention Boris' career and admiration for the now-famous poet. In his cordial response, Rilke mentioned that he had recently read and admired some of Boris' poems.

Rilke's kind words could not have come at a more opportune moment for Pasternak, who was in a period of both marital strain and severe artistic self-doubt. The poems collected in *My Sister Life* and *Themes and Variations* which had brought him sudden fame (and Tsvetaeva's admiration) had, for the most part, been written in 1917 and 1918. The following years were comparatively unproductive. Like Tsvetaeva, he nearly abandoned the short lyric after 1923 in favor of longer forms. But while Tsvetaeva's 1924 *poemy* were artistic triumphs, his first forays into the longer form[9] were more problematic. Tsvetaeva's long poems of 1924 were epic treatments of the archetypal lyric theme—love and its disappointments. Pasternak, on the other hand, turned to a more traditional epic theme: history and the individual.

According to Lazar Fleischman, Pasternak's 1922 trip to Berlin was an experiment in emigration. His return to Russia in March, 1923 (which to Tsvetaeva seemed so sudden) was the result of a conscious decision reached with a "clear understanding of the link between historical choice and the fate of the poet."[10] This would become the great theme of Pasternak's work for the rest of his life, culminating in *Dr. Zhivago*. As Pasternak phrased it in a letter to Tsvetaeva, he was trying to "return to history a generation which has evidently fallen away from it and which includes you and me . . ." (April 20, 1926)[11] In March, 1926, he had just finished the first version of "1905" and was beginning work on a *poema* about Lieutenant Schmidt, the leader of the Potemkin mutiny in that revolutionary year. Pasternak's interest in the theme of 1905 was undoubtedly motivated by concerns as much financial as creative. He now had a wife and son to support, and no income besides honoraria. The twentieth anniversary of the revolution produced a ready market for works with a jubilee theme, the best-known of which is Eisenstein's film *Battleship Potemkin* (1925). But neither Pasternak nor his editors, critics, and readers (including Tsvetaeva) were satisfied with his first efforts in this new direction; in subsequent editions he altered these poems considerably.

Suddenly, in this period of dissatisfaction with himself (a frequent mood for Pasternak) he received two emotional and creative shocks in one day.[12] The first was the tantalizing but sketchy information about Rilke's praise relayed in a letter from his father.[13] Pasternak was desperate to know exactly what Rilke had written about him, and in what context. In this state of nervous excitement, he made his first acquaintance with a typescript copy of Tsvetaeva's "Poem of the End." Pasternak was overwhelmed by her achievement, though he did confide to his sister that "a little of my influence is felt here."[14] This coincidence of events, so like those which form the fabric of his own *Dr. Zhivago*, multiplied their effect on him and forever wedded Tsvetaeva and Rilke in his imagination.

Under the dual impact of "The Poem of the End" and of his own deteriorating marriage, Pasternak began to urge Tsvetaeva toward a relationship rather more concrete than the "marriage of souls" she had imagined in her poetry. Using the intimate first-person singular ("ty") form for the first time in their nearly four-year correspondence, he wrote:

> You are filled with such beauty, you are a sister to me, you are my life, sent directly from heaven, and at the time of my soul's greatest ordeal. You are mine and have always been mine; all of my life is—you.   (March 25)

Her poem was a work of genius, he wrote, and he was "propagandizing" it among all his Moscow friends.[15] Now that Pasternak's letters to Tsvetaeva, at least for this crucial period of their correspondence, are available, we can understand one reason why she preferred "lyrical wires" to letters, and letters to real-life meetings. The Pasternak who emerges from these letters is both impetuous and indecisive, and the frequent murkiness, even wordiness of his prose suffers in comparison to the crisp dynamism of Tsvetaeva's. Their romance in letters was also a continuation of the "duel of two nightingales," and it was a duel in which Pasternak, for the moment at least, was outclassed in both prose and verse.

Pasternak's next letter precipitated a crisis in their friendship. He began by recounting in (perhaps excessive) detail an obviously erotic dream:

> I was in a bright, immaculate hotel without bedbugs or any of the usual things, or perhaps it was a mansion in which I was a servant. . . . I was told that someone was asking for me. Certain that it was you, I flew down a staircase that was bathed in quivering light. And sure enough, there you were in a kind of travelling cloak, enveloped in a mist of high determination, appearing not suddenly but on wings, gliding in much the same way that I had flown to you. . . .

It was complete harmony, experienced for the first time in my life with an intensity equalling the experience of pain. I found myself in an atmosphere so full of passion for you that I was unaware of my own brashness and evanescence. It was more than first love, as well as being the simplest thing on earth. I loved you as in life I had only *dreamed* of loving, long, long ago, loving to eternity. You were beauty in the absolute. . . . You were a mighty poet, seen in the midst of a great outpouring of loving adoration, as close as the human can get to the elemental. . . .[16]

On the next page, he undermined this paeon to her unique attraction with a frank confession:

There are *thousands* of women whom I would *have* to love if I let myself go. I am ready to run after any manifestation of femininity, and my mind swarms with such visions. Perhaps I was born with this trait so that my character would be formed by the development of a strong, almost unfailing system of brakes.

Their promised 1925 meeting in Weimar had never materialized: Tsvetaeva had a nursing infant on her hands, and Pasternak, largely for financial reasons, was unable to make the trip. Now he wrote:

I'm now going to ask you a question. . . . Answer it as you have never answered anyone, as you would answer yourself. *Shall I come to you now or in a year?* This indecision of mine is not absurd, I have real reasons to vacillate about the date, but I haven't the strength to decide on the second alternative (that is, in a year). If you will support me in this decision, then the following will result: (1) I will work through this year with all possible effort. I will move and grow closer not only to you but to some possibility of being for you (understand this in the broadest sense) something more *useful* in life and fate (to explain would be to fill volumes) than that would be now.

Then I will ask your help. You must imagine *how* I read your letters and what happens to me when I do. I will completely cease answering you—that is, I will never give head to my feelings. That is, I will see you in my dreams and you will know nothing of it. A year is a measure, I will observe it . . .

(April 20)

Like the little boy she often thought him to be, Pasternak was relying on Tsvetaeva to give him a sober answer to his impetuous proposal. He was at last offering her the meeting she had so desired (if we are to believe her lyric diary) for the last four years. But reality for Tsvetaeva was very different from poetry, or even from letters. Such a meeting, and the changed relationship it implied, seemed ill-advised and ill-timed; indeed she probably never wanted it at all, preferring to continue to meet in dreams. She later confided to a friend, "In the summer of 1926, having read somewhere my "Poem of the End," Pasternak was dying madly to see me, he wanted to come—I *warded him off*: I didn't want a *general* catastrophe.[17]

The letters (internal evidence suggests there were two) in which Tsvetaeva "warded him off" are tantalizingly omitted from the published correspondence, so we have to infer their content from Pasternak's replies.[18] According to the editors of *Letters*, Pasternak received from Tsvetaeva in early May "the strange request that she offer assistance to . . . Sofia Parnok."[19] She included with her letter a (then unpublished) 1915 poem from the "Girl Friend" cycle (I, 185) which made the nature of her friendship with Parnok all too clear. It was a tactlessly cruel way to throw cold water on Pasternak's passion. The letter cautioned Pasternak, but did not appreciably dampen his ardor:

> Forgive the excesses I allowed myself then. I should have shown restraint. I should have kept everything to myself as a vivifying secret until the day we met. Until then I could and should have hidden from you a love that can never die, for you are my only legitimate heaven and wife, so very, very legitimate that the force taking possession of the word makes me hear it in a madness that never dwelt in it before. Whenever I murmur your name, Marina, little shivers run up and down my spine from the cold and pain of it." (May 5)

He still planned to send his wife and son to his sister in Munich for the summer, and perhaps to join them in the fall. A trip to Munich meant a possible meeting with Tsvetaeva. Perhaps Tsvetaeva, in haste before her departure for St. Gilles, sent him a partial rebuff, leaving a fuller explanation for later, when she had time to write at length. For when he continued the letter three days later, Pasternak had obviously received a fuller explanation.

> Yours was a rare and splendid reply. If what I said (at an impossible distance and in a divine, noble sense) about the legitimacy of our relationship seems to be at odds with your recent words about marriage, cross it out so that you will never see it again. (May 8)[20]

Meanwhile, Pasternak had tried to arrange a kind of courtship gift for Tsvetaeva. When he finally extracted the full details of Rilke's letter from his parents, he composed a humbly ecstatic letter introducing himself and thanking Rilke for the praise. He proposed that if Rilke deigned to reply he do so through Tsvetaeva,

> . . . . A poet who loves you no less and no differently from myself and (however narrowly or broadly one may wish to conceive this) may be considered, just like myself, as a part of your own poetic history, outreach, and effort.
> (April 12)

Since Switzerland had not yet established diplomatic (or postal) relations with Soviet Russia, (one reason Pasternak proposed Tsvetaeva to Rilke as an intermediary), he forwarded this letter through his father in Berlin. Again the doting papa meddled in his son's correspondence: before sending it on to Rilke, he circulated the letter through the family, and finally sent it on to Rilke nearly three weeks after Pasternak wrote it in Moscow! (He also sent Boris his doubts about the propriety of the request to respond through Tsvetaeva.)

Pasternak, lover of meaningful coincidence, had hoped that Tsvetaeva would receive a letter from Rilke at roughly the same time as his April 20 letter, and that his answers from both Rilke and Tsvetaeva would arrive in the same envelope: "I had decided that if his reply were enclosed in the letter with your decision, I would listen **only** to my impatience and not to you or my 'other' voice." (May 19) But his father's delay ruined the timing. Pasternak's gift of Rilke had consequences he scarcely foresaw. As he proffered with one hand a relationship she did not want, he provided with the other another "spiritual brother" who was safely ensconced in his Swiss castle, who had no interest in her as a woman, and who promised the kind of friendship which Pasternak threatened to abandon. That Rilke did in fact understand Tsvetaeva and respond in her terms is a miracle which proved the possibility of the poetic communication she championed.[21] When Pasternak's letter finally reached him, Rilke immediately sent Tsvetaeva a cordial letter, a brief but warm note to forward to Pasternak, and copies of his *Sonnets to Orpheus* and *Duino Elegies*, the latter inscribed with a poem:

> We touch each other. How? With wings that beat,
> With very distance touch each other's ken.
> *One* poet only lives, and now and then
> Who bore him, and who bears him now, will meet.[22]

Rilke's letter, forwarded from her Paris address, reached Tsvetaeva in St. Gilles just as Pasternak was receiving her rebuff in Moscow. As if reaffirming that decision, she promised Rilke that Pasternak would come to France in a year and they would visit him together: "I know Boris very little, but I love him as one loves only those whom one has never seen . . ." He's not so young any more—thirty-three, I think, but he's like a little boy." (Pasternak was actually thirty-six, nearly three years *older* than Tsvetaeva, but she characteristically wanted to think of him as *younger*. His boyish impulsiveness certainly encouraged her mistake.) Tsvetaeva's letter to Rilke was as ecstatic as Pasternak's, but in her own, very different voice. Praise of poetic contemporaries was, of course, one of Tsvetaeva's favorite genres, and the letter echoes her poems to Blok, Mandel'stam, Akhmatova, and Pasternak himself.

> Rainer Maria Rilke!
>
> May I hail you like this? You, poetry incarnate, must know, after all, that your very name—is a poem. Rainer Maria, that sounds churchly—and kind-

> ly—and chivalrous. Your name does not rhyme with our time—stems from earlier or later—has always been. . . .

> You are not my dearest poet ("dearest"—a level), you are a phenomenon of nature, which cannot be mine and which one does not so much love as undergo, or (still too little) the fifth element incarnate: poetry itself or (still too little) that whence poetry comes to be and which is greater than it (you). (May 9/10[23])

As the editors of the correspondence point out in their introduction, "Tsvetaeva's conviction that poetry is the timeless, immortal, transcendent spirit made manifest in the temporal realm by its 'bearers'—poets . . . was so congenial to him that he instantly realized their spiritual affinity."[24] Indeed, he had referred to the same idea in his inscription on *Duino Elegies*. Though written in German, Tsvetaeva's letter is characteristic of her Russian voice. It is a particularly showy example of her prose style—clearly, she was trying to make an impression on Rilke, who was already in correspondence with a good many literary ladies, to impress him, even seduce him, in a manner of speaking, by her voice alone, so that he would notice her and be willing to respond with the intensity she demanded. She succeeded; Rilke answered by return mail.

> Today, Marina, I received you in my soul, in my whole consciousness, which trembles before you, before your coming, as though your great fellow reader, the ocean, had come breaking over me with you, heart's flood. . . .

> You poet, do you sense how you have overwhelmed me, you and your magnificent fellow reader; I'm writing to you and I descend like you the few steps down from the sentence into the mezzanine of parentheses, where the ceilings are so low and where it smells of roses past that never cease.   (May 10)

Even before Rilke's prompt and enthusiastic response arrived, Tsvetaeva was writing again (May 12) with her first reactions to his *Orpheus* poems, adding disparaging remarks about the Paris emigre critics whose attacks on "A Poet about Criticism" were just then appearing. If Rilke would read and understand her, she hardly needed *their* approval. She sent him inscribed copies of *Poems to Blok* and *Psyche*. The following day, after receiving his May 10 letter, she wrote again, trying unsuccessfully to differentiate between love for Rilke the poet and for the man who "bore" him. But realizing that the man, as opposed to the poet, might not be able to keep up such an intense correspondence, and afraid of losing him, she added: "Dear one, I am very obedient. If you tell me: Do not write, it excites me, I need myself badly for myself—I shall understand, and withstand, everything." (May 13) As if to demonstrate that she could control her intensity, she immediately shifted tone, and the rest of the letter could almost have been written by any clever, literary lady: she described her children, asked for his photo in exchange for hers, asked about his family and the length of his illness. She even gave him a capsule description of Sergei ("young," "sickly," "handsome: the handsomeness of suffering.") The subject of Sergei inspired some "tender lying"—she gave his age as "barely thirty-one" (he was actually almost thirty-three) and hers as thirty (instead of her actual thirty-three). Rilke again replied immediately, telling of his failed marriage ("never legally terminated"), the granddaughter he had never seen, and his life at Val-Mont. He expressed puzzlement at the bad state of his health—neither he nor his doctors realized that he suffered from leukemia, which would kill him by the end of the year. He had begun to read her poems, but it was difficult with his rusty Russian, even though she helped him with notes in the margins. He marveled, however, that she could manage feats of verbal power even in her German letters.

Meanwhile, in Moscow, Pasternak grew anxious. Tsvetaeva's letters of early May said nothing of Rilke, and then she fell silent. Unaware that his father had delayed so long in forwarding his letter, Pasternak channelled his puzzlement and anxiety into feverish work on "Lieutenant Schmidt," which he hoped would make him worthy of both Rilke and Tsvetaeva. On May 18, he submitted the first section to *Novyi mir* with a fifteen-line "Dedication"—an acrostic reading "To Marina Tsvetaeva."[25] For reasons both domestic and political, he could hardly make the dedication explicit. On the same day, he finally received Rilke's note which Tsvetaeva had belatedly forwarded, appending only two brief excerpts from Rilke's letter to her in which he described his reaction to Pasternak's letter. She added no letter of her own. Pasternak was overjoyed to have Rilke's letter, but dismayed by Tsvetaeva's silence: the mutual correspondence with Rilke, which he hoped would bring them closer together, seemed instead to be forcing them apart. He instinctively sensed that Rilke was beginning to fill his place in her life.

With only a few hours a night to herself, Tsvetaeva had neither the time nor emotional energy to write both Pasternak and Rilke at the same time. A brief remark in Rilke's third letter, however, initiated an emotional drama which temporarily shifted her attention back to Pasternak. Obliquely referring to his health, Rilke wrote: "If all of a sudden I should suddenly turn uncommunicative—[which] ought not to keep you from writing to me . . ." (May 17). Tsvetaeva's "lyrical wires" failed her on this occasion; ignoring all of Rilke's hints about his ill-health, she thought he was asking for creative solitude, and forced herself not to answer his letter. Her frustrated dialogue with Rilke, like her earlier frustrated correspondence with Pasternak, welled over into her notebooks. During the two weeks she refrained from writing to Rilke, she addressed a flood of correspondence to Pasternak on all three levels: in letters, in poetry, and along "lyrical wires." In each medium, the message was somewhat different.

We can know of their "otherworldly correspondence," of course, only what she wrote of it, and during those days she often wrote of it in her letters to Pasternak:[26]

> Not long ago I spent a beautiful day, all of it with you. I didn't let you go until late at night." (May 22)

> Boris, I write you the wrong letters. The real ones never touch paper. Today, for instance, while I was walking for two hours with Mur's carriage along an unfamiliar road . . . I talked to you all the time. Talked at you, Boris, was happy, breathed. At moments when you fell too deep into thought I took your head in both my hands and turned it toward me . . . (May 23)

> Hello, Boris! Six in the morning, everything's howling and blowing. I just ran to the well between rows of trees (two different pleasures: an empty bucket, a full bucket) and with my whole body, as I met the wind, I greeted you. By the porch (now with a full bucket—the second parentheses)—everyone was still asleep—I stopped and lifted my head to meet you. Thus I live with you, morning and evening, awaking to you, lying down to you. (May 26)

It is easy to understand how the love-sick Pasternak could mis-read such passages ("You must to imagine **how** I read your letters and what happens to me when I do.") But for Tsvetaeva, art was as much at work here as emotion. The long letter of May 23–26 is the most literary of all she addressed to Pasternak that year, its prose crafted as carefully as that in her letters to Rilke. The message of such passages was not "I am longing to be with you" but rather "How much more beautiful are such meetings than those in the real world."

Her letters to Pasternak asserted the greater satisfactions to be reached through willful renunciation of real life satisfactions—including love. The lesson, however, was as much, or more, for herself in relation to Rilke.

> I could have written about myself what you wrote about yourself: love, love, love on every hand. And it doesn't bring pleasure.

> Suddenly you have discovered America: me. That's not what I want. Be so kind as to discover America **for me.** (May 22)

How similar this is to what she told Mandel'stam ten years earlier: "Love the **world** in me and not me in the world—so that 'Marina' means the world and not the world Marina." More and more often, the theme of Rilke mixes with that of renunciation. She constructed a hypothetical conversation between herself and Pasternak in which she asked:

> "What would we do together—in life?" "We would go to see Rilke." "I tell you Rilke is overburdened; he doesn't need anything or anyone." (May 22)

> I'm not writing to Rilke. It's too tormenting. And fruitless. . . . Rilke has no need of it. It hurts me. I am no less than he (in the future) but I am younger than he. (May 23)

She answered his complaint that she had not added anything of her own to the letter from Rilke in a similar vein:

> Boris, you didn't understand me, I love your name so much that for me not to write it yet another time, accompanying Rilke's letter, was a genuine loss, a sacrifice . . . I did that deliberately. So as not to lessen the impact of joy from Rilke. Not to divide it in two. Not to mix two waters. Not to turn your event into a personal happening. Not to be less than myself. (May 25).

The letters pointedly discussed two earlier poems about her relationship to Pasternak: "The Swain," and the 1923 "Eurydice—to Orpheus." The lesson she drew from them was the same: renunciation of earthly life and love for the sake of otherworldly communication and immortality.[27]

The letter of May 23–26, a true piece of poetic prose, should be read along with its sister work in verse, Tsvetaeva's "dream-letter" "From the Sea" ("That thing about you and me"). Written in these same May days, it was addressed to Pasternak, though she gave him only the briefest of hints about its contents, and never fulfilled her promise to send it to him.[28] "From the Sea" combines two modes of correspondence—poetry and mutual dream—while mocking a third—actual letters. Its tone, very different from that of her letters, is bantering, ironic, playful, even flirtatious; the intensity of her poetry tempts us to forget how much humor— albeit often black humor—there is in it.

Снюсь тебе. Четко?	I'm in your dream. Am I distinct?
Глядко? Почище,	Can you see? A bit clearer
Чем за решеткой	Than behind a cancel
Штемпельной? Писчей —	Mark? Am I worth
Стòю? Почтовой —	The writing paper? The postage?
Стòю? Красно?	Am I fine?
Честное слово	Word of honor
Я, не письмо!	It's I, not a letter!
	(IV, 247)

Her dream journey from the Vendee to Moscow is both unreal and impossible: she comes "with the North-South wind." Her dream, like a long-distance phone call, lasts three minutes, and she must hurry. And she jokingly brushes aside a question about her weight: "A dream weighs less than ten grams." Blithely ignoring the fact that her dream-companion may be sleeping with someone else, she jests about the way she will arrive—"uncensored," "without a postage stamp." She has her fun with editors and censors (both Soviet and emigre) and with Pasternak's own domestic censor—his jealous wife. Written in code, a "dream-shorthand," her message will deceive everyone:

Всех объегоря,	Cheating them all
— Скоропись сна! —	—The shorthand of dream!
Вот тебе с моря —	Here's for you—from the sea—
Вместо письма!	Instead of a letter.

(IV, 248)

The last two lines have a double meaning, for she is offering Pasternak both "something from the sea" (herself as dream letter) and "From the Sea," the *poema* itself. The poem is indeed written in a poetic code, much of which may forever remain unbroken (one wonders how much Pasternak himself understood when he finally read it). But she did scatter a good many clues through her letter of May 23–26, which at times paraphrases "From the Sea."

The key to the poem is the symbolic equation of the sea and love. Despite her given name, Tsvetaeva did not like the sea:

> I don't love the sea. I can't. So much space, but you can't walk on it. That's one thing. It is in motion, and I watch it. That's two . . . The ocean is a dictatorship, Boris. The mountain is a divinity . . . (May 23)

> Boris, I've just come from the ocean, and I understand one thing. Constantly, from the moment when I first began not to love it, I've tried desperately to love it, in the hope that perhaps I've grown up, changed, or simply: suddenly I'll like it. Just as it is with love. Solemnly. And every time: no, it's *not* mine, I can't . . .

> On the shore I jotted in my notebook to tell you: there are things from which I am in a constant state of renunciation: the sea, love. And you know, Boris, just now as I was walking along the beach a wave was obviously licking my boots. The ocean is like a monarch, like a diamond: it hears only the one who does *not* sing his praises. But the mountains are grateful (divine) . . . (May 25)

She developed the opposition of the ocean/love to the mountain in a letter to Teskova two weeks later:

> The Ocean. I recognize its grandeur, but I *do not like it* . . . It is free, and I, beside it, am bound. . .What am I to do with the sea? Look at it? That's not enough for me. Swim? I don't like a horizontal position. To swim means to lie and ride. I like the vertical: walking, mountains. I like the resultant of forces—mine and the height's. At the ocean I am an onlooker, as at the theater, half reclining, in a loge.

> . . . Moreover, the sea either frightens or soothes. The sea is too much like love. I don't like love. (To sit and await what it will do to me.) I like friendship: the mountain . . . (June 8)

This symbolic opposition is central to Tsvetaeva's lyrics in the 1920's. The volcano/mountain, so important in her 1923 poems to Pasternak and her two Prague *poemy*, represents an active striving for spiritual heights, a masculine, or at least non-feminine, aggressiveness. The ocean, for Tsvetaeva, signified the Eros of which she had been wary since childhood and a more "feminine," passive attitude to the world. In her dream-poem, she and Pasternak sit on the beach, sifting the sand through their fingers (perhaps recalling the Koktebel' sand which Mandel'stam gave her in his verse, and from which Sergei Efron drew his first fateful gift to her.) They play a game in which the playing pieces—shells, pebbles, and other casualties of the sea—represent bits of chewed-up emotion. The ocean/Love is a mill which grinds up everything, be it mammoth or butterfly.

She took pains to underline the poem's links with the theme of childhood—that androgynous, pre-erotic ideal of her early poetry:

> Why am I so drawn to **your** childhood, and why am I drawn to draw you into mine? (Childhood is a place where all remains **where** it was and **what** it was.) Now I am here with you in the Vendee in May 1926, endlessly playing games with you . . . In the game I'm sorting out seashells with you . . . (May 23)

Tsvetaeva even proposes to invite his son to join them on the bed (since they are in a mutual dream, they are sharing a bed) as a third in the game.[29] But Rilke infiltrates even this mutual dream: she would like to send Pasternak a "handful of alpine roses"—she would rather, that is, be writing from the mountains of Switzerland, but her hut is by the ocean.

Tsvetaeva's "dream shorthand" may well have included an anagram—an answer to Pasternak's acrostic dedication (poets could play word-games with their verse that would evade the notice of censors both editorial and domestic.) Several times she used the word "crab" (*krab*), focusing attention on it in these almost indecipherable lines by rhyming it with its homonym:[30]

Не напостовцы — стоять над крабом	We're not On-Guardists: to stand over
Выеденным. Не краб:	An eaten-out crab. Not a crab:
Славы кирпичный крап.	The brick-red spot of glory.
	(IV, 249)

The letters KRAB rearrange themselves neatly into BRAK—"marriage"—the empty marriages ("eaten out-crab") she and Pasternak had contracted in "this" world. Tsvetaeva kept promising to send the poem to Pasternak, but never did; such hints at their "fated union" undermined her determination to keep physical distance between them:

> I know I should screw up my courage and copy it over, but copying it—for you—is more irrevocable than signing it for publication—it's the same in childhood—suddenly throwing some object from the window of an express train. The emptiness of the childish hand, which has just thrown out the train window—what?—Perhaps its mother's purse, something fatal . . .[31]

Immediately after she finished "From the Sea," Tsvetaeva began another *poema* in which she tried to construct in her imagination a room where she would meet with another poet. It is not entirely clear which poet it is—and, indeed, after Rilke's death, she confided to Pasternak:

> That poem about you and me . . . turned out to be a poem about him and me . . . every line. A curious substitution took place: the poem was written in the days of my extreme concentration on him, but it was directed, with my consciousness and will—to you . . . I simply told him, living, to whom I did not intend to go, how we did not meet, how we had met in another way. Thus the strange quality of dislike, of aloofness, of repudiation in every line, which distressed me even then. . .(February 9, 1927)

"An Attempt at a Room" (*Popytka komnaty*) is in fact one of Tsvetaeva's less successful works. Though there are moments of verbal and rhythmic brilliance, her meaning is too often obscure. Only after she had nearly finished it did she write to Rilke, explaining her silence. Her self-denial was excessive, he reassured her, sending as proof a long "Elegy to Marina Tsvetaeva-Efron" (June 8). His elegy (the last extended poem he wrote) reiterated his views about "the poet's role in the eternity and infinity of the complete, yet ever-changing universe" while at the same time responding quite specifically to Tsvetaeva's letters.[32] It demonstrated Rilke's surprisingly deep understanding of Tsvetaeva as both woman and poet, the more remarkable since he knew her only from her few letters. The elegy affirmed that the burden of the poet's responsibility must be borne in solitude—a theme Tsvetaeva herself had stated as early as 1922. (III, 26-8) This not only explained the slight distance Tsvetaeva had sensed in an earlier letter from Rilke, but it consoled her in her isolation, giving it a cosmic significance, and provided support for her campaign to keep Pasternak at bay.

Meanwhile, Pasternak, still in the midst of domestic turmoil and worried about exactly what Tsvetaeva had written to Rilke, could not bring himself to respond to Rilke's note. He had just received the journal publications of her "Ratcatcher" and "Poem of The Mountain" which she had sent through Ehrenburg. He in turn sent her the manuscript of the first part of "Lieutenant Schmidt" and his second collection of poems, *Above the Barriers* (1917) which he was preparing to revise. Taking his cue from her May letters, he refrained from speaking of his feelings for her as a woman and concentrated instead on her poems, writing a long critique of "The Ratcatcher" (which he liked somewhat less than "Poem of the End"). She in turn sent him her comments on "Lieutenant Schmidt."[33] His worries that she had somehow offended Rilke were assuaged when she sent him copies of Rilke's first two letters to her, from which he could judge the tenor of their correspondence. But she acknowledged his criticism of her behavior in a confession to Rilke. ("I cannot share . . . I lie . . . I renounce too easily.") (June 14).

Pasternak, too, was in a confessional mood, for as soon as his wife left for Germany he wrote Tsvetaeva about the difficulties of his celibate life in the sweltering summer city ("I love the world. I long to devour it, every bit of it.") (July 1). This letter, on top of his previous confessions, produced an amazingly frank letter from Tsvetaeva that was her final answer to Pasternak about the possibility of a physical relationship:

> I could not live with you not because we don't understand each other, but because we do. . . . Faithfulness, as a struggle with oneself, is not necessary for me . . . Faithfulness, as constancy of passion, is incomprehensible and alien to me. . . . I understand you from afar, but if I see that to which you are attracted, I'll be flooded with contempt, like a nightingale with song. I'll exult in it. I'll be cured of you in a moment.
>
> Understand me: the insatiable, primordial hatred of Psyche for Eve, of whom there is nothing in me . . .
>
> . . . I never look at men, I simply don't see them. They don't like me, they can sniff me out. The whole *sex* doesn't like me . . . They've been fascinated with me, but they've almost never fallen in love with me . . .
>
> You don't understand Adam who loved one Eve. I don't understand Eve, whom everyone loves. I don't understand the flesh as such, I don't accord it any rights, especially of voice . . .

she concluded:

> Dear one, tear out your heart which is full of me. Don't torment yourself. Live. Don't be embarrassed by your wife and son. I give you complete absolution for anyone and everything. Take all you can, while you still want to take it!
>
> Remember that blood is older than we are, especially for you, a Semite. Don't rein it in. Take it all from a lyrical—no, from an epic height. (July 10)

In a lost letter written later in the month[34] she told him that their correspondence had come to a dead end; Pasternak agreed to stop writing for a while.

Without the distraction of Pasternak, Tsvetaeva turned the full force of her spiritual passion toward Rilke in letters which almost caricature those she had once written to Pasternak:

> . . . Rainer, I want to come to you. I want it for this new I of mine (the new me) which can realize itself only with you (in you). And then Rainer ("Rainer" is the leitmotif of this letter)—don't get angry, I am still me, I want to sleep beside you—to fall asleep and sleep. Splendid common word: how profound it is, how right, without a double meaning in what it says. Simply to sleep. And nothing else. No, more: to sink my head into your left shoulder, my hand on your right shoulder and—nothing else. No, more: and even in the

most profound sleep to know you are beside me. And more: to listen to the
sound of your heart: and—to kiss it.

> . . . How much of what I tell you now must not sound like a confession: with
> me, bodies grow bored. They suspect something in me, they don't have faith
> in me (in mine) even if I did everything as others do. Too much disinterest,
> with too much benevolence. And with too much faith . . . (August 2)

Rilke understandably paused a bit before answering that one, and in his
final letter (August 19) expressed his concern that he had come between her
and Pasternak. Her next letter went unanswered; his health was deteriorating rapidly. At the beginning of October 1926, the Efrons returned from St.
Gilles and set up housekeeping in Bellvue, a lower-class suburb of Paris.
From there, Tsvetaeva sent a post card to Rilke with her new address and
the brief note: "Here's where I'm living. Do you still love me?" There was
no answer; Rilke died on December 29.

His death provided the inspiration for the last of Tsvetaeva's "otherworldly correspondences," her triumphant "New Year's Letter" (*Novogodnee*). Like "From the Sea" it overcomes space and time by addressing Rilke
in his new home. Also like "From the Sea" it is in constant dialogue with
Tsvetaeva's "real world" correspondences of 1927, particularly her last letters to and from Rilke. "From the Sea" and "A New Year's Letter" are the
apogee of Tsvetaeva's letter-lyrics. They have been undeservedly ignored,
probably because their intensely personal nature makes them so difficult
for the outside reader. Now that most of the Pasternak-Tsvetaeva-Rilke
correspondence from 1926 is available, these two poems have begun to
receive the close readings they deserve.[35]

The Last Lyrics

Efron had no other employment besides his work on *Versts*, Tsvetaeva constantly feared her Czech subsidy would be cut off, and they could afford "only the cheaper cuts of horsemeat." Their only friends were Sergei's Eurasians, but Eurasianism had no meaning for Tsvetaeva: "It's very interesting and worthwhile and correct, but there are things which are dearer than the next day of a country, even of Russia." The rest of Paris was hostile. She wrote Pasternak of her isolation and loneliness:

> Oh, Boris, Boris, how I think of you eternally, how I physically turn towards you for help! You don't know my isolation. . .I finished a big poem, I read it to one, I read it to others—total silence—not a syllable! It's indecent, it seems to me, and not at all the result of an excess of feeling—total lack of understanding . . .[1]

This work was probably the "Poem of The Air," written in May of 1927, dated "In the days of Lindberg," though it has little to do with Lindberg himself. It is the most abstract of her long poems, and it would be interesting to know whether even Pasternak understood it. She had sent him the manuscript of *After Russia*, the volume so permeated by his presence, and he liked it. With unusual modesty, Tsvetaeva replied, "You probably overestimate my book of poems. Its only worth is in its anguish. I give it as my last lyric book—I know it's the last."[2] Indeed it was her last published collection of verse, but the lyrics she wrote intermittently from 1926 until her return to Russia are, in effect, another, final book, comparable in Tsvetaeva's career to Mandel'stam's *Voronezh Notebooks* or Akhmatova's *Seventh Book.*Though intermittent, they continued the fundamental diary aspects of her earlier lyrics—each can be traced to a specific event in her life.

When *After Russia* finally appeared, it was reviewed without enthusiasm. Her old adversary Adamovich was particularly nasty, while missing the point of her poetry entirely. He could see in Tsvetaeva nothing but a woman poet; the only poem he mentions favorably is "An Attempt at Jealousy," one of the most "feminine" of her poems:

> Tsvetaeva's poetry is erotic in the highest sense of the word—it radiates love and is saturated with love, it strains toward the world and tries to include the whole world in its embrace.[3]

We can imagine how Tsvetaeva, whose whole work strains *away* from the world, reacted to this. Adamovich summarized: "All this raving is very female and very decadent." He saw her as a "quickly fading flower," compared not only to Pasternak but to "the wise and all-seeing Akhmatova."

One of the few new friends in Tsvetaeva's life was an eighteen-year-old Russian student named Nikolai Gronsky, an ardent mountain-climber who shared her love of walking. One day they hiked the 15 km. to Versailles and back. "My companion is a pedigreed eighteen-year-old puppy who teaches me everything he learned in the *gymnazium* (a great deal!). I teach him all that's in my notebook (writing is learning—you don't learn in life, after all)."[4] Under her tutelage, Gronsky developed into a promising poet. Under the influence of her own teaching, Tsvetaeva turned back to writing lyrics for the first time in more than two years. "A School for Verse" (also titled "Conversation with Genius") dramatizes the poet's struggle with her own gift. In its elliptical compactness, it is much like the *poemy* she was writing in those years.

«Пытка!» — «Терпи!»	"It's torture!"—"Endure!"
«Скошенный луг —	"My throat's a mown meadow!"
Глотка!» — «Хрипи:	"Wheeze:
Тоже ведь — звук!»	That too is a sound!"
«Львов, а не жен	"It's a business for lions,
Дело». — «*Детей:*	Not women." "It's child's play:
Распотрошен —	Even disemboweled —
Пел же — Орфей!»	Orpheus sang!"
«Так и в гробу?»	"And so to the grave?"
— «И под доской».	"And from the grave, too."
«*Петь* не могу!»	"I *can't* sing!"
— «*Это* воспой!»	"Sing of that!"

June 4, 1928

(III, 139)

The year 1928 saw a search for new directions. With "Phaedra" finished, Tsvetaeva had no large works in progress. She worked for a while on "Yegorushka," but abandoned it again. Another *poema*, the brief, elliptic, and not terribly successful "Red Bull-Calf," was inspired by the funeral of a young White Army veteran. In mid-July the Efrons went to Pontaillac, on the Atlantic coast, where she stayed with the children till the end of September. From Pontaillac, she became involved in another intensely emotional correspondence, this time with Gronsky.[5] The letters have never been published, but draft fragments show her to be a perceptive and demanding teacher:

> You don't yet have a worker's veins, you're careless, you're satisfied with the first thing that comes to hand. You're simply lazy . . .

> You are still nourished by the external world (a tribute to your sex: men are in general more external than women) while the food of the poet is 1) the internal world, 2) the external world, absorbed through the internal one . . .

The words in your poems are largely replaceable—that means, not the right ones. Your sentences, more rarely. Your verse unit is still the sentence, rather than the word (NB: mine is the syllable).[6]

Though her current work was understood by only a handful of her contemporaries, that most middle-brow of newspapers, *Poslednie novosti*, had begun publishing ten-year-old poems from *Versts* and *Swans' Encampment*. Tsvetaeva even asked Teskova to extract the manuscript of *Juvenilia* from Slonim in Prague, for she was running out of unpublished poems. But her days on the pages of *Poslednie novosti* were numbered. On November 24, 1928, the following item appeared in the first issue of the new newspaper *Eurasia*, edited by Sergei Efron:

V. V. Mayakovsky is presently visiting Paris. The poet has given several public readings of his poems. The editors of *Eurasia* print below Marina Tsvetaeva's address to him:

To Mayakovsky

On April 28, 1922, on the eve of my departure from Russia, early in the morning on a completely deserted Kuznetsky Most, I met Mayakovsky:

"Well, Mayakovsky, what shall I tell Europe from you?"

"That the truth is here."

On November 7, 1928, late at night, coming out of the Cafe Voltaire, I responded to the question, "What would you say about Russia after Mayakovsky's reading?"

Without thinking, I answered, "That the strength is there."[7]

Tsvetaeva, of course, meant "*poetic* strength," but Miliukov read this to mean support for the Bolsheviks, and stopped publishing her.

As always, it was a grave error to draw political conclusions from Tsvetaeva's statements about art. She was neither "above" nor "below" politics, simply far off to the side, and profoundly alien. Ironically, just as Miliukov banished her from his pages, the theme of the White Army returned to her work. At Pontaillac in 1928, she began a large epic poem about the final defeat of the White Army, based on Sergei's diaries. "Perekop," its title, is the name of the isthmus joining the Crimea to the mainland, where the Whites made their last stand in November 1920. Though the content may have been "white," the style—Tsvetaeva's elliptic modernism—was seen as "red:"

I know that the real listeners for my poor "Perekop" are not the White officers—to whom, every time I read the poem, in full purity of heart, I feel like telling the thing in prose—but Red students, to whom the piece—even the prayer of the priest before the attack—would get through—will get through.[8]

As she was praising the White Army, her primary source was being accused by some of his fellow Eurasians of being a "Chekist and a communist." Tsvetaeva staunchly defended him in familiar terms: "I suffer greatly for Sergei, with his purity and flaming heart. He, with the exception of two or three others, is the single *moral force* of Eurasianism."[9]

The prospects for income from prose were much better than those from verse, and so, like it or not, Tsvetaeva was becoming a prose writer. After "Perekop," Tsvetaeva began to work on a large piece she called a "non-article" commissioned by *Volia Rossii*. Its subject was Natalia Goncharova, Russia's most important woman painter. One of the major forces in the explosive development of Russian art beginning around 1907, Goncharova had been living in Paris since 1915. In undertaking the article Tsvetaeva was for the first time writing for "external" rather than "internal" reasons, though it did provide her with the opportunity to befriend and study a major woman artist, continuing her lifelong inquiry into the sources of female creativity. "Goncharova" is a work which deserves translation and further study.

During the winter of 1929–1930, Sergei's tuberculosis returned. With the help of friends, he was sent off to a sanatorium in Savoie, in the French Alps. The proceeds from an April, 1930 "evening" enabled Tsvetaeva and the children to spend a few summer months in a peasant hut nearby. It was a reinvigorating and productive interlude, during which she translated "The Swain" into French. Despairing of her reception in the emigre community, she began to hope for a French audience. Goncharova had done a set of illustrations for the poem, and prospects for publication seemed good. But like most of Tsvetaeva's attempts to write in French, or translate herself into it, it came to nothing. A far more important fruit of that summer in Savoie was a cycle of seven poems in memory of Mayakovsky, whose suicide in April had shocked and dismayed her. The cycle is both a tribute to him and an attack on his enemies in the U.S.S.R. and abroad. Tsvetaeva used a variety of voices to mimic the reaction of the Philistines, both Soviet:

В лодке, да еще в любовной	To sink in a boat—and a love boat
Запрокинуться — скандал!	At that—what a scandal!
Разин — чем тебе не ровня? —	Weren't you the equal of Razin?
Лучше с *бытом* совладал.	Better to have coped with *byt*.
Эко новшество — лекарство	Some novelty—medicine
Хлещущее, что твой кран!	Gushing out like a tap!
Парень, не по-пролетарски	Fellow, you're not acting proletarian-like,
Действуешь — а что твой пан!	But like a Polish pan!

(III, 144)

and emigre:

(Зарубежье, встречаясь:	(The emigration, hearing the news:
«Ну, казус! Каков фугас!	"Now that's a case! What a landmine!
Значит — тоже сердца есть?	You mean—*they* also have hearts?
И с той же, что и у нас?»)	And with the same love as we do?")

(III, 145)

The cycle's penultimate poem is a long, colloquial dialogue in the other world between the newly-arrived Mayakovsky and the shade of Sergei Esenin, whose suicide he had deplored only five years earlier. Esenin gently taunts him with the memory of that poem:

А помнишь, как матом	"And do you remember how you
Во весь свой эстрадный	Cussed me out
Басище — меня-то	At the top of your
Обкладывал? — Ладно	Big stage bass?"—"Alright
Уж. . . — Вот-те и шлюпка	Already"—"Some life-boat
Любовная лодка!	Your love boat's turned out to be!
Ужель из-за юбки?	You really did it for a skirt?"—
— Хужей из-за водки.	—"Better than from vodka!"

(III, 146)

"Seryozha" asks for news from home and "Volodya" concedes bitterly that it's all much the same:

А что на Рассее-	"And what's happening in
На матушке? — То есть	Mother Russia?"—Where
Где? — В Эсэсэсере	Did you say?"—"In the U.S.S.R.
Что нового? — Строят.	What's new?"—"They're building.
Родители — ро̀дят,	Parents are giving birth,
Вредители — точут,	Wreckers are preying,
Издатели — водят,	Publishers delaying,
Писатели — строчут.	Writers are scribbling.
Мост новый заложен,	A new bridge has been laid,
Да смыт половодьем.	But washed away by the flood.
Все то же, Сережа!	It's still the same, Seryozha!"
— Все то же, Володя.	—"It's still the same, Volodya!"

August, 1930
(III, 147)

Despite her husband's pro-Soviet sympathies, Tsvetaeva had no illusions at all about Soviet reality. The Mayakovsky cycle marks the return of the lyric to Tsvetaeva's work, after five years in which it was almost entirely eclipsed by long poems, and signals its return in a new key. No longer the densely allusive, private poems of *After Russia*, Tsvetaeva's late lyrics are a more *public* poetry, full of anger and fiercely polemical.

In the fall of 1930, Efron came home to Meudon after eight months in the sanatorium, but he could find no work. He enrolled in a course for film technicians with the hope of becoming a cameraman. Soon after, his increasingly sympathetic views of the U.S.S.R., under the impetus of unemployment, led him to accept assignments from the Soviet secret police. By 1932 he had became one of the founders of the Union for Return to the Homeland; as early as 1933 he was already hoping for a Soviet passport which would enable him to return home. But the Soviets exacted a high price before welcoming this former White officer back. Tsvetaeva knew nothing, and did not want to know, of Efron's political activities. During the 1930's, they usually shared the same roof, but less and less of their lives. Sergei was seldom home and Tsvetaeva mentioned him infrequently in her letters.

In March 1931, Tsvetaeva heard through friends that Pasternak had left his wife and gone off to the Caucasus with Zinaida Neihaus, whom he would later marry. She was afraid of the consequences for him, as she confided to Teskova:

> In Russia there's a *plague* on poets—what a list in ten years! A catastrophe is inevitable: in the first place there's a husband, in the second B. has a wife and son, in the third place—she's pretty (B. will be jealous), and fourth and most important—B. is *unfit for happiness in love*. For him to love means to be tormented.

But it also hurt her personally:

> For years I lived by the dream that I'd see him. Now there's an empty feeling. I have no one to go to in Russia. A wife and son I will respect. But a *new* love—I'll keep aloof. Understand me correctly, A.A.: it's *not* jealousy. But— now I've been done without.[10]

Tsvetaeva's correspondence with Pasternak had continued at a greatly reduced intensity. She simply needed to know that he was there and cared about her, but now she was not sure even of that.

Tsvetaeva's 1931 cycle of six poems to Pushkin focused on the poet's predicament in a society which hated and censored him. She accurately described them as "frighteningly shrill, frighteningly familiar, having nothing in common with the canonized Pushkin . . . Dangerous poems."[11] She didn't even try to publish them until the 1937 centennial of Pushkin's death. Her Pushkin is a hot-blooded African, in constant rebellion against the stagnation of Russian culture like his spiritual father, Peter the Great (godfather to Pushkin's great-grandfather, the Ethiopian Abram Gannibal). Her insistance on Pushkin's blackness owes something to a visit she made in May or June, 1931, to the French Colonial exhibit in Paris.

Чёрного не перекрасить   You'll never re-paint black
В белого — неисправим!   Into white—it can't be rectified!
Недурён российский классик,   He wasn't bad, that Russian
Небо Африки — своим   Classic—who called the sky of Africa

Звавший, невское — проклятым.   His own—and the Neva's sky—damned.
— Пушкин — в роли русопята?   —Pushkin, in the role of Russophile?
                                            1931

                                           (III, 149)

She rages against the academic Pushkinists, whose statuary image has nothing to do with *her* Pushkin:

Чтò вы делаете, карлы,   What are you doing, dwarfs,
Этот — голубей олив —   Branding forever this freest,
Самый вольный, самый крайний   Most extreme brow—darker than olives—
Лоб — навеки заклеймив   With the dual

Низостию двуединой   Baseness of gold
Золота и середины?   And mean?

«Пушкин — тога, Пушкин — схима,   Pushkin—toga, Pushkin—tonsure,
Пушкин — мера, — Пушкин — грань. . .» Pushkin—measure, Pushkin—boundary,
Пушкин, Пушкин, Пушкин — имя   Pushkin, Pushkin, Pushkin—they repeat the noble
Благородное — как брань   Name——like parrots

Площадную — попугаи.   Cursing on the square.

— Пушкин? Очень испугали!   Pushkin? You've really frightened us!
                                            1931

                                         (III, 150)

In spirit, and in the passion of its invective, the cycle has much in common with her Mayakovsky cycle written the previous summer. Both pay tribute to poets suffocated and killed by society. Tsvetaeva was speaking of herself as well.

"An Ode to Walking" is a three-poem cycle praising Tsvetaeva's favorite avocation. Her rejection of the automobile symbolized her alienation from a modern technological world addicted to it ("parasites of expanse!/alcoholics of versts!"). Her tone was sardonic:

Слава толстым подметкам,   Glory to thick soles,
Сапогам на гвоздях,   To hobnail boots,
Ходокам, скороходкам —   To walkers, joggers,
Божествам в сапогах!   Deities in boots!

Если есть в мире — ода   If there exists in the world an ode
Богу сил, богу гор —   To the god of strength, the god of mountains—
Это взгляд пешехода   It is the look of a pedestrian
На застрявший мотор.   At a stalled motor.
                                     August 1931

                                       (III, 157)

The machine (which in Russian means "automobile" as well) represented *byt*—passive, non-spiritual life. Walking, that same *active* force which had propelled her up the hillsides of Czechoslovakia and along the beaches of St. Gilles, was the force of the soul. A few days after the "Ode" she complained to Teskova that she herself was turning into a machine, though (at least!) a poor one:

> I live with my last bit of (spiritual) strength, without any external or internal impressions, without even the least occasion for the latter. In short: I live like a badly-functioning automaton—badly, because of the remnants of soul which hinder the machine . . .[12]

Another theme in her letters to Teskova is her increasing isolation. "When Sergei was away in the sanatorium last year, no one came by for months. The door was silent, and if there was a knock it was the gas man or the electricity."[13] This is the mood of "A House," a verse self-portrait written as her thirty-ninth birthday approached. Regarding her face in the mirror, she sees the house of her soul, and in it recognizes the traces of her youth:

Глаза — без всякого тепла:	Eyes, without any warmth:
То зелень старого стекла,	That green of old glass,
Сто лет глядящегося в сад,	Which has gazed a hundred years into a garden
Пустующий — сто пятьдесят.	Abandoned for a hundred fifty.
Стекла, дремучего, как сон,	Of glass dozing like a dream,
Окна, единственный закон	Windows, the single law of which:
Которого: гостей не ждать,	Don't expect guests,
Прохожего не отражать.	Don't reflect passers-by.

September 6, 1931
(III, 160)

It is a frightening picture of emptiness and alienation.

But this period of alienation was also a period of abstract thought about the poet and his art. Over the winter of 1931–1932, Tsvetaeva worked on two related philosophical essays, "Art in the Light of Conscience" and "The Poet and Time."[14] "Art in the Light of Conscience" sets forth—if Tsvetaeva's prose can ever be described as "setting forth"—her artistic credo. It is an example of her unique prose style—telegraphic, aphoristic, yet with a sense of organic growth, as one idea develops from another through a connection of images and sounds rather than logic:

> What does art teach? Goodness? No. Common sense? No. It cannot even teach itself, for it is given. . .All the answers we derive from art, *we* put into it. A series of answers to which there are no questions.

> The condition of creation is a condition of being overcome by a spell. Until you begin, it is a state of being obsessed; until you finish, a state of being possessed. Something, someone, lodges in you, your hand is the fulfiller not of you but of *him*. Who is that? That which through you wants to be.[15]

It was not an aesthetic to please either the emigres or the Soviets. Her view of the poet as simply an instrument for something which "wants to be written" goes against the Western glorification of the artist as autonomous creative genius. Yet her assertion that art is responsible only to itself was anathema to Marxist theories of the social role of the artist. Indeed, this and its sister essay are the two major pieces of Tsvetaeva's prose which so far have never been published, even in excerpt, in the Soviet Union. Nor were they well received in the West.[16]

"The Poet and Time" is briefer, more personal, and, to this reader, more interesting. Tsvetaeva explored in depth a theme she often touched in her letters—the paradox of her "hatred for her own age" and love for the values of a vanished age combined with a voice, a style that was clearly modern— indeed, pathbreaking. Those who could accept and value her style rejected her values:

> Not to go forward (in poetry, as in everything) is to go backwards, that is, to leave the game. The big gun [evidently Adamovich—JT] of emigre literature has experienced that which happens to a Philistine from the age of thirty—he became contemporary to the previous generation. . . . The reason X does not accept contemporary literature is because he no longer will create it.

> Contemporaneity in a poet is not the proclaiming that his age is best, nor even the simple acceptance of it. 'No' is also an answer."[17]

While her prose of 1931–1932 treated the position of the poet in general and abstract terms, the few poems she wrote concerned major choices she faced in a more immediate, personal realm. Mur would turn seven in February, 1932, and she had to confront the question of his education. Tsvetaeva disliked the long hours of French schools and their rote learning. "A child should study three hours of the day and spend the rest of the day growing." French children, she felt, were not children but "pretty little old men and ladies."[18] For Mur, such a regimen would be particularly inappropriate: she describes his character as "complex and difficult." But the question went beyond mere personality—it was really a decision about his cultural identification. Russian was his native language; she had taught him to read and write it. He had taught himself to read French, but since he had few French playmates, he still did not speak it fluently. If Mur were to remain in France, he would inevitably have to become a Frenchman. But Sergei and Ariadna were already seriously considering return to Russia, and Mur was influenced by them. "Sergei," wrote Tsvetaeva, "has completely gone over to Soviet Russia, he sees nothing else, and he sees in it only what he wants to see."[19] She was far more clear-eyed and pessimistic:

> Go to Russia? There they'll finally win over my Mur from me, and whether that will be to his benefit, I don't know. And there they'll not only stop my mouth by not publishing my things—they won't even let me write them.[20]

Tsvetaeva's "Poems to My Son" attempt to imagine and justify Mur's return without her. *Her* generation's quarrel with the Bolsheviks was not his. They had lost a Russia he had never known. Russia now beckons him as a means of salvation from the admittedly bleak prospects of emigre life in France:

Призывное: СССР, —	The inviting: USSR
Не менее во тьме небес	No less inviting in the dark heavens
Призывное, чем: SOS.	Than: SOS.
Нас родина не позовет!	The motherland does not call *us*!
Езжай, мой сын, домой — вперед —	Go, my son, home—forward—
В *свой* край, в *свой* век, в *свой* час, — от	To *your* land, *your* age, *your* hour, from us—
нас —	To the Russia of you, the Russia of masses,
В Россию — вас, в Россию — масс,	To an *our-hour* land, a *now*-land!
В *наш*-час — страну; в *сей*-час — страну!	To an on Mars-land, a without-us-land!
В на-Марс — страну! в без-нас — страну!	January 1932
	(III, 162)

She looked at the generation of emigre children and saw little for Mur to emulate. In his difficult character she saw her heritage, which would get in the way even if he became "a zero," "a pair of chewing jaws," "a Gallic rooster, his tail mortgaged to the bank," the "languid fiance of a grey-haired American lady." Yet a few months later, on the tenth anniversary of her emigration, she seemed to be considering the question of her own return:

Даль, прирожденная, как боль,	A distant land, inborn as pain,
Настолько родина и столь	So much homeland and so much
Рок, что повсюду, через всю	Fate that everywhere—through all
Даль — всю ее с собой несу!	Distance—I ever carry it with me!
Даль, отдалившая мне близь,	A distance, which alienates the near,
Даль, говорящая: «Вернись	A distance, which says: "Return
Домой!»	*Home!"*
Со всех — до горних звёзд —	Which removes me from all
Меня снимающая мест!	Places—even the mountain stars!
	May 12, 1932
	(III, 164)

The events and publishing opportunities of the next several years would decree that most of Tsvetaeva's work, and much of her attention, be focused on the events, places, and people of her own Russian past.

In August, 1932, Maximillian Voloshin died in Koktebel' at the age of 55. For the next two months, "at a gallop, never straightening my back," Tsvetaeva wrote a long prose memoir of her old friend. It is only fitting that Max, her first mentor in poetry, should, in death, have set her onto a second career. For "A Living Thing about a Living Man" is the first of her major, mature prose writings. It is both a tribute to Max himself and a formulation of the most important element in her own art, mythmaking:

Max would tell stories about events the way a people tells them, and he would tell about individuals the same way as about whole peoples. The exactness of his description was always beyond doubt for me, as the exactness of every epos is undoubtable. Achilles cannot be other than what he is, otherwise he is not Achilles. A divine measuring-standard of truth lives in each of us; only when he has sinned before it is a person a liar. Mystery-making, on certain lips, is already the beginning of truth, and when it grows into mythmaking, it is—the whole truth . . .

What is not essential—is superfluous. That is the way you get gods and heroes. Only in Max's stories did people come out like themselves, more like themselves than in life where you meet them in the wrong way, where you meet not them, where they are simply not themselves and are—unrecognizable. I remember Max telling what a little girl had said (the girl had visited a zoo for the first time and was writing a letter to her father): "I saw a lion—not at all like one."[21] Trans. J. M. King

Tsvetaeva didn't expect the piece would find a publisher in the emigre press, so she read it, for two and three-quarter hours, to an attentive hall ("primarily women") in October, 1932. Most of Tsvetaeva's major prose pieces, in fact, were first presented at such readings, before publication. It was a particularly appropriate mode, for the style of her prose is based on many devices of (good) conversation. Angela Livingstone, writing about "Art in the Light of Conscience," describes it this way:

A peculiarity of Tsvetaeva's prose is that she writes as if in mid-utterance to someone. Like Mayakovsky in many of his poems, she writes neither quietly to herself nor with the assumption of a large unknown audience, but as if to some one unspecified persona from whom she demands particular attention and response.[22]

This, of course, is exactly what we found characteristic of her poems, so many of which are addressed to a *particular* other. And, like her poems, with their exclamations and hyphenated pauses—the intonations of spoken words—her prose must have been dramatically different in a reading from the way it appears on paper. To take one example from her "Max" memoir: the passage on mythmaking quoted above, which ends with "I saw a lion—not at all like one," proceeds by an association of images rather than logic:

With Max the lion was always like one. By the way, so as not to forget. I have under the inkwell from which I am writing a plate. . .[23]

She goes on to describe the glazed lion in the middle of the plate—not surprisingly, it is the image of Max's hirsute head. The progression of topics—from Max's stories, to mythmaking in general, to the lion in the zoo, to the head of a lion which recalls Max himself, is artful and sophisticated. Yet it is motivated, halfway through, by the seemingly casual "By the way, so as not to forget." This is what we do when engaged in the oral retelling of a complex tale. The writer does *not* forget—he jots down a note and raises the question elsewhere in the manuscript, in good order. Tsvetaeva's parenthetic remark gives the illusion of oral narrative, while it justifies the less than logical (though perfectly organic) construction of her prose. But then Tsvetaeva reminds her reader that she is *not* speaking: "under the inkwell from which I am writing"—transforming the piece into a kind of written personal monologue, in other words, a letter. Indeed, the language of Tsvetaeva's prose is close to that of her remarkable letters. Like them, her prose is in some ways a substitute for those good conversations of which she was deprived. It is no wonder that emigre editors were often dismayed by the length of her prose pieces and the apparent irrelevance of their many digressions. As with her beloved Pushkin, the essence of Tsvetaeva's prose was most often in what *seemed* to be digressions. And, like a poem, her prose pieces were organic structures which could not be easily condensed.[24]

Her next prose project was the article "Epic and Lyric of Our Time: Vladimir Mayakovsky and Boris Pasternak." An emigre journal had commissioned an article on Pasternak, but soon after Tsvetaeva began writing, she asked permission to make it into a comparison of Pasternak and Mayakovsky. While "A Living Thing" was primarily a portrait of Max the *man*, "Epic and Lyric" is a contrastive study of two poetic personalities (Pasternak, we should not be surprised, comes out ahead), through the lens of their writing. The essay is one of the most extreme examples of Tsvetaeva's penchant for thinking in dichotomies: it is built entirely on a series of contrasts between the two poets.

> Neither Mayakovsky nor Pasternak, in essence, has a reader. Mayakovsky has a listener, Pasternak an eavesdropper, a spy, even a pathfinder.
>
> Two can meet at Pasternak, as at a brook, then to part, each having drunk his fill, and having bathed, carrying away the brook in himself and on himself. At Mayakovsky, as on a square, they either start a fight or sing in chorus.
>
> Pasternak is inexhaustible. Mayakovsky exhausts.
>
> "The battle hindered my being a poet."—Pasternak
> "My songs hindered my being a battler."—Mayakovsky

Many of these juxtapositions are brilliantly illustrative, though some are strained. Tsvetaeva's dichotomies provide insight into her own poetics. She is in many ways a combination of the two: one could characterize some of her longer *poemy*, such as "Poem of the End" or "Poem of the Mountain," as epic treatments of lyric themes. It is tempting to attribute the obscurity of her long poems in the late twenties to an excessive influence of Pasternak, while her new, stridently public lyrics of the thirties show a renewed respect for Mayakovsky. In proclaiming Mayakovsky and Pasternak as "the most significant poets of our time," she, in effect, relegated Akhmatova and Mandel'stam to the past, as well she might have, for they had published no new poems for ten years.

In April 1933, Tsvetaeva's half-brother Andrei died in Moscow of tuberculosis. The death of a sibling, the first of her own generation, made Tsvetaeva (now forty) aware of how distant was the world of her childhood, how fragile and vulnerable its survival in memory.

> . . . All this is finished, and finished forever. There aren't any such houses left. There aren't any such trees. . .There aren't any such as we were. All has burned to the ground, sunk into the depths. What exists is within us—you, me, Asya, a few others. Don't laugh, but we are *really* the last of the Mohicans. And I'm proud of that derisive communist term, "survivals." I'm happy to be a survival, for all of this will survive even me. (And them!)[25]

Andrei's death provided the impetus for the series of works which explore first the milieu from which she came and then the child-poet who developed in it. Four major prose pieces, "The House at Old Pimen" (1933), "Mother and Music" (1934), "The Devil" (1934), and "My Pushkin" (1937), along with the shorter prose pieces about her father and his museum (1933–1936), form what J. King terms a "mythobiography,"[26] or, to put it slightly differently, the biography of a poetic development. It is a retrospective treatment in prose of the same questions Tsvetaeva treated throughout her poetic career in her lyric diary.

In mid-January 1934, she learned of Andrey Bely's death in Moscow at the age of 53. Yet another contemporary poet had met a premature death. She had not known Bely as she had known Voloshin, but she set to work immediately on another portrait-obituary, "A Captive Spirit: My Meetings with Andrey Bely." In March she read it to an overflow hall. Her prose was meeting with modest success; but she was not resigned to abandoning poetry. She wrote vehemently to Vladislav Khodasevich, the only other major poet of the emigration:

> No, we *must* write verse. We can't let either life or the emigration, or the Vishniaks [the editor of *Contemporary Annals*—JT] nor bridge parties, nor this and that triumph . . . to force a poet to get along without poems, to make of a poet a prose writer and of a prose writer a dead man.
>
> You (we!) have been handed something which we have no right to drop, or to give over into other hands (of which there are none). For the less you write, the less you want to—between you and your desk rises a whole inability (as between you and a love from which you've emerged).[27]

Indeed, 1934 saw a modest spurt of lyrics which share the theme of her alienation from French Paris. "Homesickness" is one of Tsvetaeva's best-known poems, and rightfully so, one of the finest examples of her bitter, yet elegant invective. While she ostensibly maintains that "longing for the native land is a long-unmasked illusion," and that "it's all the same to me *where* I am entirely alone," she paints an eloquent picture of her total spiritual isolation, not only from French Paris but, if we read closely, from her family as well (who were suffering strongly from precisely that nostalgia for Russia). At the end she reveals that her protest masks a deep ambivalence:

Тàк край меня не уберег	My homeland so little protected me
Мой, что и самый зоркий сыщик	That the sharpest-eyed detective,
Вдоль всей души, всей — поперек!	Looking up and down my soul, and straight
Родимого пятна *не* сыщет!	across!
	Won't find a *single* birth-mark!
Всяк дом мне чужд, всяк храм мне пуст,	Every house is alien to me, every temple empty,
И все — равно, и все — едино.	And all's the same, and all is equal.
Но если по дороге — куст	But if along the road, a bush appears,
Встает, особенно — рябина. . .	Especially—a rowan . . .

May, 1934

(III, 175)

The same alienation is expressed in "A Garden," which concentrates Tsvetaeva's most characteristic devices (anaphora, short lines, masculine rhymes):

За этот ад,	In place of this
За этот бред,	Hell and this delirium
Пошли мне сад	Send me a garden
На старость лет.	For my old age.
На старость лет,	For my old age
На старость бед:	For my old misfortunes:
Рабочих — лет,	Of working years,
Горбатых — лет. . .	Hunchbacked years . . .
На старость лет	At the end of my dog's life—
Собачьих — клад:	A treasure:
Горячих лет —	For burning years—
Прохладный сад. . .	A cool garden . . .
Для беглеца	Send me a garden
Мне сад пошли:	For a refugee:
Без ни — лица,	Without a face
Без ни — души!	Without a soul!

October 1, 1934

(III, 178)

While "Garden" at least envisions her old age, another poem of the same months ominously foreshadows her suicide:

Уединение: уйди	Solitude: go off
В себя, как прадеды в феоды.	Into yourself, like our forefathers into their fiefs.
Уединение: в груди	Solitude: in your breast
Ищи и находи свободу.	Seek and find freedom.

Чтоб ни души, чтоб ни ноги —	So there's not a soul, not a step,
На свете нет такого саду	There's not a garden on earth
Уединению. В груди	So solitary. In your breast
Ищи и находи прохладу.	Seek and find coolness.
Ктó победил на площадú —	Who is victorious on the square?
Про то не думай и не ведай.	Don't think of it, don't know of it.
В уединении груди —	In the solitude of your breast
Справляй и погребай победу.	Deal with and bury victory.
Уединение в груди.	Solitude in the breast.
Уединение: уйди,	Solitude: go away,
Жизнь!	Life!

                                                          September 1934
                                                                (III, 177)

Thoughts of return to Russia may have prompted the uncharacteristic "The Cheliuskin Crew." The Soviet icebreaker Cheliuskin was crushed by floating ice in the Arctic, and the crew was dramatically rescued by Soviet pilots. The tenor of her poem was, to put it mildly, different from that of the nearly simultaneous "Solitude:"

Седыми бровьми	Affection constrained
Стесненная ласковость. . .	By grey brows . . .
Сегодня — смеюсь!	Today—I will laugh!
Сегодня — да здравствует	Today—long live
Советский Союз!	The Soviet Union!
За вас каждым мускулом	I hold fast to you
Держусь — и горжусь:	With every muscle, and I'm proud:
Челюскинцы — русские!	The Cheliuskin crew—are Russian!

                                                          October 3, 1934
                                                                (III, 179)

Not surprisingly, the poem was never published in the emigre press. It may have been Tsvetaeva's equivalent to Mandel'stam's "Ode to Stalin" (1937), written to save his life, or Akhmatova's cycle, "Glory to Peace" (1950), written to save her arrested son.[28] Like them, it is patently inferior to the rest of her work (the poet's protest against prostitution of her muse).

A passage from a letter to Teskova, heavily cut by the editor, sheds some light on the domestic sources of her alienation:

> Humanness, through marriage or love—through *another*, and without fail, *him* is for me worthless. Do you agree with me? Otherwise it turns out that you're some kind of half, a Lethean shadow thirsting for incarnation . . . And Selma Lagerlof, who *never* married? And you? And I, at five, and fifteen? Marriage and love rather destroy personality, they are an ordeal. That's what Goethe and Tolstoy thought. And early marriage (like mine) is in general a catastrophe, a blow against your whole life . . .[29]

Her letters to Bunina and Teskova during the winter of 1934–1935 imply that Sergei had taken up with another woman. To Teskova she wrote:

> I have another woe—not a woe, an insult—wildly undeserved . . . All these days I've felt like writing my will. In general I'd prefer *not to Exist* . . . I've lived to the age of forty, and I've never had one person who would love me more than all on earth.[30]

This personal woe was temporarily eclipsed by the death of Nikolai Gronsky in a Paris subway accident. Tsvetaeva's friendship with Gronsky had faded in 1931, and she discovered only after his death that he had indeed become the poet of which he gave promise at eighteen. "Epitaph," a cycle of poems in Gronsky's memory, mourns a meaningless, irreparable loss, with an agnostic's lack of faith in another life:

Не ты — не ты — не ты — не ты.	Not you—not you—not you—not you.
Чтò бы ни пели нам попы,	No matter what the priests sing to us
Что смерть есть жизнь и жизнь есть смерть, —	That death is life and life is death—
Бог — слишком Бог, червь — слишком червь.	God is too much God, the worm too much the worm.
На труп и призрак — неделим!	Indivisible into corpse and specter!
Не отдадим тебя за дым	We won't give you up for the smoke
Кадил,	Of censers,
Цветы	The flowers
Могил.	Of graves.

January 5–7, 1935
(III, 182)

Her long-awaited meeting with Pasternak finally took place in late June of 1935, and it was clearly a disappointment; she referred to it as a "non-meeting." Pasternak later described it guardedly:

> In the summer of 1935, when I was on the verge of mental illness after almost twelve months of insomnia, I found myself at an anti-Fascist congress in Paris. There I met Tsvetaeva's son and daughter and her husband, an enchanting, sensitive and steadfast being of whom I grew as fond as a brother.

> Tsvetaeva's family were pressing her to return to Russia. It was partly that they were homesick, partly that they sympathised with Communism and the Soviet Union, and partly that they thought Tsvetaeva had no sort of life in Paris and was going to pieces in loneliness and isolation from her readers.

> She asked me what I thought about it. I had no definite opinion. It was hard to know what to advise them; I was afraid that these remarkable people would have a difficult and troubled time at home. But the tragedy which was to strike the whole family surpassed my fears beyond all measure.[31]

Pasternak had not wanted to go to the Congress, but, seeking world-renowned figures for the delegation, the government had insisted. According to Tsvetaeva, Pasternak whispered to her at the conference: "I didn't dare not come. Stalin's secretary came to my house—I was frightened." She added, "He was terribly unwilling to come without his beautiful wife, but they sat him in an airplane and brought him."[32] Tsvetaeva was distracted, too; in the midst of the conference, Mur was operated on for appendicitis and spent ten days in the hospital.

Days later, Tsvetaeva and the convalescent Mur were on a train to the Mediterranean coast, where they spent the summer in a cheap (and stifling) attic room. It was not a vacation Tsvetaeva enjoyed. In her mood, even the beauty of the Cote d'Azur was annoying. Worst of all was the forced inactivity. Because of Mur, she spent most of her day lying on the beach, where she couldn't write ("I've never been able to write outdoors"). She was constitutionally unable to enjoy doing nothing. "Others are resting from work, from a job they obviously don't like. My rest *is* my work. When I *don't* write, I'm simply unhappy."[33]

At the end of the summer, she summarized her literary career in a long letter to Bunina:

> In the last years I've written very few poems. The fact that they're not accepted has forced me to write prose. While *Volia Rossii* was alive, I could calmly write a big long poem, knowing that they would take it . . . Fragments remained in my notebook. Now eight lines, now four, now two. Sometimes the poems broke through, or I fell into the stream. Then there were cycles, but—again—nothing ever got finished—blank spots all over—now one line missing, now a whole quatrain, i.e., in the final analysis, a rough draft.
>
> Finally I got scared. And what if I die? What will remain of the years? Why have I lived? And—another fear. And what if I've forgotten? That is, I'm no longer capable of writing a whole piece, of finishing it . . .
>
> And so, this summer, I began to finish things.[34]

Teskova urged her to collect all the poems written since *After Russia*, and the "finishing up" she did over the summer accounts for the fact that several poems begun in the early thirties bear a completion date of 1935. In "We've not gone away anywhere, you and I" (finished, ironically, during the summer when she *did* get away) Tsvetaeva voiced her resentment of the patrons of emigre culture:

С жиру лопающиеся: жир — их «лоск»,	Bursting with fat, fat is their "lustre,"
Что не только что масло едят, а мозг	For they eat not just butter but brains—
Наш — в поэмах, в сонатах, в сводах:	Ours—in *poemy*, sonatas, collections,
Людоеды в парижских модах!	Cannibals in Paris fashions!

Нами — лакомящиеся: франк — за вход.	They treat themselves to us—for a franc a ticket.
О, урод, как водой туалетной — рот	Oh, you freak, rinsing your mouth
Сполоснувший — бессмертной песней!	With immortal song—as with toilet water!
Будьте прокляты вы — за весь мой	May you be damned—for all my shame
Стыд: вам руку жать, когда зуд в горсти, —	At shaking your hand, when my fist itches—
Пятью пальцами — да от всех пяти	To give you an autograph—with five fingers,
Чувств — на память о чувствах добрых —	From all five senses, in memory of good feelings—
Через всё вам лицо — автограф!	Right across your face!

1932—Summer 1935
(III, 187)

Back in Vanves, she vented her anger on *Poslednie novosti* and its readers in the gloriously vicious "Readers of Newspapers." Transported by an "underground snake" (the metro), they have lost their identities behind their papers:

Кто — чтец? Старик? Атлет?	Who's the reader? Old man? Athlete?
Солдат? — Ни чёрт, ни лиц,	Soldier? Neither features, nor faces,
Ни лет. Скелет — раз нет	Nor years. A skeleton—since there's no
Лица: газетный лист!	Face: a newsprint page!
Которым — весь Париж	With which all Paris
С лба до пупа одет.	Is dressed from brow to navel.
Брось, девушка!	Quit it, girl!
Родишь —	You'll give birth
Читателя газет.	To a newspaper reader!

She imitates the swaying of the strap-hangers by breaking the word in half and inserting snatches of headline:

Кача — «живет с сестрой» —	Sway—"Lives with sister"—
ются — «убил отца!» —	Ing—"Killed his father"—
Качаются — тщетой	Swaying—they are soused
Накачиваются.	With trivia.

November 15, 1935
(III, 190)

Tsvetaeva preferred the past, and paid tribute to the older generation in two poems titled, "To the Fathers:"

В мире, ревущем:	In a world which roars:
— Слава грядущим!	—"Praise the men of the future!"
Чтò во мне шепчет:	Something in me whispers:
— Слава прошедшим!	—"Praise the men of the past!"

September 14-15, 1935
(III, 187)

But she continued her deliberations about return to the land which saluted the "men of the future." She had absolutely no illusions about what she would find:

> Moscow has become a New York: an ideological New York—no open land,
> no hillocks. Asphalt lakes with loudspeakers and colossal posters. No—I
> didn't begin with the most important thing: Mur, whom this Moscow will
> take away immediately, entirely, headfirst. And secondly, also important: I,
> with my *Furchtlosigkeit*, I, *not knowing how* not to answer, I incapable of
> signing a congratulatory address to the great Stalin, for it is *not I* who called
> him great and—even if he is—it is not my grandeur and—perhaps most
> important—I hate every solemn, state church.[35]

Her literary activity had already taken on a schizophrenic quality, for she
was now certain she would return sooner or later. She found it very difficult
to write under this uncertainty. Of her husband she wrote:

> I can hold S.Ya. here no longer—but I don't hold him. He won't go without
> me, he's waiting for something (my "recovery of sight") not understanding
> that I'll *die the way I am*.[36]

The summer of 1936 was consumed by one last brief, emotionally-
oversaturated correspondence with a young male poet. Anatolii Shteiger,
fifteen years her junior, was a middling poet of the Adamovich-dominated
Paris school. Of Shteiger, Vladimir Nabokov said:

> His talent has been greatly exaggerated. He was a very minor poet. *Very*
> minor poet. With a very limited gift and a very limited emotional life. A nice
> person. A charming person. A well-bred person. That's all.[37]

Tsvetaeva had a passing acquaintance with his sister, the poetess Alla
Golovina, but she had met Shteiger himself only briefly. A year or more
later, Shteiger suddenly wrote her from a Swiss sanatorium, a letter which
she described as a "wail." He had just been through a disastrous (homosexual) love affair, and was seriously ill with tuberculosis. Tsvetaeva responded
to his plea for friendship with much more than the fragile Shteiger had
bargained for—a flood of vigorous maternal protectiveness, love, and letters. Shortly after their correspondence began, Shteiger underwent a serious
operation; Tsvetaeva wrote him daily postcards as he recovered, keeping a
longer, more serious letter growing in her notebook until he was well
enough to cope with it.

When he recovered, he sent her a sixteen-page confession[38] about his life,
designed to ward her off gently. But it had no effect. Her letters to Shteiger
sometimes echo those to Pasternak and Rilke: mutual dreams, a "dream
room" where they could live an imaginary life together. But Shteiger was
neither Pasternak nor Rilke, and the light of reality inevitably came, fore-
shadowed by a slowing down of letters from Shteiger.[39] Characteristically,
most of her poems to him were written during this slowdown and in
response to a failed plan for a meeting. Between early August and mid-
September, when the correspondence took place, Tsvetaeva (and Mur) were

in the French Alps. Shteiger's sanatorium was only kilometers away, but it was across the border in Switzerland, and Tsvetaeva had left her Nansen passport back in Vanves. In the cycle, she *becomes* both the medieval castle in which her *pension* was located and the mountain range which surrounded her, taking him into her monumental embrace as she had hoped to enclose Bakhrakh in the protective seashell of her palms:

Обнимаю тебя кругозором	I embrace you with the mountain
Гор, гранитной короною скал.	Horizon, with the granite crown of cliffs.
(Занимаю тебя разговором —	(I occupy you with conversation—
Чтобы легче дышал, крепче спал.)	So you'll breathe easier, sleep deeper.)

August 21–24, 1936
(III, 192)

In the most eloquent of these poems, Tsvetaeva speaks with folk-song simplicity of the heart of the matter, her need to be needed:

Наконец-то встретила	Finally I've met
Надобного — мне:	The one I need:
У кого-то смертная	Someone one has
Надоба — во мне.	Mortal need of me.
Чтò для ока — радуга,	What the rainbow's for the eye,
Злаку — чернозем —	Black earth for seeds of grain—
Человеку — надоба	So each of us needs
Человека — в нем.	Another's need of him.

September 11, 1936
(III, 195)

But Shteiger made it perfectly clear that he did *not* need her or her concern. As soon as he could, he planned to slip out from the watchful gaze of his parents and doctors and return to Paris, "the most tubercular city in the world," back to the Bohemian circle surrounding Adamovich. There is surely a memory of this episode in a short lyric of mid-October, Tsvetaeva's last "autumnal" self-portrait—a picture of a woman and poet needed by no one:

Когда я гляжу на летящие листья,	When I gaze at the flying leaves,
Слетающие на булыжный торец,	Floating down on the cobblestone street,
Сметаемые — как художника кистью,	Swept away, as by the brush of the artist,
Картину *кончающего* наконец,	Finishing his picture at last,
Я думаю (уж никому не по нраву	I think (no longer does anyone like
Ни стан мой, ни весь мой задумчивый вид),	My carriage or my pensive look)
Что явственно желтый, решительно ржавый	That one distinctly yellow, decisively rusty
Один такой лист на вершине — забыт.	Such leaf at the top—is forgotten.

Between Oct. 20 and 30, 1936
(III, 196)

With its theme of oncoming age and uncharacteristically long line, the poem recalls Shakespeare's last sonnets.

In 1937, the final tragedy began to unfold. On March 15, Alya returned to the USSR. She left with a dowry of clothing collected by family and friends, and a grammophone Tsvetaeva had bought her at the Paris flea market. "The departure was gay, as if she were leaving on a honeymoon."[40] Alya wrote that she was living in Moscow with Sergei's sister, studying English, and earning money. That fall, one Ignacy Reiss, A KGB defector, was found murdered near Lausanne, and the investigation led to Sergei Efron, who was also implicated in the murder of Andrei Sedov, Trotsky's son. Efron disappeared before the police could find him, fleeing through Spain to the USSR. Tsvetaeva, when questioned by the French police, denied any knowledge of her husband's activities. But guilt by association was not the exclusive province of *Soviet* Russians. If Tsvetaeva had been largely ignored by emigre Paris before Efron's disappearance, now she was shunned by all but a very few friends. Some months later, she wrote that she was only received in two households. Because of general ostracism (and her lack of resources) Mur no longer attended school, but was given lessons by an emigre tutor. This probably implies that Tsvetaeva had shifted the language of his formal education from French to Russian, in anticipation of his return to the homeland he had never seen. Tsvetaeva was no longer writing. The literary work she accomplished that winter and spring consisted of putting her archive in order and finding a safe haven for those works she could not take with her.[41]

In these bleakest months of her emigration, Nazi Germany annexed the Czechoslovakia she had transformed into myth. She wrote Teskova a letter full of horror and sympathy, expressing an unfounded hope in her own native land: "Russia will *not* let Czechoslovakia be swallowed up." Later, she had to phrase her letters in Aesopian language to get past the censor. "I am happy to know I have been able to console you—if only a bit—in your family grief, with which all my family sympathize. . . ." In November, 1938, she sent Anna Antonovna three poems of a new cycle, "Poems for Bohemia."[42] In this, her last known poetic cycle, Tsvetaeva's love and indignation find eloquent expression. With their short lines, strongly marked rhythms, strict and simple rhyme schemes, and generous use of anaphora, the poems are vintage Tsvetaeva. She contrasted Czechoslovakia's three hundred years under the Hapsburgs to the twenty years of the Czech republic in a ballad-like refrain:

Полон и просторен	A full and spacious
Край. Одно лишь горе:	Land. With only one woe:
Нет у чехов — моря.	The Czechs have no ocean.
Стало чехам — море	The Czechs now have an ocean
Слёз: не надо соли!	Of tears: they need no salt!
Запаслись на годы!	Their supply will last for years!
Триста лет неволи,	Three hundred years of slavery
Двадцать лет свободы.	Twenty years of freedom.

November 12, 1938
(III, 197)

Czechoslovakia is both "the homeland of my son" and "the home-land of all who are without a country," and she curses both those who seized Bohemia and those who gave her away. The world in which this small and noble country could be so wantonly trampled was becoming unliveable for her; ominously, she recalled Ivan Karamozov's phrase about "returning his ticket to God:"

О слезы на глазах!	Oh, tears in the eyes!
Плач гнева и любви!	Cry of anger and love!
О Чехия в слезах!	Oh, Bohemia in tears!
Испания в крови!	Spain in blood!
О черная гора,	Oh, black mountain
Затмившая — весь свет!	Which has shadowed the whole world!
Пора — пора — пора	It's time—it's time—it's time
Творцу вернуть билет.	To return my ticket to the creator.

March 15–May 11, 1939
(III, 208)

On May 31, 1939, Tsvetaeva wrote to Teskova of her imminent departure: "We are probably leaving soon for the countryside, far away, and for a long time." She summarized her reasons: "I had no choice: you can't abandon a person in need—I was born believing that—and for Mur in a city like Paris there's no life, no growth."[43] One final postcard was postmarked at Le Havre on June 12, 1939, at 4:30 p.m. Tsvetaeva and Mur were already aboard a boat to Poland.

Return to Russia

Tsvetaeva arrived in the USSR on June 18, 1939. The reunited Efrons spent the summer together in the suburban village of Bolshevo, in a dacha provided by the NKVD, along with the family of another returned agent. Quarters were cramped, the mood was ominous. Tsvetaeva recalled the summer in a cryptic journal entry made more than a year later:

> . . . Meeting with the ill Sergei. Bleak. I go for kerosene. Sergei buys apples. Gradual oppression of the heart. Ordeals by telephone. The enigmatic Alya, her false good cheer. I live without papers, not showing myself to anyone . . . My isolation. Dishwater and tears. The overtone, the undertone of it all—terror. They promise to build a partition—days go by. School for Mur—days go by. Sergei's illness. Fear of his mortal terror. Snatches of his life without me—I don't have time to listen: my hands are full of tasks, I listen as if on a spring. The cellar: one hundred times a day. When can I write?[1]

On August 27, 1939, Ariadna was arrested, and on October 10 they came for Sergei. Tsvetaeva was now not only a returned emigree, but the wife and mother of "enemies of the people." Would she be arrested as well, leaving Mur, at fourteen, to fend for himself in the strange country that was now his home? Mandel'stam had been arrested for the second time in mid-1938; he was already dead in a Siberian transit camp, though no one yet knew his fate. Her sister Anastasia was in Siberian exile as well. Why should she expect to remain untouched? And where was she to live? The dacha was sealed after Sergei's arrest. How could she support herself and her son? To whom could she turn for help? Her fellow writers, cowed by the raging purges, saw her as a pariah. The only offer of help was from Pasternak. He took her to the Goslitizdat publishing house, introduced her to the editors, and arranged for her to receive translation work. These poetic translations, from Baudelaire and Garcia Lorca, from Georgian, Polish, Bulgarian, and Czech poetry, from German, English, and Breton folk ballads, were her work during the last two years of her life. Verse translation has always paid decently in the Soviet Union, and it was a means of survival for many poets, including Pasternak himself, in the darkest years when they could publish nothing of their own. A few of Tsvetaeva's translations were published in Soviet journals in 1940 and 1941. It was long thought she had written no poetry of her own after her return, that she had, as she complained more than once, "forgotten how to write poems." But we now know of at least five poems written in 1940 and 1941, and there may be others.

In December, with Pasternak's help, Tsvetaeva and Mur settled in Golitsyno, about an hour from Moscow on a main railway line, where she and Mur shared one meal-ticket in the dining-room of a writers' retreat. Mur enrolled in the local school, Tsvetaeva worked long hours each day on her translations. Her major effort that winter was her work on Georgian epics. For reasons not hard to guess, translations from the Georgian were readily published in Stalin's time. Fortunately for poet-translators, the Georgians have an ancient and rich heritage.

What must her mood have been like? Only four days before Ariadna's arrest in August, Stalin had concluded his infamous pact with Hitler. Translating from Czech and Polish poetry must have seemed a noble but futile gesture when Czechoslovakia and Poland no longer existed. Three brief original poems written in January 1940 testify to her mood. With a brevity echoing that of the folk-songs she was translating (the more easily to be camouflaged among them in her notebooks) she wrote of her husband's arrest:

Ушел — не ем:	He's gone—I don't eat.
Пуст — хлеба вкус	Empty—the taste of bread
Всё — мел,	All is chalk
За чем ни потянусь	For which I reach.
. . . Мне хлебом был,	. . . He was my bread
И снегом был.	And my snow.
И снег не бел,	And the snow's not white
И хлеб не мил.	The bread's not sweet.

January 23, 1940
(III, 211)

"The pain that is in my breast," she wrote on the same day, "is older than love." That pain was mortal terror. Despite it, she kept doggedly at work and even kept up a brave mask for her fellow writers at Golitsyno. One of them recalled :

> Despite the mark left in her voice and her eyes by what she had been through, she easily held the attention of our small company at supper or after supper in the small dining-room of the Golitsyno retreat. Her conversation was always interesting and substantive.[2]

Marietta Shaginian recalled her as "somehow old-fashioned, helpless, in the old Moscow way . . . in her habit of deliberation, heedless of the minutes running by, as if they would wait for her." Physically, she was "thin, with a kerchief on her shoulders, with brownish bags under her eyes, a mother's eyes, worn out by life."[3] Yet where her work was concerned, she was highly professional, and in a businesslike way, gave Shaginian collegial advice on translating. (Did either remember Shaginian's review of her first book, published nearly thirty years earlier?) Tsvetaeva had always been as reserved in company as she was unreserved in her poems. Now she was understandably even more reluctant to confide in chance acquaintances. While at work on her translations, she was also making frantic appeals for help and information about her loved ones, like her millions of sisters across Russia, the wives and mothers Akhmatova immortalized in her *Requiem:*

Как трехсотая, с передачею,	Three-hundreth in line, with a parcel,
Под Крестами будешь стоять	You will stand beneath the prison wall
И своей слезою горячею	And your hot tears
Новогодний лед прожигать.	Will burn a hole in the New-year ice.[4]

Tsvetaeva and Mur left Golytsino in June and sublet a room in Moscow for the summer. In the fall, she moved in for a while with Efron's sister Lilya, sleeping on the trunk which contained her archive. In her search for a room of her own in Moscow, she turned to one literary bureaucrat after another.

> I cannot rid myself of the feeling that I have a **right** (not to mention the fact that in the Rumiantsev Museum [which had long since been renamed the Lenin Library—JT] there are **three** of our libraries: that of my grandfather, . . . of my mother, . . . and of my father. . . . We have generously endowed Moscow . . .)[5]

Her mood was dismal, suicide was constantly on her mind, and her thoughts about it were quite concrete:

> No one sees or knows that for a year now (or thereabouts) I've been looking for a hook—but there aren't any, because everywhere they've put in electricity—no chandeliers. For a year I've been trying on death. Every way is ugly and frightening. To take poison is an abomination; to jump—my hatred, my inborn revulsion of water . . . I don't want to die, I want not to exist.[6]

She finally managed to sublet a room in a communal apartment on Pokrovsky Boulevard, where, in this mood, she began to put together a collection of her poetry. It is not at all clear where or with whom the idea originated. Tsvetaeva herself had little hope it would be published:

> Here I am putting together a book; I insert things, proofread them, pay money for a typist, correct them again and—I'm almost certain that they *won't* take it, it would be a miracle if they took it. Well—I've done my job, shown complete good will (I've obeyed).[7]

But even in the depths of depression and fear, she never lost faith in her own worth as a poet: "I know that the poems are good and necessary to someone —perhaps even as necessary as bread."[8]

The plan for this collection has survived. It consists of poems written between 1920 and 1925: fourteen from before *Craft*, thirty-four from *Craft*, and one hundred from *After Russia*. In her analysis of the plan,[9] Viktoria Schweitzer weighs the conflicting evidence about Tsvetaeva's intentions. On the one hand, she changed individual words in the poems, and gave titles to most of them, probably to make them more comprehensible. On the other hand, Schweitzer points out, by concentrating on the poems of 1920–1925, she chose to present the Soviet reader with the most difficult poems of her entire oeuvre. The individual lyrics written after 1930, as we have seen, have a severe simplicity. While they are very different from the poems of 1916–1920, they are similar in their accessibility to a wider readership. Many of the poems of the '30's might indeed seem destined to please a Soviet censor: "Homesickness," "Poems for my Son," or "Newspaper Readers," for instance. Strangely, as Schweitzer points out, Tsvetaeva excluded from her projected volume those few poems from *After Russia* which speak most clearly about the poverty and frustrations of emigre life. Most arrogantly courageous was the opening, dedicatory poem, "I wrote on a slate board . . ." addressed to the one "whose initials are engraved within my [wedding] ring," i.e. to the imprisoned Sergei. Even in her most desperate moments, Tsvetaeva worked *against* her own interests, as defined by *this* world.

There may have been another motivation: her lifelong rivalry with Akhmatova. In early September, 1940, she read Akhmatova's new collection, *From Six Books*. The first book of Akhmatova's in nearly twenty years, it was a very timid collection of her most familiar poems, containing almost nothing of what she had written since 1922. Many of those newer poems, of course, could scarcely have been published in Stalin's Russia, least of all *Requiem*. But Tsvetaeva, ignorant of their existence, expressed her deep disappointment:

> Yesterday I read, reread, almost the whole of Akhmatova's book—and it's old, it's weak. Often (a bad and true sign) entirely weak endings adding up (and leading) to nothing. The poem about Lot's wife has been ruined . . . But what has she done from 1917 to 1940? *Within* herself. This book is an irreparably white page. Too bad.[10]

Even for the sake of getting her own book published by Goslitizdat, Tsvetaeva was not willing to compromise. She wanted her Soviet reader to know what *she* had been doing since 1920. Less than three weeks after Tsvetaeva met her November 1 deadline, the manuscript received a predictable response from Goslitizdat's internal reader, the well-known critic Kornely Zelinsky. Schweitzer ferreted this review out of Zelinsky's archive:

> The real tragedy of Marina Tsvetaeva is that, gifted with a talent for writing verse, she has nothing to say to readers. Tsvetaeva's poetry is non-humanistic and devoid of real human content. And that is why, evidently slaking her need to versify, she needs to pile up complex, encoded verse constructions within which is emptiness, lack of content. Thus poetry takes stern revenge on those who try to "write themselves out of the breadth of real, historical life."[11]

That real, historical life was in fact bearing down heavily on Tsvetaeva. But another sort of life, a more personal one, was also continuing. In the published fragments from her notebook, tucked between entries for October 9 (her forty-eighth birthday) and October 24, is the draft of a letter which begins, "Dear Comrade T . . . Your book is delightful . . ." Comrade T. was the distinguished Soviet poet and translator Arseny Tarkovsky, father of the film director Andrey Tarkovsky. Their friendship in the last year of Tsvetaeva's life was something close to a last love for this greying woman of forty-eight. A December, 1940 rough draft complains:

Когда-то сверстнику (о медь	Once, to my contemporary
Волос моих! Живая жила!)	(O copper of my hair—Living vein!)
Я поклялася не стареть,	I vowed never to age—
Увы: не поседеть — забыла.	Alas: I forgot not to turn grey.
	(III, 222)

Tarkovsky, fifteen years her junior, had a wife and children, but the friendship was important to him as well. Tsvetaeva left her mark on several of his poems:

Марина стирает белье.	Marina is doing the laundry
В гордыне шипучую пену	Her working hands arrogantly
Рабочие руки ее	Fling hissing foam
Швыряют на голую стену.	On the blank wall. . . .[12]

It was to Tarkovsky that Tsvetaeva's last known poem, the longest and most important of her 1940–1941 poems, is addressed. It takes a line from one of his poems as its epigraph.

«Я стол накрыл на шестерых»	*"I set the table for six ..."*
Всё повторяю первый стих	I keep repeating the first line
И всё переправляю слово:	And keep correcting a word:
— «Я стол накрыл на шестерых . . .»	"—I set the table for six . . ."
Ты одного забыл — седьмого.	You forgot one—the seventh.
Невесело вам вшестером.	It's somber for the six of you.
На лицах — дождевые струи . . .	Rivulets rain down your faces . . .
Как мог ты за таким столом	How could you, at such a table,
Седьмого позабыть — седьмую . . .	Forget her—the seventh.
Невесело твоим гостям,	It's somber for all your guests,
Бездействует графин хрустальный.	The crystal decanter sits idle.
Печально — им, печален — сам,	It's sad for them, you're sad yourself.
Непозванная — всех печальней.	Sadder than all is the uninvited.
Невесело и несветло.	It's somber and gloomy.
Ах! не едите и не пьете.	Ah! You're not eating or drinking.
— Как мог ты позабыть число?	—How could you forget the date?
Как мог ты ошибиться в счете?	How could you mis-count the guests?

Как мог, как смел ты не понять,	How could you, dare you, not understand
Что шестеро (два брата, третий —	That six (two brothers, you yourself,
Ты сам — с женой, отец и мать)	Your wife, your parents both),
Есть семеро — раз я на свете!	Is seven—since I'm on the earth!

Ты стол накрыл на шестерых,
Но шестерыми мир не вымер.
Чем пугалом среди жиых —
Быть призраком хочу — с твоими,

You set the table for six of you.
But the world doesn't end with six.
Rather than a scarecrow among the living
I want to be a ghost—among your kin,

(Своими) . . .
　　　　　　　Робкая, как вор,
О — ни души не задевая! —
За непоставленный прибор
Сажусь незваная, седьмая.

(My kin) . . .
　　　　　　　Timid, as a thief,
Oh—not offending a soul!
I'll sit at the unset place
The uninvited seventh.

Раз! — опрокинула стакан!
И всё, что жаждало пролиться, —
Вся соль из глаз, вся кровь из ран —
Со скатерти — на половицы.

There!—I've tipped over a glass!
And all that was thirsting to spill out—
All the salt from my eyes, all the blood from
　　my wounds—
Off the tablecloth—onto the floorboards . . .

И — гроба нет! Разлуки — нет!
Стол расколдован, дом разбужен.
Как смерть — на свадебный обед,
Я — жизнь, пришедшая на ужин.

And—there is no grave! No separation!
The table's freed of its spell, the house
　　awakened.
Like death at a wedding feast
I am life, come to sit at your supper.

. . . Никто: не брат, не сын, не муж,
Не друг — и всё же укоряю:
— Ты, стол накрывший нà шесть — душ,
Меня не посадивший — с краю.

I'm no one: not brother, nor son, nor husband,
Not friend—and still I reproach you:
Setting the table for six—souls
You didn't put me at the corner.
　　　　　　　March 6, 1941
　　　　　　　(III, 212-3)

Like all of Tsvetaeva's late lyrics, the poem is poignant in its severe simplicity, in the boldness with which she reveals her hurt, refusing to let pride hide any of it. The poem itself *is* the "spilled glass," "all that was thirsting to spill out." It is the poem of a woman lonely in the extreme, who fears (or knows) herself to be "a scarecrow among the living."

Exactly how isolated was she? The writer N.Ya. Moskvin and his wife, Tatania Kvanina, met her in Golitsyno, and were somewhat surprised that, given the newness of their acquaintance and the magnitude of her talent, their friendship seemed so important to Tsvetaeva. True, Kvanina reminded Tsvetaeva of Sonechka Holliday. Tsvetaeva read Kvanina excerpts of the "Povest' o Sonechke" and ceremoniously presented her with the remaining coral beads from a string Holliday had given her. When Tsvetaeva's original three month discount stay at the Golitsyno retreat ran out in late March, 1940, she turned to Moskvin, who used his connections to continue it for her into June. Yet Kvanina, in her memoir, realizes that her reliance on their friendship was a sign of her isolation, whose depth Kvanina did not realize at the time:

> . . . The famous names—of writers and actors, whom Marina Ivanovna mentioned in her conversations—had a hypnotic effect. I was convinced that there were old, firm ties of friendship, reliable defense, and help. And nothing of the sort existed.[13]

How many of Tsvetaeva's acquaintances let themselves be deluded by the belief—or the hope—that others were helping? Pasternak himself, on learning of her suicide, reproached himself:

> . . . I shall never be forgiven for it. During this last year I no longer showed any interest in her. She was very highly thought of among the intelligentsia and was becoming fashionable among people who understood poetry—my friends Garrik [Neigaus], Asmus, Kolia Villyam—not to mention Aseev—had taken her up. Since people were flattered to be numbered among her friends, and for many other reasons, I had drifted away from her and didn't impose myself on her—and during the last year almost completely forgot about her. . . .[14]

"She was becoming fashionable," "since people were flattered to be among her friends" . . . Pasternak seems to try to excuse himself while confessing his guilt. Except for this letter, there is little evidence that Tsvetaeva had become so fashionable. Aseev was a friend of Pasternak's from their futurist days, a close friend and collaborator of Mayakovsky, who had recently won the Stalin prize for his *poema* "Mayakovsky Begins." His friendship with Tsvetaeva began in the spring of 1941; she and Mur were often at his home. Another of her old friends, the still-influential Il'ya Ehrenburg, met with her only in the last few days before her evacuation, when the war was already on. The meeting was clearly a failure—Ehrenburg could or would not do anything to help, but in his memoir he tries to slough blame onto his preoccupation with the war.[15]

Sometime during these two years, she also turned to Akhmatova, less for help (Akhmatova was scarcely among the influential) than for advice—Akhmatova, with a son imprisoned since 1935, had had much experience in the writing of petitions and appeals. The meeting took place in June, probably June of 1940, but possibly 1941. (Akhmatova herself gave conflicting accounts). Rumors of Tsvetaeva's plight had already moved Akhmatova to write a prophetic poem about her:

Невидимка, двойник, пересмешник,	Invisible double, mocking-bird,
Что ты прячешься в черных кустах,	Why do you hide in black bushes
То забьешься в дырявый скворешник,	Or in a starling-house full of holes,
То мелькнешь на погибших крестах.	Or perch flittingly on the crosses of the dead,
То кричишь из Маринкиной башни:	Or cry from Marinka's tower:

«Я сегодня вернулась домой,
Полюбуйтесь, родимые пашни,
Что за это случилось со мной.
Поглотила любимых пучина
И разграблен родительский дом».
Мы сегодня с тобою, Марина,
По столице полнощной идем,
А за нами таких миллионы,
И безмолвнее шествия нет,
А вокруг погребальные звоны
Да Московские дикие стоны
Вьюги, наш заметающей след.

"Today I've come home.
Feast your eyes on me, native fields,
And see what has become of me.
An abyss has swallowed my loved ones
And my parents' home has been pillaged."
I walk with you today, Marina,
Through the midnight capitol.
And behind, millions like us,
And there's no more silent procession,
All around there are funeral bells
And the wild Moscow groans
Of the blizzard which covers our traces.

March, 1940[16]

When they finally met, Akhmatova did not dare read the poem to Tsvetaeva because of the line "An abyss has swallowed my loved ones." (Sergei and Ariadna, though imprisoned, were still presumably alive.) She did, however, read excerpts from the "Poem without a Hero," which did not make much of an impression. Tsvetaeva in turn read her "Poem of the Air," that difficult and abstract work which she often used as a touchstone for her listeners. Akhmatova, like so many others, failed the test. Ultimately, it was their family tragedies, rather than their poetry, which gave them common ground.

We have few glimpses of Tsvetaeva that last winter of 1940–1941. A brief fragment of four lines, ten words, is dated February, 1941:

Пора снимать янтарь,
Пора менять словарь,
Пора гасить фонарь
Наддверный . . .

Time to take off the amber,
Time to change vocabulary,
Time to turn out the light
Over the door . . .

February, 1941
(III, 212)

Why "take off the amber?" The answer is in a letter she wrote the previous summer:

. . . My only joy—you will laugh—is an oriental Islamic amber (which I bought two years ago, at a Paris flea market—totally dead, waxen, covered with mould, and which, every day, to my joy, is returning to life—it plays and glows from within.) I wear it on my body, unseen. It's like a rowan-berry.[17]

Tsvetaeva took comfort in the ability of her body to give life to something else, even if only a piece of amber. The fragment hints even this hope was gone—there was not enough life for herself left in that body. After putting together her collection of poetry, she returned to translating. This time her task was a group of Breton folk songs. Her versions of folk-songs are particularly successful, for they bring her back to the strong folk-song element which inspired the best of her early poetry.

Twenty months after Ariadna's arrest, Tsvetaeva finally received a letter. A phrase in Tsvetaeva's reply leaps out: "On the tenth I carried a parcel to

Papa. They accepted it."[18] Refusal by the authorities to accept a parcel was the way many prisoners' wives discovered they were widows—no other official notice was given. Mur's letters to his sister, in stark contrast, reveal a handsome young man much enjoying youth and life:

> I have two new interests: a girl and soccer. The girl had to repeat the ninth grade, she's eighteen years old, Ukrainian, she was in Tashkent, and now she has nothing to do. We go out, share books, go to the movies, etc. Mama is angry that she knows nothing about my 'friend', but that's all nonsense. In any case, I have a good time with this girl, she's clever and elegant—what more do I need?[19]

It is understandable that Tsvetaeva was worried about Mur's attraction to a school drop-out two years his senior. Mur, on the threshold of manhood, was asserting his independence, no matter how difficult a time it may have been for his mother and his country.

On June 18, 1941, Alexsei Kruchennykh organized an outing to Kuskovo, the former Sheremetev estate outside Moscow, with its museum of fine porcelain. Kruchennykh invited Tsvetaeva, Mur, and Lidia Tolstaia, later the wife of the well-known Soviet writer Jurii Libedinsky.[20] On a whim, the quartet had themselves photographed by a street photographer. The photo, probably Tsvetaeva's last, shows her wearing a beret and an enigmatic smile. On Libedinskaia's copy, she wrote a two-line epigram:

Хороший дом,   A nice house—
Хочу жить в нем . . .   I'd like to live in it.

Four days later, Hitler attacked Russia. By July, Moscow was under air attack. Mur spent nights with his friends on firewatch atop their tall apartment building. Tsvetaeva was terrified that some harm would come to him, her only remaining reason for living. When civilian evacuation began, Tsvetaeva chose to go, over Mur's objections: he had no desire to leave Moscow. They departed from the Moscow riverboat station in early August. Libedinskaia and Pasternak saw her off. The Moscow writers, including Pasternak's own family and the Aseevs, were being evacuated to Chistopol', a provincial center on the Kama river. But Tsvetaeva, not a member of the Writer's Union, was to go further upriver, to the smaller town of Elabuga.[21]

They arrived in Elabuga on August 21, and chose a room in a small house owned by an elderly couple named Brodel'shchikov. The wife's name and patronymic, Anastasia Ivanovna, were, coincidentally, the same as those of the sister she had not seen since 1927. Did Tsvetaeva see that as a good omen? Finding there was utterly no work for her in Elabuga, she left a few days later for Chistopol' to plead with the writers' organizations for permission to settle there, and for work—any kind of work. The only position in prospect was that of dishwasher in a proposed cafeteria for writers. The dining room would not open for several months, but there were already plenty of applicants for the job. On August 26, in Chistopol', Tsvetaeva was introduced to Lidia Chukovskia, daughter of the childrens' writer and critic Kornei Chukovsky. Chukovskaia, Akhmatova's self-appointed Boswell, had already begun the ciphered diaries which have given us her invaluable chronicle of Akhmatova's later years. Her chance meeting with Tsvetaeva in Chistopol' has left us with a reliable witness to Tsvetaeva's state of mind only a few days before her death. On the morning of the 27th, Chukovskaia stood by to give moral, and perhaps political, support as Tsvetaeva waited in the corridor outside the meeting room where the twinned issues of residence and work were being decided by the local committee of the Litfond, a support organization for writers.

> "Right now my fate is being decided," she greeted Chukovskaia. "If they refuse me permission to register in Chistopol', I'll die. I sense they're bound to refuse. I'll throw myself in the Kama . . . Here, in Chistopol', at least there are people, there [in Elabuga] there is no one.[22]

Human sympathy and companionship were Tsvetaeva's greatest need, though her own manner often drove away those most anxious to help.

As it turned out, the committee decided to allow her to register in Chistopol'; a letter from Aseev, who could not attend because of illness, turned the tide. The question of the dishwasher's job remained open. Chukovskaia took her in hand and the two set out to find a room, or more likely, a corner of a room, to rent. It was at this moment that the conversation about Akhmatova took place: (". . . And you think *I* can cope?") Chukovskaia was amazed that the permission to live in Chistopol' seemed not to hearten Tsvetaeva at all. "But is it worth looking for a room? I won't find one anyway. I'd best give up right away and go back to Elabuga." Chukovskaia assured her that rooms could still be found. "It's all the same. If I find a room, they won't give me work. I'll have nothing to live on." Tsvetaeva's suicidal mood was clear:

> When I was leaving Moscow, I took nothing with me. I understood clearly that my life is finished. I didn't even take Boren'ka Pasternak's letters to me. . . . Tell me, please, why do you think it's still worth living? Don't you understand what's coming?[23]

Chukovskaia, whose husband had been shot in 1938 (evidently only because he had the misfortune to share with Trotsky the name "Bronstein") replied that she could not ask such questions, for she was responsible for two small children.

> "To live for the children" . . . retorted Tsvetaeva. "If you only knew what a son I have, what a talented, gifted boy! But there's no way I can help him. It's only worse for him with me. I'm even more helpless than he. I'm down to my last two hundred rubles. If I could only sell this wool I have. . . . If they'd

take me as a dishwasher, that would be wonderful. Washing dishes is something I can still do. You can't imagine how helpless I am. I used to know how to write poems, but I've forgotten."[24]

Chukovskaia took her to the room of friends, the Schneiders. Schneider and his wife Tatiana Alekseevna welcomed Tsvetaeva with enthusiasm, thanking Chukovskaia for bringing them such an honored guest. Once provided with tea and sympathetic company, a bit of life returned to Tsvetaeva's face and manner: she seemed younger, and offered her hosts an account of her history (most of which they already knew by rumor). Chukovskaia was struck by the "precision with which she realized how terribly misguided were her husband and daughter in their desire to return to Russia."[25] When asked to read from her "Poems to Blok," she replied, "That's old," and offered instead "Homesickness," but broke it off before the end of the poem. The subject was too close. Excusing herself for the interruption, she proposed to read "The Poem of the Air" later in the evening. Neither Chukovskaia nor the Schneiders, like most poetry-loving Soviets, knew anything of her long poems, or her other work in emigration.

It was decided that Tsvetaeva would remain at the Schneiders to rest on their folding cot, while Chukovskaia sent a telegram to Mur in Elabuga. She would stop by the dormitory where Tsvetaeva had spent the night to let them know Tsvetaeva would be sleeping at the Schneiders. Meanwhile, Tatiana Alekseevna would ask around in her neighborhood about rooms to rent. After checking in with her children and their nurse, Chukovskaia would return at eight in the evening for dinner, after which, as promised, Tsvetaeva would read. But when Chukovskaia returned, she learned that Tsvetaeva had rested a bit, eaten dinner, and then suddenly announced that she had to meet with someone immediately at the dormitory. Tatiana Alekseevna had escorted her there; she promised to return and spend the night. But she never came back. In the morning, Chukovskaia learned that Tsvetaeva had spent the night in the dormitory and left first thing for Elabuga. Why had she not waited? Was it that the hospitality and help of Chukovskaia and her friends showed her that life *was* still possible, and, already irrevocably committed to suicide, this was something she did not want to accept? Or had she, resting in the calm at the Schneiders', suddenly realized that the day, August 27, was the second anniversary of Ariadna's arrest, and been overcome by a new wave of despair?

Tsvetaeva left Chistopol' on the morning of August 28. On Saturday, August 31, Anastasia Ivanovna Brodel'shchikova and Mur went off to do volunteer labor clearing an airfield on the outskirts of Elabuga. Brodel'shchikov went fishing; Tsvetaeva remained alone. When Anastasia Ivanovna returned, she found Tsvetaeva's body hanging from a nail in the enclosed entryway. She had acted with deliberation—chosen the entryway so as not to "spoil" the interior rooms for her landlords, curtained the entryway windows and tied up the door with string, so she would not be seen or rescued till the deed was done. She left three notes: one to Aseev and his family, asking them to take Mur and raise him as one of their own, one to Sergei and Ariadna, which Mur took with him, and one to Mur himself: "Forgive me. I love you madly, but it would only have been worse in the future. . . . If you ever see [Sergei and Alya], tell them I loved them to the last moment." [26] The police arrived; her body was taken to the local morgue, and buried in an unmarked grave in the Elabuga cemetery. Mur did not remain for the funeral: he left Elabuga for Chistopol' the next day.

Any suicide is a reproach to the living, the cause of soul-searching and guilt-placing. The search for the reason for Tsvetaeva's final act goes on among Russians even today. Libedinskaia felt, "It would not have happened had I accompanied her into evacuation." Pasternak blamed himself for his lack of attention in the last year. Anastasia Tsvetaeva goes to great pains to prove that her sister did it for the sake of Mur, to save *him* from suicide. She takes her cue from a reported retort of Mur's to his mother in Elabuga: *One* of us will leave here feet first!" Was Mur to blame for his mother's death? Or, conversely, was he the only reason she postponed that final act for so many years? Anastasia asserts that, in Elabuga, Tsvetaeva finally realized not only that her adored son no longer needed her, but that she was now only a burden to him and a barrier in his path. It is undoubtedly true that she desperately wanted to get out of Elabuga as much for his sake as for hers. War or no war, the school year was about to begin, and the talented, sophisticated Mur was not anxious to be stuck in a dreary small-town school. Even at sixteen, his command of Russian was extraordinary, but so, it appears, was his ego. That spring he had written to his sister:

> I led a rather interesting life in the period I lived in Golitsyno . . . I attended the village school, took lessons in mathematics from the director, and right after school I came straight to the writers' retreat, where I had breakfast and dinner in the company of a chorus of writers, critics, playwrights, scenarists, poets, etc. Such a somersault (from school to writer) was rather picturesque and gave rich material for interesting observations and acquaintances. The ceaseless change of people in the retreat, the colorful cocktail, the round dance of changing faces—all this constituted, at times, an interesting spectacle.[27]

Mur clearly had literary aspirations and talent. He was also, by all accounts, outrageously rude and cruel to his mother in their last years alone together. Those who would defend his behavior recall that he was fourteen, fifteen, and sixteen in those years, the most difficult period of adolescence, when children struggling for independence see their parents as the enemy. Tsvetaeva was an overprotective mother to this much-desired and badly spoiled son.

Mur survived his mother by less than three years. From Elabuga, he went to the Aseevs in Chistopol', then to his Aunt Lilya in Moscow, and on to Tashkent, to which the Leningrad writers had been evacuated. In Tashkent, he lived alone while finishing the last two years of school. According to one account, he earned money working, a la Mayakovsky, making cartoons and slogans for the windows of the local telegraph agency. He must have been helped financially by his mother's friends, chief among them Pasternak and Aseev. He was also helped by Akhmatova, who lived in the same building and took her rival's orphaned son under her wing. In the fall of 1943, he moved in with his aunt in Moscow and enrolled in the evening division of the Literary Institute. During the day, he earned money working as a designer in a factory. On February 1, 1944, he turned 19, and soon after was called into the army.

By mid-June, 1944, he was at the front, pursuing the retreating Germans along the left bank of the Western Dvina. On the eve of his first battle, he wrote his sister with naive optimism: "I am absolutely certain that my star will carry me unharmed from this war, and success will come without fail." Two weeks of battle brought him face-to-face with reality:

> I've seen death for the first time in my life: until now I refused to look at the dead, including even M.I. [Marina Ivanovna—this was the way Mur referred to his mother in all his letters after her death.—JT] And now I've confronted death head on. It's terrible, ugly: danger is everywhere, but everyone hopes that he won't be killed.[28]

On July 7, 1944, his regiment was battling the Germans for a slight rise outside the village of Druik. The regimental record book contains a brief entry: "Red Army soldier Georgii Efron left for the medical station after being wounded." There the army record breaks off. According to Anastasia Ivanovna, a wartime grave marked "Efron, Georgii Sergeevich, killed in July, 1944" was recently located outside Druik.[29]

Having served her term of eight years in the camps, Ariadna was released and moved to Riazan'. She found a job teaching at the local art school, and began a ten-year correspondence with Boris Pasternak[30] and a friendship which lasted until his death in 1960. In February of 1949, she was resentenced and sent to the remote Turukhansk region in the Siberian north, finally to be rehabilitated only in 1955. She devoted the last twenty years of her life to collecting, preserving, and publishing her mother's literary heritage. She died of a heart attack in 1975, and is buried in Tarusa, where she lived her last years.

Sergei Efron's death date is given in Soviet sources as 1941. He was apparently shot in the same month Tsvetaeva met her death.

NOTES

INTRODUCTION

1. In a prose piece taken from her diary of the revolutionary years, Marina Tsvetaeva, *Izbrannaia proza* (Hereafter cited as IP) N.Y. 1979, II, p.21, she wrote, "If God performs this miracle—leaves you among the living, I will follow after you like a dog." In 1938, a year before her return to the Soviet Union, she wrote in the margin of an offprint at this spot, "And here I am, about to go—like a dog (21 years later)." See Marina Tsvetaeva, *The Demesne of the Swans*, ed. and trans. Robin Kemball, (Ann Arbor, 1980) p.156.

2. First published in *Zvezda* (1973 #3 and 1976 #6) and *Literaturnaia Armenia* (1967, #8), they were reprinted in Paris (Lev, 1979) as *Stranitsy vospominanii*, (hereafter cited as AE).

3. IP1 and IP2, cited above, and Tsvetaeva, *Stikhotvoreniia i poemy v piati tomakh* (SP) (N.Y. 1980–.) All citations of Tsvetaeva's poetry, when possible, will be from SP, by volume number. In the notes which follow, I have used the abbreviations adopted in SP; a chart is provided in the Appendix.

4. Paris (Sintaxis) 1988.

5. Berkeley (California University Press) 1966, and New York (Cambridge University Press) 1985.

6. Anya M. Kroth, "Androgyny as an Exemplary Feature of Marina Tsvetaeva's Dichotomous Poetic Vision," *Slavic Review* (Volume 38, No. 4) Dec. 1979, p.580.

7. True to her own credo, she slightly improved Trediakovsky while quoting him, as Michael Naydan has noted in his recent dissertation "Time in the Composition of Tsvetaeva's *Posle Rossii*" (Columbia U. 1984) p.32n.

8. Irma Kudrova has written an extremely thoughtful essay on Tsvetaeva's mythmaking, though largely in terms of her prose rather than her poetry, in "Voskreshenie i postizhenie," *Neva*, (1982, #12) pp.151-160. See also Anna Saakiants, "O pravde 'letopisi' i pravde poeta," *Voprosy literatury* (1983, #11) pp.208-214.

9. Clarence Brown, *Mandelstam* (Cambridge University Press, 1973)

10. The most influential theory of influence now current is, of course, Harold Bloom's, as set out in his *The Anxiety of Influence* (N.Y. 1973) and developed in *A Map of Misreading* (N.Y. 1975) and *Poetry and Repression* (N.Y. 1976).

11. For a feminist critique of Bloom on these grounds, see Joanne Feit Diehl, "'Come Slowly—Eden': An Exploration of Women Poets and Their Muse," *Signs* (1978 vol. 3 no.3) pp.572-587.

12. IP 1, p.199.

13. For two excellent recent studies of these women and their *milieu*, see Richard Stites, *The Women's Liberation Movement in Russia* (Princeton, 1978) and Barbara Alpern Engel, *Mothers and Daughters: Women of the Intelligentsia in Nineteenth-Century Russia* (N.Y. 1983).

14. For a somewhat different view of the question, see Antonina Filonov Gove, "The Feminine Stereotype and Beyond: Role Conflict and Resolution in the Poetics of Marina Tsvetaeva" *Slavic Review*, Vol. 36 #2 (June, 1977).

15. Sandra M. Gilbert and Susan Gubar, "Gender, Creativity, and the Woman Poet," in Gilbert and Gubar, ed, *Shakespeare's Sisters: Feminist Essays on Women Poets*, Indiana University Press, 1979. p.xvi.

16. Gilbert and Gubar, p.xxi.

17. See Daly's *Pure Lust* (Boston, 1984).

18. Jeanne Kammer, "The Art of Silence and the Forms of Women's Poetry" in Gilbert and Gubar, op. cit., p.153-4.

19. Kammer, p.156.

20. Kammer, p.156-7.

21. Kammer, p.159.

22. Letter to Alexander Bakhrakh, June 9, 1923, in *Mosty*, V, Munich, 1960 p.305.

CHAPTER ONE — MAMA AND PAPA

1. Phyllis Rose, *Woman of Letters: A Life of Virginia Woolf* (N.Y. 1978) p.4.

2. Perdita Schaffner, "Unless a Bomb Falls . . . " preface to H.D.'s autobiographical novel *The Gift* (N.Y. 1982) p.xi. It is interesting to compare this novel with Tsvetaeva's "childhood prose", written roughly ten years earlier. There are many parallels.

3. "List'ia i korni," *Zvezda* (1976 #4) p.191.

4. These issues, however, are treated in detail by Lilly Feiler in an unpublished paper, "The Double Beat of Heaven and Hell: Marina Tsvetaeva's God/Devil", part of a forthcoming psychobiography of Tsvetaeva.

5. Letter from Tsvetaeva to the writer Vasily Rozanov, a friend of her father's, April 8, 1914. *NP* p.27.

6. Ibid. p. 28-29.

7. ATsV p.21.

8. ATsV p.228.

9. NP p.26.

10. NP p.29.

11. Karlinsky (1985, p.22) cites an unpublished 1930 letter of Tsvetaeva's to shed interesting light on the issue. Maria Mein, fearing in 1905 that her then-radical daughters would grow up, "join a party, and donate it all for the destruction of the country" stipulated they not have access to the principal until they turned forty.

12. IP2 p.174

13. IP2 p.180. Translated by J. M. King in *A Captive Spirit*, (Ann Arbor, 1980).

14. IP2 p.172. Trans. J.M. King.

15. IP2 p.201. Trans. J.M. King.

16. IP1 p.137. Trans. by Angela Livingstone in *Pasternak: Modern Judgements* ed. Donald Davie & Angela Livingstone (London, 1969).

17. Anastasia Tsvetaeva's *Vospominaniia* have gone through three editions: 1971, 1974, and 1983, with additional material included in the second and third editions.

18. ATsV p.71.

19. For a polemical exchange about the "truth" of Anastasia's memoirs vs. Marina's, see I. Kudrova, "List'ia i korny," A. Tsvetaeva, "Korni i plody," *Zvezda* (1979, #4) and the articles by Kudrova and Saakiants cited above in my Introduction. Viktoria Schweitzer summarized and analyzed the debate in "Zerno zerna poeta: spor o detstve Mariny Tsvetaevoi," in *Russkaia mysl'* Paris, May 3 and May 10, 1984.

CHAPTER TWO — AFTER MAMA

1. ATsV p.284.

2. Ellis was a founder of the Symbolist publishing house *Musagetes*; his book *Russian Symbolists* would appear in 1910, and his first collection of poems, *Stigmata*, in 1911.

3. Andrei Belyi, *Nachalo veka* p.37.

4. Karlinsky (1985), p.30. For Anastasia's version see pp.313ff.

5. IP1 p.186.

6. For the most detailed study of Tsvetaeva's *logaed*, see G.S. Smith, "Logaoedic metres in the lyric poetry of Marina Tsvetayeva," *SEER* LIII, #132 (1975) pp. 330-354.

7. IP2 p.86. Trans. J.M.King.

8. *Novyi mir* (1969 #4) p.186.

9. IP1 p.185.

10. The Briusov dedication, Dated Dec.4, is mentioned in Saakiants, "O pravde poeta. . ." p.213. The copy dedicated to Voloshin on Dec. 1, 1910 was mentioned in EPO75, p.157n.

11. *Russkaia mysl'* (Moscow, 1911) #2, p.233.

12. Ibid.

13. See her memoir, "Chelovek i vremia," in *Novyi mir* (1977 #1) pp.85-86ff. Six years later, however, Shaginian herself republished that early review in *Voprosy literatury* (1983, #12) pp.203-209.

14. "Paradise" from *Magic Lantern*.

15. IP1 p. 191.

16. *Russkaia mysl'* (Moscow, 1911) #7 pp.24-25.

CHAPTER THREE — MAX AND SERYOZHA

1. IP2 p.48.

2. "Zhenskaia poeziia" in *Utro Rossii*, December 11, 1910, quoted by Irma Kudrova in *Novyi mir* (1977, #7) p. 231 (henceforth cited as "Kudrova").

3. See "Zhivoe o Zhivom" and the poem "Posle chteniia 'Les Rencontres de M. de Breot' Regner" (I, 310).

4. Kudrova, p.239.

5. Ibid. p.240.

6. ATsV p.377.

7. Ibid. p.382.

8. My main source for this information on Sergei Efron and his family is Ariadna Efron's memoir. There is little other reliable information available about him.

9. NP p.25.

10. SP1 pp.89,90.

11. There are some indications that here again Tsvetaeva fudged the facts slightly to make a better story.

12. Kudrova, p.241.

13. EPO75 p.169.

14. Kudrova p.242.

15. Kudrova, p.243.

16. Kudrova, p.244.

17. EPO75 p.173n.

18. IP2 p.54.

19. Kudrova p.244.

20. It was first published by Anna Saakiants in S80, Vol.1, p.491.

21. See I, 137, and I, 252.

22. NP p.23.

23. The 1912 poem which opens *Junosheskie stikhi* may be the only remnant of the Bashkirtseva poems. It describes the death of a young woman.

24. Karlinsky (1985) attributes the silence of this period entirely to the "happiness" of her life, to her affluence and knowledge that she was "attractive and secure about her place in the human community." (p.43) This seems to equate poetry with social pathology.

25. *Vestnik Evropy* (Moscow, 1913, #3) p.355-6.

CHAPTER FOUR — POEMS OF A FEMALE YOUTH: MARRIAGE AND MOTHERHOOD

1. *Iunosheskie stikhi*. The collection was never published in its entirety during Tsvetaeva's lifetime. The first definitive edition is in SP1.

2. It is the poem Ariadna Efron chose to begin her 1965 selection of her mother's verse, and the first of six Tsvetaeva poems set to music by Shostakovich (op. 143a, 1974).

3. NP p.23-24.

4. Years later, she discovered the portrait was actually her *great*-grandmother. No matter.

5. For the best account of Pavlova's life and work in English, see Barbara Heldt Monter's introduction in Karolina Pavlova, *A Double Life* (Ann Arbor, 1978).

6. AE p.30.

7. "Alia: zapisi o moei pervoi docheri," ed. and introd. Veronika Losskaia, *Vestnik* #135 (1981) pp.181-192.

8. See Ellendea Proffer, ed. *Tsvetaeva: A Pictorial Biography* (Ann Arbor, 1980) particularly p.45.

9. Sergei Efron, *Detstvo* (Moscow, 1912) p.127.

10. Nikolai Elenev, "Kem byla Marina Tsvetaeva," *Grani* XXXIX (Frankfurt-Main, 1958) p.148.

11. See SP1, p.295.

12. Oddly, the second stanza is identical with the final stanza of the poem to Pyotr Efron cited above.

CHAPTER FIVE — MARINA AND SONIA

1. E.P. Voloshina to Ju. L. Obolenskaia, Dec. 30, 1914. Quoted in Sofia Poliakova, *Zakatnye ony dni: Tsvetaeva i Parnok* (Ann Arbor, 1983) p.47.

2. Poliakova, p.58.
3. Letter of January, 1915, quoted in Poliakova, p.50.
4. Op.cit. p.48.
5. Poliakova, p.57.
6. Quoted in Poliakova, pp.106-107.
7. Sofia Parnok, *Sobranie stikhotvorenii* ed. S. Poliakova, (Ann Arbor, 1979) p.234.

CHAPTER SIX — PETERSBURG

1. IP2, p.136.
2. The best study of Kuzmin in English (or in any language) is John E. Malmstad's "Mikhail Kuzmin: A Chronicle of His Life and Times," p.7-319 of M. A. Kuzmin, *Sobranie stikhotvorenii*, Vol.III (Munich, 1977).
3. In her letter to Kuzmin, Tsvetaeva created an imaginary interlocutor, presumably a Muscovite, to whom she recounted the events of the "Petersburg evening." This device allowed her to say things *about* Kuzmin in the third persto him. Her use of such a literary device in a personal letter is another reminder that her letters are part of her art.
4. For the full Russian text of this letter, see Poliakova, pp.110-114.
5. Poliakova, p.68.
6. IP2, 134. Trans. J.M. King.
7. Esenin, best known in the West for his short-lived marriage to Isadora Duncan, was bisexual, as Tsvetaeva was undoubtedly aware.
8. EPO75, p.176.

CHAPTER SEVEN — MANDEL'STAM AND MOSCOW

1. See *Tsvetaeva: A Pictorial Biography*, pp.83 and 135.
2. IP1, p.358.
3. The source of this information is Tsvetaeva herself, who, in 1941, marked the poems in question in copies of *Versts* and *Tristia* owned by the poet and bibliophile Aleksei Kruchenykh. See Viktoria Schweitzer's extensive note in SP1, pp.300-301.
4. N. Mandel'stam, *Vtoraia kniga* (Paris, 1972) p.33 and p.522; Nadezhda Yakovlevna's book was translated by Clarence Brown as *Hope Abandoned*.
5. Ibid., p.522-523.
6. L. Ginzburg, "O poetike O. Mandel'stama," *Izvestiia akademii nauk SSSR, Seriia literatury i iakyka* (July-August 1972: 310-327). Translated in Victor Erlich, ed., *Twentieth-Century Russian Literary Criticism* (New Haven, 1975) p.285.
7. Kiril Taranovsky, *Essays on Mandel'stam* (Cambridge, Ma., 1976) p.1.
8. In her 1922 essay on Pasternak, "A Downpour of Light," IP1, p.136.
9. All citations of Mandel'stam's poems will be given according to the numeration in the Struve-Fillipov edition (Washington, 1967-1969).
10. A.S. Pushkin, *Stikhotvoreniia* (Moscow, 1963) Vol.II, p.215. The subtext was noted by Khardzhiev in O. Mandel'stam, *Stikhotvoreniia* (Leningrad, 1978) p.310.
11. Akhmatova's "Don Juan list" of Mandel'stam's loves mentions only one

woman before Tsvetaeva, who left no trace in his poetry.

12. In his *Mandelstam*, op. cit.

13. Ibid., p.68.

14. Parnok, a year earlier, pointedly mentioned Mniszek in her verbal portrait of Tsvetaeva.

15. Mandel'stam, *Stikhotvoreniia*, p.270 n.71.

16. Elena Tager, a friend of Sergei's older sister in Petersburg refers to "Sergei's friend Mandel'stam" in her memoir of Mandel'stam in *Novyi zhurnal* (N.Y. 1965, #81) p.178.

17. See Brown, op.cit., and Taranovsky, pp.116-120.

18. A. Saakiants, "O pravde 'letopisi' i pravde poeta," cited above, p.209.

19. Letter of July 25, 1923 to Aleksandr Bakhrakh, *Mosty* (Munich, 1960) V, p.313.

20. BP65, p.737. Here I disagree with Taranovsky who, perhaps misled by her 1916 poems, claims she "was always a devout Orthodox believer." (Taranovsky, op.cit., p.118).

21. Noted by Anna Saakiants, 1980 I, p.492.

22. See the Nov. 30, 1916 poem dedicated to Sergei where she develops this theme (II, 139-140).

23. For a discussion of Mandel'stam's attitude to his own Jewish heritage, see Chapter III of Taranovsky, op.cit.

24. See Mandel'stam, *Stikhotvoreniia*, p.311, n.271.

25. This cluster of poems has attracted the attention of few critics. They take on an interesting dimension in Svetlana Elnitskaya's "Tsvetaeva i chort," *Russian Language Journal* (forthcoming).

26. IP1, p.352.

27. IP1, p.354.

28. The letter was published in Saakiants, "O pravde . . ."

29. O. Mandel'stam, Vol. II, p.370. Translated by Constance Link in Jane Gary Harris, ed. *The Complete Critical Prose and Letters of Mandel'stam*, p.146. His brief review of the 1916 *Almanakh muz*, where several of their poems to each other appeared, does not mention her. (That review is translated in Harris, pp.105-107).

30. For an excellent analysis of Mandel'stam's "Ne veria," see Ieva Vitins, "Mandel'stam's Farewell to Marina Tsvetaeva" *Slavic Review* Vol. 46 #2 (Summer, 1987) pp.266-280.

CHAPTER EIGHT — BLOK

1. AE p.63.

2. See Victor Erlich's chapter on Blok and Briusov, "The Maker and the Seer" in his *The Double Image: Concepts of the Poet in Slavic Literatures* (Baltimore, 1964) pp.68-119.

3. N.S. Gumilev, "A Review of Alexander Blok's *Collected Poems in Three Volumes*," translated in *Blok: Essays and Memoirs* ed. Lucy Vogel (Ann Arbor, 1982) p.103.

4. See Isaiah Berlin's essay, "A Remarkable Decade: The Birth of the Russian Intelligentsia" in *Russian Thinkers*, particularly pp.127-131.

5. Lecture at Amherst College, Spring, 1984.

6. Liubov' Mendeleeva-Blok, "Facts and Myths about Blok and Myself" in *Blok: Essays and Memoirs.*

7. For a study of Blok's versification, see Robin Kemball, *Alexander Blok: A Study in Rhythm and Metre* (The Hague, 1965). Kemball also appended a study of Tsvetaeva's meters in *Swans' Encampment* to his translation of that collection (Ann Arbor, 1980) and treated the subject more broadly in "Innovatory features of Tsvetaeva's Lyric Verse," *Russian Literature and Criticism* ed. Evelyn Bristol (Berkeley, 1982), pp.79-100.

8. See chapter 12.

9. In the pre-revolutionary orthography.

10. Angela Livingstone points to the "smooth-flowing melodious line and lulling repetition of stressed vowels in a verse that is made (unlike much of her later, more rugged verse) of entire sentences in which the syntax is relatively inconspicuous . . ." as characteristics of Tsvetaeva's early verse which link her to the heritage of Symbolism. Livingstone particularly notes the poems to Blok and Mandel'stam, where these qualities, I feel, are part of her intentional imitation. Livingstone also observes that the attitude of adoration was characteristic of Symbolist poetics. "Marina Tsvetaeva and Russian Poetry," *Melbourne Slavonic Studies* (1971) pp.178-93.

11. Aleksandr Blok, *Sobranie sochinenii* (Moscow, 1960) Vol.I p.81.

12. Freiderich Scholz has found a good many sources in Blok's own verse for the imagery of this poem, from the "blizzard covering up his tracks" to the "quiet," "last nail," and "stately tread" (which both echoes Blok and predates his use of the phrase in the ending of "The Twelve.") Scholz, "'Ty prokhodish' na zapad solntsa': Kirchenslavisches bei Marina Cvetaeva" *Orbis Scriptus* (Munich, 1966) pp.673-678.

13. Tsvetaeva was nearly twenty-four when she wrote the poem in 1916, four years (not seven), almost to the day, before Blok's 1920 reading in Moscow.

14. NP p.282.

15. 1980 I, p.494.

16. AE p.63

CHAPTER NINE — AKHMATOVA

1. AE p.64.

2. N. Mandel'stam, *Vtoraia kniga* p.512.

3. O. Mandel'stam, "A Letter about Russian Poetry," Translated in Harris, op.cit., p.158.

4. Sam Driver, *Anna Akhmatova* (New York, 1972) p.64.

5. Driver, p.60 and n.16.

6. A. Blok, *Sobranie sochinenii* (M-L 1960) III, p.143.

7. Joseph Brodsky, "Introduction" to Anna Akhmatova, *Poems* selected and translated by Lyn Coffin (N.Y. 1983) p.xiv.

8. IP2, p.130.

9. Karlinsky (1966) p.183, and again in (1985) p.64.

10. See Viktoria Schweitzer's note in SP1, pp.300-301.

11. On Sept. 8, she addressed a poem to her "rival (f.)." Plutser-Sarna, judging by his name, was Jewish; the poem "Valley of Roses" cryptically dated simply "1917" is full of Hebraic motifs. From these clues, we might hypothesize that Plutser-Sarna, under pressure from his family, renounced Tsvetaeva to return to his family-approved wife/fiancee.

12. *The New Yorker* Oct. 17, 1983, p.48.

13. BP65, p.736.

14. SP3, p.406-7.

CHAPTER TEN — 1917: GYPSIES AND STENKA RAZIN

1. Pasternak, letter to Tsvetaeva of June 14, 1922. Quoted in AE, p.107.

2. Ariadna Efron, too, was reticent about her younger sister. In an unpublished letter to Pavel Antokolsky (cited in 1980, I, p.500) she described her as "an exceedingly pretty little girl with ash-grey curls, with a large forehead, snub-nosed, with her father's large eyes."

3. AE p.89-90.

4. See BP65, p.737.

5. *The Role of the Reader and Translator of Marina Tsvetaeva's Lyrics, With a Translation of Vyorsty II*, unpublished PhD dissertation, Comparative Literature, University of Massachusetts, 1985, pp.1-2.

6. See my Introduction.

7. IP1 p.23.

CHAPTER ELEVEN — DUTY AND DALLIANCE

1. IP1 p.105.

2. IP1 p.82.

3. She stubbornly continued to use the old calendar and write in the old orthography. Of all the collections published during her lifetime, only *After Russia* is dated according to the New Style. In this work, all dates after February 1, 1918, have been converted to New Style, including those of Tsvetaeva's poems.

4. Literally "to the devil's dozen"—the Russian equivalent of "baker's dozen"— Tsvetaeva's playful reference to the thirteen added days.

5. Ilya Ehrenburg, *People, Years, and Life* p.254.

6. The motif of female as "blank page" open to the phallic male authorial pen has been much discussed in recent feminist criticism. See, for example, Sandra M. Gilbert and Susan Gubar, *The Madwoman in the Attic: The Woman Writer and the Nineteenth-Century Literary Imagination* (New Haven, 1979).

7. IP2 p.166-7.

8. For Ariadna Efron's account of the genesis of this poem, see AE p.38.

9. BP65 p.779.

10. She described her five and one-half months of "servitude" with wit and humor in her prose reminiscence "My Service," IP1, pp.50-71.

CHAPTER TWELVE — A FAREWELL TO ROMANTICISM: TSVETAEVA AND THE THEATER (1918-1919)

1. *Konets Kazanovy* (Moscow, 1920) p.6.
2. Curious readers can see Zavadsky in the role of a young Martian officer in *Aelita*, a 1926 Soviet science-fiction film.
3. IP1 p.99.
4. *Tainii zhar* (Moscow, 1986) p.14.
5. Karlinsky (1966) p.240, also (1985) p.89.
6. The play's title recalled Blok's collections "Snow mask" (1907) and "The Earth in Snow" (1908), even more the central metaphor—the Revolution as blizzard—of his masterpiece, "The Twelve," (January, 1918) which made a deep impression on Tsvetaeva.
7. Karlinsky (1966), p.249, also (1985) p.90.
8. N76 p.346-7. Sonechka did, in fact, get married—to the director of the provincial theater where she worked until her death of cancer in 1935. It was news of that death, sent back from Moscow by the repatriated Alya, which provided the impetus for "A Tale About Sonechka."
9. (Paris, Mercure de France, 1979) with an introduction by G. Limont. A Russian version circulating in *samizdat*, judging by its style, is probably a translation into Russian from Tsvetaeva's French, perhaps done by Ariadna Efron. I am grateful to V. Schweitzer for providing me with a copy.
10. Two biographies of Natalie Barney have appeared in recent years, *The Amazon of Letters: The Life and Loves of Natalie Barney* by George Wickes (N.Y. 1976) and *Portrait of a Seductress* by Jean Chalon, trans. Carol Barko (N.Y. 1979).
11. Were the putative date of composition one year later, *Mon Frere Feminin* might have been inspired by Sofia Parnok's death in 1933.

CHAPTER THIRTEEN — TRAGEDY AND GUILT (1919-1920)

1. N76 p.287.
2. A portrait of her father—Tsvetaeva's note.
3. AE p.36-7.
4. Letter to Evgeny Lann, *Wiener Slawistischer Almanach* Sonderband 3, (Wien, 1981) p.186-7.
5. IP1 p.82.
6. IP1 p.84.
7. From an unpublished original in TsGALI. Quoted by Viktoria Schweitzer in her "Stranitsy k biografii M. Tsvetaevoi," *Russian Literature* IX (1981) p.334.
8. Quoted in Schweitzer, op.cit. p.337.
9. Quoted in Schweitzer, p.335.
10. Quoted in Schweitzer, p.338.
11. Boris Trukhachev, the first husband of her sister Anastasia, of whom Tsvetaeva remained extremely fond. He did of typhus in the Crimea in 1919.

12. Letter to E. Lann, WSA p.166.

13. Pavel Antokolsky, *Sobranie sochinenii* (Moscow, 1973) IV, p.39.

14. Poliakova analyzed the poem's relationship to its sources, as well as its links with Tsvetaeva's 1922 *poema* "Sidestreets" (*Pereulochki*), in "K voprosu ob istochnikakh poemy Tsvetaevoi 'Tsar-Devitsa,' Almanakh *Russika* (N.Y. 1981) p.222-228.

15. Op.cit.

16. G.S. Smith, "Characters and Narrative Modes in Marina Tsvetaeva's 'Tsar-Devitsa'" *Oxford Slavonic Papers*, New Series, Vol. 12 (1979) p.123.

17. Quoted by Schweitzer, op.cit. p.342.

18. Volkenstein was probably the addressee of "The Wolf" (*Volk*, II, 293) which begins: "It was friendship, it's become a job. God be with thee, my brother wolf!"

19. Letter to Voloshin, EPO75 p.181.

CHAPTER FOURTEEN — RETREAT FROM EROS: (1921-1922)

1. "Marina Cvetaeva's *Remeslo:* A Commentary." Unpublished doctoral dissertation, (Harvard, 1974) p.70. I am indebted to Margaret Troupin for granting me access to her thesis, which clarified many of my insights into the poems of *Remeslo*.

2. SP2 p.364.

3. Letter to Ju. P. Ivask, RLA p.220.

4. IP1 p.223.

5. Karolina Pavlova, *Polnoe sobranie stikhotvorenii* (Moscow-Leningrad, 1964) p.154.

6. Tsvetaeva published two versions of the *poema*, first in *Razluka* (Berlin, 1922) and then in *Psikheia* (Berlin, 1923). In the second version, she eliminated 78 lines which recount the sacrifice of lover and son.

7. Karlinsky (1966), p.210.

8. Anna Akhmatova, *Stikhotvoreniia i poemy* (Leningrad, 1976) p.93.

9. So far, the only study of this subject is Viktoria Schweitzer's pioneering "Maiakovskii i Tsvetaeva" *Prostor* (Alma-Ata, 1966, #8) pp.86-90.

10. AE p.65.

11. WSA p.168.

12. He had been a friend of Anastasia Tsvetaeva in the Crimea during the Civil War, and was a disciple of Tikhon Churilin, the poet who was Mandelstam's rival in the spring of 1916.

13. WSA p.167.

14. Surviving fragments from this unfinished work appeared in *Novyi mir* (1971 #10) pp.119-131, and in *Ogonek* (October 16, 1982, #42).

15. WSA p.182.

16. Ibid.

17. WSA p.185.

18. IP1 p.201.

19. He resigned in 1902 as director of the Imperial theaters when Nicholas II pressured him to rescind a disciplinary fine laid on the ballerina Ksheshinskaia (the mistress of one of the Grand Dukes).

20. Vera Zviagintseva, quoted by V. Schweitzer in "Stranitsy" p.341.

21. They were published in English translation as *My Reminiscences*, by Prince Serge Wolkonsky (London, 1924). Americans will find of particular interest the accounts of Volkonsky's two trips to America in the 1890's, during which he was feted by Chicago tycoons, visited a school for Jewish immigrant children ("Do you miss Russia, my child?") and gave the 1896 Lowell Lectures at Harvard, published as *Russian History and Literature* (Boston, 1897).

22. IP2 p.136.

23. NP p.56-7.

24. Ibid.

25. My translation borrows somewhat from that of George L. Kline in *Arroy* (May, 1969) p.4.

26. AE p.87.

27. Ibid.

28. EPO75 p.182.

CHAPTER FIFTEEN — BERLIN (MAY–JULY, 1922)

1. IP2 p.99. Bely attempted to analyze that melody in an abstruse formalist manner totally foreign to Tsvetaeva's aesthetic, and published his analysis in the Berlin Russian newspaper *Golos Rossii* (No.971, May 21, 1922).

2. Published, with a parallel Italian translation, by Serena Vitale, *Le notti Fiorentine, Lettera all'amazone* (Milan, 1983). A Russian translation from the French, with brief introduction by A. Saakiants, appeared in *Novyi mir* (1985 #8). The original letters have evidently been lost.

3. AE p.91-92.

4. Evgeny Mindlin, who tells the story of his acquaintance with Tsvetaeva in his book, *Neobyknovennye sobesedniki* (Moscow, 1968).

5. *Le notti Fiorentine* p.4.

6. Twenty-two Berlin poems have been published; Ariadna Efron said there were thirty altogether.

7. *zhimolost'* (honeysuckle), *smol'* (jet-black), "*shchebet*" (twitter), the neologism "*levogrudyi*" (left-breasted—referring to the heart, and also to the one-breasted Amazons).

8. "*ruka*" (hand), "*zhizn'*" (life), "*svet*" (light) "*liubov'*" (love), "*zemnoi*" (earthly), "*usta/guby*" (lips), "*son*" (dream), "*den'*" (day), "*lob*" (forehead), "*plecho*" (shoulder), "*noch'*" (night), "*vzmakh*" (wave).

9. AE p.107.

10. NP p.266.

11. IP1 p.147.

12. IP1 p.135.

13. IP1 p.136.

14. IP1 p.141.

15. IP1 p.143.

16. IP2 p.18.

17. "Poety s istoriei i poety bez istorii" 1980 II, p.433. Another reverse translation of the article (it was originally published in Serbian translation, and the Russian

original is lost) appeared in *Glagol 3* (Ann Arbor, 1981) pp.197-240. The *Glagol* translation is complete; that in 1980 II has been abridged.

18. IP1 p.147.

19. The first, fourth, and final lines of the poem end with it. The first eight lines repeat the consonant "zh" no less than eighteen times, ten of those followed by the vowel "i".

20. Letter of November 19, 1922. NP p.273.

21. Letter of February 10, 1923. *Vestnik* #128 pp.169-174.

22. AE p.94-95.

23. AE p.96.

24. IP1 p.144.

25. Unpublished paper.

CHAPTER SIXTEEN — THE CZECH FOREST
(AUGUST–SEPTEMBER, 1922)

1. Letter of July 20, 1923 to Alexander Bakhrakh in *Mosty* V (Munich, 1960) p.312.

2. Ibid.

3. BP65 p.746.

4. For an excellent close reading of the "Sibilla" poems, see Olga Peters Hasty, "Cvetaeva's Sibylline Lyrics," *Russian Literature* XIX (May, 1986) pp.323-340.

5. The rowan tree, by the way, played a similar symbolic role in Pasternak's *Doctor Zhivago*. Tsvetaeva's poem may well be an important source of that image. Galina Vaneckova discusses the symbolic use of the rowan throughout Tsvetaeva's poetry in "Simvol riabiny v poezii Mariny Tsvetaevoi i ego perevod," Ceskoslovenska rusistika, Vol 27, no.5 (1982) pp.197-201.

6. BP65 p.747.

7. It is one of the very few known poems from the years 1922-1925 which were not included in *After Russia*.

8. This is an important feature of Tsvetaeva's poetry. See the discussion of it in G.S. Smith, "Marina Cvetaeva's *Poema Gory*: An Analysis," *Russian Literature* (Vol. VI, no.4, Oct. 1978) pp.103-123.

CHAPTER SEVENTEEN — PASTERNAK IN BERLIN:
SO NEAR AND YET SO FAR
(OCTOBER, 1922–FEBRUARY, 1923)

1. Letter of February 10, 1923, *Vestnik* #128 p.171.

2. AE p.108

3. Letter of November 19, 1922, NP p.271.

4. NP p.273.

5. Ibid.

6. Letter of December 12, 1922 *Novyi zhurnal* #58 (N.Y. 1959) p.170.

7. Aleksandr N. Afanas'ev, *Narodnye russkie skazki* (Moscow, 1958) III, p.127.

8. IP1 p.240.

9. Ibid.

10. Letter of March 9, NP p.285.

11. Pasternak, *Stikhotvoreniia i poemy* (Moscow-Leningrad, 1965) p.644. The same note also indicates that the manuscript of the poem contains the subtitle "Poety." Did Tsvetaeva know this when she wrote the 1923 cycle of the same name, which is clearly about herself and Pasternak? (See III, pp.67-68).

12. Pasternak, op.cit., p. 179-180. Akhmatova consciously echoed him nearly forty years later, when she began a poem, "There are few of us, perhaps four" (her quartet included Pasternak, Mandel'stam, and Tsvetaeva), and Andrei Voznesenskii sadly echoed them both when he ironically began a poem to Bella Akhmadullina, "There are many of us, perhaps four."

13. IP1 p.136.

14. NP p.277.

15. Letter of February 14, 1923, NP p. 281.

16. This line is an echo—undoubtedly intentional—from a poem to the other most important Russian poet in her life—Alexander Blok. See I, 230.

17. The volcano has been an important theme in recent feminist criticism. See particularly Adrienne Rich's essay "Vesuvius at Home: the Power of Emily Dickinson" in *On Lies, Secrets, and Silence: Selected Prose, 1966-1978* (N.Y. 1979) A comparative study of Tsvetaeva's and Dickinson's poetics remains to be done.

18. *Vestnik* #128, p.172.

19. IP1 p.137.

20. NP p.278.

21. 1980 I p. 512.

22. Each logaoedic line begins with two anapests and finishes with a dactyl, repeating that rare event in Russian poetry, the conjunction of two stressed syllables.

23. Letter of February 14, 1923. NP p.281.

CHAPTER EIGHTEEN — A MISSED MEETING: PASTERNAK'S RETURN TO RUSSIA (MARCH–JUNE, 1923)

1. Letter of February 9, 1923, Gul', p.173.

2. Vestnik #128 p.171.

3. Letter of March 5/6, 1923, NP p.283.

4. Letter of March 3, 1923, NP p.282.

5. Letter of March 9, 1923 NP p.283.

6. NP p.285.

7. NP p.286.

8. NP p.287.

9. Letter of March 11, 1923, Gul', p.178.

10. In a series of as yet unpublished papers, Liza Knapp has been exploring the related concepts of poetry/translation/communication in Tsvetaeva.

11. This particular word-play had yet another function. As she was writing the cycle, three of her 1916 poems to Mandel'stam appeared in an emigre journal, grouped as a cycle titled "Leave-Taking" (*provody*). The title should alert the observant reader (and Tsvetaeva had no patience for any other) that the two cycles were

somehow connected.

12. In her close reading of the cycle, Ieva Vitins points out that the persona's shift from "assault to capitulation" is paralleled by a turn from predominantly Greek myth and folklore to Biblical motifs and Church Slavonic diction (Unpublished paper presented at the Yale Tsvetaeva colloquium, April, 1984).

13. BP65 p.749.

14. BP65 p.749.

15. Most of the remaining April poems can be read in the context of the ongoing poetic drama. "Ariadna" explores the experience of abandonment. "Words and Meanings," "Pedal," "Palm," and "Speak through the Hills" are united by a "drift" of sounds and meanings: "*dal'*" (distance), "*bol'*" (pain), "*pedal'*" (pedal), "*ladon'*" (palm of the hand), "*iudol'*" (valley). The image of the piano is central to most of the poems in this nest. This common element in both Tsvetaeva's and Pasternak's childhoods was a frequent presence in her juvenilia, but seldom appears elsewhere in her mature verse. She uses its ringing wires and long pedal to express the perverse sweetness of drawn-out pain. Perhaps it is simply the inertia of this series of words ending in soft "L" which evoked the archaic "*iudol'*" (vale). Tsvetaeva had used the word in one of her first Berlin poems (III, 11); its reappearance here brings something full circle.

16. Letter of April 27, 1923 to L. Chirikova, *Novyi zhurnal* #124 p.148.

17. Ibid.

18. Time is a central concern in the poetry of Joseph Brodsky, and his essays on Tsvetaeva highlight her treatment of it. For a detailed study of the theme of time in the collection, see Michael M. Naydan, "Time in the Composition of Marina Cvetaeva's *Posle Rossii*," Unpublished doctoral dissertation, Columbia University, 1984.

19. Another pun. When used of musical instruments, this word also means "to go out of tune."

CHAPTER NINETEEN — THE SEARCH FOR A SUBSTITUTE: BACHRACH AND RODZEVICH

1. *Dni*, April 21, 1923

2. Letter of June 9, 1923 in *Mosty* V p.304.

3. *Dni*, June 24, 1923.

4. Letter of June 30, 1923, *Mosty* V p.306.

5. Letter of July 14-15, 1923, *Mosty* V p.309.

6. They are long and intimate enough as published, and Bachrach made lengthy cuts for reasons of discretion.

7. Letter of August 17, 1923 *Mosty* V p.318.

8. *Mosty* VI p.325.

9. Letter of August 28, 1923, *Mosty* VI p.320.

10. *Novyi zhurnal* #100 (1970) p.167.

11. Ariadna's favorable opinion of Rodzevich was influenced both by his politics (Rodzevich, who is still alive at this writing, has long been a member of the French Communist Party) and his discretion: he has refused to discuss the affair in any way, and, in the 1960's, entrusted his letters from Tsvetaeva to the (closed) Soviet archive.

12. AE p.151.

13. *Mosty* VI p.327.

14. AE p.150. It is another of the very few poems from 1922-1925 not included in *After Russia*.

15. A pun on the Latin *memento mori*—the Russian for "sea" is "*more*," and perhaps on her own name as well. She is also playing on the similarity between the Russian for "mountain" (*gora*) and for "grief" (*gore*).

16. N.Y., 1983, p.3.

17. With one important exception, a cycle inspired by Pasternak discussed in the next chapter.

CHAPTER TWENTY — A MARRIAGE OF SOULS

1. Letter of October 4, 1923 *Mosty* VI p.338.

2. AE p.116.

3. Letter of June 14, 1924, quoted in AE p.113.

4. AE p.116.

5. AE does not provide the exact date of this letter, but we know Tsvetaeva wrote to Pasternak through Gul' on June 29, and that in November she told Chernova she hadn't written him in six months, since sending the news of "my future Boris."

6. Tsvetaeva, by the way, feels no need to explain how, in the same cycle, Achilles could be part of *two* fated pairs.

7. One other poem, written two days later, seems related to the cycle, though it is not among the Pasternak poems identified by Ariadna Efron in BP65. "The Island" (III, 109) describes a "virgin, uninhabited" island, as yet undiscovered, its location recorded "only in your Columbus-like eyes." This is the unreal world she will someday share with Pasternak.

8. His first published effort in this genre, excerpts from "A Lofty Malady," would soon appear in the journal *Lef*.

9. Letter of February 11, 1923, NP p.278.

10. NP p.279.

11. The shawls, incidentally, were an important element in Tsvetaeva's life at the time. One of her neighbors had taught her how to knit, and she spent the early months of her pregnancy turning out shawls and scarves for herself, her family, and friends—it became a kind of obsession and family joke.

12. *Novyi zhurnal* #100 pp.176-177.

13. Letter to Chernova of November 25, 1924 NP p.92.

14. A two-poem cycle dated November 24 and 26 describes what must be that dream. (III,113).

15. AE p.117.

16. Letter of December 27, 1924 to Chernova, NP p.104-105.

17. NP p.105-106.

18. Letter to Chernova of December 3, 1924, NP p.98.

19. Letter to Chernova of January 2, 1925, NP p.109.

20. Letter to Chernova of January 26, 1925, NP p.126.

21. NP p.127.

22. Though it is not among those Ariadna Efron identifies as "Pasternak" poems.

23. Gregory Altshuller, son of the famous Yalta physician who treated both Chekhov and Tolstoy.

24. Gregory I. Altschuller, M.D. "Marina Tsvetaeva: A Physician's Memoir" *Sun* Vol. IV, no.3 (Winter, 1979-1980) p.119. The translator does not identify the Russian original.

25. Veronique Lossky, "Marina Cvetaeva. Souvenirs de contemporains" in *WSA* pp.227-228.

26. AE p.117.

27. Letter to Chernova of February (?) 29 [obviously a misprint or Tsvetaeva's error, since 1925 was not a leap year] NP p.139-40.

28. See BP65 p.770.

29. *Rul'*, June 10, 1925.

30. Letter of July 19, 1925, NP p.291.

31. NP p.291-292.

32. Teskova was a maiden lady nearly twenty years older than Tsvetaeva. She had spent her childhood in Moscow, where her father worked as an engineer. After her return to Prague, she taught at a Czech girls' school, translated Russian literature, and wrote memoirs and short stories in Czech. Her childhood left her with a mastery of Russian and a fondness for Russian culture.

33. Tsvetaeva's letters to Teskova, polite but revealing, are one of our best biographical sources after 1925.

34. Letter to Teskova of October 1, 1925, PT p.33.

35. BP65 p.762.

CHAPTER TWENTY-ONE — PARIS

1. Their very first issue included four Tsvetaeva poems which Bal'mont had brought with him when he left Russia.

2. For a detailed account of this episode, and of Tsvetaeva's literary debut in Paris, see I.V. Kudrova, "Polgoda v Parizhe (K biografii Mariny Tsvetaevoi)" *WSA* p.129-159 and A. Saakiants' notes, 1980, II, p.502.

3. His two-volume *History of Russian Literature* (1926-1927) is still standard for English-speaking students of Russian literature.

4. The late Elisabeth Schouvaloff, private conversation with the author. This was confirmed by the late Salomea Gal'pern in a conversation with V. Schweitzer, June, 1980.

5. *Contemporary Russian Literature* (N.Y. 1926) p.263.

6. *Sovremennye zapiski* #27 (1926) p.569, translated in *Tri-Quarterly* #27 (Spring, 1973) pp.88-93.

7. The "Mandel'stam connection" through Andronikova was one factor behind the project Tsvetaeva accomplished during her working holiday in London: a "big article" (still unpublished) titled "My Answer to Mandel'stam." We know only that it was Tsvetaeva's response to a chapter of Mandel'stam's autobiographical prose, "Theodosia," which enraged Tsvetaeva by its account of the Civil War in the Crimea. According to Kudrova, Tsvetaeva never sent the piece to *Volia Rossii*, its intended publisher, because Efron, on reading it, found it too sharply worded. See Kudrova, *WSA* p.145.

8. *Slavonic Review* Vol. VI no.17 (December, 1927) p.315.

9. She eventually arranged an extension of the subsidy in absentia, though it was reduced by half.

10. Letter to Pasternak of June 21, 1926.

CHAPTER TWENTY-TWO — PASTERNAK AND RILKE

1. For an English version of the correspondence, see *Letters: Summer 1926*, edited by Evgeny Pasternak, Elena Pasternak, and Konstantin M. Azadovsky, translated by Margaret Wettlin and Walter Arndt (San Diego, Harcourt Brace Jovanovich, 1985). The German edition (Insel Verlag, 1983) includes the original letters to and from Rilke.

2. "Iz perepiski Ril'ke, Tsvetaevoi i Pasternaka v 1926 godu," *Voprosy literatury* (4:1978) p.268. This publication includes roughly one-fifth of the entire correspondence. Some of Tsvetaeva's letters from this period are also in NP. When this book was already in press, a full Russian version of the correspondence appeared in *Druzhba narodov* (1987, Nos. 6-9).

3. "From the Sea," "An Attempt at a Room," and "A New Year's Letter."

4. For a thoughtful approach to this problem, see the Amherst College honors essay of David G. Kropf, "Rhetorical Ambiguity in the Correspondence between Marina Tsvetaeva and Rainer Maria Rilke" (1985).

5. See my "Between Letter and Lyric: The Epistolary-Poetic Friendships of Marina Cvetaeva" unpublished doctoral dissertation, Yale University (1972).

6. The the three-way correspondence and its complexities have already been the subject of scholarly attention, and warrant a good deal more. I will have space here only to touch those aspects which cast light on our central concern: Tsvetaeva's transformation of life into art.

7. See Patricia Pollock Brodsky, *Russia in the Works of Rainer Maria Rilke* (Detroit, 1984).

8. Letter (in French) to Michel Aucouturier of Feb. 4, 1959, in *Cahiers du monde russe et sovietique* (Paris) XV:1-2 (1974):232. Quoted in *Letters*, p.5.

9. "A Lofty Malady" (1923), "The Year 1905" (July 1925-February 1926), and "Spektorskii" (1925-1931).

10. *Boris Pasternak v dvadtsatye gody* (Munich, 1980) p.26.

11. *Voprosy Literatury* (4:1978) pp.240-241. Whenever possible, I have translated letters written in Russian from this publication or NP. For passages not included in *Vlit*, or letters originally written in German, I will cite *Letters*.

12. Judging from internal evidence in the correspondence, probably March 21, 1926.

13. The Pasternaks were either incredibly careless or insensitive to the importance the news had for Boris, for they circulated Rilke's letter among his sisters without first sending a copy to him. They prudently chose not to send the famous poet's letter through the mail for fear it would be confiscated or mutilated by Soviet censors.

14. *Letters* p.49.

15. In a gesture asserting she was still part of that circle, he sent her a questionnaire for a biographical encyclopedia of twentieth-century writers, to be published in Moscow. For her reply—a four-page manifesto of her life—see *Letters* pp.62-65.

16. A staircase had occupied an equally important place in one of Tsvetaeva's dreams of Pasternak, which she used as the basis for the two poems of "The Dream" (November 24-26, 1924; III, 113-114). For the symbolic significance of flight, consult Freud.

17. Letter to Anna Teskova, March 20, 1931.

18. If they have survived in draft form, it is possible they spoke too intimately about Pasternak's marriage and her own to be published even now. After all, the literary heirs of that correspondence, Ariadna Efron and Evgenii Pasternak, are the children of those other marriages.

19. *Letters* p.101.

20. Given Pasternak's characteristic vagueness and the missing Tsvetaeva letter(s), it is hard to make out the exact sequence of events. He began the May 5 letter, "Your reply will come any day now," evidently still awaiting a reply to his April 20 letter, yet he "already knew before her [letter from Paris] arrived that he would not see her in St. Gilles." Was it just intuition or something else which told him?

21. For a detailed study of the Tsvetaeva-Rilke relationship, see Olga Peters Hasty, "Marina Cvetaeva's Encounters with Rainer Maria Rilke," unpublished dissertation (Yale, 1980). I am grateful to Prof. Hasty for making the manuscript available to me.

22. *Letters*, p.81.

23. Though the letter was postmarked May 8, Tsvetaeva post-dated it for the day when Rilke would receive it, to emphasize the instantaneous nature of communication between poets.

24. *Letters* p.26.

25. See Boris Pasternak, *Izbrannoe* (Moscow, 1985) I, p.494.

26. One letter dated May 22, and another long one, in three parts, dated May 23, 25, and 26. NP does not have the May 22 letter, and treats the other as three separate letters, misdating the first part "May 29" and placing it last.

27. These commentaries provide tempting clues for reading the earlier poems, but we should not forget that the poems and her commentaries belong to two different stages of her relationship with Pasternak, as well as two different stages of her creative biography.

28. See her draft letter of July, 1927, cited below. The poem was published in 1928, in the third and final number of *Versty*.

29. Does she actually mean Pasternak's son Evgeny, then about three years old? The particle "*by*" inserted between the words "your" and "son" allows the reading: the son who would be yours—either the son whom she had wanted to have by Pasternak, or her own Mur, his honorary progeny.

30. "*Krap*"—spots, specks, like those used by card sharks to mark a deck.

31. From a rough draft in her notebook, mid-July, 1927, *Novyi mir* (1969 #4) p.197.

32. Hasty, p.70-71.

33. After its first publication, Pasternak made extensive changes in the poem, in almost every case following her advice. There is ample material for an intensive study of Pasternak and Tsvetaeva as readers of each other's work.

34. See *Letters* p.185.

35. "Novogodnee" received a brilliant and provocative analysis by Joseph Brodsky (SP1, pp.[39]-[80]). For an English version of the essay, see Brodsky's *Less Than One* (N.Y. 1986).

CHAPTER TWENTY-THREE — THE LAST LYRICS

1. Draft letter of mid-July, 1927, *Novyi mir* (1969 #4) p.196.
2. Ibid.
3. *Poslednie novosti* June 21, 1928.
4. Letter to Teskova of April 10, 1928, PT p.64.
5. According to Saakiants (1980, I, p.527) there are 99 of her letters to him and 41 of his to her, probably located in TsGALI. See also PT p.122.
6. Draft letter of August 1928, *Novyi mir* (1969 #4) p.203.
7. For a photocopy of the article, see *The Demesne of the Swans* (Ann Arbor, 1980) p.155.
8. IP1 p.371.
9. Letter to Teskova of January 22, 1929, PT p.71.
10. Letter of March 20, 1931, PT p.90.
11. Letter to Teskova of January 26, 1937, PT p.149.
12. Letter to Teskova of August 1931, PT p.92.
13. Letter to Teskova of February 25, 1931, PT p.88.
14. They were evidently first part of one work which, like much of Tsvetaeva's prose, grew beyond its original bounds.
15. IP1 pp.381-406.
16. *Sovremennye zapiski* did finally publish "Iskusstvo," but, according to Tsvetaeva, "following the demands of the editors, it was cut in half. I read it and I myself don't understand [the links which were there in the original]." RLA p.214.
17. IP1 p.370.
18. Letter to Teskova of October 8, 1931, PT p.95.
19. Letter to Teskova of October, 1932, PT p.101.
20. Letter to Teskova of January 1, 1932, PT p.97.
21. In *A Captive Spirit*.
22. *Russian Literature Triquarterly* #11, p.362.
23. *A Captive Spirit* p.81.
24. An interesting case in point is the comparison of "Skazka materi" as it was published in *Poslednie novosti*, February 17, 1935, with her original version in IP2 pp.167-171. See also her letter to Bunina about the cuts (NP pp.481-2) and PT p.120.
25. Letter to Vera Bunina of August 19, 1933, NP p.415.
26. *A Captive Spirit* pp.17-22 and pp.443-445.
27. Letter of May, 1934, *Novyi mir* (1969 #4) p.207.
28. Akhmatova, *Sochineniia* (Washington, 1968) pp.147-154. For Mandel'stam's Ode, not included in the four-volume edition of his work, see *Slavic Review* Vol. 34 #4 (1975) and Clarence Brown's article in *Slavic Review* (Dec. 1967).
29. Letter to Teskova, May 26, 1934, PT p.112.
30. Letter of November 21, 1934, PT p.116-117.
31. *An Essay in Autobiography* pp.107-108.
32. Letter to Teskova of February 15, 1936, PT p.134.
33. Letter to Bunina of August 28, 1935, NP p.502.
34. Letter to Bunina, August 23, 1935, NP p.503.
35. Letter to Teskova of February 15, 1936, PT p.135.
36. Letter to Teskova of March 29, 1936, PT p.137-8.
37. Quoted by Andrew Field in *Nabokov: His Life in Part* (N.Y. 1977) p.216.

38. See Kirill Vil'chkovskii, "Perepiska Mariny Tsvetaevoi s Anatoliem Shteigerom" *Opyty* V (N.Y. 1955) p.42.

39. Of Tsvetaeva's 25 letters to Shteiger, 13 were published in three numbers of *Opyty* (V, VII, VIII) in 1955. Another version of the letter in *Opyty* VIII, and a previously unpublished letter, were published in *Novyi mir* (1969 #4). All Tsvetaeva's letters to Shteiger, and a collection of his poetry, are now in press at Russica.

40. Letter to Teskova, May 2, 1937, PT p.152.

41. *Swans' Encampment* was dispatched to a library in Switzerland; another part of the archive, left with friends in Paris, perished during the war when pipes froze and broke, flooding the cellar where it was kept.

42. For a detailed discussion of this cycle, see Gleb Zekulin, "Marina Tsvetaeva's Cycle 'Poems for Bohemia'" *Melbourne Slavonic Studies* 9/10 (1975) pp.30-38.

43. Letter of June 7, 1939, PT p.183.

CHAPTER TWENTY-FOUR — RETURN TO RUSSIA

1. SP3, p. 390.

2. V. Ardov, "Vstrecha Anny Akhmatovoi s Marinoi Tsvetaevoi," *Grani* (Munchen) #76 (July, 1970), p.112.

3. "Chelovek i vremia," *Novy mir* (1977, #1) pp.85-90.

4. Anna Akhmatova, *Sochineniia*, (Washington, 1967) Vol.I, p. 364.

5. Letter to V.A. Merkur'eva, *NP* p.611.

6. SP3, p.391.

7. SP3, p.392.

8. SP3, p.425-428.

9. SP3, p.419-424.

10. SP3,p.391-392.

11. SP3, p.423.

12. Arseny Tarkovsky, *Izbrannoe* (Moscow, 1982) p.154-158.

13. *Oktiabr'*, (1982, #9).

14. Letter to his wife, Zinaida, quoted by Olga Ivinskaia in *A Captive of Time*, trans. Max Hayward, (N.Y., 1978) p.159.

15. Il'ia Ehrenburg, *Liudi, gody, zhizn'*, translated as *People and Life*, trans. A. Bostock and Y. Kapp, (N.Y., 1962) Vol. I, p. 258.

16. Anna Akhmatova, *Sochineniia*, second ed. Washington, 1967, p.342.

17. Letter to V.A. Merkur'eva, *NP*, p.612.

18. NP, p.618.

19. Letter of July 19, 1941, quoted in Stanislav Gribanov, "Stroka Tsvetaevoi," *Neman* (1975, #8) p.114.

20. Lidia Libedinskaia, *Zelenaia lampa* (Moscow, 1966) pp.120-140.

21. On August 16, as the boat neared Kazan', Tsvetaeva wrote to the chair of the Tatar Republic Writer's Union, asking to be given work as a poetic translator. She never received an answer. Until and unless her suicide notes ever come to light, it is the last writing we have from Tsvetaeva's hand. First published in *Komsomolets Tatarii* March 20, 1966, no. 34 (3148) it was reprinted in *Vestnik*, #149 (1986) pp.162-163.

22. Lidia Chukovskaia, "Predsmertie," SP3, p.402.
23. SP3, p.404.
24. SP3, p.406.
25. SP2, p.409.
26. ATsV, p.727.
27. Gribanov, p.114.
28. Gribanov, p.118.
29. ATsV, p.761.
30. Ariadna Efron B. Pasternaku: *Pis'ma iz ssylki* (Paris, 1982).

Appendix: Abbreviations Used in the Notes

ATsV   Анастаия Цветаева. Воспоминания. Изд. второе, дополненное. М., «Советский писатель», 1974.

AE   Ариадна Эфрон. Станицы воспоминаний. Париж, «Лев», 1979.

BP   М. Цветаева. Избранные произведения. М.-Л., 1965. (Библиотека поэта. Большая серия).

ERO75   Ежегодник рукописного отдела Пушкинского Дома на 1975 год. Л., «Наука», 1977.

IP1, IP2   М. Цветаева. Избранная проза в двух томах. Нью-Йорк, «Russica», 1979.

NP   М. Цветаева. Неизданные письма. Под общей ред. проф. Г. Струве и Н. Струве. Париж, ИМКА-Пресс, 1972.

N76   М. Цветаева. Неизданные. Париж, 1976.

SP   М. Цветаева. Стихотворения и поэмы в пяти томах. Нью-Йорк, «Russica», (1980-)

WSA   Marina Cvetaeva. Studien und Materialen. (Wiener Slawistischer Almanach. Sonderband 3). Wien, 1981.